Linear Math
Math 151
COMMUNITY COLLEGE OF PHILADELPHIA

Taken from:

Finite Mathematics, **Ninth Edition**
by Margaret L. Lial, Raymond N. Greenwell, and Nathan P. Ritchey

Intermediate Algebra, **Fifth Edition**
by Elayn Martin-Gay

*Finite Mathematics for Business, Economics,
Life Sciences, and Social Sciences,* **Twelfth Edition**
by Raymond A. Barnett, Michael R. Ziegler, and Karl E. Byleen

Learning Solutions

New York   Boston   San Francisco
London   Toronto   Sydney   Tokyo   Singapore   Madrid
Mexico City   Munich   Paris   Cape Town   Hong Kong   Montreal

Cover Art: Seashell 03, by Micheal Lary.

Taken from:

Finite Mathematics, Ninth Edition
by Margaret L. Lial, Raymond N. Greenwell, and Nathan P. Ritchey
Copyright © 2008 by Pearson Education, Inc.
Published by Addison-Wesley
Boston, Massachusetts 02116

Intermediate Algebra, Fifth Edition
by Elayn Martin-Gay
Copyright © 2009, 2005, 2001, 1997, 1993 by Pearson Education, Inc.
Published by Prentice Hall
Upper Saddle River, New Jersey 07458

Finite Mathematics for Business, Economics, Life Sciences, and Social Sciences, Twelfth Edition
by Raymond A. Barnett, Michael R. Ziegler, and Karl E. Byleen
Copyright © 2011, 2008 by Pearson Education, Inc.
Published by Prentice Hall

This special edition published in cooperation with Pearson Learning Solutions.

Pearson Learning Solutions, 501 Boylston Street, Suite 900, Boston, MA 02116
A Pearson Education Company
www.pearsoned.com

Printed in the United States of America

1 2 3 4 5 6 7 8 9 10 XXXX 15 14 13 12 11 10

000200010270587214

LB

ISBN 10: 0-558-80879-4
ISBN 13: 978-0-558-80879-2

Contents

Chapters 1–4 taken from *Finite Mathematics,* Ninth Edition, by Margaret L. Lial, Raymond N. Greenwell, and Nathan P. Ritchey.

Appendixes A and C taken from *Intermediate Algebra,* Fifth Edition, by Elayn-Martin Gay.

This book is a thorough, application-oriented text for students majoring in business, management, economics, or the life or social sciences. A prerequisite of two to three semesters of high school algebra is assumed. New exercises, new applications, and other new features make this latest edition a richer, stronger learning resource for students.

▸ New and Enhanced Features

Expanded Chapter Summaries We have expanded the information at the end of each chapter to summarize important concepts, rules, and formulas, helping students review and summarize what they have learned. We have also added Concept Check Exercises so students can verify their mastery of the important chapter concepts.

Updated Real-Data Applications This edition has many updated application exercises and examples using real data. We have added many new applications, with references to articles appearing in newspapers, books, and journals. Examples with recent data help students learn how extensively mathematics is applied, how it relates to the world around them, and how they might use it in their daily lives. We believe the real-data applications, both in quantity and quality, set this book apart from others available for this course.

Updated Exercises Approximately 30% of the exercises in each section are new or changed from the previous edition.

Increased Use of Actuarial Problems This edition includes many more problems from actuarial exams, enabling students to see how the mathematics introduced in the book is used by professionals in this field. These novel exercises often require students to connect a variety of topics to solve the problem. These exercises tend to be more challenging than the other exercises in this book, and we have provided hints for many of them.

Improved Pedagogy There are numerous changes throughout this edition, some small and some more significant, based on suggestions from reviewers and our own classroom experience. We believe that the result is a textbook that increases students' learning even more than previous editions.

Improved Notation To agree with standard usage, we now write decimals less than 1 with a leading zero, as in 0.234.

▶ Continuing Features

This edition continues to offer the many popular features of the previous edition:

Pedagogical Features

▶ Careful explanation of the mathematics behind each problem

▶ Fully developed examples with explanatory annotations in color to the right

▶ Think About It questions open most sections and are answered in an application within the section or the section exercises. The location of the answer is denoted by the ? icon.

▶ For Reviews in the margin provide "just-in-time" short explanations or comments reminding students of skills or techniques learned earlier that are needed to master the material.

▶ Cautions appear within each chapter and highlight common student difficulties and errors.

▶ Notes emphasize important treatments and asides.

▶ An index of applications shows the abundant variety of real-data applications used in the text and allows direct reference to particular topics.

▶ Multiple representations of a topic, whenever possible, examine each topic symbolically, numerically, graphically, and verbally.

▶ Multiple methods of solutions for some topics

▶ Use of graphing calculators and spreadsheets wherever appropriate

▶ Use of four-color graphics makes the book livelier and more enjoyable to read, enhances the exposition, and clarifies different parts of figures.

▶ In-depth applied exercises, called "Extended Applications," appear at the end of most chapters to stimulate student interest. These include Directions for Group Project for instructors who wish to use the Extended Applications in that way. A larger collection of Extended Applications is available in the MyMathLab® online course for this book.

Exercises

▶ Exercises are carefully arranged according to the material in the section, with the more challenging exercises placed near the end.

▶ Applied exercises (labeled "Applications") are grouped by subject, with subheads indicating the specific topic.

▶ Technology exercises, labeled with the ⬛ icon, explore concepts using a graphing calculator or spreadsheet.

▶ Writing exercises, labeled with the ✎ icon, provide students with an opportunity to explain important mathematical ideas.

▶ Connections exercises, labeled with the ⟳ icon, integrate topics presented in different sections or chapters.

▶ Problems from entrance examinations for Japanese universities give students a glimpse of international standards in math education.

► **Flexible Syllabus**

The flexibility of the text is indicated in the following chart of chapter prerequisites.

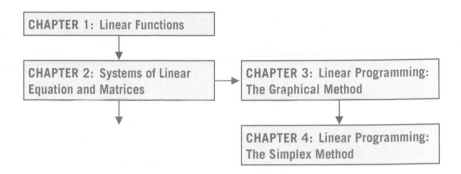

▶ Supplements

▶ Student Supplements

Student's Solutions Manual

- ▶ Provides detailed solutions to all odd-numbered text exercises and sample chapter tests with answers.

  ISBN-13: 978-0-321-44718-0
  ISBN-10: 0-321-44718-2

Graphing Calculator and Excel® Spreadsheet Manual

- ▶ Provides instructions and keystroke operations for the TI-82, TI-83/84 Plus, TI-85, TI-86, and TI-89 as well as for the Excel spreadsheet program.

  ISBN-13: 978-0-321-45067-8
  ISBN-10: 0-321-45067-1

Addison-Wesley Math Tutor Center

- ▶ Provides free tutoring through a registration number that can be packaged with a new textbook or purchased separately.
- ▶ Staffed by qualified college mathematics instructors.
- ▶ Accessible via toll-free telephone, toll-free fax, e-mail, and the Internet.
- ▶ www.aw-bc.com/tutorcenter

▶ Instructor Supplements

NEW! Instructor's Edition

- ▶ This edition of the text provides a complete answer section to both even- and odd-numbered exercises at the back of the text.

  ISBN-13: 978-0-321-46093-6
  ISBN-10: 0-321-46093-6

Instructor's Resource Guide and Solutions Manual

- ▶ Provides complete solutions to *all* exercises, two versions of a pre-test and final exam as well as teaching tips.

  ISBN-13: 978-0-321-44881-1
  ISBN-10: 0-321-44881-2

PowerPoint Lecture Presentation

- ▶ Classroom presentation software oriented specifically to the text's topic sequence.
- ▶ Available within MyMathLab® or on the Internet at www.aw-bc.com/irc.

Supplementary Chapter

- ▶ *Digraphs and Networks* chapter available within MyMathLab® or at www.aw-bc.com/irc.

NEW! Adjunct Support Center

- ▶ Offers consultation on suggested syllabi, helpful tips on using the textbook support package, assistance with content, and advice on classroom strategies.
- ▶ Available Sunday through Thursday evenings from 5 P.M. to midnight EST; telephone: 1-800-435-4084; e-mail: AdjunctSupport@aw.com; fax: 1-877-262-9774.

► Technology Supplements

MyMathLab®

MyMathLab is a series of text-specific, easily customizable online courses for Pearson Education's textbooks in mathematics and statistics. Powered by CourseCompass™ (our online teaching and learning environment) and MathXL® (our online homework, tutorial, and assessment system), MyMathLab gives you the tools you need to deliver all or a portion of your course online, whether your students are in a lab setting or working from home. MyMathLab provides a rich and flexible set of course materials, featuring free-response exercises that are algorithmically generated for unlimited practice and mastery. Students can also use online tools, such as video lectures, animations, and a multimedia textbook, to independently improve their understanding and performance. Instructors can use MyMathLab's homework and test managers to select and assign online exercises correlated directly to the textbook, and they can also create and assign their own online exercises and import TestGen® tests for added flexibility. MyMathLab's online gradebook—designed specifically for mathematics and statistics—automatically tracks students' homework and test results and gives the instructor control over how to calculate final grades. Instructors can also add off-line (paper-and-pencil) grades to the gradebook. MyMathLab is available to qualified adopters. For more information, visit our Web site at www.mymathlab.com or contact your sales representative.

MathXL®

MathXL is a powerful online homework, tutorial, and assessment system that accompanies Pearson Education's textbooks in mathematics or statistics. With MathXL, instructors can create, edit, and assign online homework and tests using algorithmically generated exercises correlated at the objective level to the textbook. They can also create and assign their own online exercises and import TestGen tests for added flexibility. All student work is tracked in MathXL's online gradebook. Students can take chapter tests in MathXL and receive personalized study plans based on their test results. The study plan diagnoses weaknesses and links students directly to tutorial exercises for the objectives they need to study and retest. Students can also access supplemental animations and video clips directly from selected exercises. MathXL is available to qualified adopters. For more information, visit our Web site at www.mathxl.com, or contact your sales representative.

InterAct Math® Tutorial Web site: www.interactmath.com

Get practice and tutorial help online! This interactive tutorial Web site provides algorithmically generated practice exercises that correlate directly to the exercises in the textbook. Students can retry an exercise as many times as they like with new values each time for unlimited practice and mastery. Every exercise is accompanied by an interactive guided solution that provides helpful feedback for incorrect answers, and students can also view a worked-out sample problem that steps them through an exercise similar to the one they're working on.

TestGen®

TestGen enables instructors to build, edit, print, and administer tests using a computerized bank of questions developed to cover all the objectives of the text. TestGen is algorithmically based, allowing insructors to create multiple but equivalent versions of the same question or test with the click of a button. Instructors can also modify test bank questions or add new questions. Tests can be printed or administered online. The software and testbank are available for download from Pearson Education's online catalog.

Acknowledgments

We wish to thank the following professors for their contributions in reviewing portions of this text.

Kevin Farrell, *Lyndon State College*
JoBeth Harney, *South Plains College*
Debbie Hewitt, *McLennan Community College*
Lynette King, *Gadsden State Community College*
Jean-Pierre Liamba, *Ball State University*
Rama Rao, *University of North Florida*
Nancy Ressler, *Oakton Community College*
Thomas Riedel, *University of Louisville*
Sandra Rucker, *Clark Atlanta University*
Fred Tramell, *University of Central Florida*
Mary Treanor, *Valparaiso University*
Zhijian Wu, *University of Alabama*

We are grateful to Nesbitt Graphics, Inc., especially our wonderful Project Manager, Bonnie Boehme, for a remarkable job as the compositor. We want to thank the talented team at Laurel Tech Services, especially Hal Whipple and Steven Fenton, for doing an excellent job coordinating the Student's Solutions Manual and Instructor's Resource Guide and Solutions Manual, an enormous and time-consuming task. We also thank Judy Martinez and Sherri Minker for typesetting these manuals. Eleanor Kuljian has created an accurate and complete index for us, and Becky Troutman has compiled the Index of Applications. We thank Hofstra University professors Peter Grassi and David Knee for their numerous suggestions. We are indebted to J. Laurie Snell of Dartmouth College, whose electronic newsletter *Chance* alerted us to many applications in probability and statistics. We also want to thank Karla Harby and Mary Ann Ritchey for their editorial assistance. Further thanks go to our accuracy checkers, Paul Lorczak and Tom Wegleitner. We especially appreciate the staff at Pearson/Addison-Wesley, whose contributions have been very important in bringing this project to a successful conclusion: Greg Tobin, Bill Hoffman, Joanne Dill, Susan Whalen, Caroline Celano, Kathy Manley, Barbara Atkinson, Christine Stavrou, Beth Anderson, and Shannon Barbe.

Margaret L. Lial
Raymond N. Greenwell
Nathan P. Ritchey

Dear Student,

Hello! The fact that you're reading this preface is good news. One of the keys to success in a math class is to read the book. Another is to answer all the questions correctly on your professor's tests. You've already started doing the first; doing the second may be more of a challenge, but by reading this book and working out the exercises, you'll be in a much stronger position to ace the tests. One last essential key to success is to go to class and actively participate.

You'll be happy to discover that we've provided the answers to the odd-numbered exercises in the back of the book. When you work out the exercises, you might have the tendency to immediately look up the answer in the back of the book, and then figure out how to get that answer. It is an easy solution that has a consequence—you won't learn to do the exercises without that extra hint. Then, when you take a test, you'll look in the back of the test but won't find any answers there, unless your professor is a lot more indulgent than we are to our students. You will then be forced to answer the questions without knowing what the answer is. Believe us, this is a lot harder! In math, the answer is too much of a hint; it tells you what you want to know without telling you how to figure it out. The learning comes from figuring out the exercises. Once you have an answer, look in the back and see if your answer agrees with ours. If it does, you're on the right path. If it doesn't, try to figure out what you did wrong. Once you've discovered your error, continue to work out more exercises to master the concept and skill.

Equations are a mathematician's way of expressing ideas in concise shorthand. The problem in reading mathematics is unpacking the shorthand. One useful technique is to read with paper and pencil at hand so you can work out calculations as you go along. When you are baffled, and you wonder, "How did they get that result?" try doing the calculation yourself and see what you get. You'll be amazed (or at least mildly satisfied) at how often that answers your question. Remember, math is not a spectator sport. You don't learn math by passively reading it or watching your professor. You learn mathematics by doing mathematics.

Finally, if there is anything you would like to see changed in the book, feel free to write to us at matrng@hofstra.edu or npritchey@ysu.edu. We're constantly trying to make this book even better. If you'd like to know more about us, we have Web sites that we invite you to visit: http://people.hofstra.edu/rgreenwell and http://www.as.ysu.edu/~nate/.

Marge Lial
Ray Greenwell
Nate Ritchey

Index of Applications

1

Linear Functions

▶ Over short time intervals, many changes in the economy are well modeled by linear functions. In an exercise in the first section of this chapter, we will examine a linear model that predicts the number of cellular telephone users in the United States. Such predictions are important tools for cellular telephone company executives and planners.

Before using mathematics to solve a real-world problem, we must usually set up a **mathematical model**, a mathematical description of the situation. Constructing such a model requires a solid understanding of the situation to be modeled, as well as familiarity with relevant mathematical ideas and techniques.

Much mathematical theory is available for building models, but the very richness and diversity of contemporary mathematics often prevents people in other fields from finding the mathematical tools they need. There are so many useful parts of mathematics that it can be hard to know which to choose.

To avoid this problem, it is helpful to have a thorough understanding of the most basic and useful mathematical tools available for constructing mathematical models. In this chapter we look at some mathematics of *linear* models, which are used for data whose graphs can be approximated by straight lines.

1.1 Slopes and Equations of Lines

? THINK ABOUT IT

How fast has tuition at public colleges been increasing in recent years, and how well can we predict tuition in the future?

In Example 15 of this section, we will answer these questions using the equation of a line.

There are many everyday situations in which two quantities are related. For example, if a bank account pays 6% simple interest per year, then the interest I that a deposit of P dollars would earn in one year is given by

$$I = 0.06 \cdot P, \quad \text{or} \quad I = 0.06P.$$

The formula $I = 0.06P$ describes the relationship between interest and the amount of money deposited.

Using this formula, we see, for example, that if $P = \$100$, then $I = \$6$, and if $I = \$12$, then $P = \$200$. These corresponding pairs of numbers can be written as **ordered pairs**, $(100, 6)$ and $(200, 12)$, pairs of numbers whose order is important. The first number denotes the value of P and the second number the value of I.

Ordered pairs are graphed with the perpendicular number lines of a **Cartesian coordinate system**, shown in Figure 1. The horizontal number line, or **x-axis**, represents the first components of the ordered pairs, while the vertical or **y-axis** represents the second components. The point where the number lines cross is the zero point on both lines; this point is called the **origin**.

The name "Cartesian" honors René Descartes (1596–1650), one of the greatest mathematicians of the seventeenth century. According to legend, Descartes was lying in bed when he noticed an insect crawling on the ceiling and realized that if he could determine the distance from the bug to each of two perpendicular walls, he could describe its position at any given moment. The same idea can be used to locate a point in a plane.

Each point on the *xy*-plane corresponds to an ordered pair of numbers, where the *x*-value is written first. From now on, we will refer to the point corresponding to the ordered pair (a, b) as "the point (a, b)."

Locate the point $(-2, 4)$ on the coordinate system by starting at the origin and counting 2 units to the left on the horizontal axis and 4 units upward, parallel to the vertical axis. This point is shown in Figure 1, along with several other sample points. The number -2 is the ***x*-coordinate** and the number 4 is the ***y*-coordinate** of the point $(-2, 4)$.

The x-axis and y-axis divide the plane into four parts, or **quadrants**. For example, quadrant I includes all those points whose x- and y-coordinates are both positive. The quadrants are numbered as shown in Figure 1. The points on the axes themselves belong to no quadrant. The set of points corresponding to the ordered pairs of an equation is the **graph** of the equation.

The x- and y-values of the points where the graph of an equation crosses the axes are called the ***x*-intercept** and ***y*-intercept**, respectively.* See Figure 2.

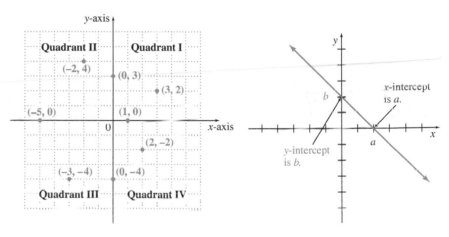

FIGURE 1　　　　　　　　　　　FIGURE 2

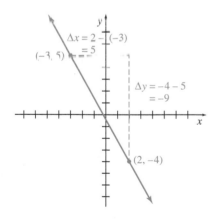

FIGURE 3

Slope of a Line

An important characteristic of a straight line is its *slope*, a number that represents the "steepness" of the line. To see how slope is defined, look at the line in Figure 3. The line goes through the points $(x_1, y_1) = (-3, 5)$ and $(x_2, y_2) = (2, -4)$. The difference in the two x-values,

$$x_2 - x_1 = 2 - (-3) = 5$$

in this example, is called the **change in x**. The symbol Δx (read "delta x") is used to represent the change in x. In the same way, Δy represents the **change in y**. In our example,

$$\begin{aligned} \Delta y &= y_2 - y_1 \\ &= -4 - 5 \\ &= -9. \end{aligned}$$

*Some people prefer to define the intercepts as ordered pairs, rather than as numbers.

These symbols, Δx and Δy, are used in the following definition of slope.

SLOPE OF A LINE

The **slope** of a line is defined as the vertical change (the "rise") over the horizontal change (the "run") as one travels along the line. In symbols, taking two different points (x_1, y_1) and (x_2, y_2) on the line, the slope is

$$m = \frac{\text{Change in } y}{\text{Change in } x} = \frac{\Delta y}{\Delta x} = \frac{y_2 - y_1}{x_2 - x_1},$$

where $x_1 \neq x_2$.

By this definition, the slope of the line in Figure 3 is

$$m = \frac{\Delta y}{\Delta x} = \frac{-4 - 5}{2 - (-3)} = -\frac{9}{5}.$$

The slope of a line tells how fast y changes for each unit of change in x.

NOTE Using similar triangles, it can be shown that the slope of a line is independent of the choice of points on the line. That is, the same slope will be obtained for *any* choice of two different points on the line.

EXAMPLE 1 **Slope**

Find the slope of the line through each pair of points.

(a) $(7, 6)$ and $(-4, 5)$

▶Solution Let $(x_1, y_1) = (7, 6)$ and $(x_2, y_2) = (-4, 5)$. Use the definition of slope.

$$m = \frac{\Delta y}{\Delta x} = \frac{5 - 6}{-4 - 7} = \frac{-1}{-11} = \frac{1}{11}$$

(b) $(5, -3)$ and $(-2, -3)$

▶Solution Let $(x_1, y_1) = (5, -3)$ and $(x_2, y_2) = (-2, -3)$. Then

$$m = \frac{-3 - (-3)}{-2 - 5} = \frac{0}{-7} = 0.$$

Lines with zero slope are horizontal (parallel to the x-axis).

(c) $(2, -4)$ and $(2, 3)$

▶Solution Let $(x_1, y_1) = (2, -4)$ and $(x_2, y_2) = (2, 3)$. Then

$$m = \frac{3 - (-4)}{2 - 2} = \frac{7}{0},$$

which is undefined. This happens when the line is vertical (parallel to the y-axis).

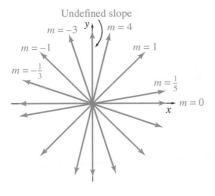

Undefined slope
$m = -3$ $m = 4$
$m = -1$ $m = 1$
$m = -\frac{1}{3}$ $m = \frac{1}{5}$
$m = 0$

FIGURE 4

CAUTION The phrase "no slope" should be avoided; specify instead whether the slope is zero or undefined. ∎

In finding the slope of the line in Example 1(a), we could have let $(x_1, y_1) = (-4, 5)$ and $(x_2, y_2) = (7, 6)$. In that case,

$$m = \frac{6 - 5}{7 - (-4)} = \frac{1}{11},$$

the same answer as before. The order in which coordinates are subtracted does not matter, as long as it is done consistently.

Figure 4 shows examples of lines with different slopes. Lines with positive slopes go up from left to right, while lines with negative slopes go down from left to right.

It might help you to compare slope with the percent grade of a hill. If a sign says a hill has a 10% grade uphill, this means the slope is 0.10, or 1/10, so the hill rises 1 foot for every 10 feet horizontally. A 15% grade downhill means the slope is -0.15.

Equations of a Line
An equation in two first-degree variables, such as $4x + 7y = 20$, has a line as its graph, so it is called a **linear equation**. In the rest of this section, we consider various forms of the equation of a line.

EXAMPLE 2 Equation of a Line
Find the equation of the line through $(0, -3)$ with slope $3/4$.

▶Solution We can use the definition of slope, letting $m = 3/4$, $(x_1, y_1) = (0, -3)$, and (x, y) represent another point on the line.

$$m = \frac{y_2 - y_1}{x_2 - x_1}$$
$$\frac{3}{4} = \frac{y - (-3)}{x - 0} = \frac{y + 3}{x} \quad \text{Substitute.}$$
$$3x = 4(y + 3) \quad \text{Cross multiply.}$$
$$3x = 4y + 12$$
$$3x - 4y = 12$$

A generalization of the method of Example 2 can be used to find the equation of any line, given its y-intercept and slope. Assume that a line has y-intercept b, so that it goes through the point $(0, b)$. Let the slope of the line be represented by m. If (x, y) is any point on the line *other* than $(0, b)$, then the definition of slope can be used with the points $(0, b)$ and (x, y) to get

$$m = \frac{y - b}{x - 0}$$
$$m = \frac{y - b}{x}$$
$$mx = y - b$$
$$y = mx + b.$$

This result is called the *slope-intercept form* of the equation of a line, because b is the y-intercept of the graph of the line.

> **SLOPE-INTERCEPT FORM**
>
> If a line has slope m and y-intercept b, then the equation of the line in **slope-intercept form** is
>
> $$y = mx + b.$$

When $b = 0$, we say that y is **proportional** to x.

EXAMPLE 3   **Slope-Intercept Form**

Find the equation of the line in slope-intercept form having y-intercept $-9/4$ and slope $3/2$.

▶**Solution** Use the slope-intercept form with $b = -9/4$ and $m = 3/2$.

$$y = mx + b$$

$$y = \frac{3}{2}x - \frac{9}{4}$$

The slope-intercept form shows that we can find the slope of a line by solving its equation for y. In that form, the coefficient of x is the slope and the constant term is the y-intercept. For instance, in Example 2 the slope of the line $3x - 4y = 12$ was given as $3/4$. This slope also could be found by solving the equation for y.

$$3x - 4y = 12$$

$$-4y = -3x + 12 \qquad \text{Subtract } 3x \text{ from both sides.}$$

$$y = \frac{3}{4}x - 3 \qquad \text{Divide both sides by } -4.$$

The coefficient of x, $3/4$, is the slope of the line. The y-intercept is -3.

The slope-intercept form of the equation of a line involves the slope and the y-intercept. Sometimes, however, the slope of a line is known, together with one point (perhaps *not* the y-intercept) that the line goes through. The *point-slope form* of the equation of a line is used to find the equation in this case. Let (x_1, y_1) be any fixed point on the line and let (x, y) represent any other point on the line. If m is the slope of the line, then by the definition of slope,

$$\frac{y - y_1}{x - x_1} = m,$$

or

$$y - y_1 = m(x - x_1). \qquad \text{Multiply both sides by } x - x_1.$$

> **POINT-SLOPE FORM**
>
> If a line has slope m and passes through the point (x_1, y_1), then an equation of the line is given by
>
> $$y - y_1 = m(x - x_1),$$
>
> the **point-slope form** of the equation of a line.

EXAMPLE 4 **Point-Slope Form**

Find an equation of the line that passes through the point $(3, -7)$ and has slope $m = 5/4$.

▶Solution Use the point-slope form.

$$y - y_1 = m(x - x_1)$$

$$y - (-7) = \frac{5}{4}(x - 3) \quad \text{$y_1 = -7, m = \frac{5}{4}, x_1 = 3$}$$

$$y + 7 = \frac{5}{4}(x - 3)$$

$$4y + 28 = 5(x - 3) \qquad \text{Multiply both sides by 4.}$$

$$4y + 28 = 5x - 15 \qquad \text{Distribute.}$$

$$4y = 5x - 43 \qquad \text{Combine constants.}$$

$$y = \frac{5}{4}x - \frac{43}{4} \qquad \text{Divide both sides by 4.}$$

The equation of the same line can be given in many forms. To avoid confusion, the linear equations used in the rest of this section will be written in slope-intercept form, $y = mx + b$, which is often the most useful form.

The point-slope form also can be useful to find an equation of a line if we know two different points that the line goes through. The procedure for doing this is shown in the next example.

EXAMPLE 5 **Using Point-Slope Form to Find an Equation**

Find an equation of the line through $(5, 4)$ and $(-10, -2)$.

▶Solution Begin by using the definition of slope to find the slope of the line that passes through the given points.

$$\text{Slope} = m = \frac{-2 - 4}{-10 - 5} = \frac{-6}{-15} = \frac{2}{5}$$

Either $(5, 4)$ or $(-10, -2)$ can be used in the point-slope form with $m = 2/5$. If $(x_1, y_1) = (5, 4)$, then

$$y - y_1 = m(x - x_1)$$

$$y - 4 = \frac{2}{5}(x - 5) \quad \text{$y_1 = 4, m = \frac{2}{5}, x_1 = 5$}$$

$$5y - 20 = 2(x - 5) \qquad \text{Multiply both sides by 5.}$$

$$5y - 20 = 2x - 10 \qquad \text{Distributive property}$$

$$5y = 2x + 10 \qquad \text{Add 20 to both sides.}$$

$$y = \frac{2}{5}x + 2 \qquad \text{Divide by 5 to put in slope-intercept form.}$$

Check that the same result is found if $(x_1, y_1) = (-10, -2)$.

EXAMPLE 6 **Horizontal Line**

Find an equation of the line through $(8, -4)$ and $(-2, -4)$.

▶**Solution** Find the slope.

$$m = \frac{-4 - (-4)}{-2 - 8} = \frac{0}{-10} = 0$$

Choose, say, $(8, -4)$ as (x_1, y_1).

$$y - y_1 = m(x - x_1)$$
$$y - (-4) = 0(x - 8) \qquad y_1 = -4, m = 0, x_1 = 8$$
$$y + 4 = 0 \qquad\qquad 0(x - 8) = 0$$
$$y = -4$$

Plotting the given ordered pairs and drawing a line through the points, show that the equation $y = -4$ represents a horizontal line. See Figure 5(a). Every horizontal line has a slope of zero and an equation of the form $y = k$, where k is the y-value of all ordered pairs on the line.

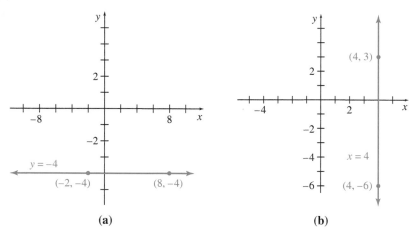

(a)   (b)

FIGURE 5

EXAMPLE 7 **Vertical Line**

Find an equation of the line through $(4, 3)$ and $(4, -6)$.

▶**Solution** The slope of the line is

$$m = \frac{-6 - 3}{4 - 4} = \frac{-9}{0},$$

which is undefined. Since both ordered pairs have x-coordinate 4, the equation is $x = 4$. Because the slope is undefined, the equation of this line cannot be written in the slope-intercept form.

Again, plotting the given ordered pairs and drawing a line through them show that the graph of $x = 4$ is a vertical line. See Figure 5(b).

The slope of a horizontal line is 0.

The slope of a vertical line is undefined.

The different forms of linear equations discussed in this section are summarized below. The slope-intercept and point-slope forms are equivalent ways to express the equation of a nonvertical line. The slope-intercept form is simpler for a final answer, but you may find the point-slope form easier to use when you know the slope of a line and a point through which the line passes.

EQUATIONS OF LINES

Equation	Description
$y = mx + b$	**Slope-intercept form:** slope m, y-intercept b
$y - y_1 = m(x - x_1)$	**Point-slope form:** slope m, line passes through (x_1, y_1)
$x = k$	**Vertical line:** x-intercept k, no y-intercept (except when $k = 0$), undefined slope
$y = k$	**Horizontal line:** y-intercept k, no x-intercept (except when $k = 0$), slope 0

Parallel and Perpendicular Lines   One application of slope involves deciding whether two lines are parallel. Since two parallel lines are equally "steep," they should have the same slope. Also, two lines with the same "steepness" are parallel.

PARALLEL LINES

Two lines are **parallel** if and only if they have the same slope, or if they are both vertical.

EXAMPLE 8   **Parallel Line**

Find the equation of the line that passes through the point $(3, 5)$ and is parallel to the line $2x + 5y = 4$.

▶**Solution**   The slope of $2x + 5y = 4$ can be found by writing the equation in slope-intercept form.

$$2x + 5y = 4$$
$$y = -\frac{2}{5}x + \frac{4}{5}$$

This result shows that the slope is $-2/5$. Since the lines are parallel, $-2/5$ is also the slope of the line whose equation we want. This line passes through $(3, 5)$. Substituting $m = -2/5$, $x_1 = 3$, and $y_1 = 5$ into the point-slope form gives

$$y - y_1 = m(x - x_1)$$

$$y - 5 = -\frac{2}{5}x + \frac{6}{5}$$

$$y = -\frac{2}{5}x + \frac{6}{5} + 5$$

$$y = -\frac{2}{5}x + \frac{31}{5}.$$

As already mentioned, two nonvertical lines are parallel if and only if they have the same slope. Two lines having slopes with a product of -1 are perpendicular. A proof of this fact, which depends on similar triangles from geometry, is given as Exercise 43 in this section.

> **PERPENDICULAR LINES**
>
> Two lines are **perpendicular** if and only if the product of their slopes is -1, or if one is vertical and the other horizontal.

EXAMPLE 9 **Perpendicular Line**

Find the slope of the line L perpendicular to the line having the equation $5x - y = 4$.

▶**Solution** To find the slope, write $5x - y = 4$ in slope-intercept form:

$$y = 5x - 4.$$

The slope is 5. Since the lines are perpendicular, if line L has slope m, then

$$5m = -1$$

$$m = -\frac{1}{5}.$$

The next two examples use different forms of the equation of a line to analyze real-world data. In both examples, we are looking at how one variable changes over time. To simplify the arithmetic, we will *rescale* the variable representing time, although computers and calculators have made rescaling less important than in the past. Here it allows us to work with smaller numbers, and, as you will see, find the y-intercept of the line more easily. We will use rescaling on many examples throughout this book. When we do, it is important to be consistent.

EXAMPLE 10 **Prevalence of Cigarette Smoking**

In recent years, the percentage of the U.S. population age 18 and older who smoke has decreased at a roughly constant rate, from 23.3% in 2000 to 20.9% in 2004.*

(a) Find the equation describing this linear relationship.

*U.S. Department of Health and Human Services.

▶**Solution** Let x represent time in years, with $x = 0$ for 2000. With this rescaling, the year 2000 corresponds to $x = 0$ and the year 2004 corresponds to $x = 2004 - 2000 = 4$. Let y represent the percentage of the population who smoke. The two ordered pairs representing the given information are $(0, 23.3)$ and $(4, 20.9)$. The slope of the line through these points is

$$m = \frac{20.9 - 23.3}{4 - 0} = \frac{-2.4}{4} = -0.6.$$

This means that, on average, the percentage of the adult population who smoke is decreasing by about 0.6% per year.

Using $m = -0.6$ and $(x_1, y_1) = (0, 23.3)$ in the point-slope form gives the required equation,

$$y - 23.3 = -0.6(x - 0)$$
$$y = -0.6x + 23.3.$$

This result could also have been obtained by observing that $(0, 23.3)$ is the y-intercept.

(b) One of the objectives of Healthy People 2010 (a campaign of the U.S. Department of Health and Human Services) is to reduce the percentage of U.S. adults who smoke to 12% or less by the year 2010. If this decline in smoking continues at the same rate, will they meet this objective?

▶**Solution** Using the same rescaling, $x = 10$ corresponds to the year 2010. Substituting this value into the above equation gives

$$y = -0.6(10) + 23.3, \quad \text{or} \quad y = 17.3.$$

Continuing at this rate, an estimated 17.3% of the adult population will still smoke and the objective of Healthy People 2010 will not be met. ▬

Notice that if this formula is valid for all nonnegative x, then eventually y becomes 0:

$$-0.6x + 23.3 = 0$$
$$-0.6x = -23.3 \qquad \text{Subtract 23.3 from both sides.}$$
$$x = \frac{-23.3}{-0.6} = 38.8333 \approx 38*, \qquad \text{Divide both sides by } -0.6.$$

which indicates that 38 years from 2000 (in the year 2038), 0% of the U.S. adult population will smoke. Of course, it is still possible that in 2038 there will be adults who smoke; the trend of recent years may not continue. Most equations are valid for some specific set of numbers. It is highly speculative to extrapolate beyond those values.

On the other hand, people in business and government often need to make some prediction about what will happen in the future, so a tentative conclusion based on past trends may be better than no conclusion at all. There are also circumstances, particularly in the physical sciences, in which theoretical reasons imply that the trend will continue.

---

*The symbol $\approx$ means "is approximately equal to."

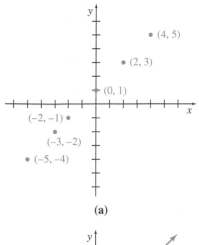

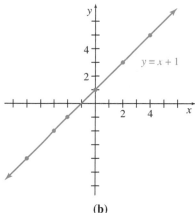

(a)

(b)

FIGURE 6

EXAMPLE 11 **Graduate Degrees**

The number of African Americans earning doctorate degrees has risen at an approximately constant rate from 1987 to 2005. The linear equation $y = 63.6x + 787$, where x represents the number of years since 1987, can be used to estimate the annual number of African Americans earning doctorate degrees.*

(a) Determine this number in 2006.

▶**Solution** Rescaling the year, let $x = 2006 - 1987 = 19$. Evaluating the equation at $x = 19$ gives

$$y = 63.6x + 787$$
$$= 63.6(19) + 787 = 1995.4 \approx 1995.$$

This means that about 1995 African Americans earned doctorate degrees in 2006.

(b) Find and interpret the slope.

▶**Solution** The equation is given in slope-intercept form, so the slope is the coefficient of x, which is 63.6. The slope indicates the change in the number of doctorate degrees earned annually by African Americans from 1987 to 2005. Because the slope is positive, the number of doctorate degrees is increasing by about 64 per year.

Graph of a Line We can graph the linear equation defined by $y = x + 1$ by finding several ordered pairs that satisfy the equation. For example, if $x = 2$, then $y = 2 + 1 = 3$, giving the ordered pair $(2, 3)$. Also, $(0, 1)$, $(4, 5)$, $(-2, -1), (-5, -4), (-3, -2)$, among many others, satisfy the equation.

To graph $y = x + 1$, we begin by locating the ordered pairs obtained above, as shown in Figure 6(a). All the points of this graph appear to lie on a straight line, as in Figure 6(b). This straight line is the graph of $y = x + 1$.

It can be shown that every equation of the form $ax + by = c$ has a straight line as its graph. Although just two points are needed to determine a line, it is a good idea to plot a third point as a check. It is often convenient to use the x- and y-intercepts as the two points, as in the following example.

EXAMPLE 12 **Graph of a Line**

Graph $3x + 2y = 12$.

▶**Solution** To find the y-intercept, let $x = 0$.

$$3(0) + 2y = 12$$
$$2y = 12 \qquad \text{Divide both sides by 2.}$$
$$y = 6$$

Similarly, find the x-intercept by letting $y = 0$, which gives $x = 4$. Verify that when $x = 2$, the result is $y = 3$. These three points are plotted in Figure 7(a). A line is drawn through them in Figure 7(b).

---

*The Journal of Blacks in Higher Education, Issue 54, 2007, http://www.jbhe.com.

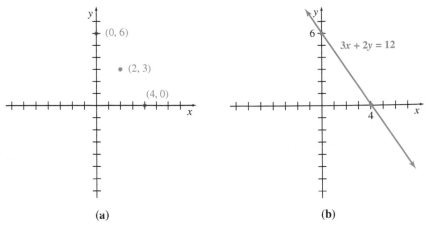

FIGURE 7

Not every line has two distinct intercepts; the graph in the next example does not cross the x-axis, and so it has no x-intercept.

EXAMPLE 13   **Graph of a Horizontal Line**
Graph $y = -3$.

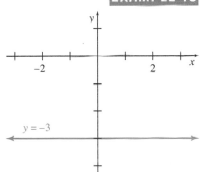

FIGURE 8

▶**Solution** The equation $y = -3$, or equivalently, $y = 0x - 3$, always gives the same y-value, -3, for any value of x. Therefore, no value of x will make $y = 0$, so the graph has no x-intercept. As we saw in Example 6, the graph of such an equation is a horizontal line parallel to the x-axis. In this case the y-intercept is -3, as shown in Figure 8.

In general, the graph of $y = k$, where k is a real number, is the horizontal line having y-intercept k.

The graph in Example 13 has only one intercept. Another type of linear equation with coinciding intercepts is graphed in Example 14.

EXAMPLE 14   **Graph of a Line Through the Origin**
Graph $y = -3x$.

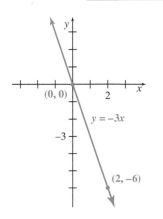

FIGURE 9

▶**Solution** Begin by looking for the x-intercept. If $y = 0$, then

$$y = -3x$$
$$0 = -3x \qquad \text{Let } y = 0.$$
$$0 = x. \qquad \text{Divide both sides by } -3.$$

We have the ordered pair $(0, 0)$. Starting with $x = 0$ gives exactly the same ordered pair, $(0, 0)$. Two points are needed to determine a straight line, and the intercepts have led to only one point. To get a second point, we choose some other value of x (or y). For example, if $x = 2$, then

$$y = -3x = -3(2) = -6, \qquad \text{Let } x = 2.$$

giving the ordered pair $(2, -6)$. These two ordered pairs, $(0, 0)$ and $(2, -6)$, were used to get the graph shown in Figure 9.

Linear equations allow us to set up simple mathematical models for real-life situations. In almost every case, linear (or any other reasonably simple) equations provide only approximations to real-world situations. Nevertheless, these are often remarkably useful approximations.

EXAMPLE 15

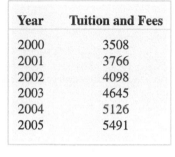

Tuition

The table on the left lists the average annual cost (in dollars) of tuition and fees at public four-year colleges for selected years.*

(a) Plot the cost of public colleges by letting $x = 0$ correspond to 2000. Are the data *exactly* linear? Could the data be *approximated* by a linear equation?

▶**Solution** Use a scale from 3000 to 6000 on the y-axis. The graph is shown in Figure 10(a) in a figure known as a **scatterplot**. Although it is not exactly linear, it is approximately linear and could be approximated by a linear equation, as shown by the calculator-generated graph in Figure 10(b).

Year	Tuition and Fees
2000	3508
2001	3766
2002	4098
2003	4645
2004	5126
2005	5491

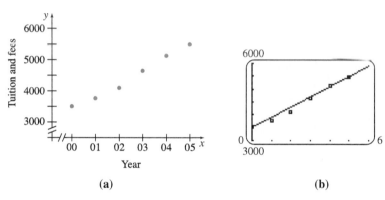

(a) (b)

FIGURE 10

(b) Use the points (0, 3508) and (5, 5491) to determine an equation that models the data.

▶**Solution** We first find the slope of the line as follows:

$$m = \frac{5491 - 3508}{5 - 0} = \frac{1983}{5} = 396.6.$$

Using the slope-intercept form of the line, $y = mx + b$, with $m = 396.6$ and $b = 3508$, gives

$$y = 396.6x + 3508.$$

(c) Discuss the accuracy of using this equation to estimate the cost of public colleges in the year 2030.

▶**Solution** The year 2030 corresponds to the year $x = 30$, for which the equation predicts a cost of

$$396.6(30) + 3508 = 15,406, \quad \text{or} \quad \$15,406.$$

*Annual Survey of Colleges 2005–2006, The College Board.

The year 2030 is many years in the future, however. Many factors could affect the tuition, and the actual figure for 2030 could turn out to be very different from our prediction.

You can plot data with a TI-83/84 Plus graphing calculator using the following steps.

1. Store the data in lists.
2. Define the stat plot.
3. Turn off $Y =$ functions (unless you also want to graph a function).
4. Turn on the plot you want to display.
5. Define the viewing window.
6. Display the graph.

Consult the calculator's instruction booklet or *The Graphing Calculator Manual*, available with this book, for specific instructions. See the calculator-generated graph in Figure 10(b), which includes the points and line from Example 15. Notice how the line closely approximates the data.

▶ 1.1 Exercises

Find the slope of each line that has a slope.

1. Through $(4, 5)$ and $(1, 2)$

2. Through $(5, -4)$ and $(1, 3)$

3. Through $(8, 4)$ and $(8, -7)$

4. Through $(1, 5)$ and $(-2, 5)$

5. $y = x$

6. $y = 3x - 2$

7. $5x - 9y = 11$

8. $4x + 7y = 1$

9. $x = 5$

10. The x-axis

11. $y = 8$

12. $y = -6$

13. A line parallel to $6x - 3y = 12$

14. A line perpendicular to $8x = 2y - 5$

Find an equation in slope-intercept form (where possible) for each line in Exercises 15–34.

15. Through $(1, 3)$, $m = -2$

16. Through $(2, 4)$, $m = -1$

17. Through $(-5, -7)$, $m = 0$

18. Through $(-8, 1)$, with undefined slope

19. Through $(4, 2)$ and $(1, 3)$

20. Through $(8, -1)$ and $(4, 3)$

21. Through $(2/3, 1/2)$ and $(1/4, -2)$

22. Through $(-2, 3/4)$ and $(2/3, 5/2)$

23. Through $(-8, 4)$ and $(-8, 6)$

24. Through $(-1, 3)$ and $(0, 3)$

25. x-intercept -6, y-intercept -3

26. x-intercept -2, y-intercept 4

27. Vertical, through $(-6, 5)$

28. Horizontal, through $(8, 7)$

29. Through $(-4, 6)$, parallel to $3x + 2y = 13$

30. Through $(2, -5)$, parallel to $y - 4 = 2x$

31. Through $(3, -4)$, perpendicular to $x + y = 4$

32. Through $(-2, 6)$, perpendicular to $2x - 3y = 5$

33. The line with y-intercept 4 and perpendicular to $x + 5y = 7$

34. The line with x-intercept $-2/3$ and perpendicular to $2x - y = 4$

35. Do the points $(4, 3)$, $(2, 0)$, and $(-18, -12)$ lie on the same line? (*Hint:* Find the slopes between the points.)

36. Find k so that the line through $(4, -1)$ and $(k, 2)$ is

    a. parallel to $2x + 3y = 6$,

    b. perpendicular to $5x - 2y = -1$.

37. Use slopes to show that the quadrilateral with vertices at $(1, 3)$, $(-5/2, 2)$, $(-7/2, 4)$, and $(2, 1)$ is a parallelogram.

38. Use slopes to show that the square with vertices at $(-2, 5)$, $(4, 5)$, $(4, -1)$, and $(-2, -1)$ has diagonals that are perpendicular.

For the lines in Exercises 39 and 40, which of the following is closest to the slope of the line?
(a) 1   (b) 2   (c) 3   (d) 21   (e) 22   (f) -3

39.

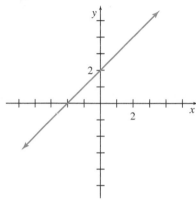

40.

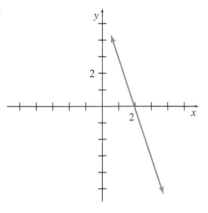

Estimate the slope of the lines in Exercises 41 and 42.

41.

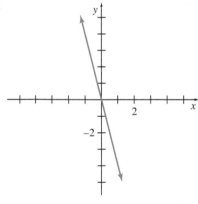

42.

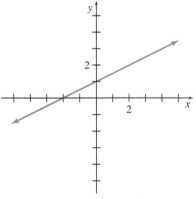

43. To show that two perpendicular lines, neither of which is vertical, have slopes with a product of -1, go through the following steps. Let line L_1 have equation $y = m_1 x + b_1$, and let L_2 have equation $y = m_2 x + b_2$. Assume that L_1 and L_2 are perpendicular, and use right triangle MPN shown in the figure. Prove each of the following statements.

    a. MQ has length m_1.

    b. QN has length $-m_2$.

    c. Triangles MPQ and PNQ are similar.

    d. $m_1/1 = 1/(-m_2)$ and $m_1 m_2 = -1$

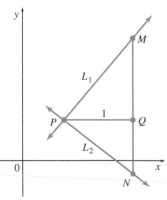

Graph each equation.

44. $y = x - 1$ **45.** $y = 4x + 5$ **46.** $y = -4x + 9$ **47.** $y = -6x + 12$

48. $2x - 3y = 12$ **49.** $3x - y = -9$ **50.** $3y - 7x = -21$ **51.** $5y + 6x = 11$

52. $y = -2$ **53.** $x = 4$ **54.** $x + 5 = 0$ **55.** $y + 8 = 0$

56. $y = 2x$ **57.** $y = -5x$ **58.** $x + 4y = 0$ **59.** $3x - 5y = 0$

▶ Applications

BUSINESS AND ECONOMICS

60. *Sales* The sales of a small company were \$27,000 in its second year of operation and \$63,000 in its fifth year. Let y represent sales in the xth year of operation. Assume that the data can be approximated by a straight line.

   a. Find the slope of the sales line, and give an equation for the line in the form $y = mx + b$.

   b. Use your answer from part a to find out how many years must pass before the sales surpass \$100,000.

61. *Use of Cellular Telephones* The following table shows the subscribership of cellular telephones in the United States (in millions) between 1994 and 2004.*

Year	Subscribers (in millions)
1994	24.13
1995	33.77
1996	44.04
1997	55.31
1998	69.21
1999	86.05
2000	109.48
2001	128.38
2002	140.77
2003	158.72
2004	182.14

   a. Plot the data by letting $x = 0$ correspond to 1993. What can we conclude about the number of U.S. subscribers over this time period?

   b. Determine a linear equation that approximates the number of subscribers using the points $(3, 44.04)$ and $(11, 182.14)$.

   c. Using the equation from part b, approximate the number of cellular phone subscribers in the year 2005. Compare your result with the actual value of 207.9 million.

62. *Hybrid Cars* As hybrid car sales rise in the United States, automobile manufacturers are expected to increase the number of available models in America. In 2006, 12 models were available. It is predicted that there will be 52 models available in 2012.[†]

   a. Find an equation for the number of available models in terms of time t, where t represents the number of years since 2000.

   b. If this growth follows a linear trend, in what year will the number of models reach at least 72?

   c. Discuss the practicality of using this equation to predict the number of models in 2025.

63. *Consumer Price Index* The Consumer Price Index (CPI) is a measure of the change in the cost of goods over time. If 1982 is used as the base year of comparison (CPI = 100 in 1982), then the CPI of 201.6 in 2006[‡] would indicate that an item that cost \$1.00 in 1982 would cost \$2.02 in 2006. The CPI has been increasing at an approximately linear rate for the past 30 years.

   a. Use this information to determine a linear function for this data, letting x be the years since 1982.

   b. Based on your function, what was the CPI in 2000? Compare this estimate to the actual CPI of 172.2.

   c. How is the annual CPI changing?

LIFE SCIENCES

64. *HIV Infection* The time interval between a person's initial infection with HIV and that person's eventual development of AIDS symptoms is an important issue. The method of infection with HIV affects the time interval before AIDS develops. One study of HIV patients who were infected by intravenous drug use found that 17% of the patients had

---

*The World Almanac and Book of Facts 2006, p. 380, and http://www.ctia.org/.

†Winslow, Lance, "Where Is the Hybrid Car Market Going in the Future?" http://ezinearticles.com.

‡U.S. Department of Labor, Bureau of Labor Statistics.

AIDS after 4 years, and 33% had developed the disease after 7 years. The relationship between the time interval and the percentage of patients with AIDS can be modeled accurately with a linear equation.*

a. Write a linear equation $y = mx + b$ that models this data, using the ordered pairs $(4, 0.17)$ and $(7, 0.33)$.

b. Use your equation from part a to predict the number of years before half of these patients will have AIDS.

65. *Exercise Heart Rate* To achieve the maximum benefit for the heart when exercising, your heart rate (in beats per minute) should be in the target heart rate zone. The lower limit of this zone is found by taking 70% of the difference between 220 and your age. The upper limit is found by using 85%.[†]

a. Find formulas for the upper and lower limits (u and l) as linear equations involving the age x.

b. What is the target heart rate zone for a 20-year-old?

c. What is the target heart rate zone for a 40-year-old?

d. Two women in an aerobics class stop to take their pulse and are surprised to find that they have the same pulse. One woman is 36 years older than the other and is working at the upper limit of her target heart rate zone. The younger woman is working at the lower limit of her target heart rate zone. What are the ages of the two women, and what is their pulse?

e. Run for 10 minutes, take your pulse, and see if it is in your target heart rate zone. (After all, this is listed as an exercise!)

66. *Ponies Trotting* A 1991 study found that the peak vertical force on a trotting Shetland pony increased linearly with the pony's speed, and that when the force reached a critical level, the pony switched from a trot to a gallop.[‡] For one pony, the critical force was 1.16 times its body weight. It experienced a force of 0.75 times its body weight at a speed of 2 meters per second, and a force of 0.93 times its body weight at 3 meters per second. At what speed did the pony switch from a trot to a gallop?

67. *Life Expectancy* Some scientists believe there is a limit to how long humans can live. One supporting argument is that during the last century, life expectancy from age 65 has increased more slowly than life expectancy from birth, so

eventually these two will be equal, at which point, according to these scientists, life expectancy should increase no further. In 1900, life expectancy at birth was 46 yr, and life expectancy at age 65 was 76 yr. In 2004, these figures had risen to 77.8 and 83.7, respectively.[§] In both cases, the increase in life expectancy has been linear. Using these assumptions and the data given, find the maximum life expectancy for humans.

68. *Deer Ticks* Deer ticks cause concern because they can carry Lyme disease. One study found a relationship between the density of acorns produced in the fall and the density of deer tick larvae the following spring.[||] The relationship can be approximated by the linear equation

$$y = 34x + 230,$$

where x is the number of acorns per square meter (m^2) in the fall, and y is the number of deer tick larvae per 400 m^2 the following spring. According to this formula, approximately how many acorns per square meter would result in 1000 deer tick larvae per 400 m^2?

SOCIAL SCIENCES

69. *Marriage* The following table lists the U.S. Median Age at First Marriage for men and women.[#] The age at which both groups marry for the first time seems to be increasing at a roughly linear rate since 1965. Let x correspond to the number of years since 1960.

Year	Men	Women
1965	22.8	20.6
1970	23.2	20.8
1975	23.5	21.1
1980	24.7	22.0
1985	25.5	23.3
1990	26.1	23.9
1995	26.9	24.5
2000	26.8	25.1
2005	27.4	25.8

*Alcabes, P., A. Munoz, D. Vlahov, and G. Friedland, "Incubation Period of Human Immunodeficiency Virus," *Epidemiologic Review*, Vol. 15, No. 2, The Johns Hopkins University School of Hygiene and Public Health, 1993, pp. 303–318.

[†]Hockey, Robert V., *Physical Fitness: The Pathway to Healthful Living*, Times Mirror/Mosby College Publishing, 1989, pp. 85–87.

[‡]*Science*, Vol. 253, No. 5017, July 19, 1991, pp. 306–308.

[§]*Science*, Vol. 254, No. 5034, Nov. 15, 1991, pp. 936–938, and http://www.cdc.gov/nchs/data.

[||]*Science*, Vol. 281, No. 5375, July 17, 1998, pp. 350–351.

[#]U. S. Census Bureau, http://www.census.gov/population/socdemo/hh-fam/ms2.pdf.

a. Find a linear equation that approximates the data for men, using the points (5, 22.8) and (45, 27.4).

b. Find a linear equation that approximates the data for women, using the points (5, 20.6) and (45, 25.8).

c. Which group seems to have the faster increase in median age at first marriage?

d. In what year will the men's median age at first marriage reach 30?

e. When the men's median age at first marriage is 30, what will the median age be for women?

70. *Immigration* In 1974, there were 86,821 people from other countries who immigrated to the state of California. In 2004, the number of immigrants was 252,920.[*]

a. If the change in foreign immigration to California is considered to be linear, write an equation expressing the number of immigrants, y, in terms of the number of years after 1974, x.

b. Use your result in part a to predict the foreign immigration to California in the year 2014.

71. *Cohabitation* The number of unmarried, opposite sex couples in the United States who are living together has been rising at a roughly linear rate in recent years. The number of cohabiting adults was 1.59 million in 1980 and 5.08 million in 2004.[†]

a. Write an equation expressing the number of cohabiting adults (in millions), y, in terms of the number of years after 1980, x.

b. Use your result in part a to predict the number of cohabiting adults in the year 2010.

PHYSICAL SCIENCES

72. *Global Warming* In 1990, the Intergovernmental Panel on Climate Change predicted that the average temperature on Earth would rise 0.3°C per decade in the absence of international controls on greenhouse emissions.[‡] Let t measure the time in years since 1970, when the average global temperature was 15°C.

a. Find a linear equation giving the average global temperature in degrees Celsius in terms of t, the number of years since 1970.

b. Scientists have estimated that the sea level will rise by 65 cm if the average global temperature rises to 19°C. According to your answer to part a, when would this occur?

73. *Galactic Distance* The table lists the distances (in megaparsecs where 1 megaparsec $\approx 3.1 \times 10^{19}$ km) and velocities (in kilometers per second) of four galaxies moving rapidly away from Earth.[§]

Galaxy	Distance	Velocity
Virga	15	1600
Ursa Minor	200	15,000
Corona Borealis	290	24,000
Bootes	520	40,000

a. Plot the data points letting x represent distance and y represent velocity. Do the points lie in an approximately linear pattern?

b. Write a linear equation $y = mx$ to model this data, using the ordered pair (520, 40,000).

c. The galaxy Hydra has a velocity of 60,000 km per sec. Use your equation to determine how far away it is from Earth.

d. The value of m in the equation is called the *Hubble constant*. The Hubble constant can be used to estimate the age of the universe A (in years) using the formula

$$A = \frac{9.5 \times 10^{11}}{m}.$$

Approximate A using your value of m.

GENERAL INTEREST

74. *Radio Stations* The graph on the next page shows the number of U.S. radio stations on the air along with the graph of a linear equation that models the data.[‖]

a. Let x be the number of years since 1990. Use the two ordered pairs (0, 10,770) and (15, 13,660) to find the approximate slope of the line shown. Interpret your answer.

b. Use the same two ordered pairs to write an equation of the line that models the data.

---

[*]*Legal Immigration to California in Federal Fiscal Year 1996*, State of California Demographic Research Unit, June 1999, and *The World Almanac and Book of Facts 2006*, p. 482.
[†]U.S. Bureau of the Census, Population Division, Current Population Survey, 2004 Annual Social and Economic Supplement.
[‡]*Science News*, June 23, 1990, p. 391.
[§]Acker, A. and C. Jaschek, *Astronomical Methods and Calculations*, John Wiley & Sons, 1986; Karttunen, H. (editor), *Fundamental Astronomy*, Springer-Verlag, 1994.
[‖]http://www.stateofthemedia.org.

c. Estimate the year when it is expected that the number of stations will first exceed 15,000.

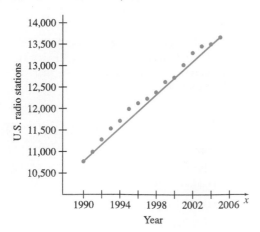

Year	Tuition and Fees
2000	16,072
2001	17,377
2002	18,060
2003	18,950
2004	20,045
2005	21,235

a. Sketch a graph of the data. Do the data appear to lie roughly along a straight line?

b. Let $x = 0$ correspond to the year 2000. Use the points (0, 16,072) and (5, 21,235) to determine a linear equation that models the data. What does the slope of the graph of the equation indicate?

75. *Tuition* The table lists the annual cost (in dollars) of tuition and fees at private four-year colleges for selected years.* (See Example 15.)

c. Discuss the accuracy of using this equation to estimate the cost of private college in 2025.

1.2 Linear Functions and Applications

? THINK ABOUT IT

How many units must be sold for a firm to break even?

Later in this section, this question will be answered using a linear function.

As we saw in the previous section, many situations involve two variables related by a linear equation. For such a relationship, when we express the variable y in terms of x, we say that y is a **linear function** of x. This means that for any allowed value of x (the **independent variable**), we can use the equation to find the corresponding value of y (the **dependent variable**). Examples of linear functions include $y = 2x + 3$, $y = -5$, and $2x - 3y = 7$, which can be written as $y = (2/3)x - (7/3)$. Equations in the form $x = k$, where k is a constant, are not linear functions. All other linear equations define linear functions.

$f(x)$ Notation

Letters such as f, g, or h are often used to name functions. For example, f might be used to name the function

$$y = 5 - 3x.$$

To show that this function is named f, it is common to replace y with $f(x)$ (read "f of x") to get

$$f(x) = 5 - 3x.$$

By choosing 2 as a value of x, $f(x)$ becomes $5 - 3 \cdot 2 = 5 - 6 = -1$, written

$$f(2) = -1.$$

Annual Survey of Colleges 2005–2006, The College Board.

The corresponding ordered pair is $(2, -1)$. In a similar manner,

$$f(-4) = 5 - 3(-4) = 17, \quad f(0) = 5, \quad f(-6) = 23,$$

and so on.

EXAMPLE 1 **Function Notation**

Let $g(x) = -4x + 5$. Find $g(3)$, $g(0)$, $g(-2)$, and $g(b)$.

▶**Solution** To find $g(3)$, substitute 3 for x.

$$g(3) = -4(3) + 5 = -12 + 5 = -7$$

Similarly,

$$g(0) = -4(0) + 5 = 0 + 5 = 5,$$
$$g(-2) = -4(-2) + 5 = 8 + 5 = 13,$$

and

$$g(b) = -4b + 5.$$

We summarize the discussion below.

LINEAR FUNCTION

A relationship f defined by

$$y = f(x) = mx + b,$$

for real numbers m and b, is a **linear function**.

Supply and Demand Linear functions are often good choices for supply and demand curves. Typically, as the price of an item increases, consumers are less likely to buy an increasingly expensive item, and so the demand for the item decreases. On the other hand, as the price of an item increases, producers are more likely to see a profit in selling the item, and so the supply of the item increases. The increase in supply and decrease in demand can eventually result in a surplus, which causes the price to fall. These countervailing trends tend to move the price, as well as the supply and demand, toward an equilibrium value.

For example, during the late 1980s and early 1990s, the consumer demand for cranberries (and all of their healthy benefits) soared. The demand surpassed the supply, causing a shortage, and cranberry prices rose dramatically. As prices increased, growers wanted to increase their profits, so they planted more acres of cranberries. Unfortunately, cranberries take 3 to 5 years from planting until they can first be harvested. As growers waited and prices increased, consumer demand decreased. When the cranberries were finally harvested, the supply overwhelmed the demand and a huge surplus occurred, causing the price of cranberries to drop in the late 1990s.* Other factors were involved in this situation, but the relationship between price, supply, and demand was nonetheless typical. Some

*http://www.umass.edu/agcenter/census/cran-prices.html.

commodities, such as medical care, college education, and certain luxury items, however, may be exceptions to these typical relationships.

Although economists consider price to be the independent variable, they have the unfortunate habit of plotting price, usually denoted by p, on the vertical axis, while everyone else graphs the independent variable on the horizontal axis. This custom was started by the English economist Alfred Marshall (1842–1924). In order to abide by this custom, we will write p, the price, as a function of q, the quantity produced, and plot p on the vertical axis. But remember, it is really *price* that determines how much consumers demand and producers supply, not the other way around.

Supply and demand functions are not necessarily linear, the simplest kind of function. Yet most functions are approximately linear if a small enough piece of the graph is taken, allowing applied mathematicians to often use linear functions for simplicity. That approach will be taken in this chapter.

EXAMPLE 2   **Supply and Demand**

Suppose that Greg Tobin, manager of a giant supermarket chain, has studied the supply and demand for watermelons. He has noticed that the demand increases as the price decreases. He has determined that the quantity (in thousands) demanded weekly, q, and the price (in dollars) per watermelon, p, are related by the linear function

$$p - D(q) = 9 - 0.75q. \quad \text{Demand function}$$

(a) Find the demand at a price of \$5.25 per watermelon and at a price of \$3.75 per watermelon.

▶**Solution**   To find the demand at a price of \$5.25 per watermelon, replace p in the demand function with 5.25 and solve for q.

$$5.25 = 9 - 0.75q$$
$$-3.75 = -0.75q \qquad \text{Subtract 9 from both sides.}$$
$$5 = q \qquad \text{Divide both sides by } -0.75.$$

Thus, at a price of \$5.25, the demand is 5000 watermelons.

Similarly, replace p with 3.75 to find the demand when the price is \$3.75. Verify that this leads to $p = 7$. When the price is lowered from \$5.25 to \$3.75 per watermelon, the demand increases from 5000 to 7000 watermelons.

(b) Greg also noticed that the supply of watermelons decreased as the price decreased. Price p and supply q are related by the linear function

$$p = S(q) = 0.75q. \quad \text{Supply function}$$

Find the supply at a price of \$5.25 per watermelon and at a price of \$3.00 per watermelon.

▶**Solution**   Substitute 5.25 for p in the supply function, $p = 0.75q$, to find that $q = 7$, so the supply is 7000 watermelons. Similarly, replacing p with 3 in the supply equation gives a supply of 4000 watermelons. If the price decreases from \$5.25 to \$3.00 per watermelon, the supply also decreases, from 7000 to 4000 watermelons.

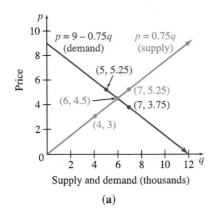

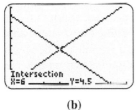

(b)

FIGURE 11

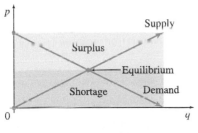

FIGURE 12

(c) Graph both functions on the same axes.

▶**Solution** The results of part (a) are written as the ordered pairs (5, 5.25) and (7, 3.75). The line through those points is the graph of the demand function, $p = 9 - 0.75q$, shown in red in Figure 11(a). We used the ordered pairs (7, 5.25) and (4, 3) from the work in part (b) to graph the supply function, $p = 0.75q$, shown in blue in Figure 11(a). ▬

A calculator-generated graph of the lines representing the supply and demand functions in Example 2 is shown in Figure 11(b). To get this graph, the equation of each line, using x and y instead of q and p, was entered, along with an appropriate window. A special menu choice gives the coordinates of the intersection point, as shown at the bottom of the graph.

NOTE   Not all supply and demand problems will have the same scale on both axes. It helps to consider the intercepts of both the supply graph and the demand graph to decide what scale to use. For example, in Figure 11, the y-intercept of the demand function is 9, so the scale should allow values from 0 to at least 9 on the vertical axis. The x-intercept of the demand function is 12, so the values on the x-axis must go from 0 to 12. ▪

As shown in the graphs of Figure 11, both the supply graph and the demand graph pass through the point (6, 4.5). If the price of a watermelon is more than $4.50, the supply will exceed the demand and there will be a **surplus** of watermelons. At a price less than $4.50, the demand will exceed the supply and there will be a **shortage** of watermelons. Only at a price of $4.50 will demand and supply be equal. For this reason, $4.50 is called the *equilibrium price*. When the price is $4.50, demand and supply both equal 6000 watermelons, the *equilibrium quantity*. In general, the **equilibrium price** of the commodity is the price found at the point where the supply and demand graphs for that commodity intersect. The **equilibrium quantity** is the demand and supply at that same point. Figure 12 illustrates a general supply and demand situation.

EXAMPLE 3   **Equilibrium Quantity**
Use algebra to find the equilibrium quantity for the watermelons in Example 2.

▶**Solution** The equilibrium quantity is found when the prices from both supply and demand are equal. Set the two expressions for p equal to each other and solve.

$$9 - 0.75q = 0.75q$$
$$9 = 1.5q \quad \text{Add 0.75q to both sides.}$$
$$6 = q$$

The equilibrium quantity is 6000 watermelons, the same answer found earlier. ▬

You may prefer to find the equilibrium quantity by solving the equation with your calculator. Or, if your calculator has a TABLE feature, you can use it to find the value of q that makes the two expressions equal.

Another important issue is how, in practice, the equations of the supply and demand functions can be found. This issue is important for many problems involving linear functions in this section and the next. Data need to be collected, and if they lie perfectly along a line, then the equation can easily be found with any two points. What usually happens, however, is that the data are scattered, and there is no line that goes through all the points. In this case we must find a line that approximates the linear trend of the data as closely as possible (assuming the points lie approximately along a line) as in Example 15 in the previous section. This is usually done by the *method of least squares*, also referred to as *linear regression*. We will discuss this method in Section 1.3.

Cost Analysis   The cost of manufacturing an item commonly consists of two parts. The first is a **fixed cost** for designing the product, setting up a factory, training workers, and so on. Within broad limits, the fixed cost is constant for a particular product and does not change as more items are made. The second part is a *cost per item* for labor, materials, packing, shipping, and so on. The total value of this second cost *does* depend on the number of items made.

EXAMPLE 4   Cost Analysis

Suppose that the cost of producing video games can be approximated by

$$C(x) = 12x + 500,$$

where $C(x)$ is the cost in dollars to produce x games. The cost to produce 0 games is

$$C(0) = 12(0) + 500 = 500,$$

or \$500. This sum, \$500, is the fixed cost.

Once the company has invested the fixed cost into the video game project, what will be the additional cost per game? As an example, let's compare the costs of making 5 games and 6 games:

$$C(5) = 12(5) + 500 = 560 \quad \text{and} \quad C(6) = 12(6) + 500 = 572,$$

or \$560 and \$572, respectively.

So the 6th game itself costs \$572 − \$560 = \$12 to produce. In the same way, the 81st game costs $C(81) − C(80) = \$1472 − \$1460 = \$12$ to produce. In fact, the $(n + 1)$st game costs

$$C(n + 1) - C(n) = [12(n + 1) + 500] - (12n + 500)$$
$$= 12n + 12 + 500 - 12n - 500$$
$$= 12,$$

or \$12, to produce. The number 12 is also the slope of the graph of the cost function $C(x) = 12x + 500$; the slope gives us the cost to produce an additional item.

In economics, **marginal cost** is the rate of change of cost $C(x)$ at a level of production x and is equal to the slope of the cost function at x. It approximates the cost of producing one additional item. In fact, some books define the marginal cost to be the cost of producing one additional item. With *linear functions*, these two definitions are equivalent, and the marginal cost, which is equal to the slope of the cost function, is *constant*. For instance, in the video game example, the marginal cost of each game is \$12. For other types of functions, these two definitions are only approximately equal. Marginal cost is important to management in making decisions in areas such as cost control, pricing, and production planning.

The work in Example 4 can be generalized. Suppose the total cost to make x items is given by the linear cost function $C(x) = mx + b$. The fixed cost is found by letting $x = 0$:

$$C(0) = m \cdot 0 + b = b;$$

thus, the fixed cost is b dollars. The additional cost of the $(n + 1)$st item, the marginal cost, is m, the slope of the line $C(x) = mx + b$.

LINEAR COST FUNCTION

In a cost function of the form $C(x) = mx + b$, the m represents the marginal cost per item and b the fixed cost. Conversely, if the fixed cost of producing an item is b and the marginal cost is m, then the **linear cost function** $C(x)$ for producing x items is $C(x) = mx + b$.

EXAMPLE 5 **Cost Function**

The marginal cost to make x batches of a prescription medication is \$10 per batch, while the cost to produce 100 batches is \$1500. Find the cost function $C(x)$, given that it is linear.

▶**Solution** Since the cost function is linear, it can be expressed in the form $C(x) = mx + b$. The marginal cost is \$10 per batch, which gives the value for m, leading to $C(x) = 10x + b$. To find b, use the fact that the cost of producing 100 batches of tablets is \$1500, or $C(100) = 1500$. Substituting $C(x) = 1500$ and $x = 100$ into $C(x) = 10x + b$ gives

$$1500 = 10 \cdot 100 + b$$

$$1500 = 1000 + b$$

$$500 = b. \qquad \text{Subtract 1000 from both sides.}$$

The cost function is given by $C(x) = 10x + 500$, where the fixed cost is \$500.

Break-Even Analysis The **revenue** $R(x)$ from selling x units of an item is the product of the price per unit p and the number of units sold (demand) x, so that

$$R(x) = px.$$

The corresponding **profit** $P(x)$ is the difference between revenue $R(x)$ and cost $C(x)$. That is,

$$P(x) = R(x) - C(x).$$

A company can make a profit only if the revenue received from its customers exceeds the cost of producing and selling its goods and services. The number of units at which revenue just equals cost is the **break-even quantity**; the corresponding ordered pair gives the **break-even point**.

EXAMPLE 6

?

Break-Even Analysis

A firm producing poultry feed finds that the total cost $C(x)$ in dollars of producing and selling x units is given by

$$C(x) = 20x + 100.$$

Management plans to charge $24 per unit for the feed.

(a) How many units must be sold for the firm to break even?

▶**Solution** The firm will break even (no profit and no loss) as long as revenue just equals cost, or $R(x) = C(x)$. From the given information, since $R(x) = px$ and $p = \$24$,

$$R(x) = 24x.$$

Substituting for $R(x)$ and $C(x)$ in the equation $R(x) = C(x)$ gives

$$24x = 20x + 100,$$

from which $x = 25$. The firm breaks even by selling 25 units, which is the break-even quantity. The graphs of $C(x) = 20x + 100$ and $R(x) = 24x$ are shown in Figure 13. The break-even point (where $x = 25$) is shown on the graph. If the company sells more than 25 units (if $x > 25$), it makes a profit. If it sells fewer than 25 units, it loses money.

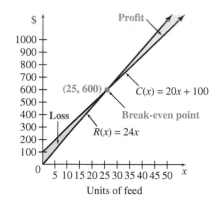

FIGURE 13

(b) What is the profit if 100 units of feed are sold?

▶**Solution** Use the formula for profit $P(x)$.

$$\begin{aligned} P(x) &= R(x) - C(x) \\ &= 24x - (20x + 100) \\ &= 4x - 100 \end{aligned}$$

Then $P(100) = 4(100) - 100 = 300$. The firm will make a profit of $300 from the sale of 100 units of feed.

(c) How many units must be sold to produce a profit of $900?

▶**Solution** Let $P(x) = 900$ in the equation $P(x) = 4x - 100$ and solve for x.

$$\begin{aligned} 900 &= 4x - 100 \\ 1000 &= 4x \\ x &= 250 \end{aligned}$$

Sales of 250 units will produce $900 profit.

Temperature   One of the most common linear relationships found in everyday situations deals with temperature. Recall that water freezes at 32° Fahrenheit and 0° Celsius, while it boils at 212° Fahrenheit and 100° Celsius.* The ordered pairs $(0, 32)$ and $(100, 212)$ are graphed in Figure 14 on axes showing Fahrenheit (F) as a function of Celsius (C). The line joining them is the graph of the function.

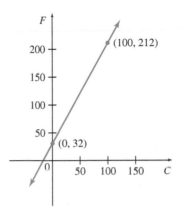

FIGURE 14

EXAMPLE 7   Temperature

Derive an equation relating F and C.

▶**Solution**   To derive the required linear equation, first find the slope using the given ordered pairs, $(0, 32)$ and $(100, 212)$.

$$m = \frac{212 - 32}{100 - 0} = \frac{9}{5}$$

The F-intercept of the graph is 32, so by the slope-intercept form, the equation of the line is

$$F = \frac{9}{5}C + 32.$$

With simple algebra this equation can be rewritten to give C in terms of F:

$$C = \frac{5}{9}(F - 32).$$

---

*Gabriel Fahrenheit (1686–1736), a German physicist, invented his scale with 0° representing the temperature of an equal mixture of ice and ammonium chloride (a type of salt), and 96° as the temperature of the human body. (It is often said, erroneously, that Fahrenheit set 100° as the temperature of the human body. Fahrenheit's own words are quoted in *A History of the Thermometer and Its Use in Meteorology* by W. E. Knowles, Middleton: The Johns Hopkins Press, 1966, p. 75.) The Swedish astronomer Anders Celsius (1701–1744) set 0° and 100° as the freezing and boiling points of water.

► 1.2 Exercises

For Exercises 1–10, let $f(x) = 7 - 5x$ and $g(x) = 2x - 3$. Find the following.

1. $f(2)$ **2.** $f(4)$

3. $f(-3)$ **4.** $f(-1)$

5. $g(1.5)$ **6.** $g(2.5)$

7. $g(-1/2)$ **8.** $g(-3/4)$

9. $f(t)$ **10.** $g(k^2)$

In Exercises 11–14, decide whether the statement is true or false.

11. To find the *x*-intercept of the graph of a linear function, we solve $y = f(x) = 0$, and to find the *y*-intercept, we evaluate $f(0)$.

12. The graph of $f(x) = -5$ is a vertical line.

13. The slope of the graph of a linear function cannot be undefined.

14. The graph of $f(x) = ax$ is a straight line that passes through the origin.

15. Describe what fixed costs and marginal costs mean to a company.

16. In a few sentences, explain why the price of a commodity not already at its equilibrium price should move in that direction.

17. Explain why a linear function may not be adequate for describing the supply and demand functions.

18. In your own words, describe the break-even quantity, how to find it, and what it indicates.

Write a linear cost function for each situation. Identify all variables used.

19. A Lake Tahoe resort charges a snowboard rental fee of $10 plus $2.25 per hour.

20. An Internet site for downloading music charges a $10 registration fee plus 99 cents per downloaded song.

21. A parking garage charges 2 dollars plus 75 cents per half-hour.

22. For a one-day rental, a car rental firm charges $44 plus 28 cents per mile.

Assume that each situation can be expressed as a linear cost function. Find the cost function in each case.

23. Fixed cost: $100; 50 items cost $1600 to produce.

24. Fixed cost: $35; 8 items cost $395 to produce.

25. Marginal cost: $75; 50 items cost $4300 to produce.

26. Marginal cost: $120; 700 items cost $96,500 to produce.

▶ Applications

27. *Supply and Demand* Suppose that the demand and price for a certain model of a youth wristwatch are related by

$$p = D(q) = 16 - 1.25q,$$

where p is the price (in dollars) and q is the demand (in hundreds). Find the price at each level of demand.

a. 0 watches   **b.** 400 watches   **c.** 800 watches

Find the demand for the watch at each price.

d. $8   **e.** $10   **f.** $12

g. Graph $p = 16 - 1.25q$.

Suppose the price and supply of the watch are related by

$$p = S(q) = 0.75q,$$

where p is the price (in dollars) and q is the supply (in hundreds) of watches. Find the supply at each price.

h. $0   **i.** $10   **j.** $20

k. Graph $p = 0.75q$ on the same axis used for part g.

l. Find the equilibrium quantity and the equilibrium price.

28. *Supply and Demand* Suppose that the demand and price for strawberries are related by

$$p = D(q) = 5 - 0.25q,$$

where p is the price (in dollars) and q is the demand (in hundreds of quarts). Find the price at each level of demand.

a. 0 quarts   **b.** 400 quarts   **c.** 840 quarts

Find the demand for the strawberries at each price.

d. $4.50   **e.** $3.25   **f.** $2.40

g. Graph $p = 5 - 0.25q$.

Suppose the price and supply of strawberries are related by

$$p = S(q) = 0.25q,$$

where p is the price (in dollars) and q is the supply (in hundreds of quarts) of strawberries. Find the supply at each price.

h. $0   **i.** $2   **j.** $4.50

k. Graph $p = 0.75q$ on the same axis used for part g.

l. Find the equilibrium quantity and the equilibrium price.

29. *Supply and Demand* Let the supply and demand functions for butter pecan ice cream be given by

$$p = S(q) = \frac{2}{5}q \quad \text{and} \quad p = D(q) = 100 - \frac{2}{5}q,$$

where p is the price in dollars and q is the number of 10-gallon tubs.

a. Graph these on the same axes.

b. Find the equilibrium quantity and the equilibrium price. (*Hint:* The way to divide by a fraction is to multiply by its reciprocal.)

30. *Supply and Demand* Let the supply and demand functions for sugar be given by

$$p = S(q) = 1.4q - 0.6 \quad \text{and}$$
$$p = D(q) = -2q + 3.2,$$

where p is the price per pound and q is the quantity in thousands of pounds.

a. Graph these on the same axes.

b. Find the equilibrium quantity and the equilibrium price.

31. *T-Shirt Cost* Joanne Ha sells silk-screened T-shirts at community festivals and crafts fairs. Her marginal cost to produce one T-shirt is $3.50. Her total cost to produce 60 T-shirts is $300, and she sells them for $9 each.

a. Find the linear cost function for Joanne's T-shirt production.

b. How many T-shirts must she produce and sell in order to break even?

c. How many T-shirts must she produce and sell to make a profit of $500?

32. *Publishing Costs* Juan Santiago owns a small publishing house specializing in Latin American poetry. His fixed cost to produce a typical poetry volume is $525, and his total cost to produce 1000 copies of the book is $2675. His books sell for $4.95 each.

a. Find the linear cost function for Juan's book production.

b. How many poetry books must he produce and sell in order to break even?

c. How many books must he produce and sell to make a profit of $1000?

33. *Marginal Cost of Coffee* The manager of a restaurant found that the cost to produce 100 cups of coffee is $11.02, while the cost to produce 400 cups is $40.12. Assume the cost $C(x)$ is a linear function of x, the number of cups produced.

a. Find a formula for $C(x)$.

b. What is the fixed cost?

c. Find the total cost of producing 1000 cups.

d. Find the total cost of producing 1001 cups.

e. Find the marginal cost of the 1001st cup.

f. What is the marginal cost of *any* cup and what does this mean to the manager?

34. *Marginal Cost of a New Plant* In deciding whether to set up a new manufacturing plant, company analysts have decided that a linear function is a reasonable estimation for the total cost $C(x)$ in dollars to produce x items. They estimate the cost to produce 10,000 items as \$547,500, and the cost to produce 50,000 items as \$737,500.

  a. Find a formula for $C(x)$.

  b. Find the fixed cost.

  c. Find the total cost to produce 100,000 items.

  d. Find the marginal cost of the items to be produced in this plant and what does this mean to the manager?

35. *Bread Sales* Panera Bread, a national chain, has become a popular coffee house specializing in baked breads and other tasty consumables. During its first 5 years, the company claimed a sales growth of 5000%.*

  a. Suppose sales were \$100,000 in 1991. At this growth rate, what would sales have been in 1996?

  b. Let x correspond to the number of years since 1990. Write two ordered pairs representing sales in 1991 and 1996. Assuming sales increased linearly, write a linear sales function for this company using these two ordered pairs.

  c. Use the equation in part b to predict when sales should reach one billion dollars. The actual sales were expected to be \$1 billion in 2003. Discuss the assumption that the growth rate has been linear.

  d. Actual sales were \$356 million in 2003 and \$479 million in 2004.† Letting x correspond to the number of years since 1990, use these more recent sales figures to write a new linear sales function.

  e. Use the function from part d to estimate sales for 2005 and compare these to the actual sales of \$640 million.

  f. Using the linear function found in part d, estimate the year in which sales will reach \$1 billion.

36. *Break-Even Analysis* Producing x units of tacos costs $C(x) = 5x + 20$; revenue is $R(x) = 15x$, where $C(x)$ and $R(x)$ are in dollars.

  a. What is the break-even quantity?

  b. What is the profit from 100 units?

  c. How many units will produce a profit of \$500?

37. *Break-Even Analysis* To produce x units of a religious medal costs $C(x) = 12x + 39$. The revenue is $R(x) = 25x$. Both $C(x)$ and $R(x)$ are in dollars.

  a. Find the break-even quantity.

  b. Find the profit from 250 units.

  c. Find the number of units that must be produced for a profit of \$130.

Break-Even Analysis You are the manager of a firm. You are considering the manufacture of a new product, so you ask the accounting department for cost estimates and the sales department for sales estimates. After you receive the data, you must decide whether to go ahead with production of the new product. Analyze the data in Exercises 38–41 (find a break-even quantity) and then decide what you would do in each case. Also write the profit function.

38. $C(x) = 85x + 900$; $R(x) = 105x$; no more than 38 units can be sold.

39. $C(x) = 105x + 6000$; $R(x) = 250x$; no more than 400 units can be sold.

40. $C(x) = 70x + 500$; $R(x) = 60x$ (*Hint*: What does a negative break-even quantity mean?)

41. $C(x) = 1000x + 5000$; $R(x) = 900x$

PHYSICAL SCIENCES

42. *Temperature* Use the formula for conversion between Fahrenheit and Celsius derived in Example 7 to convert each temperature.

  a. 58°F to Celsius

  b. −20°F to Celsius

  c. 50°C to Fahrenheit

43. *Body Temperature* You may have heard that the average temperature of the human body is 98.6°. Recent experiments show that the actual figure is closer to 98.2°.‡ The figure of 98.6 comes from experiments done by Carl Wunderlich in 1868. But Wunderlich measured the temperatures in degrees Celsius and rounded the average to the nearest degree, giving 37°C as the average temperature.§

  a. What is the Fahrenheit equivalent of 37°C?

  b. Given that Wunderlich rounded to the nearest degree Celsius, his experiments tell us that the actual average human body temperature is somewhere between 36.5°C and 37.5°C. Find what this range corresponds to in degrees Fahrenheit.

44. *Temperature* Find the temperature at which the Celsius and Fahrenheit temperatures are numerically equal.

---

*The New York Times, November 18, 1995, pp. 19 and 21.
†http://money.excite.com.
‡Science News, Sept. 26, 1992, p. 195.
§Science News, Nov. 7, 1992, p. 399.

1.3 The Least Squares Line

How has the accidental death rate in the United States changed over time?

In this section, we show how to answer such questions using the method of least squares. We use past data to find trends and to make tentative predictions about the future. The only assumption we make is that the data are related linearly—that is, if we plot pairs of data, the resulting points will lie close to some line. This method cannot give exact answers. The best we can expect is that, if we are careful, we will get a reasonable approximation.

The table lists the number of accidental deaths per 100,000 people in the United States through the past century.* If you were a manager at an insurance company, these data could be very important. You might need to make some predictions about how much you will pay out next year in accidental death benefits, and even a very tentative prediction based on past trends is better than no prediction at all.

The first step is to draw a scatterplot, as we have done in Figure 15. Notice that the points lie approximately along a line, which means that a linear function may give a good approximation of the data. If we select two points and find the line that passes through them, as we did in Section 1.1, we will get a different line for each pair of points, and in some cases the lines will be very different. We want to draw one line that is simultaneously close to all the points on the graph, but many such lines are possible, depending upon how we define the phrase "simultaneously close to all the points." How do we decide on the best possible line? Before going on, you might want to try drawing the line you think is best on Figure 15.

The line used most often in applications is that in which the sum of the squares of the vertical distances from the data points to the line is as small as possible. Such a line is called the **least squares line**. The least squares line for the data in Figure 15 is drawn in Figure 16. How does the line compare with the one you drew on Figure 15? It may not be exactly the same, but should appear similar.

In Figure 16, the vertical distances from the points to the line are indicated by d_1, d_2, and so on, up through d_{10} (read "d-sub-one, d-sub-two, d-sub-three," and so on). For n points, corresponding to the n pairs of data, the least squares line is found by minimizing the sum $(d_1)^2 + (d_2)^2 + (d_3)^2 + \cdots + (d_n)^2$.

Year	Death Rate
1910	84.4
1920	71.2
1930	80.5
1940	73.4
1950	60.3
1960	52.1
1970	56.2
1980	46.5
1990	36.9
2000	34.0

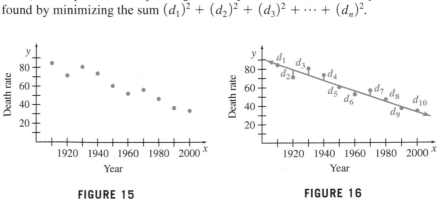

FIGURE 15

FIGURE 16

*U.S. Department of Health and Human Services, National Center for Health Statistics.

We often use **summation notation** to write the sum of a list of numbers. The Greek letter sigma, Σ, is used to indicate "the sum of." For example, we write the sum $x_1 + x_2 + \cdots + x_n$, where n is the number of data points, as

$$x_1 + x_2 + \cdots + x_n = \Sigma x.$$

Similarly, Σxy means $x_1 y_1 + x_2 y_2 + \cdots + x_n y_n$, and so on.

CAUTION Note that Σx^2 means $x_1^2 + x_2^2 + \cdots + x_n^2$, which is *not* the same as squaring Σx. When we square Σx, we write it as $(\Sigma x)^2$. ∎

For the least squares line, the sum of the distances we are to minimize, $d_1^2 + d_2^2 + \cdots + d_n^2$, is written as

$$d_1^2 + d_2^2 + \cdots + d_n^2 = \Sigma d^2.$$

To calculate the distances, we let $(x_1, y_1), (x_2, y_2), \ldots, (x_n, y_n)$ be the actual data points and we let the least squares line be $Y = mx + b$. We use Y in the equation instead of y to distinguish the predicted values (Y) from the y-value of the given data points. The predicted value of Y at x_1 is $Y_1 = mx_1 + b$, and the distance, d_1, between the actual y-value y_1 and the predicted value Y_1 is

$$d_1 = |Y_1 - y_1| = |mx_1 + b - y_1|.$$

Likewise,

$$d_2 = |Y_2 - y_2| = |mx_2 + b - y_2|,$$

and

$$d_n = |Y_n - y_n| = |mx_n + b - y_n|.$$

The sum to be minimized becomes

$$\Sigma d^2 = (mx_1 + b - y_1)^2 + (mx_2 + b - y_2)^2 + \cdots + (mx_n + b - y_n)^2$$
$$= \Sigma (mx + b - y)^2,$$

where $(x_1, y_1), (x_2, y_2), \ldots, (x_n, y_n)$ are known and m and b are to be found.

The method of minimizing this sum requires advanced techniques and is not given here. To obtain the equation for the least squares line, a system of equations must be solved, producing the following formulas for determining the slope m and y-intercept b.*

LEAST SQUARES LINE

The **least squares line** $Y = mx + b$ that gives the best fit to the data points $(x_1, y_1), (x_2, y_2), \ldots, (x_n, y_n)$ has slope m and y-intercept b given by

$$m = \frac{n(\Sigma xy) - (\Sigma x)(\Sigma y)}{n(\Sigma x^2) - (\Sigma x)^2} \quad \text{and} \quad b = \frac{\Sigma y - m(\Sigma x)}{n}.$$

---

*Also see Exercise 5, at the end of this section.

EXAMPLE 1

?

Least Squares Line

Calculate the least squares line for the accidental death rate data.

▶Solution

METHOD 1
Calculating by Hand

To find the least squares line for the given data, we first find the required sums. To reduce the size of the numbers, we rescale the year data. Let x represent the years since 1900, so that, for example, $x = 10$ corresponds to the year 1910. Let y represent the death rate. We then calculate the values in the xy, x^2, and y^2 columns and find their totals. (The column headed y^2 will be used later.) Note that the number of data points is $n = 10$.

x	y	xy	x^2	y^2
10	84.4	844	100	7123.36
20	71.2	1424	400	5069.44
30	80.5	2415	900	6480.25
40	73.4	2936	1600	5387.56
50	60.3	3015	2500	3636.09
60	52.1	3126	3600	2714.41
70	56.2	3934	4900	3158.44
80	46.5	3720	6400	2162.25
90	36.9	3321	8100	1361.61
100	34.0	3400	10,000	1156.00
$\Sigma x = 550$	$\Sigma y = 595.5$	$\Sigma xy = 28,135$	$\Sigma x^2 = 38,500$	$\Sigma y^2 = 38,249.41$

Putting the column totals into the formula for the slope m, we get

$$m = \frac{n(\Sigma xy) - (\Sigma x)(\Sigma y)}{n(\Sigma x^2) - (\Sigma x)^2}$$ Formula for m

$$= \frac{10(28,135) - (550)(595.5)}{10(38,500) - (550)^2}$$ Substitute from the table.

$$= \frac{281,350 - 327,525}{385,000 - 302,500}$$ Multiply.

$$= \frac{-46,175}{82,500}$$ Subtract.

$$= -0.5596970 \approx -0.560.$$

The significance of m is that the death rate per 100,000 people is tending to drop (because of the negative) at a rate of 0.560 per year.

Now substitute the value of m and the column totals in the formula for b:

$$b = \frac{\Sigma y - m(\Sigma x)}{n} \qquad \text{Formula for } b$$

$$= \frac{595.5 - (-0.559697)(550)}{10} \qquad \text{Substitute.}$$

$$= \frac{595.5 - (-307.83335)}{10} \qquad \text{Multiply.}$$

$$= \frac{903.33335}{10} = 90.333335 \approx 90.3$$

Substitute m and b into the least squares line, $Y = mx + b$; the least squares line that best fits the 10 data points has equation

$$Y = -0.560x + 90.3.$$

This gives a mathematical description of the relationship between the year and the number of accidental deaths per 100,000 people. The equation can be used to predict y from a given value of x, as we will show in Example 2. As we mentioned before, however, caution must be exercised when using the least squares equation to predict data points that are far from the range of points on which the equation was modeled.

CAUTION In computing m and b, we rounded the final answer to three digits because the original data were known only to three digits. It is important, however, *not* to round any of the intermediate results (such as Σx^2) because round-off error may have a detrimental effect on the accuracy of the answer. Similarly, it is important not to use a rounded-off value of m when computing b. ∎

METHOD 2
Graphing Calculator

The calculations for finding the least squares line are often tedious, even with the aid of a calculator. Fortunately, many calculators can calculate the least squares line with just a few keystrokes. For purposes of illustration, we will show how the least squares line in the previous example is found with a TI-83/84 Plus graphing calculator.

We begin by entering the data into the calculator. We will be using the first two lists, called L_1 and L_2. Choosing the STAT menu, then choosing the fourth entry ClrList, we enter L_1, L_2, to indicate the lists to be cleared. Now we press STAT again and choose the first entry EDIT, which brings up the blank lists. As before, we will only use the last two digits of the year, putting the numbers in L_1. We put the death rate in L_2, giving the two screens shown in Figure 17.

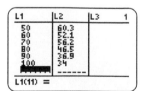

FIGURE 17

Press STAT again and choose CALC instead of EDIT. Then choose item 4 LinReg $(ax + b)$ to get the values of a (the slope) and b (the y-intercept) for the least squares line, as shown in Figure 18. With *a* and *b* rounded to three decimal places, the least squares line is $Y = -0.560x + 90.3$. A graph of the data points and the line is shown in Figure 19.

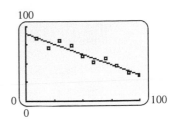

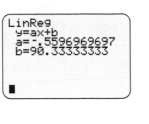

FIGURE 18   **FIGURE 19**

For more details on finding the least squares line with a graphing calculator, see *The Graphing Calculator Manual* available with this book.

METHOD 3
Spreadsheet

Many computer spreadsheet programs can also find the least squares line. Figure 20 shows the scatterplot and least squares line for the accidental death rate data using an Excel spreadsheet. The scatterplot was found using the XY(Scatter) command under Chart Wizard, and the line was found using the Add Trendline command under the Chart menu. For details, see *The Spreadsheet Manual* available with this book.

Accidental Deaths

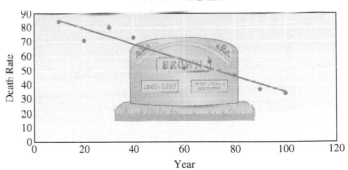

FIGURE 20

EXAMPLE 2   **Least Squares Line**

What do we predict the accidental death rate to be in 2007?

▶**Solution** Use the least squares line equation given above with $x = 107$.

$$Y = -0.560x + 90.3$$
$$= -0.56(107) + 90.3$$
$$= 30.38$$

The accidental death rate in 2007 is predicted to be about 30.4 per 100,000 population. In this case, we will have to wait until the 2007 data become available to see how accurate our prediction is. We have observed, however, that data for

2001, 2002, and 2003 indicate that the actual accidental death rate is going up slightly. This could be a simple short-term anomaly or an actual upward trend, which will certainly be determined as time goes by.

EXAMPLE 3   **Least Squares Line**

In what year is the death rate predicted to drop below 26 per 100,000 population?

▶**Solution** Let $Y = 26$ in the equation above and solve for x.

$$26 = -0.560x + 90.3$$

$$-64.3 = -0.560x \qquad \text{Subtract 90.3 from both sides.}$$

$$x = 114.8 \qquad \text{Divide both sides by } -0.560.$$

This means that after 114 years, the rate will not have quite reached 26 per 100,000, so we must wait 115 years for this to happen. This corresponds to the year 2015 (115 years after 1900), when our equation predicts the death rate to be $-0.560(115) + 90.3 = 25.9$ per 100,000 population.

Correlation   Once an equation is found for the least squares line, we need to have some way of judging just how good the equation is for predictive purposes. If the points from the data fit the line quite closely, then we have more reason to expect future data pairs to do so. But if the points are widely scattered about even the best-fitting line, then predictions are not likely to be accurate.

In order to have a quantitative basis for confidence in our predictions, we need a measure of the "goodness of fit" of the original data to the prediction line. One such measure is called the **coefficient of correlation**, denoted r.

COEFFICIENT OF CORRELATION

$$r = \frac{n(\Sigma xy) - (\Sigma x)(\Sigma y)}{\sqrt{n(\Sigma x^2) - (\Sigma x)^2} \cdot \sqrt{n(\Sigma y^2) - (\Sigma y)^2}}$$

Although the expression for r looks daunting, remember that each of the summations, Σx, Σy, Σxy, and so on, are just the totals from a table like the one we prepared for the data on accidental deaths. Also, with a calculator, the arithmetic is no problem!

The coefficient of correlation r is always equal to or between 1 and -1. Values of exactly 1 or -1 indicate that the data points lie *exactly* on the least squares line. If $r = 1$, the least squares line has a positive slope; $r = -1$ gives a negative slope. If $r = 0$, there is no linear correlation between the data points (but some *nonlinear* function might provide an excellent fit for the data). A correlation of zero may also indicate that the data fit a horizontal line. To investigate what is happening, it is always helpful to sketch a scatterplot of the data. Some scatterplots that correspond to these values of r are shown in Figure 21.

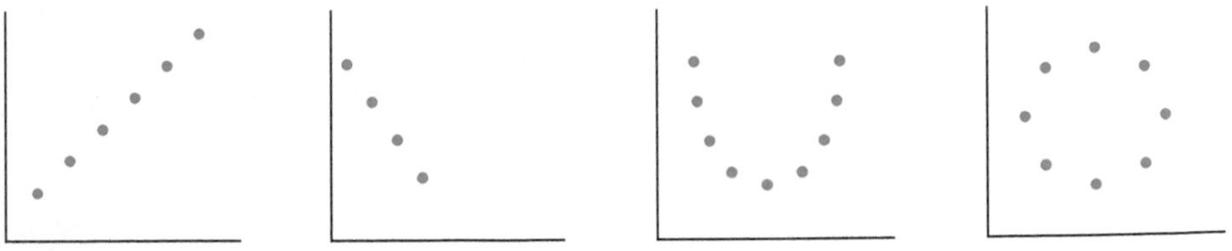

r close to 1   r close to –1   r close to 0   r close to 0

FIGURE 21

A value of r close to 1 or -1 indicates the presence of a linear relationship. The exact value of r necessary to conclude that there is a linear relationship depends upon n, the number of data points, as well as how confident we want to be of our conclusion. For details, consult a text on statistics.*

EXAMPLE 4

Coefficient of Correlation

Find r for the data on accidental death rates in Example 1.

▶**Solution**

METHOD 1
Calculating by Hand

From the table in Example 1,

$\Sigma x = 550$, $\Sigma y = 595.5$, $\Sigma xy = 28{,}135$, $\Sigma x^2 = 38{,}500$,

$\Sigma y^2 = 38{,}249.41$, and $n = 10$.

Substituting these values into the formula for r gives

$$r = \frac{n(\Sigma xy)-(\Sigma x)(\Sigma y)}{\sqrt{n(\Sigma x^2)-(\Sigma x)^2} \cdot \sqrt{n(\Sigma y^2)-(\Sigma y)^2}}$$ Formula for r

$$= \frac{10(28{,}135)-(550)(595.5)}{\sqrt{10(38{,}500)-(550)^2} \cdot \sqrt{10(38{,}249.41)-(595.5)^2}}$$ Substitute.

$$= \frac{281{,}350 - 327{,}525}{\sqrt{385{,}000 - 302{,}500} \cdot \sqrt{382{,}494.1 - 354{,}620.25}}$$ Multiply.

$$= \frac{-46{,}175}{\sqrt{82{,}500} \cdot \sqrt{27{,}873.85}}$$ Subtract.

$$= \frac{-46{,}175}{47{,}954.06787}$$ Take square roots and multiply.

$$= -0.9629005849 \approx -0.963.$$

This is a high correlation, which agrees with our observation that the data fit a line quite well.

METHOD 2
Graphing Calculator

Most calculators that give the least squares line will also give the coefficient of correlation. To do this on the TI-83/84 Plus, press the second function CATALOG and go down the list to the entry DiagnosticOn. Press ENTER at that

*For example, see *Introductory Statistics*, 7th edition, by Neil A. Weiss, Boston, Mass.: Addison-Wesley, 2005.

point, then press STAT, CALC, and choose item 4 to get the display in Figure 22. The result is the same as we got by hand. The command DiagnosticOn need only be entered once, and the coefficient of correlation will always appear in the future.

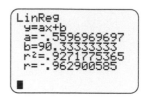

FIGURE 22

METHOD 3
Spreadsheet

Many computer spreadsheet programs have a built-in command to find the coefficient of correlation. For example, in Excel, use the command "= CORREL(A1:A10,B1:B10)" to find the correlation of the 10 data points stored in columns A and B. For more details, see *The Spreadsheet Manual* available with this text.

EXAMPLE 5 **Airline Passengers**

The following table shows the number of airline passengers in the United States (in millions) from 1996 to 2005.*

Year	1996	1997	1998	1999	2000	2001	2002	2003	2004	2005
Passengers	581.2	594.7	612.9	636.0	666.2	622.1	611.9	655.4	712.6	745.7

(a) Create a scatterplot of the data.

▶**Solution** A graphing calculator graph of the data is shown in Figure 23(a).

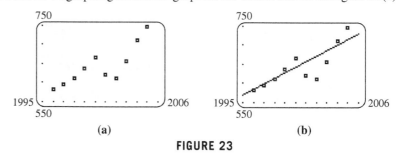

(a)   **(b)**

FIGURE 23

Notice that the data appear to be increasing linearly from 1996 to 2000, but there is a downward decline from 2000 to 2002. The most likely explanation for this downward spiral is the terrorist attack on September 11, 2001. The data again begin to increase linearly from 2002 to 2005. The scatterplot indicates that a significant event has occurred that temporarily stopped the increase.

(b) Find the correlation coefficient and the line that best fits the data.

▶**Solution** Figure 24 shows the result of the LinReg command on the TI-83/84 Plus calculator. The graph of the least squares line is shown in Figure 23(b).

The correlation coefficient is $r = 0.843$, which indicates a fairly strong linear correlation. The equation for the least squares line is $Y = 14.55697x - 28,477.35$.

FIGURE 24

*http://www.bts.gov.

Using this equation, however, we would predict the number of passengers in 2005 to be about 709,400,000. This equation does not appear to be a good predictor for recent years, as illustrated in Figure 23(b).

There is little doubt that the events of 2001 greatly affected the airline industry. A question now arises as to how to handle the data from that time period. One option would be to simply start over with data from 2002. For example, if the same analysis had been done using data from 2002 to 2005, we would get $r = 0.995$ and $Y = 45.86x - 91,199.11$. (Verify this on your calculator.) The prediction for the number of passengers in 2005 is about 750,200,000, which is much closer to the actual value.

A second option would be to determine that the data points from 2001 and 2002 do not accurately reflect normal airline traffic patterns and perform the analysis without these data points. In this case, the resulting least squares line would be $Y = 16.01541x - 31,384.23$ and $r = 0.947$. The prediction for the number of passengers in 2005 is about 726,700,000, which is also closer to the actual value.

EXAMPLE 6 **Average Expenditure per Pupil Versus Test Scores**

Many states and school districts debate whether or not increasing the amount of money spent per student will guarantee academic success. The following table lists the 2003 average per pupil expenditure and the average eighth grade reading score on the National Assessment of Education Progress (NAEP) for the 50 states and the District of Columbia.*

	Expenditure (dollars)	Score		Expenditure (dollars)	Score		Expenditure (dollars)	Score
AL	6553	253	LA	7209	253	OH	8963	267
AK	10,114	256	ME	9534	268	OK	6176	262
AZ	6036	255	MD	9212	262	OR	7619	264
AR	6740	258	MA	10,693	273	PA	9979	264
CA	7748	251	MI	9072	264	RI	9903	261
CO	7412	268	MN	8359	268	SC	7184	258
CT	10,788	267	MS	6237	255	SD	6949	270
DE	10,228	265	MO	7331	267	TN	6504	258
FL	6784	257	MT	7763	270	TX	7104	259
GA	7733	258	NE	8032	266	UT	5008	264
HI	8533	251	NV	6399	252	VT	11,128	271
ID	6028	264	NH	8860	271	VA	8225	268
IL	8656	266	NJ	12,981	268	WA	7243	264
IN	8280	265	NM	7331	252	WV	8475	260
IA	7631	268	NY	12,930	265	WI	9226	266
KS	7518	266	NC	6702	262	WY	9363	267
KY	6888	266	ND	7727	270	DC	12,801	239

*U.S. Census Bureau: Annual Survey of Local Government Finances and National Center for Education Statistics, Common Core of Data and Nation's Report Card.

Draw a scatterplot of the data and calculate the correlation coefficient.

▶Solution A spreadsheet was used to plot the points, and the scatterplot is shown in Figure 25(a).

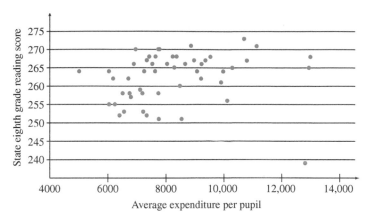

FIGURE 25(a)

The correlation coefficient is $r = 0.144$. Notice that one data point (corresponding to DC) is way off by itself. As shown in Example 5, sometimes, by removing such a point from the graph, we can achieve a higher correlation.* Figure 25(b) shows the scatterplot with the remaining 50 points. The correlation coefficient has almost tripled to $r = 0.396$, but it still does not indicate that NAEP eighth grade reading scores and per pupil expenditure have a strong linear correlation.

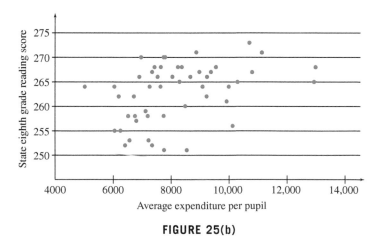

FIGURE 25(b)

*Before discarding a point, we should investigate the reason it is an outlier.

▶ 1.3 Exercises

1. Suppose a positive linear correlation is found between two quantities. Does this mean that one of the quantities increasing causes the other to increase? If not, what does it mean?

2. Given a set of points, the least squares line formed by letting x be the independent variable will not necessarily be the same as the least squares line formed by letting y be the independent variable. Give an example to show why this is true.

3. For the following table of data,

   a. Draw a scatterplot.

   b. Calculate the correlation coefficient.

   c. Calculate the least squares line and graph it on the scatterplot.

   d. Predict the y-value when x is 11.

x	1	2	3	4	5	6	7	8	9	10
y	0	0.5	1	2	2.5	3	3	4	4.5	5

*The following problem is reprinted from the November 1989 Actuarial Examination on Applied Statistical Methods.**

4. You are given

X	6.8	7.0	7.1	7.2	7.4
Y	0.8	1.2	0.9	0.9	1.5

Determine r^2, the coefficient of determination for the regression of Y on X. (Choose one of the following. *Note:* The coefficient of determination is defined as the square of the coefficient of correlation.)

   a. 0.3   **b.** 0.4   **c.** 0.5   **d.** 0.6   **e.** 0.7

5. The formulas for the least squares line were found by solving the system of equations

$$nb + (\Sigma x)m = \Sigma y$$
$$(\Sigma x)b + (\Sigma x^2)m = \Sigma xy.$$

Solve the above system for b and m to show that

$$m = \frac{n(\Sigma xy) - (\Sigma x)(\Sigma y)}{n(\Sigma x^2) - (\Sigma x)^2} \quad \text{and} \quad b = \frac{\Sigma y - m(\Sigma x)}{n}.$$

*"November 1989 Course 120 Examination Applied Statistical Methods" of the *Education and Examination Committee of The Society of Actuaries.* Reprinted by permission of The Society of Actuaries.

▶ **Applications**

BUSINESS AND ECONOMICS

6. *Recreation Spending* The U.S. Department of Commerce, Bureau of Economic Analysis, has reported the total U.S. expenditures on recreational goods (hobbies, music, sports, spectator admissions, etc.). From 1998 to 2004, expenditures have grown at an approximately linear rate. The results of the report, in which x represents the years since 1900 and y represents the total expenditures (in billions of dollars), provide the following summations.*

$$n = 7 \quad \Sigma x^2 = 71,435 \quad \Sigma x = 707$$

$$\Sigma xy = 223,963.8 \quad \Sigma y = 2212 \quad \Sigma y^2 = 709,879.52$$

a. Find an equation for the least squares line.

b. Predict the recreational expenditures in 2010.

c. If this growth continues linearly, when will recreational expenditures reach 750 billion dollars?

d. Find and interpret the coefficient of correlation.

7. *Decrease in Banks* The number of banks in the United States has dropped about 25% since 1995. The following data are from a survey in which x represents the years since 1900 and y corresponds to the number of banks, in thousands, in the United States.[†]

$$n = 10 \quad \Sigma x^2 = 99,085 \quad \Sigma x = 995$$

$$\Sigma xy = 8501.39 \quad \Sigma y = 85.65 \quad \Sigma y^2 = 739.08$$

a. Find an equation for the least squares line.

b. If the trend continues, how many banks will there be in 2010?

c. Find and interpret the coefficient of correlation.

8. *Air Fares* In 2006, for passengers who made early reservations, American Airlines offered lower prices on one-way fares from New York to various cities. Fourteen of the cities are listed in the following table, with the distances from New York to the cities included.[‡]

a. Plot the data. Do the data points lie in a linear pattern?

b. Find the correlation coefficient. Combining this with your answer to part a, does the cost of a ticket tend to go up with the distance flown?

c. Find the equation of the least squares line, and use it to find the approximate marginal cost per mile to fly.

d. For similar data in a January 2000 *New York Times* ad, the equation of the least squares line was $Y = 113 + 0.0243x$.[§] Use this information and your answer to part b to compare the cost of flying American Airlines for these two time periods.

e. Identify the outlier in the scatterplot. Discuss the reason why there would be a difference in price to this city.

City	Distance (x) (miles)	Price (y) (dollars)
Boston	206	95
Chicago	802	138
Denver	1771	228
Kansas City	1198	209
Little Rock	1238	269
Los Angeles	2786	309
Minneapolis	1207	202
Nashville	892	217
Phoenix	2411	109
Portland	2885	434
Reno	2705	399
St. Louis	948	206
San Diego	2762	239
Seattle	2815	329

9. *Consumer Debt* Credit card debt has risen steadily over the years. The following table gives the average U.S. credit card debt (in dollars) per household in recent years.[‖] Let x represent the number of years since 1900. (The table includes all credit cards and U.S. households with at least one credit card.)

Years	Debt	Years	Debt
1997	6247	2001	8234
1998	6618	2002	8940
1999	7031	2003	9205
2000	7842	2004	9312

---

*The World Almanac and Book of Facts 2006, p. 83.
[†]FDIC, Historical Statistics on Banking, http://www2.fdic.gov/hsob/index, Table CB01.
[‡]American Airlines, http://www.aa.com.
[§]The New York Times, Jan. 7, 2000.
[‖]"Low Credit Card Rates Getting Rare," posted 9/20/2004, http://www.usatoday.com, and "Is the American Dream Still Possible?" April 23, 2006, http://www.parade.com/.

a. Plot the data. Does the graph show a linear pattern?

b. Find the equation of the least squares line and graph it on the same axes. Does the line appear to be a good fit?

c. Find and interpret the coefficient of correlation.

d. If this linear trend continues, when will credit card debt per household reach $12,000?

10. *New Car Sales* New car sales have increased at a roughly linear rate. Sales, in millions of vehicles, from 1992 to 2005, are given in the table below.* Let x represent the number of years since 1900.

Year	Sales	Year	Sales
1992	12.8	1999	17.0
1993	13.9	2000	17.4
1994	15.0	2001	17.2
1995	14.7	2002	16.8
1996	15.1	2003	16.7
1997	15.2	2004	16.9
1998	15.6	2005	17.0

a. Find the equation of the least squares line and the coefficient of correlation.

b. Find the equation of the least squares line using only the data for every other year starting with 1993, 1995, and so on. Find the coefficient of correlation.

c. Compare your results for parts a and b. What do you find? Why do you think this happens?

LIFE SCIENCES

11. *Size of Hunting Parties* In the 1960s, the famous researcher Jane Goodall observed that chimpanzees hunt and eat meat as part of their regular diet. Sometimes chimpanzees hunt alone, while other times they form hunting parties. The following table summarizes research on chimpanzee hunting parties, giving the size of the hunting party and the percentage of successful hunts.[†]

Number of Chimps in Hunting Party	Percentage of Successful Hunts
1	20
2	30
3	28
4	42
5	40
6	58
7	45
8	62
9	65
10	63
12	75
13	75
14	78
15	75
16	82

a. Plot the data. Do the data points lie in a linear pattern?

b. Find the correlation coefficient. Combining this with your answer to part a, does the percentage of successful hunts tend to increase with the size of the hunting party?

c. Find the equation of the least squares line, and graph it on your scatterplot.

12. *Bird Eggs* The average length and width of various bird eggs are given in the following table.[‡]

Bird Name	Width (cm)	Length (cm)
Canada goose	5.8	8.6
Robin	1.5	1.9
Turtledove	2.3	3.1
Hummingbird	1.0	1.0
Raven	3.3	5.0

*"The 2006 Used Car Market Report," http://www.manheimconsulting.com.
†Stanford, Craig B., "Chimpanzee Hunting Behavior and Human Evolution," *American Scientist,* Vol. 83, May–June 1995, pp. 256–261, and Goetz, Albert, "Using Open-Ended Problems for Assessment," *Mathematics Teacher*, Vol. 99, No. 1, August 2005, pp.12–17.
‡www.nctm.org/wlme/wlme6/five.htm.

a. Plot the points, putting the length on the y-axis and the width on the x-axis. Do the data appear to be linear?

b. Find the least squares line, and plot it on the same graph as the data.

c. Suppose there are birds with eggs even smaller than those of hummingbirds. Would the equation found in part b continue to make sense for all positive widths, no matter how small? Explain.

d. Find the coefficient of correlation.

13. *Crickets Chirping* Biologists have observed a linear relationship between the temperature and the frequency with which a cricket chirps. The following data were measured for the striped ground cricket.*

Temperature °F (x)	Chirps per Second (y)
88.6	20.0
71.6	16.0
93.3	19.8
84.3	18.4
80.6	17.1
75.2	15.5
69.7	14.7
82.0	17.1
69.4	15.4
83.3	16.2
79.6	15.0
82.6	17.2
80.6	16.0
83.5	17.0
76.3	14.4

a. Find the equation for the least squares line for the data.

b. Use the results of part a to determine how many chirps per second you would expect to hear from the striped ground cricket if the temperature were 73°F.

c. Use the results of part a to determine what the temperature is when the striped ground crickets are chirping at a rate of 18 times per sec.

d. Find the coefficient of correlation.

SOCIAL SCIENCES

14. *Pupil-Teacher Ratios* The following table gives the national average pupil-teacher ratio in public schools over selected years.[†]

Year	Ratio	Year	Ratio
1955	26.9	1985	17.9
1960	25.8	1990	17.2
1965	24.7	1995	17.3
1970	22.3	2000	16.0
1980	18.7	2005	15.5

a. Find the equation for the least squares line. Let x correspond to the number of years since 1950 and let y correspond to the average number of pupils per 1 teacher.

b. Use your answer from part a to predict the pupil-teacher ratio in 2010. Does this seem realistic?

c. Calculate and interpret the coefficient of correlation.

15. *Poverty Levels* The following table lists how poverty level income cutoffs (in dollars) for a family of four have changed over time.[‡]

Year	Income
1970	3968
1975	5500
1980	8414
1985	10,989
1990	13,359
1995	15,569
2000	17,604
2005	19,961

Let x represent the year, with $x = 0$ corresponding to 1970 and y represent the income in thousands of dollars. (*Note:* $n = 8$, $\Sigma x = 140$, $\Sigma x^2 = 3500$, $\Sigma xy = 2159.635$, $\Sigma y = 95.364$, $\Sigma y^2 = 1366.748$.)

a. Plot the data. Do the data appear to lie along a straight line?

b. Calculate the coefficient of correlation. Does your result agree with your answer to part a?

---

*Pierce, George W., *The Songs of Insects*, Cambridge, Mass., Harvard University Press, Copyright © 1948 by the President and Fellows of Harvard College.
[†]*Digest of Education Statistics 2005*, Table 63.
[‡]U.S. Census Bureau, *Historical Poverty Tables*.

c. Find the equation of the least squares line.

d. Use your answer from part c to predict the poverty level in the year 2020.

16. *SAT Scores* At Hofstra University, all students take the math SAT before entrance, and most students take a mathematics placement test before registration. Recently, one professor collected the following data for 19 students in his Finite Mathematics class:

Math SAT	Placement Test	Math SAT	Placement Test	Math SAT	Placement Test
540	20	580	8	440	10
510	16	680	15	520	11
490	10	560	8	620	11
560	8	560	13	680	8
470	12	500	14	550	8
600	11	470	10	620	7
540	10				

a. Find an equation for the least squares line. Let x be the math SAT and y be the placement test score.

b. Use your answer from part a to predict the mathematics placement test score for a student with a math SAT score of 420.

c. Use your answer from part a to predict the mathematics placement test score for a student with a math SAT score of 620.

d. Calculate the coefficient of correlation.

e. Based on your answer to part d, what can you conclude about the relationship between a student's math SAT and mathematics placement test score?

PHYSICAL SCIENCES

17. *Air Conditioning* While shopping for an air conditioner, Adam Bryer consulted the following table, which gives a machine's BTUs and the square footage (ft²) that it would cool.

a. Find the equation for the least squares line for the data.

b. To check the fit of the data to the line, use the results from part a to find the BTUs required to cool a room of 150 ft², 280 ft², and 420 ft². How well does the actual data agree with the predicted values?

ft² (x)	BTUs (y)
150	5000
175	5500
215	6000
250	6500
280	7000
310	7500
350	8000
370	8500
420	9000
450	9500

c. Suppose Adam's room measures 230 ft². Use the results from part a to decide how many BTUs it requires. If air conditioners are available only with the BTU choices in the table, which would Adam choose?

d. Why do you think the table gives ft² instead of ft³, which would give the volume of the room?

18. *Length of a Pendulum* Grandfather clocks use pendulums to keep accurate time. The relationship between the length of a pendulum L and the time T for one complete oscillation can be determined from the data in the table.*

L (ft)	T (sec)
1.0	1.11
1.5	1.36
2.0	1.57
2.5	1.76
3.0	1.92
3.5	2.08
4.0	2.22

a. Plot the data from the table with L as the horizontal axis and T as the vertical axis.

b. Find the least squares line equation and graph it simultaneously, if possible, with the data points. Does it seem to fit the data?

c. Find the coefficient of correlation and interpret it. Does it confirm your answer to part b?†

*Data provided by Gary Rockswold, Mankato State University, Minnesota.
†The actual relationship is $L = 0.81T^2$, which is not a linear equation. This illustrates that even if the relationship is not linear, a line can give a good approximation.

19. *Athletic Records* The table shows the men's and women's outdoor world records (in seconds) in the 800-m run.*

Year	Men's Record	Women's Record
1905	113.4	—
1915	111.9	—
1925	111.9	144
1935	109.7	135.6
1945	106.6	132
1955	105.7	125
1965	104.3	118
1975	103.7	117.48
1985	101.73	113.28
1995	101.11	113.28
2005	101.11	113.28

Let x be the year, with $x = 0$ corresponding to 1900.

a. Find the equation for the least squares line for the men's record (y) in terms of the year (x).

b. Find the equation for the least squares line for the women's record.

c. Suppose the men's and women's records continue to improve as predicted by the equations found in parts a and b. In what year will the women's record catch up with the men's record? Do you believe that will happen? Why or why not?

d. Calculate the coefficient of correlation for both the men's and the women's record. What do these numbers tell you?

e. Draw a plot of the data, and discuss to what extent a linear function describes the trend in the data.

20. *Football* The following data give the expected points for a football team with first down and 10 yards to go from various points on the field.[†] (*Note:* $\sum x = 500$, $\sum x^2 = 33,250$, $\sum y = 20.668$, $\sum y^2 = 91.927042$, $\sum xy = 399.16$.)

a. Calculate the coefficient of correlation. Does there appear to be a linear correlation?

b. Find the equation of the least squares line.

c. Use your answer from part a to predict the expected points when a team is at the 50-yd line.

Yards from Goal (x)	Expected Points (y)
5	6.041
15	4.572
25	3.681
35	3.167
45	2.392
55	1.538
65	0.923
75	0.236
85	−0.637
95	−1.245

21. *Baseball* The average length of Major League Baseball games has increased as indicated by the table on the next page. Many fans and television executives have indicated a desire to significantly reduce the length of a game. Since 2002, league officials have even taken several steps to reduce the length of the game, including giving umpires the authority to call a ball if a pitch is not delivered within 12 seconds when no one is on base.[‡]

*Whipp, Brian J. and Susan Ward, "Will Women Soon Outrun Men?" *Nature*, Vol. 355, Jan. 2, 1992, p. 25. The data are from Peter Matthews, *Track and Field Athletics: The Records*, Guinness, 1986, pp. 11, 44; from Robert W. Schultz and Yuanlong Liu, in *Statistics in Sports*, edited by Jay Bennett, Arnold, 1998, p. 189; and from *The World Almanac and Book of Facts 2006*, p. 880.
[†]Carter, Virgil and Robert E. Machol, *Operations Research*, Vol. 19, 1971, pp. 541–545.
[‡]http://www.usatoday.com/sports/baseball/.

Year	Average Completion Time	Year	Average Completion Time
1982	2:34	1992	2:49
1984	2:35	1994	2:54
1986	2:44	1996	2:51
1988	2:45	1998	2:48
1990	2:48	2000	2:58

Let x be the number of years since 1980 and let y be the number of minutes an average game lasts beyond 2 hours. (*Note:* $\Sigma x = 110$, $\Sigma x^2 = 1540$, $\Sigma y = 466$, $\Sigma y^2 = 22{,}232$, $\Sigma xy = 5496$.)

a. Find the equation of the least squares line.

b. Calculate the coefficient of correlation. Does there appear to be a positive linear correlation?

c. Assuming the steps taken by the Major League Baseball did not decrease the length of the average baseball game and the previous trend continued, estimate the length of a game in 2005.

d. The average length of a Major League Baseball game in 2005 was 2:46. Compare this value with the one obtained in part c. Has the average length of baseball games decreased?

22. *Running* If you think a marathon is a long race, consider the Hardrock 100, a 101.7-mile running race held in southwestern Colorado. The following table lists the times that the 2000 winner, Kirk Apt, arrived at various mileage points along the way.*

a. What was Apt's average speed?

b. Graph the data, plotting time on the x-axis and distance on the y-axis. You will need to convert the time from hours and minutes into hours. Do the data appear to lie approximately on a straight line?

c. Find the equation for the least squares line, fitting distance as a linear function of time.

d. Calculate the coefficient of correlation. Does it indicate a good fit of the least squares line to the data?

e. Based on your answer to part d, what is a good value for Apt's average speed? Compare this with your answer to part a. Which answer do you think is better? Explain your reasoning.

Miles	Time (hr:min)
0	0
9.6	2:14
16.5	4:08
21.6	6:10
31.6	7:10
42.4	10:51
49.8	12:42
58.0	14:20
65.2	16:30
68.4	18:02
73.7	19:25
83.1	23:07
89.6	26:09
95.8	28:18
101.7	29:35

*Hardrock Hundred Mile Endurance Run, 2000 Hardrock Results Spreadsheet, http://www.run100s.com/HR/.

Chapter 1 Review

► Chapter Summary

In this chapter we studied linear functions, whose graphs are straight lines. We developed the slope-intercept and point-slope formulas, which can be used to find the equation of a line, given a point and the slope or given two points. We saw that lines have many applications in virtually every discipline. Lines are used through the rest of this book, so fluency in their use is important. We concluded the chapter by introducing the method of least squares, which is used to find an equation of the line that best fits a given set of data.

LINEAR FUNCTIONS SUMMARY

Slope of a Line   The slope of a line is defined as the vertical change (the "rise") over the horizontal change (the "run") as one travels along the line. In symbols, taking two different points (x_1, y_1) and (x_2, y_2) on the line, the slope is

$$m = \frac{y_2 - y_1}{x_2 - x_1},$$

where $x_1 \neq x_2$.

Equations of Lines

Equation	Description
$y = mx + b$	Slope intercept form: slope m and y-intercept b.
$y - y_1 = m(x - x_1)$	Point-slope form: slope m and line passes through (x_1, y_1).
$x = k$	Vertical line: x-intercept k, no y-intercept (except when $k = 0$), undefined slope.
$y = k$	Horizontal line: y-intercept k, no x-intercept (except when $k = 0$), slope 0.

Parallel Lines   Two lines are parallel if and only if they have the same slope, or if they are both vertical.

Perpendicular Lines   Two lines are perpendicular if and only if the product of their slopes is -1, or if one is vertical and the other horizontal.

Linear Function   A relationship f defined by

$$y = f(x) = mx + b,$$

for real numbers m and b, is a linear function.

Linear Cost Function   In a cost function of the form $C(x) = mx + b$, the m represents the marginal cost per item and b represents the fixed cost.

Least Squares Line   The least squares line $Y = mx + b$ that gives the best fit to the data points
$(x_1, y_1), (x_2, y_2), \ldots, (x_n, y_n)$ has slope m and y-intercept b given by the equations

$$m = \frac{n(\Sigma xy) - (\Sigma x)(\Sigma y)}{n(\Sigma x^2) - (\Sigma x)^2}$$

$$b = \frac{\Sigma y - m(\Sigma x)}{n}$$

Coefficient of Correlation

$$r = \frac{n(\Sigma xy) - (\Sigma x)(\Sigma y)}{\sqrt{n(\Sigma x^2) - (\Sigma x)^2} \; \sqrt{n(\Sigma y^2) - (\Sigma y)^2}}$$

▶  Key Terms

To understand the concepts presented in this chapter, you should know the meaning and use of the following terms. For easy reference, the section in the chapter where a word (or expression) was first used is provided.

mathematical model	intercepts	**1.2** linear function	linear cost function
1.1 ordered pair	slope	independent variable	revenue
Cartesian coordinate	linear equation	dependent variable	profit
system	slope-intercept form	surplus	break-even quantity
axes	proportional	shortage	break-even point
origin	point-slope form	equilibrium price	**1.3** least squares line
coordinates	parallel	equilibrium quantity	summation notation
quadrants	perpendicular	fixed cost	coefficient of
graph	scatterplot	marginal cost	correlation

▶ *Concept Check*

Determine whether each of the following statements is true or false, and explain why.

1. A given line can have more than one slope.

2. The equation $y = 3x + 4$ represents the equation of a line with slope 4.

3. The line $y = -2x + 5$ intersects the point $(3, -1)$.

4. The line that intersects the points $(2, 3)$ and $(2, 5)$ is a horizontal line.

5. The line that intersects the points $(4, 6)$ and $(5, 6)$ is a horizontal line.

6. The x-intercept of the line $y = 8x + 9$ is 9.

7. The function $f(x) = \pi x + 4$ represents a linear function.

8. The function $f(x) = 2x^2 + 3$ represents a linear function.

9. The lines $y = 3x + 17$ and $y = -3x + 8$ are perpendicular.

10. The lines $4x + 3y = 8$ and $4x + y = 5$ are parallel.

11. A correlation coefficient of zero indicates a perfect fit with the data.

12. It is not possible to get a correlation coefficient of -1.5 for a set of data.

▶ Chapter 1 Review Exercises

1. What is marginal cost? Fixed cost?

2. What six quantities are needed to compute a coefficient of correlation?

Find the slope for each line that has a slope.

3. Through $(-3, 7)$ and $(2, 12)$

4. Through $(4, -1)$ and $(3, -3)$

5. Through the origin and $(11, -2)$

6. Through the origin and $(0, 7)$

7. $4x + 3y = 6$

8. $4x - y = 7$

9. $y + 4 = 9$

10. $3y - 1 = 14$

11. $y = 5x + 4$

12. $x = 5y$

Find an equation in the form $y = mx + b$ (where possible) for each line.

13. Through $(5, -1)$; slope $= 2/3$

14. Through $(8, 0)$; slope $= -1/4$

15. Through $(-6, 3)$ and $(2, -5)$

16. Through $(2, -3)$ and $(-3, 4)$

17. Through $(-1, 4)$; undefined slope

18. Through $(-2, 5)$; slope $= 0$

19. Through $(3, -4)$, parallel to $4x - 2y = 9$

20. Through $(0, 5)$, perpendicular to $8x + 5y = 3$

21. Through $(2, -10)$, perpendicular to a line with undefined slope

22. Through $(3, -5)$, parallel to $y = 4$

23. Through $(-3, 5)$, perpendicular to $y = -2$

Graph each linear equation defined as follows.

24. $y = 4x + 3$

25. $y = 6 - 2x$

26. $3x - 5y = 15$

27. $4x + 6y = 12$

28. $x - 3 = 0$

29. $y = 1$

30. $y = 2x$

31. $x + 3y = 0$

▶ Applications

BUSINESS AND ECONOMICS

32. *Profit* To manufacture x thousand computer chips requires fixed expenditures of $352 plus $42 per thousand chips. Receipts from the sale of x thousand chips amount to $130 per thousand.

a. Write an expression for expenditures.

b. Write an expression for receipts.

c. For profit to be made, receipts must be greater than expenditures. How many chips must be sold to produce a profit?

33. *Supply and Demand* The supply and demand for crabmeat in a local fish store are related by the equations

$$\text{Supply: } p = S(q) = 6q + 3$$

and

$$\text{Demand: } p = D(q) = 19 - 2q,$$

where p represents the price in dollars per pound and q represents the quantity of crabmeat in pounds per day. Find the supply and demand at each of the following prices.

a. $10   **b.** $15   **c.** $18

d. Graph both the supply and the demand functions on the same axes.

e. Find the equilibrium price.

f. Find the equilibrium quantity.

34. *Supply* For a new diet pill, 60 pills will be supplied at a price of $40, while 100 pills will be supplied at a price of $60. Write a linear supply function for this product.

35. *Demand* The demand for the diet pills in Exercise 34 is 50 pills at a price of $47.50 and 80 pills at a price of $32.50. Determine a linear demand function for these pills.

36. *Supply and Demand* Find the equilibrium price and quantity for the diet pills in Exercises 34 and 35.

Cost Find a linear cost function in Exercises 37–40.

37. Eight units cost $300; fixed cost is $60.

38. Fixed cost is $2000; 36 units cost $8480.

39. Twelve units cost $445; 50 units cost $1585.

40. Thirty units cost $1500; 120 units cost $5640.

41. *Break-Even Analysis* The cost of producing x cartons of CDs is $C(x)$ dollars, where $C(x) = 200x + 1000$. The CDs sell for $400 per carton.

    a. Find the break-even quantity.

    b. What revenue will the company receive if it sells just that number of cartons?

42. *Break-Even Analysis* The cost function for flavored coffee at an upscale coffeehouse is given in dollars by $C(x) = 3x + 160$, where x is in pounds. The coffee sells for $7 per pound.

    a. Find the break-even quantity.

    b. What will the revenue be at that point?

43. *U.S. Imports from China* The United States is China's largest export market. Imports from China have grown from about 102 billion dollars in 2001 to 243 billion dollars in 2005.* This growth has been approximately linear. Use the given data pairs to write a linear equation that describes this growth in imports over the years. Let $x = 1$ represent 2001 and $x = 5$ represent 2005.

44. *U.S. Exports to China* U.S. exports to China have grown (although at a slower rate than imports) since 2001. In 2001, about 19 billion dollars of goods were exported to China. By 2005, this amount had grown to 42 billion dollars.* Write a linear equation describing the number of exports each year, with $x = 1$ representing 2001 and $x = 5$ representing 2005.

45. *Median Income* The U.S. Census Bureau reported that the median income for all U.S. households in 2005 was $46,326. In 1997, the median income (in 2005 dollars) was

$44,883.[†] The median income is approximately linear and is a function of time. Find a formula for the median income, I, as a function of the year x, where x is the number of years since 1900.

46. *New Car Cost* The average new car cost for selected years from 1980 to 2005 is given in the table.[‡]

Year	1980	1985	1990	1995	2000	2005
Cost	7500	12,000	16,000	20,450	24,900	28,400

    a. Let x represent the number of years since 1900 and let y be the cost in thousands of dollars. Find an equation for the least squares line.

    b. Use your equation from part a to predict the average cost of a new car in the year 2010 ($x = 110$).

    c. Find and interpret the coefficient of correlation. Does it indicate that the line is a good fit for the data?

    d. Plot the data. Does the scatterplot suggest the trend might not be linear?

LIFE SCIENCES

47. *World Health* In general, people tend to live longer in countries that have a greater supply of food. Listed below is the 2002 daily caloric supply and 2002 life expectancy at birth for 10 randomly selected countries.[§]

Country	Calories (x)	Life Expectancy (y)
Tanzania	1960	43
Belize	2840	74
Cambodia	2060	54
France	3630	79
India	2420	63
Mexico	3160	74
New Zealand	3220	78
Peru	2550	70
Sweden	3140	80
United States	3790	77

    a. Find the coefficient of correlation. Do the data seem to fit a straight line?

*TradeStats Express™—National Trade Data, http://tse.export.gov.
[†]U.S. Census Bureau, Historical Income Tables—Households, Table H-6, 2005.
[‡]*Chicago Tribune*, Feb. 4, 1996, Sec. 5, p. 4, and NADA Industry Analysis Division, 2006.
[§]Food and Agriculture Organization Statistical Yearbook, Table D1, Table G5, http://www.fao.org/es/ess/yearbook/vol_1_1/.

b. Draw a scatterplot of the data. Combining this with your results from part a, do the data seem to fit a straight line?

c. Find the equation of the least squares line.

d. Use your answer from part c to predict the life expectancy in the United Kingdom, which has a daily calorie supply of 3400. Compare your answer with the actual value of 78 years.

e. Briefly explain why countries with a higher daily calorie supply might tend to have a longer life expectancy.

f. (For the ambitious!) Find the coefficient of correlation and least squares line using the data for a larger sample of countries, as found in an almanac or other reference. Is the result in general agreement with the previous results?

48. *Blood Sugar and Cholesterol Levels* The following data show the connection between blood sugar levels and cholesterol levels for eight different patients.

Patient	Blood Sugar Level (x)	Cholesterol Level (y)
1	130	170
2	138	160
3	142	173
4	159	181
5	165	201
6	200	192
7	210	240
8	250	290

For the data given in the preceding table, $\Sigma x = 1394$, $\Sigma y = 1607$, $\Sigma xy = 291,990$, $\Sigma x^2 = 255,214$, and $\Sigma y^2 = 336,155$.

a. Find the equation of the least squares line, $Y = mx + b$.

b. Predict the cholesterol level for a person whose blood sugar level is 190.

c. Find r.

SOCIAL SCIENCES

49. *Red Meat Consumption* The per capita consumption of red meat in the United States decreased from 142.3 lb in 1974 to 118.4 lb in 2004.* Assume a linear function describes the decrease. Write a linear equation defining the function. Let x represent the number of years since 1900 and y represent the number of pounds of red meat consumed.

50. *Marital Status* More people are staying single longer in the United States. In 1995, the number of never-married adults, age 15 and over, was 55.0 million. By 2005, it was 67.0 million.[†] Assume the data increase linearly, and write an equation that defines a linear function for this data. Let x represent the number of years since 1900.

51. *Governors' Salaries* In general, the larger a state's population, the more the governor earns. Listed in the table below are the estimated 2005 populations (in millions) and the salary of the governor (in thousands of dollars) for eight randomly selected states.[‡]

a. Find the coefficient of correlation. Do the data seem to fit a straight line?

b. Draw a scatterplot of the data. Compare this with your answer from part a.

c. Find the equation for the least squares line.

d. Based on your answer to part c, how much does a governor's salary increase, on average, for each additional million in population?

e. Use your answer from part c to predict the governor's salary in your state. Based on your answers from parts a and b, would this prediction be very accurate? Compare with the actual salary, as listed in an almanac or other reference.

f. (For the ambitious!) Find the coefficient of correlation and least squares line using the data for all 50 states, as found in an almanac or other reference. Is the result in general agreement with the previous results?

State	AZ	DE	MD	MA	NY	PA	TN	WY
Population (x)	5.94	0.84	5.60	6.40	19.25	12.43	5.96	0.51
Governor's Salary (y)	95	114	145	135	179	145	85	105

*USDA Economic Research Service, http://www.ers.usda.gov/data/.
[†]U.S. Census Bureau, http://www.census.gov/population/socdemo/hh-fam/ms1.xls.
[‡]*The World Almanac and Book of Facts 2006*, p. 65, and U.S. Census Bureau, http://www.census.gov/popest/estimates.php.

Using Extrapolation to Predict Life Expectancy

One reason for developing a mathematical model is to make predictions. If your model is a least squares line, you can predict the *y*-value corresponding to some new *x* by substituting this *x* into an equation of the form $Y = mx + b$. (We use a capital *Y* to remind us that we're getting a predicted value rather than an actual data value.) Data analysts distinguish between two very different kinds of prediction, *interpolation* and *extrapolation*. An interpolation uses a new *x* inside the *x* range of your original data. For example, if you have inflation data at 5-year intervals from 1950 to 2000, estimating the rate of inflation in 1957 is an interpolation problem. But if you use the same data to estimate what the inflation rate was in 1920, or what it will be in 2020, you are extrapolating.

In general, interpolation is much safer than extrapolation, because data that are approximately linear over a short interval may be nonlinear over a larger interval. One way to detect nonlinearity is to look at *residuals,* which are the differences between the actual data values and the values predicted by the line of best fit. Here is a simple example:

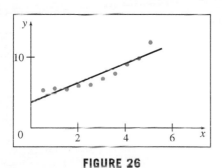

FIGURE 26

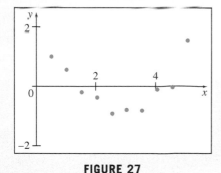

FIGURE 27

The regression equation for the linear fit in Figure 26 is $Y = 3.431 + 1.334x$. Since the *r*-value for this regression line is 0.93, our linear model fits the data very well. But we might notice that the predictions are a bit low at the ends and high in the middle. We can get a better look at this pattern by plotting the residuals. To find them, we put each value of the independent variable into the regression equation, calculate the predicted value *Y*, and subtract it from the actual *y*-value. The residual plot is shown in Figure 27, with the vertical axis rescaled to exaggerate the pattern. The residuals indicate that our data have a nonlinear, U-shaped component that is not captured by the linear fit. Extrapolating from this data set is probably not a good idea; our linear prediction for the value of *y* when *x* is 10 may be much too low.

EXERCISES

The following table gives the life expectancy at birth of females born in the United States in various years from 1970 to 2005. *

Year of Birth	Life Expectancy (years)
1970	74.7
1975	76.6
1980	77.4
1985	78.2
1990	78.8
1995	78.9
2000	79.5
2005	80.8

1. Find an equation for the least squares line for these data, using year of birth as the independent variable.

2. Use your regression equation to guess a value for the life expectancy of females born in 1900.

3. Compare your answer with the actual life expectancy for females born in 1900, which was 48.3 years. Are you surprised?

4. Find the life expectancy predicted by your regression equation for each year in the table, and subtract it from the actual value in the second column. This gives you a table of residuals. Plot your residuals as points on a graph.

5. Now look at the residuals as a fresh data set and see if you can sketch the graph of a smooth function that fits the residuals well. How easy do you think it will be to predict the life expectancy at birth of females born in 2015?

*The World Almanac and Book of Facts 2006, p. 181, and http://www.cia.gov/cia/publications/ factbook/geos/us.html.

6. What will happen if you try linear regression on the *residuals*? If you're not sure, use your calculator or software to find the regression equation for the residuals. Why does this result make sense?

7. Since most of the females born in 1995 are still alive, how did the Public Health Service come up with a life expectancy of 78.9 years for these women?

DIRECTIONS FOR GROUP PROJECT

Assume that you and your group (3–5 students) are preparing a report for a local health agency that is interested in using linear regression to predict life expectancy. Using the questions above as a guide, write a report that addresses the spirit of each question and any issues related to that question. The report should be mathematically sound, grammatically correct, and professionally crafted. Provide recommendations as to whether the health agency should proceed with the linear equation or whether it should seek other means of making such predictions.

2

Systems of Linear Equations and Matrices

▶ The synchronized movements of band members marching on a field can be modeled using matrix arithmetic. An exercise in Section 5 in this chapter shows how multiplication by a matrix inverse transforms the original positions of the marchers into their new coordinates as they change direction.

Many mathematical models require finding the solutions of two or more equations. The solutions must satisfy *all* of the equations in the model. A set of equations related in this way is called a **system of equations**. In this chapter we will discuss systems of equations, introduce the idea of a *matrix*, and then show how matrices are used to solve systems of equations.

2.1 Solution of Linear Systems by the Echelon Method

 **? THINK ABOUT IT**

How much of each ingredient should be used in an animal feed to meet dietary requirements?

Suppose that an animal feed is made from three ingredients: corn, soybeans, and cottonseed. One gram of each ingredient provides the number of grams of protein, fat, and fiber shown in the table. For example, the entries in the first column, 0.25, 0.4, and 0.3, indicate that one gram of corn provides twenty-five hundredths (one-fourth) of a gram of protein, four-tenths of a gram of fat, and three-tenths of a gram of fiber.

	Corn	Soybeans	Cottonseed
Protein	0.25	0.4	0.2
Fat	0.4	0.2	0.3
Fiber	0.3	0.2	0.1

?

Now suppose we need to know the number of grams of each ingredient that should be used to make a feed that contains 22 g of protein, 28 g of fat, and 18 g of fiber. To find out, we let x represent the required number of grams of corn, y the number of grams of soybeans, and z the number of grams of cottonseed. Each gram of corn provides 0.25 g of protein, so the amount of protein provided by x grams of corn is $0.25x$. Similarly, the amount of protein provided by y grams of soybeans is $0.4y$, and the amount of protein provided by z grams of cottonseed is $0.2z$. Since the total amount of protein is to be 22 g,

$$0.25x + 0.4y + 0.2z = 22.$$

The feed must supply 28 g of fat, so

$$0.4x + 0.2y + 0.3z = 28,$$

and 18 g of fiber, so

$$0.3x + 0.2y + 0.1z = 18.$$

To solve this problem, we must find values of x, y, and z that satisfy this system of equations. Verify that $x = 40$, $y = 15$, and $z = 30$ is a solution of the system, since these numbers satisfy all three equations. In fact, this is the only solution of this system. Many practical problems lead to such systems of *first-degree equations*.

A **first-degree equation in n unknowns** is any equation of the form

$$a_1x_1 + a_2x_2 + \cdots + a_nx_n = k,$$

where $a_1, a_2, \ldots, a_n$ and k are real numbers and $x_1, x_2, \ldots, x_n$ represent variables.* Each of the three equations from the animal feed problem is a first-degree equation. For example, the first equation

$$0.25x + 0.4y + 0.2z = 22$$

is a first-degree equation where

$$a_1 = 0.25, \qquad a_2 = 0.4, \qquad a_3 = 0.2, \qquad k = 22$$

and the variables are x, y, and z.

A *solution* of the first-degree equation

$$a_1 x_1 + a_2 x_2 + \cdots + a_n x_n = k$$

is a sequence of numbers $s_1, s_2, \ldots, s_n$ such that

$$a_1 s_1 + a_2 s_2 + \cdots + a_n s_n = k.$$

A solution of an equation is usually written in parentheses as $(s_1, s_2, \ldots, s_n)$. For example, $(1, 6, 2)$ is a solution of the equation $3x_1 + 2x_2 - 4x_3 = 7$, since $3(1) + 2(6) - 4(2) = 7$. This is an extension of the idea of an ordered pair, which was introduced in Chapter 1. A solution of a first-degree equation in two unknowns is an ordered pair, and the graph of the equation is a straight line. For this reason, all first-degree equations are also called linear equations.

Because the graph of a linear equation in two unknowns is a straight line, there are three possibilities for the solutions of a system of two linear equations in two unknowns.

POSSIBLE TYPES OF SOLUTIONS

1. The two graphs are lines intersecting at a single point. The system has a **unique solution**, and it is given by the coordinates of this point. See Figure 1(a).

2. The graphs are distinct parallel lines. When this is the case, the system is **inconsistent**; that is, there is no solution common to both equations. See Figure 1(b).

3. The graphs are the same line. In this case, the equations are said to be **dependent**, since any solution of one equation is also a solution of the other. There are infinitely many solutions. See Figure 1(c).

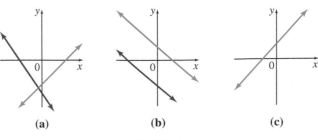

(a)   (b)   (c)

FIGURE 1

---

*a_1 is read "a-sub-one." The notation $a_1, a_2, \ldots, a_n$ represents n real-number coefficients (some of which may be equal), and the notation $x_1, x_2, \ldots, x_n$ represents n different variables, or unknowns.

In larger systems, with more equations and more variables, there also may be exactly one solution, no solutions, or infinitely many solutions. If no solution satisfies every equation in the system, the system is inconsistent, and if there are infinitely many solutions that satisfy all the equations in the system, the equations are dependent.

Methods for solving systems of linear equations with two unknowns are usually introduced in algebra courses. The graphing method shows geometrically how solutions are found, but it may not be possible to determine the exact solution from the graph, especially if the answer does not involve integers. The substitution method, which we used in Chapter 1 to find the equilibrium point, determines the solution algebraically but becomes too difficult with larger systems with many unknowns. The elimination method determines solutions by using the addition property of equality to eliminate variables. We will expand this method to solve systems of linear equations. Although the discussion will be confined to equations with only a few variables, the method of solution can be extended to systems with many variables.

Transformations

To solve a linear system of equations, we use properties of algebra to change, or transform, the system into a simpler *equivalent* system. An **equivalent system** is one that has the same solutions as the given system. Algebraic properties are the basis of the following transformations.

TRANSFORMATIONS OF A SYSTEM

The following transformations can be applied to a system of equations to get an equivalent system:

1. exchanging any two equations;
2. multiplying both sides of an equation by any nonzero real number;
3. replacing any equation by a nonzero multiple of that equation plus a nonzero multiple of any other equation.

Use of these transformations leads to an equivalent system because each transformation can be reversed or "undone," allowing a return to the original system.

The Echelon Method

A systematic approach for solving systems of equations using the three transformations is called the **echelon method**. The goal of the echelon method is to use the transformations to rewrite the equations of the system until the system has a triangular form. For a system of three equations in three variables, for example, the system should have the form

$$x + ay + bz = c$$
$$y + dz = e$$
$$z = f,$$

where a, b, c, d, e, and f are constants. Then the value of z from the third equation can be substituted into the second equation to find y, and the values of y and z can be substituted into the first equation to find x. This is called **back-substitution**.

EXAMPLE 1

Solving a System of Equations with a Unique Solution
Solve the system

$$2x + 3y = 12 \tag{1}$$

$$3x - 4y = 1. \tag{2}$$

▶**Solution** We will first use transformation 3 to eliminate the x-term from equation (2). We multiply equation (1) by 3 and add the results to -2 times equation (2).

$$
\begin{array}{ll}
3(2x + 3y) = 3 \cdot 12 & \quad 6x + 9y = 36 \\
-2(3x - 4y) = -2 \cdot 1 \quad \longrightarrow & \quad \underline{-6x + 8y = -2} \\
& \quad 17y = 34
\end{array}
$$

We will indicate this process by the notation $3R_1 + (-2)R_2 \rightarrow R_2$. (R stands for row.) The new system is

$$2x + 3y = 12 \tag{1}$$

$$3R_1 + (-2)R_2 \rightarrow R_2 \qquad 17y = 34. \tag{3}$$

Now we use transformation 2 to make the coefficient of the first term in each row equal to 1. Here, we must multiply equation (1) by 1/2 and equation (3) by 1/17 to accomplish this.

We get the system

$$\tfrac{1}{2}R_1 \rightarrow R_1 \qquad x + \frac{3}{2}y = 6$$

$$\tfrac{1}{17}R_2 \rightarrow R_2 \qquad \phantom{x + \frac{3}{2}}y = 2.$$

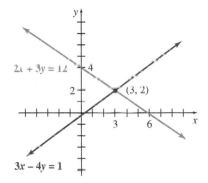

$2x + 3y = 12$

(3, 2)

$3x - 4y = 1$

FIGURE 2

Back-substitution gives

$$x + \frac{3}{2}(2) = 6 \qquad \text{Substitute } y = 2.$$

$$x + 3 = 6$$

$$x = 3.$$

The solution of the system is (3, 2). The graphs of the two equations in Figure 2 suggest that (3, 2) satisfies both equations in the system. Verify that (3, 2) does indeed satisfy both original equations.

EXAMPLE 2

Solving a System of Equations with No Solution
Solve the system

$$2x - 3y = 6 \tag{1}$$

$$-4x + 6y = 8. \tag{2}$$

▶**Solution** Eliminate x in equation (2) to get the system

$$2x - 3y = 6 \tag{1}$$

$$2R_1 + R_2 \rightarrow R_2 \qquad 0 = 20. \tag{3}$$

In equation (3), both variables have been eliminated, leaving a *false statement*. This is a signal that these two equations have no common solution. This system is

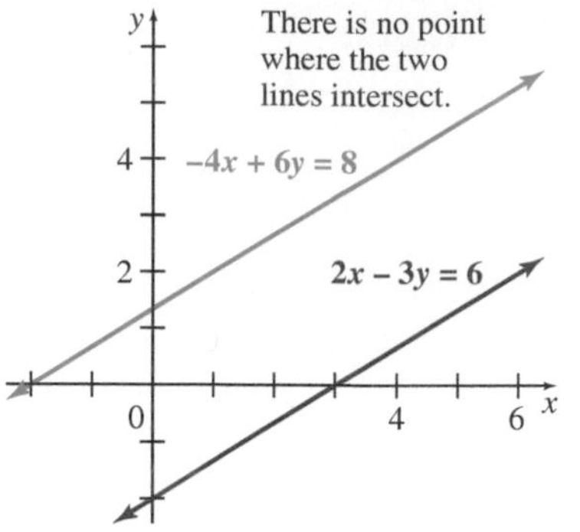

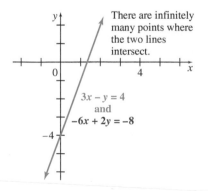

y↑
There is no point
where the two
lines intersect.

4 — $-4x + 6y = 8$

2 — $2x - 3y = 6$

0   4   6   x

FIGURE 3

inconsistent and has no solution, As Figure 3 shows, the graph of the system is made up of two distinct parallel lines. ▬▬

EXAMPLE 3 **Solving a System of Equations with an Infinite Number of Solutions**
Solve the system

$$3x - y = 4 \tag{1}$$
$$-6x + 2y = -8. \tag{2}$$

▶**Solution** We use transformation 3 to eliminate x in equation (2), getting the system

$$3x - y = 4 \tag{1}$$
$$2R_1 + R_2 \rightarrow R_2 \qquad 0 = 0. \tag{3}$$

The system becomes

$$\tfrac{1}{3}R_1 \rightarrow R_1 \qquad x - \frac{1}{3}y = \frac{4}{3} \tag{4}$$

$$0 = 0. \tag{3}$$

y↑
There are infinitely
many points where
the two lines
intersect.

0   4   x

$3x - y = 4$
and
$-6x + 2y = -8$

−4

FIGURE 4

In equation (3), both variables have been eliminated, leaving a *true statement*. If we graph the original equations of the system on the same axes, as shown in Figure 4, we see that the graphs are the same line, and any point on the line will satisfy the system. This system is dependent and has an infinite number of solutions.

We will express the solutions in terms of y, where y can be any real number. The variable y in this case is called a **parameter**. (We could also let x be the parameter. In this text, we will follow the common practice of letting the rightmost variable be the parameter.) Solving equation (4) for x gives $x = (1/3)y + 4/3 = (y + 4)/3$, and all ordered pairs of the form

$$\left(\frac{y + 4}{3}, y \right)$$

are solutions. For example, if we let $y = 5$, then $x = (5 + 4)/3 = 3$ and one solution is $(3, 5)$. Similarly, letting $y = -10$ and $y = 3$ gives the solutions $(-2, -10)$ and $(7/3, 3)$.

Note that the original two equations are solved not only by the particular solutions like $(3, 5)$, $(-2, -10)$, and $(7/3, 3)$, but also by the general solution $(x, y) = ((y + 4)/3, y)$. For example, substituting this general solution into the first equation gives

$$3\left(\frac{y + 4}{3}\right) - y = y + 4 - y = 4,$$

which verifies that this general solution is indeed a solution. ▬▬

In some applications, x and y must be nonnegative integers. For instance, in Example 3, if x and y represent the number of male and female workers in a factory, it makes no sense to have $x = 7/3$ or $x = -2$. To make both x and y nonnegative, we solve the inequalities

$$\frac{y + 4}{3} \geq 0 \quad \text{and} \quad y \geq 0,$$

yielding

$$y \geq -4 \quad \text{and} \quad y \geq 0.$$

To make these last two inequalities true, we require $y \geq 0$, from which $y \geq -4$ automatically follows. Furthermore, to ensure $(y + 4)/3$ is an integer, it is necessary that y be 2 more than a whole-number multiple of 3. Therefore, the possible values of y are 2, 5, 8, 11, and so on, and the corresponding values of x are 2, 3, 4, 5, and so on.

The echelon method can be generalized to systems with more equations and unknowns. Because systems with three or more unknowns are complicated, however, we will only do a few in this section. In the next section, we will show a procedure based on the echelon method that is useful for solving large systems of equations. Meanwhile, the following example illustrates the additional steps needed to solve a system with three equations in three unknowns by the echelon method.

EXAMPLE 4 **Solving a System of Equations**
Solve the system

$$2x + y - z = 2 \tag{1}$$
$$x + 3y + 2z = 1 \tag{2}$$
$$x + y + z = 2. \tag{3}$$

▶**Solution** As in the previous examples, begin by eliminating the term with x, this time from equations (2) and (3), as follows.

$$2x + y - z = 2 \tag{1}$$
$$R_1 + (-2)R_2 \rightarrow R_2 \qquad -5y - 5z = 0 \tag{4}$$
$$R_1 + (-2)R_3 \rightarrow R_3 \qquad -y - 3z = -2 \tag{5}$$

In the same way, use equation (4) to eliminate y in equation (5). The new system is

$$2x + y - z = 2$$
$$-5y - 5z = 0$$

$R_2 + (-5)R_3 \rightarrow R_3$ $\qquad 10z = 10.$

Make the coefficient of the first term in each equation equal to 1.

$\frac{1}{2}R_1 \rightarrow R_1$ $\qquad x + \frac{1}{2}y - \frac{1}{2}z = 1$ (6)

$(-\frac{1}{5})R_2 \rightarrow R_2$ $\qquad y + z = 0$ (7)

$\frac{1}{10}R_3 \rightarrow R_3$ $\qquad z = 1$ (8)

Substitute 1 for z in equation (7) to get $y = -1$. Finally, substitute 1 for z and -1 for y in equation (6) to get $x = 2$. The solution of the system is $(2, -1, 1)$. Verify that $(2, -1, 1)$ satisfies all three equations in the original system. Note the triangular form of the last system. This is the typical echelon form.   ■

In summary, to solve a linear system in n variables by the echelon method, perform the following steps using the three transformations given earlier.

ECHELON METHOD OF SOLVING A LINEAR SYSTEM

1. If possible, arrange the equations so that there is an x_1-term in the first equation, an x_2-term in the second equation, and so on.
2. Eliminate the x_1-term in all equations after the first equation.
3. Eliminate the x_2-term in all equations after the second equation.
4. Eliminate the x_3-term in all equations after the third equation.
5. Continue in this way until the last equation has the form $ax_n = k$, for constants a and k, if possible.
6. Multiply each equation by the reciprocal of the coefficient of its first term.
7. Use back-substitution to find the value of each variable.

Applications   The mathematical techniques in this text will be useful to you only if you are able to apply them to practical problems. To do this, always begin by reading the problem carefully. Next, identify what must be found. Let each unknown quantity be represented by a variable. (It is a good idea to *write down* exactly what each variable represents.) Now reread the problem, looking for all necessary data. Write those down, too. Finally, look for one or more sentences that lead to equations or inequalities. The next example illustrates these steps.

EXAMPLE 5   **Flight Time**

A flight leaves New York at 8 P.M. and arrives in Paris at 9 A.M. (Paris time). This 13-hour difference includes the flight time plus the change in time zones. The return flight leaves Paris at 1 P.M. and arrives in New York at 3 P.M. (New York time). This 2-hour difference includes the flight time *minus* time zones, plus an extra hour due to the fact that flying westward is against the wind. Find the actual flight time eastward and the difference in time zones.

▶**Solution** Let x be the flight time and y be the difference in time zones. For the trip east, the flight time plus the change in time zones is 13 hours, so

$$x + y = 13.$$

For the trip west, the flight time (which is $x + 1$ hours due to the wind) minus the time zone is 2 hours, so

$$(x + 1) - y = 2.$$

Subtract 1 from both sides of this equation, and then solve the system

$$x + y = 13$$
$$x - y = 1$$

using the echelon method.

$$x + y = 13$$
$$R_1 + (-1)R_2 \to R_2 \qquad 2y = 12$$

Dividing the last equation by 2 gives $y = 6$. Substituting this into the first equation gives $x + 6 = 13$, so $x = 7$. Therefore, the flight time eastward is 7 hours, and the difference in time zones is 6 hours.

EXAMPLE 6   **Integral Solutions**

A restaurant owner orders a replacement set of knives, forks, and spoons. The box arrives containing 40 utensils and weighing 141.3 oz (ignoring the weight of the box). A knife, fork, and spoon weigh 3.9 oz, 3.6 oz, and 3.0 oz, respectively.

(a) How many solutions are there for the number of knives, forks, and spoons in the box?

▶**Solution** Let

$$x = \text{the number of knives};$$
$$y = \text{the number of forks};$$
$$z = \text{the number of spoons}.$$

A chart is useful for organizing the information in a problem of this type.

	Knives	Forks	Spoons	Total
Number	x	y	z	40
Weight	3.9	3.6	3.0	141.3

Because the box contains 40 utensils,

$$x + y + z = 40.$$

The x knives weigh $3.9x$ ounces, the y forks weigh $3.6y$ ounces, and the z spoons weigh $3.0z$ ounces. Since the total weight is 141.3 oz, we have the system

$$x + y + z = 40$$
$$3.9x + 3.6y + 3.0z = 141.3.$$

Solve using the echelon method.

$$x + y + z = 40$$

$$3.9R_1 + (-1)R_2 \rightarrow R_2 \qquad 0.3y + 0.9z = 14.7$$

We do not have a third equation to solve for z, as we did in Example 4. This system, then, has an infinite number of solutions. Letting z be the parameter, solve the second equation for y to get

$$y = \frac{14.7 - 0.9z}{0.3} = 49 - 3z.$$

Substituting this into the first equation, we get

$$x + (49 - 3z) + z = 40.$$

Solving this for x gives

$$x = 2z - 9.$$

Thus, the solutions are $(2z - 9, 49 - 3z, z)$, where z is any real number.

Now that we have solved for x and y in terms of z, let us investigate what values z can take on. This application demands that the solutions be non-negative integers. The number of forks cannot be negative, so set

$$49 - 3z \geq 0.$$

Solving for z gives

$$z \leq \frac{49}{3} \approx 16.33.$$

Also, the number of knives cannot be negative, so set

$$2z - 9 \geq 0.$$

Solving for z gives

$$z \geq \frac{9}{2} = 4.5.$$

Therefore, the permissible values of z are 5, 6, 7, . . . , 16, for a total of 12 solutions.

(b) Find the solution with the smallest number of spoons.

▶**Solution**   The smallest value of z is $z = 5$, from which we find $x = 2(5) - 9 = 1$ and $y = 49 - 3(5) = 34$. This solution has 1 knife, 34 forks, and 5 spoons.

▶ 2.1 Exercises

Use the echelon method to solve each system of two equations in two unknowns. Check your answers.

1. $x + y = 5$
$2x - 2y = 2$

2. $4x + y = 9$
$3x - y = 5$

3. $3x - 2y = -3$
$5x - y = 2$

4. $2x + 7y = -8$
$-2x + 3y = -12$

5. $3x + 2y = -6$
$5x - 2y = -10$

6. $-3x + y = 4$
$2x - 2y = -4$

7. $6x - 2y = -4$
$3x + 4y = 8$

8. $4m + 3n = -1$
$2m + 5n = 3$

9. $5p + 11q = -7$
$3p - 8q = 25$

10. $12s - 5t = 9$
$3s - 8t = -18$

11. $6x + 7y = -2$
$7x - 6y = 26$

12. $3a - 8b = 14$
$a - 2b = 2$

13. $3x + 2y = 5$
$6x + 4y = 8$

14. $9x - 5y = 1$
$-18x + 10y = 1$

15. $3x - 2y = -4$
$-6x + 4y = 8$

16. $3x + 5y + 2 = 0$
$9x + 15y + 6 = 0$

17. An inconsistent system has _____ solutions.

18. The solution of a system with two dependent equations in two variables is _____.

Use the echelon method to solve each system. Check your answers.

19. $x - \dfrac{3y}{2} = \dfrac{5}{2}$
$\dfrac{4x}{3} + \dfrac{2y}{3} = 6$

20. $\dfrac{x}{5} + 3y = 31$
$2x - \dfrac{y}{5} = 8$

21. $\dfrac{x}{2} + y = \dfrac{3}{2}$
$\dfrac{x}{3} + y = \dfrac{1}{3}$

22. $\dfrac{x}{9} + \dfrac{y}{6} = \dfrac{1}{3}$
$2x + \dfrac{8y}{5} = \dfrac{2}{5}$

Use the echelon method to solve each system of three equations in three unknowns. Check your answers.

23. $x + y + z = 2$
$2x + y - z = 5$
$x - y + z = -2$

24. $2x + y + z = 9$
$-x - y + z = 1$
$3x - y + z = 9$

25. $x + 3y + 4z = 14$
$2x - 3y + 2z = 10$
$3x - y + z = 9$

26. $4x - y + 3z = -2$
$3x + 5y - z = 15$
$-2x + y + 4z = 14$

27. $2x + 5y + 4z = 10$
$8x + 2y + 3z = 27$
$4x + y + z = 13$

28. $2x + y + 4z = 5$
$-3x + y + 3z = 14$
$4x + 2y + z = 3$

29. In your own words, describe the echelon method as used to solve a system of three equations in three variables.

Solve each system of equations. Let z be the parameter.

30. $2x + 3y - z = 1$
$3x + 5y + z = 3$

31. $3x + y - z = 0$
$2x - y + 3z = -7$

32. $x + 2y + 3z = 11$
$2x - y + z = 2$

33. $-x + y - z = -7$
$2x + 3y + z = 7$

34. In an exercise in Section 1.3, you were asked to solve the system of least squares line equations

$$nb + (\Sigma x)m = \Sigma y$$
$$(\Sigma x)b + (\Sigma x^2)m = \Sigma xy$$

by the method of substitution. Now solve the system by the echelon method to get

$$m = \frac{n(\Sigma xy) - (\Sigma x)(\Sigma y)}{n(\Sigma x^2) - (\Sigma x)^2}$$

$$b = \frac{\Sigma y - m(\Sigma x)}{n}.$$

35. The examples in this section did not use the first transformation. How might this transformation be used in the echelon method?

▶ Applications

BUSINESS AND ECONOMICS

36. *Groceries* If 20 lb of rice and 10 lb of potatoes cost $16.20, and 30 lb of rice and 12 lb of potatoes cost $23.04, how much will 10 lb of rice and 50 lb of potatoes cost?

37. *Sales* An apparel shop sells skirts for $45 and blouses for $35. Its entire stock is worth $51,750. But sales are slow and only half the skirts and two-thirds of the blouses are sold, for a total of $30,600. How many skirts and blouses are left in the store?

38. *Sales* A theater charges $8 for main floor seats and $5 for balcony seats. If all seats are sold, the ticket income is $4200. At one show, 25% of the main floor seats and 40% of the balcony seats were sold and ticket income was $1200. How many seats are on the main floor and how many are in the balcony?

39. *Stock* Lorri Morgan has $16,000 invested in Disney and Exxon stock. The Disney stock currently sells for $30 a share and the Exxon stock for $70 a share. Her stockbroker points out that if Disney stock goes up 50% and Exxon stock goes up by $35 a share, her stock will be worth $25,500. Is this possible? If so, tell how many shares of each stock she owns. If not, explain why not.

40. *Production* A company produces two models of bicycles, model 201 and model 301. Model 201 requires 2 hours of assembly time and model 301 requires 3 hours of assembly time. The parts for model 201 cost $18 per bike and the parts for model 301 cost $27 per bike. If the company has a total of 34 hours of assembly time and $335 available per day for these two models, how many of each should be made in a day to use up all available time and money? If it is not possible, explain why not.

41. *Banking* A bank teller has a total of 70 bills in five-, ten-, and twenty-dollar denominations. The number of fives is three times the number of tens, while the total value of the money is $960. Find the number of each type of bill.

42. *Investments* Katherine Chong invests $10,000 received from her grandmother in three ways. With one part, she buys U.S. savings bonds at an interest rate of 2.5% per year. She uses the second part, which amounts to twice the first, to buy mutual funds that offer a return of 6% per year. She puts the rest of the money into a money market account paying 4.5% annual interest. The first year her investments bring a return of $470. How much did she invest in each way?

43. *Production* Felsted Furniture makes dining room furniture. A buffet requires 30 hours for construction and 10 hours for finishing. A chair requires 10 hours for construction and 10 hours for finishing. A table requires 10 hours for construction and 30 hours for finishing. The construction department has 350 hours of labor and the finishing department has 150 hours of labor available each week. How many pieces of each type of furniture should be produced each week if the factory is to run at full capacity?

44. *Rug Cleaning Machines* Kelly Karpet Kleaners sells rug cleaning machines. The EZ model weighs 10 lb and comes in a 10-cubic-ft box. The compact model weighs 20 lb and comes in an 8-cubic-ft box. The commercial model weighs 60 lb and comes in a 28-cubic-ft box. Each of their delivery vans has 248 cubic ft of space and can hold a maximum of 440 lb. In order for a van to be fully loaded, how many of each model should it carry?

45. *Production* Turley Tailor Inc. makes long-sleeve, short-sleeve, and sleeveless blouses. A long-sleeve blouse requires 1.5 hours of cutting and 1.2 hours of sewing. A short-sleeve blouse requires 1 hour of cutting and 0.9 hour of sewing. A sleeveless blouse requires 0.5 hour of cutting and 0.6 hour of sewing. There are 380 hours of labor available in the cutting department each day and 330 hours in the sewing department. If the plant is to run at full capacity, how many of each type of blouse should be made each day?

46. *Broadway Economics* When Neil Simon opens a new play, he has to decide whether to open the show on Broadway or Off Broadway. For example, in his play *London Suite*, he decided to open it Off Broadway. From information provided by Emanuel Azenberg, his producer, the following equations were developed:

$$43,500x - y = 1,295,000$$
$$27,000x - y = 440,000,$$

where x represents the number of weeks that the show has run and y represents the profit or loss from the show (first equation is for Broadway and second equation is for Off Broadway).*

a. Solve this system of equations to determine when the profit/loss from the show will be equal for each venue. What is the profit at that point?

b. Discuss which venue is favorable for the show.

LIFE SCIENCES

47. *Birds* The date of the first sighting of robins has been occurring earlier each spring over the past 25 years at the Rocky Mountain Biological Laboratory. Scientists from this laboratory have developed two linear equations that estimate the date of the first sighting of robins:

$$y = 759 - 0.338x$$
$$y = 1637 - 0.779x,$$

where x is the year and y is the estimated number of days into the year when a robin can be expected.[†]

a. Compare the date of first sighting in 2000 for each of these equations. (*Hint:* 2000 was a leap year.)

b. Solve this system of equations to find the year in which the two estimates agree.

PHYSICAL SCIENCES

48. *Stopping Distance* The stopping distance of a car traveling 25 mph is 61.7 ft, and for a car traveling 35 mph it is 106 ft.[‡] The stopping distance in feet can be described by the equation $y = ax^2 + bx + c$, where x is the speed in mph.

a. Find the values of a and b.

b. Use your answers from part a to find the stopping distance for a car traveling 55 mph.

GENERAL INTEREST

49. *Basketball* Wilt Chamberlain holds the record for the highest number of points scored in a single NBA basketball game. Chamberlain scored 100 points for Philadelphia against the New York Knicks on March 2, 1962. This is an amazing feat, considering he scored all of his points without the help of three-point shots. Chamberlain made a total of 64 baskets, consisting of free throws (worth two points) and foul shots (worth one point).[§] Find the number of free throws and the number of foul shots that Chamberlain made.

50. *Basketball* Kobe Bryant has the second highest single game point total in the NBA. Bryant scored 81 points for the Los Angeles Lakers on January 22, 2006, against the Toronto Raptors. Bryant made a total of 46 baskets, including foul shots (worth one point), free throws (worth two points), and three-point shots (worth three points). The number of free throw shots he made is equal to three times the number of three pointers he made.[§] Find the number of foul shots, free throws, and three pointers Bryant made.

51. *The 24® Game* The object of the 24® Game, created by Robert Sun, is to combine four numbers, using addition, subtraction, multiplication, and/or division, to get the number 24.[‖] For example, the numbers 2, 5, 5, 4 can be combined as $2(5 + 5) + 4 = 24$. For the algebra edition of the game and the game card shown below, the object is to find single-digit positive integer values x and y so the four numbers $x + y$, $3x + 2y$, 8, and 9 can be combined to make 24.

a. Using the game card, write a system of equations that, when solved, can be used to make 24 from the game card. What is the solution to this system, and how can it be used to make 24 on the game card?

b. Repeat part a and develop a second system of equations.

*Goetz, Albert, "Basic Economics: Calculating Against Theatrical Disaster," *The Mathematics Teacher*, Vol. 89, No. 1, Jan. 1996, pp. 30–32.

[†]Inouye, David, Billy Barr, Kenneth Armitage, and Brian Inouye, "Climate Change Is Affecting Altitudinal Migrants and Hibernating Species," *Proceedings of the National Academy of Science*, Vol. 97, No. 4, Feb. 15, 2000, pp. 1630–1633.

[‡]*National Traffic Safety Institute Student Workbook*, 1993, p. 7.

[§]"Kobe's 81-Point Game Second Only to Wilt," http://sports.espn.go.com.

[‖]Source: Copied with permission. 24® is a registered trademark of Suntex International Inc., all rights reserved. Suntex Int. Inc., Easton, PA, http://www.24game.com.

2.2 Solution of Linear Systems by the Gauss-Jordan Method

? THINK ABOUT IT

How can an auto manufacturer with more than one factory and several dealers decide how many cars to send to each dealer from each factory?

Questions like this are called *transportation problems*; they frequently lead to a system of equations that must be satisfied. In this section we use a further refinement of the echelon method to answer this question. When we use the echelon method, since the variables are in the same order in each equation, we really need to keep track of just the coefficients and the constants. For example, look at the system solved in Example 4 of the previous section.

$$2x + y - z = 2$$
$$x + 3y + 2z = 1$$
$$x + y + z = 2$$

This system can be written in an abbreviated form as

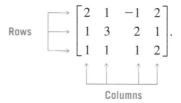

Such a rectangular array of numbers enclosed by brackets is called a **matrix** (plural: **matrices**).* Each number in the array is an **element** or **entry**. To separate the constants in the last column of the matrix from the coefficients of the variables, we use a vertical line, producing the following **augmented matrix**.

$$\left[\begin{array}{ccc|c} 2 & 1 & -1 & 2 \\ 1 & 3 & 2 & 1 \\ 1 & 1 & 1 & 2 \end{array}\right]$$

The rows of the augmented matrix can be transformed in the same way as the equations of the system, since the matrix is just a shortened form of the system. The following **row operations** on the augmented matrix correspond to the transformations of systems of equations given earlier.

---

*The word matrix, Latin for "womb," was coined by James Joseph Sylvester (1814–1897) and made popular by his friend Arthur Cayley (1821–1895). Both mathematicians were English, although Sylvester spent much of his life in the United States.

> **ROW OPERATIONS**
>
> For any augmented matrix of a system of equations, the following operations produce the augmented matrix of an equivalent system:
>
> 1. interchanging any two rows;
> 2. multiplying the elements of a row by any nonzero real number;
> 3. adding a nonzero multiple of the elements of one row to the corresponding elements of a nonzero multiple of some other row.

In steps 2 and 3, we are replacing a row with a new, modified row, which the old row helped to form, just as we replaced an equation with a new, modified equation in the previous section.

Row operations, like the transformations of systems of equations, are reversible. If they are used to change matrix A to matrix B, then it is possible to use row operations to transform B back into A. In addition to their use in solving equations, row operations are very important in the simplex method to be described in Chapter 4.

In the examples in this section, we will use the same notation as in Section 1 to show the row operation used. For example, the notation R_1 indicates row 1 of the previous matrix, and $-3R_1 + R_2$ means that row 1 is multiplied by -3 and added to row 2.

By the first row operation, interchanging two rows, the matrix

$$\begin{bmatrix} 0 & 1 & 2 & 3 \\ -2 & -6 & -10 & -12 \\ 2 & 1 & -2 & -5 \end{bmatrix} \text{ becomes } \begin{bmatrix} -2 & -6 & -10 & -12 \\ 0 & 1 & 2 & 3 \\ 2 & 1 & -2 & -5 \end{bmatrix} \quad \text{Interchange } R_1 \text{ and } R_2$$

by interchanging the first two rows. Row 3 is left unchanged.

The second row operation, multiplying a row by a number, allows us to change

$$\begin{bmatrix} -2 & -6 & -10 & -12 \\ 0 & 1 & 2 & 3 \\ 2 & 1 & -2 & -5 \end{bmatrix} \text{ to } \begin{bmatrix} 1 & 3 & 5 & 6 \\ 0 & 1 & 2 & 3 \\ 2 & 1 & -2 & -5 \end{bmatrix} \quad (-1/2)R_1 \to R_1$$

by multiplying the elements of row 1 of the original matrix by $-1/2$. Note that rows 2 and 3 are left unchanged.

Using the third row operation, adding a multiple of one row to another, we change

$$\begin{bmatrix} 1 & 3 & 5 & 6 \\ 0 & 1 & 2 & 3 \\ 2 & 1 & -2 & -5 \end{bmatrix} \text{ to } \begin{bmatrix} 1 & 3 & 5 & 6 \\ 0 & 1 & 2 & 3 \\ 0 & -5 & -12 & -17 \end{bmatrix} \quad -2R_1 + R_3 \to R_3$$

by first multiplying each element in row 1 of the original matrix by -2 and then adding the results to the corresponding elements in the third row of that matrix. Work as follows.

$$\begin{bmatrix} 1 & 3 & 5 & 6 \\ 0 & 1 & 2 & 3 \\ (-2)1+2 & (-2)3+1 & (-2)5-2 & (-2)6-5 \end{bmatrix} = \begin{bmatrix} 1 & 3 & 5 & 6 \\ 0 & 1 & 2 & 3 \\ 0 & -5 & -12 & -17 \end{bmatrix}$$

Notice that rows 1 and 2 are left unchanged, *even though the elements of row 1 were used to transform row 3.*

The Gauss-Jordan Method

The **Gauss-Jordan method** is an extension of the echelon method of solving systems.* Before the Gauss-Jordan method can be used, the system must be in proper form: the terms with variables should be on the left and the constants on the right in each equation, with the variables in the same order in each equation.

The system is then written as an augmented matrix. Using row operations, the goal is to transform the matrix so that it has zeros above and below a diagonal of 1's on the left of the vertical bar. Once this is accomplished, the final solution can be read directly from the last matrix. The following example illustrates the use of the Gauss-Jordan method to solve a system of equations.

EXAMPLE 1 **Gauss-Jordan Method**

Solve the system

$$3x - 4y = 1 \tag{1}$$

$$5x + 2y = 19. \tag{2}$$

▶**Solution**

METHOD 1
1's on Diagonal

The system is already in the proper form to use the Gauss-Jordan method. To begin, we change the 3 in the first row to 1 using the second row operation. (Notice that the same notation is used to indicate each transformation, as in the previous section.)

$$\begin{bmatrix} 3 & -4 & 1 \\ 5 & 2 & 19 \end{bmatrix} \quad \text{Augmented matrix}$$

$$\tfrac{1}{3}R_1 \to R_1 \quad \begin{bmatrix} 1 & -\frac{4}{3} & \frac{1}{3} \\ 5 & 2 & 19 \end{bmatrix}$$

Using the third row operation, we change the 5 in row 2 to 0.

$$-5R_1 + R_2 \to R_2 \quad \begin{bmatrix} 1 & -\frac{4}{3} & \frac{1}{3} \\ 0 & \frac{26}{3} & \frac{52}{3} \end{bmatrix}$$

*The great German mathematician Carl Friedrich Gauss (1777–1855), sometimes referred to as the "Prince of Mathematicians," originally developed his elimination method for use in finding least squares coefficients. (See Section 1.3.) The German geodesist Wilhelm Jordan (1842–1899) improved his method and used it in surveying problems. Gauss's method had been known to the Chinese at least 1800 years earlier and was described in the *Jiuahang Suanshu* (*Nine Chapters on the Mathematical Art*).

We now change 26/3 in row 2 to 1 to complete the diagonal of 1's.

$$\frac{3}{26}R_2 \rightarrow R_2 \quad \begin{bmatrix} 1 & -\frac{4}{3} & \Big| & \frac{1}{3} \\ 0 & 1 & \Big| & 2 \end{bmatrix}$$

The final transformation is to change the $-4/3$ in row 1 to 0.

$$\tfrac{4}{3}R_2 + R_1 \rightarrow R_1 \quad \begin{bmatrix} 1 & 0 & \Big| & 3 \\ 0 & 1 & \Big| & 2 \end{bmatrix}$$

The last matrix corresponds to the system

$$x = 3$$
$$y = 2,$$

so we can read the solution directly from the last column of the final matrix. Check that (3, 2) is the solution by substitution in the equations of the original matrix.

METHOD 2
Fraction-Free

An alternate form of Gauss-Jordan is to first transform the matrix so that it contains zeros above and below the main diagonal. Then, use the second transformation to get the required 1's. When doing calculations by hand, this second method simplifies the calculations by avoiding fractions and decimals. We will use this method when doing calculations by hand throughout the remainder of this chapter.

To begin, we change the 5 in row 2 to 0.

$$\begin{bmatrix} 3 & -4 & \Big| & 1 \\ 5 & 2 & \Big| & 19 \end{bmatrix} \quad \text{Augmented matrix}$$

$$5R_1 + (-3)R_2 \rightarrow R_2 \quad \begin{bmatrix} 3 & -4 & \Big| & 1 \\ 0 & -26 & \Big| & -52 \end{bmatrix}$$

We change the -4 in row 1 to 0.

$$-4R_2 + 26R_1 \rightarrow R_1 \quad \begin{bmatrix} 78 & 0 & \Big| & 234 \\ 0 & -26 & \Big| & -52 \end{bmatrix}$$

Then we change the first nonzero number in each row to 1.

$$\begin{matrix} \frac{1}{78}R_1 \rightarrow R_1 \\ -\frac{1}{26}R_2 \rightarrow R_2 \end{matrix} \quad \begin{bmatrix} 1 & 0 & \Big| & 3 \\ 0 & 1 & \Big| & 2 \end{bmatrix}$$

The solution is read directly from this last matrix: $x = 3$ and $y = 2$, or (3, 2).

NOTE   If your solution does not check, the most efficient way to find the error is to substitute back through the equations that correspond to each matrix, starting with the last matrix. When you find a system that is not satisfied by your (incorrect) answers, you have probably reached the matrix just before the error occurred. Look for the error in the transformation to the next matrix. ∎

When the Gauss-Jordan method is used to solve a system, the final matrix always will have zeros above and below the diagonal of 1's on the left of the vertical bar. To transform the matrix, it is best to work column by column from left to right. Such an orderly method avoids confusion and going around in circles. For each column, first perform the steps that give the zeros. When all columns have zeros in place, multiply each row by the reciprocal of the coefficient of the remaining nonzero number in that row to get the required 1's. With dependent equations or inconsistent systems, it will not be possible to get the complete diagonal of 1's.

EXAMPLE 2   **Gauss-Jordan Method**
Use the Gauss-Jordan method to solve the system

$$x + 5z = -6 + y$$
$$3x + 3y = 10 + z$$
$$x + 3y + 2z = 5.$$

▶**Solution**

METHOD 1
Calculating by Hand

First, rewrite the system in proper form, as follows.

$$x - y + 5z = -6$$
$$3x + 3y - z = 10$$
$$x + 3y + 2z = 5$$

Begin to find the solution by writing the augmented matrix of the linear system.

$$\begin{bmatrix} 1 & -1 & 5 & | & -6 \\ 3 & 3 & -1 & | & 10 \\ 1 & 3 & 2 & | & 5 \end{bmatrix}$$

Row transformations will be used to rewrite this matrix in the form

$$\begin{bmatrix} 1 & 0 & 0 & | & m \\ 0 & 1 & 0 & | & n \\ 0 & 0 & 1 & | & p \end{bmatrix},$$

where m, n, and p are real numbers (if this form is possible). From this final form of the matrix, the solution can be read: $x = m, y = n, z = p$, or (m, n, p).

In the first column, we need zeros in the second and third rows. Multiply the first row by -3 and add to the second row to get a zero there. Then multiply the first row by -1 and add to the third row to get that zero.

$$\begin{array}{c} \\ -3R_1 + R_2 \rightarrow R_2 \\ -1R_1 + R_3 \rightarrow R_3 \end{array} \begin{bmatrix} 1 & -1 & 5 & | & -6 \\ 0 & 6 & -16 & | & 28 \\ 0 & 4 & -3 & | & 11 \end{bmatrix}$$

Now get zeros in the second column in a similar way. We want zeros in the first and third rows. Row 2 will not change.

$$\begin{array}{c} R_2 + 6R_1 \rightarrow R_1 \\ \\ 2R_2 + (-3)R_3 \rightarrow R_3 \end{array} \quad \begin{bmatrix} 6 & 0 & 14 & | & -8 \\ 0 & 6 & -16 & | & 28 \\ 0 & 0 & -23 & | & 23 \end{bmatrix}$$

In transforming the third row, you may have used the operation $4R_2 + (-6)R_3 \rightarrow R_3$ instead of $2R_2 + (-3)R_3 \rightarrow R_3$. This is perfectly fine; the last row would then have -46 and 46 in place of -23 and 23. To avoid errors, it helps to keep the numbers as small as possible. We observe at this point that all of the numbers can be reduced in size by multiplying each row by an appropriate constant. This next step is not essential, but it simplifies the arithmetic.

$$\begin{array}{c} \tfrac{1}{2}R_1 \rightarrow R_1 \\ \tfrac{1}{2}R_2 \rightarrow R_2 \\ -\tfrac{1}{23}R_3 \rightarrow R_3 \end{array} \quad \begin{bmatrix} 3 & 0 & 7 & | & -4 \\ 0 & 3 & -8 & | & 14 \\ 0 & 0 & 1 & | & -1 \end{bmatrix}$$

Next, we want zeros in the first and second rows of the third column. Row 3 will not change.

$$\begin{array}{c} -7R_3 + R_1 \rightarrow R_1 \\ 8R_3 + R_2 \rightarrow R_2 \end{array} \quad \begin{bmatrix} 3 & 0 & 0 & | & 3 \\ 0 & 3 & 0 & | & 6 \\ 0 & 0 & 1 & | & -1 \end{bmatrix}$$

Finally, get 1's in each row by multiplying the row by the reciprocal of (or dividing the row by) the number in the diagonal position.

$$\begin{array}{c} \tfrac{1}{3}R_1 \rightarrow R_1 \\ \tfrac{1}{3}R_2 \rightarrow R_2 \end{array} \quad \begin{bmatrix} 1 & 0 & 0 & | & 1 \\ 0 & 1 & 0 & | & 2 \\ 0 & 0 & 1 & | & -1 \end{bmatrix}$$

The linear system associated with the final augmented matrix is

$$x = 1$$
$$y = 2$$
$$z = -1,$$

and the solution is $(1, 2, -1)$. Verify that this is the solution to the original system of equations.

CAUTION Notice that we have performed two or three operations on the same matrix in one step. This is permissible as long as we do not use a row that we are changing as part of another row operation. For example, when we changed row 2 in the first step, we could not use row 2 to transform row 3 in the same step. To avoid difficulty, use *only* row 1 to get zeros in column 1, row 2 to get zeros in column 2, and so on. ∎

METHOD 2
Graphing Calculators

The row operations of the Gauss-Jordan method can also be done on a graphing calculator. For example, Figure 5 shows the result when the augmented matrix is entered into a TI-83/84 Plus. Figures 6 and 7 show how row operations can be used to get zeros in rows 2 and 3 of the first column.

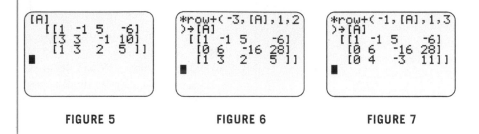

FIGURE 5   **FIGURE 6**   **FIGURE 7**

Calculators typically do not allow any multiple of a row to be added to any multiple of another row, such as in the operation $2R_2 + 6R_1 \rightarrow R_1$. They normally allow a multiple of a row to be added only to another unmodified row. To get around this restriction, we can convert the diagonal element to a 1 before changing the other elements in the column to 0, as we did in the first method of Example 1. In this example, we change the 6 in row 2, column 2, to a 1 by dividing by 6. The result is shown in Figure 8. (The right side of the matrix is not visible, but can be seen by pressing the right arrow key.) Notice that this operation introduces decimals. Converting to fractions is preferable on calculators that have that option; 1/3 is certainly more concise than 0.3333333333. Figure 9 shows such a conversion on the TI-83/84 Plus.

FIGURE 8   **FIGURE 9**

When performing row operations without a graphing calculator, it is best to avoid fractions and decimals, because these make the operations more difficult and more prone to error. A calculator, on the other hand, encounters no such difficulties.

Continuing in the same manner, the solution $(1, 2, -1)$ is found as shown in Figure 10.

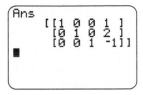

FIGURE 10

Some calculators can do the entire Gauss-Jordan process with a single command; on the TI-83/84 Plus, for example, this is done with the `rref` command. This is very useful in practice, although it does not show any of the intermediate steps.

METHOD 3
Spreadsheets

The Gauss-Jordan method can be done using a spreadsheet either by using a macro or by developing the pivot steps using formulas with the copy and paste commands. However, spreadsheets also have built-in methods to solve systems of equations. Although these solvers do not usually employ the Gauss-Jordan method for solving systems of equations, they are, nonetheless, efficient and practical to use.

The Solver included with Excel can solve systems of equations that are both linear and nonlinear. The Solver is located in the Tools menu and requires that cells be identified ahead of time for each variable in the problem. It also requires that the left-hand side of each equation be placed in the spreadsheet as a formula. For example, to solve the above problem, we could identify cells A1, B1, and C1 for the variables x, y, and z, respectively. The Solver requires that we place a guess for the answer in these cells. It is convenient to place a zero in each of these cells. The left-hand side of each equation must be placed in a cell. We could choose A3, A4, and A5 to hold each of these formulas. Thus, in cell A3, we would type "$=A1 - B1 + 5*C1$" and put the other two equations in cells A4 and A5.

We now click on the Tools menu and choose Solver. Since this solver attempts to find a solution that is best in some way, we are required to identify a cell with a formula in it that we want to optimize. In this case, it is convenient to use the cell with the left-hand side of the first constraint in it, A3. Figure 11 illustrates the Solver box and the items placed in it.

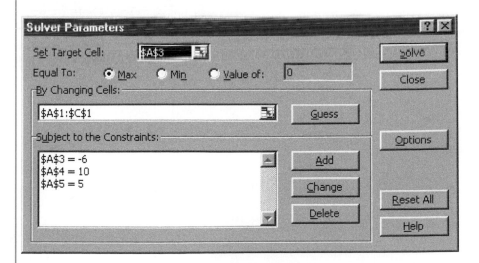

FIGURE 11

To obtain a solution, click on Solve. The solution is located in cells A1, B1, and C1, and these correspond to x, y, and z, respectively.

In summary, the Gauss-Jordan method of solving a linear system requires the following steps.

GAUSS-JORDAN METHOD OF SOLVING A LINEAR SYSTEM

1. Write each equation so that variable terms are in the same order on the left side of the equals sign and constants are on the right.
2. Write the augmented matrix that corresponds to the system.
3. Use row operations to transform the first column so that all elements except the element in the first row are zero.
4. Use row operations to transform the second column so that all elements except the element in the second row are zero.
5. Use row operations to transform the third column so that all elements except the element in the third row are zero.
6. Continue in this way, when possible, until the last row is written in the form

$$[0 \quad 0 \quad 0 \quad \cdots \quad 0 \quad j \mid k],$$

where j and k are constants with $j \neq 0$. When this is not possible, continue until every row has more zeros on the left than the previous row (except possibly for any rows of all zero at the bottom of the matrix), and the first nonzero entry in each row is the only nonzero entry in its column.
7. Multiply each row by the reciprocal of the nonzero element in that row.

Systems without a Unique Solution   In the previous examples, we were able to get the last row in the form $[0 \quad 0 \quad 0 \quad \cdots \quad 0 \quad j \mid k]$, where j and k are constants with $j \neq 0$. We will now look at examples where this is not the case.

EXAMPLE 3   **Solving a System of Equations with No Solution**

Use the Gauss-Jordan method to solve the system

$$x - 2y = 2$$
$$3x - 6y = 5.$$

▶Solution   Begin by writing the augmented matrix.

$$\begin{bmatrix} 1 & -2 & \mid 2 \\ 3 & -6 & \mid 5 \end{bmatrix}$$

To get a zero for the second element in column 1, multiply the numbers in row 1 by -3 and add the results to the corresponding elements in row 2.

$$-3R_1 + R_2 \rightarrow R_2 \quad \begin{bmatrix} 1 & -2 & \mid & 2 \\ 0 & 0 & \mid & -1 \end{bmatrix}$$

This matrix corresponds to the system

$$x - 2y = 2$$
$$0x + 0y = -1.$$

Since the second equation is $0 = -1$, the system is inconsistent and therefore has no solution. The row $\begin{bmatrix} 0 & 0 \mid k \end{bmatrix}$ for any nonzero k is a signal that the given system is inconsistent.

EXAMPLE 4

Solving a System of Equations with an Infinite Number of Solutions
Use the Gauss-Jordan method to solve the system

$$x + 2y - z = 0$$
$$3x - y + z = 6$$
$$-2x - 4y + 2z = 0.$$

▶**Solution** The augmented matrix is

$$\begin{bmatrix} 1 & 2 & -1 & \mid & 0 \\ 3 & -1 & 1 & \mid & 6 \\ -2 & -4 & 2 & \mid & 0 \end{bmatrix}.$$

We first get zeros in the second and third rows of column 1.

$$\begin{matrix} -3R_1 + R_2 \rightarrow R_2 \\ 2R_1 + R_3 \rightarrow R_3 \end{matrix} \quad \begin{bmatrix} 1 & 2 & -1 & \mid & 0 \\ 0 & -7 & 4 & \mid & 6 \\ 0 & 0 & 0 & \mid & 0 \end{bmatrix}$$

To continue, we get a zero in the first row of column 2 using the second row, as usual.

$$2R_2 + 7R_1 \rightarrow R_1 \quad \begin{bmatrix} 7 & 0 & 1 & \mid & 12 \\ 0 & -7 & 4 & \mid & 6 \\ 0 & 0 & 0 & \mid & 0 \end{bmatrix}$$

We cannot get a zero for the first-row, third-column element without changing the form of the first two columns. We must multiply each of the first two rows by the reciprocal of the first nonzero number.

$$\begin{matrix} \frac{1}{7}R_1 \rightarrow R_1 \\ -\frac{1}{7}R_2 \rightarrow R_2 \end{matrix} \quad \begin{bmatrix} 1 & 0 & \frac{1}{7} & \mid & \frac{12}{7} \\ 0 & 1 & -\frac{4}{7} & \mid & -\frac{6}{7} \\ 0 & 0 & 0 & \mid & 0 \end{bmatrix}$$

To complete the solution, write the equations that correspond to the first two rows of the matrix.

$$x + \frac{1}{7}z = \frac{12}{7}$$

$$y - \frac{4}{7}z = -\frac{6}{7}$$

Because both equations involve z, let z be the parameter. There are an infinite number of solutions, corresponding to the infinite number of values of z. Solve the first equation for x and the second for y to get

$$x = \frac{12 - z}{7} \quad \text{and} \quad y = \frac{4z - 6}{7}.$$

As shown in the previous section, the general solution is written

$$\left(\frac{12 - z}{7}, \frac{4z - 6}{7}, z\right),$$

where z is any real number. For example, $z = 2$ and $z = 12$ lead to the solutions $(10/7, 2/7, 2)$ and $(0, 6, 12)$.

EXAMPLE 5 **Solving a System of Equations with an Infinite Number of Solutions**
Consider the following system of equations.

$$\begin{aligned} x + 2y + 3z - w &= 4 \\ 2x + 3y + w &= -3 \\ 3x + 5y + 3z &= 1 \end{aligned}$$

(a) Set this up as an augmented matrix, and verify that the result after the Gauss-Jordan method is

$$\begin{bmatrix} 1 & 0 & -9 & 5 & \bigm| & -18 \\ 0 & 1 & 6 & -3 & \bigm| & 11 \\ 0 & 0 & 0 & 0 & \bigm| & 0 \end{bmatrix}$$

(b) Find the solution to this system of equations.

▶**Solution** To complete the solution, write the equations that correspond to the first two rows of the matrix.

$$\begin{aligned} x \quad - 9z + 5w &= -18 \\ y + 6z - 3w &= 11 \end{aligned}$$

Because both equations involve both z and w, let z and w be parameters. There are an infinite number of solutions, corresponding to the infinite number of values of z and w. Solve the first equation for x and the second for y to get

$$x = -18 + 9z - 5w \quad \text{and} \quad y = 11 - 6z + 3w.$$

In an analogous manner to problems with a single parameter, the general solution is written

$$(-18 + 9z - 5w, 11 - 6z + 3w, z, w),$$

where z and w are any real numbers. For example, $z = 1$ and $w = -2$ leads to the solution $(1, -1, 1, -2)$.

Although the examples have used only systems with two equations in two unknowns, three equations in three unknowns, or three equations in four unknowns, the Gauss-Jordan method can be used for any system with n equations and m unknowns. The method becomes tedious with more than three equations in three unknowns; on the other hand, it is very suitable for use with graphing calculators and computers, which can solve fairly large systems quickly. Sophisticated computer programs modify the method to reduce round-off error. Other methods used for special types of large matrices are studied in a course on numerical analysis.

EXAMPLE 6 **Soda Sales**
A convenience store sells 23 sodas one summer afternoon in 12-, 16-, and 20-oz cups (small, medium, and large). The total volume of soda sold was 376 oz.

(a) Suppose that the prices for a small, medium, and large soda are $1, $1.25, and $1.40, respectively, and that the total sales were $28.45. How many of each size did the store sell?

▶**Solution**　As in Example 6 of the previous section, we will organize the information in a table.

	Small	Medium	Large	Total
Number	x	y	z	23
Volume	12	16	20	376
Price	1.00	1.25	1.40	28.45

The three rows of the table lead to three equations: one for the total number of sodas, one for the volume, and one for the price.

$$
\begin{aligned}
x + y + z &= 23 \\
12x + 16y + 20z &= 376 \\
1.00x + 1.25y + 1.40z &= 28.45
\end{aligned}
$$

Set this up as an augmented matrix, and verify that the result after the Gauss-Jordan method is

$$
\begin{bmatrix}
1 & 0 & 0 & | & 6 \\
0 & 1 & 0 & | & 9 \\
0 & 0 & 1 & | & 8
\end{bmatrix}.
$$

The store sold 6 small, 9 medium, and 8 large sodas.

(b) Suppose the prices for small, medium, and large sodas are changed to $1, $2, and $3, respectively, but all other information is kept the same. How many of each size did the store sell?

▶**Solution**　Change the third equation to

$$x + 2y + 3z = 28.45$$

and go through the Gauss-Jordan method again. The result is

$$
\begin{bmatrix}
1 & 0 & -1 & | & 2 \\
0 & 1 & 2 & | & 25 \\
0 & 0 & 0 & | & -19.55
\end{bmatrix}.
$$

(If you do the row operations in a different order in this example, you will have different numbers in the last column.) The last row of this matrix says that $0 = -19.55$, so the system is inconsistent and has no solution. (In retrospect, this is clear, because each soda sells for a whole number of dollars, and the total amount of money is not a whole number of dollars. In general, however, it is not easy to tell whether a system of equations has a solution or not by just looking at it.)

(c) Suppose the prices are the same as in part (b), but the total revenue is $48. Now how many of each size did the store sell?

▶**Solution**　The third equation becomes

$$x + 2y + 3z = 48,$$

and the Gauss-Jordan method leads to

$$\begin{bmatrix} 1 & 0 & -1 & -2 \\ 0 & 1 & 2 & 25 \\ 0 & 0 & 0 & 0 \end{bmatrix}.$$

The system is dependent, similar to Example 4. Let z be the parameter, and solve the first two equations for x and y, yielding

$$x = z - 2 \quad \text{and} \quad y = 25 - 2z.$$

Remember that in this problem, x, y, and z must be nonnegative integers. From the equation for x, we must have

$$z \geq 2,$$

and from the equation for y, we must have

$$25 - 2z \geq 0,$$

from which we find

$$z \leq 12.5.$$

We therefore have 11 solutions corresponding to $z = 2, 3, \ldots, 12$.

(d) Give the solutions from part (c) that have the smallest and largest numbers of large sodas.

▶**Solution** For the smallest number of large sodas, let $z = 2$, giving $x = 2 - 2 = 0$ and $y = 25 - 2(2) = 21$. There are 0 small, 21 medium, and 2 large sodas.

For the largest number of large sodas, let $z = 12$, giving $x = 12 - 2 = 10$ and $y = 25 - 2(12) = 1$. There are 10 small, 1 medium, and 12 large sodas.

▶ 2.2 Exercises

Write the augmented matrix for each system. **Do not solve.**

1. $3x + y = 6$
$2x + 5y = 15$

2. $4x - 2y = 8$
$-7y = -12$

3. $2x + y + z = 3$
$3x - 4y + 2z = -7$
$x + y + z = 2$

4. $2x - 5y + 3z = 4$
$-4x + 2y - 7z = -5$
$3x - y = 8$

Write the system of equations associated with each augmented matrix.

5. $\begin{bmatrix} 1 & 0 & 2 \\ 0 & 1 & 3 \end{bmatrix}$

6. $\begin{bmatrix} 1 & 0 & 5 \\ 0 & 1 & -3 \end{bmatrix}$

7. $\begin{bmatrix} 1 & 0 & 0 & 4 \\ 0 & 1 & 0 & -5 \\ 0 & 0 & 1 & 1 \end{bmatrix}$

8. $\begin{bmatrix} 1 & 0 & 0 & 4 \\ 0 & 1 & 0 & 2 \\ 0 & 0 & 1 & 3 \end{bmatrix}$

9. _____ on a matrix correspond to transformations of a system of equations.

10. Describe in your own words what $2R_1 + R_3 \to R_3$ means.

Use the indicated row operations to change each matrix.

11. Replace R_2 by $R_1 + (-3)R_2$.

$$\begin{bmatrix} 3 & 7 & 4 & | & 10 \\ 1 & 2 & 3 & | & 6 \\ 0 & 4 & 5 & | & 11 \end{bmatrix}$$

12. Replace R_3 by $(-1)R_1 + 3R_3$.

$$\begin{bmatrix} 3 & 2 & 6 & | & 18 \\ 2 & -2 & 5 & | & 7 \\ 1 & 0 & 5 & | & 20 \end{bmatrix}$$

13. Replace R_1 by $(-2)R_2 + R_1$.

$$\begin{bmatrix} 1 & 6 & 4 & | & 7 \\ 0 & 3 & 2 & | & 5 \\ 0 & 5 & 3 & | & 7 \end{bmatrix}$$

14. Replace R_1 by $R_3 + (-3)R_1$.

$$\begin{bmatrix} 1 & 0 & 4 & | & 21 \\ 0 & 6 & 5 & | & 30 \\ 0 & 0 & 12 & | & 15 \end{bmatrix}$$

15. Replace R_1 by $\frac{1}{3}R_1$.

$$\begin{bmatrix} 3 & 0 & 0 & | & 18 \\ 0 & 5 & 0 & | & 9 \\ 0 & 0 & 4 & | & 8 \end{bmatrix}$$

16. Replace R_3 by $\frac{1}{6}R_3$.

$$\begin{bmatrix} 1 & 0 & 0 & | & 30 \\ 0 & 1 & 0 & | & 17 \\ 0 & 0 & 6 & | & 162 \end{bmatrix}$$

Use the Gauss-Jordan method to solve each system of equations.

17.
$$\begin{aligned} x + y &= 5 \\ 3x + 2y &= 12 \end{aligned}$$

18.
$$\begin{aligned} x + 2y &= 5 \\ 2x + y &= -2 \end{aligned}$$

19.
$$\begin{aligned} x + y &= 7 \\ 4x + 3y &= 22 \end{aligned}$$

20.
$$\begin{aligned} 4x - 2y &= 3 \\ -2x + 3y &= 1 \end{aligned}$$

21.
$$\begin{aligned} 2x - 3y &= 2 \\ 4x - 6y &= 1 \end{aligned}$$

22.
$$\begin{aligned} 2x + 3y &= 9 \\ 4x + 6y &= 7 \end{aligned}$$

23.
$$\begin{aligned} 6x - 3y &= 1 \\ -12x + 6y &= -2 \end{aligned}$$

24.
$$\begin{aligned} x - y &= 1 \\ -x + y &= 1 \end{aligned}$$

25.
$$\begin{aligned} y &= x - 3 \\ y &= 1 + z \\ z &= 4 - x \end{aligned}$$

26.
$$\begin{aligned} x &= 1 - y \\ 2x &= z \\ 2z &= 2 - y \end{aligned}$$

27.
$$\begin{aligned} 2x - 2y &= -5 \\ 2y + z &= 0 \\ 2x + z &= -7 \end{aligned}$$

28.
$$\begin{aligned} x - z &= -3 \\ y + z &= 9 \\ -2x + 3y + 5z &= 33 \end{aligned}$$

29.
$$\begin{aligned} 4x + 4y - 4z &= 24 \\ 2x - y + z &= -9 \\ x - 2y + 3z &= 1 \end{aligned}$$

30.
$$\begin{aligned} x + 2y - 7z &= -2 \\ -2x - 5y + 2z &= 1 \\ 3x + 5y + 4z &= -9 \end{aligned}$$

31.
$$\begin{aligned} 3x + 5y - z &= 0 \\ 4x - y + 2z &= 1 \\ 7x + 4y + z &= 1 \end{aligned}$$

32.
$$\begin{aligned} 3x - 6y + 3z &= 11 \\ 2x + y - z &= 2 \\ 5x - 5y + 2z &= 6 \end{aligned}$$

33.
$$\begin{aligned} 5x - 4y + 2z &= 6 \\ 5x + 3y - z &= 11 \\ 15x - 5y + 3z &= 23 \end{aligned}$$

34.
$$\begin{aligned} 3x + 2y - z &= -16 \\ 6x - 4y + 3z &= 12 \\ 5x - 2y + 2z &= 4 \end{aligned}$$

35.
$$\begin{aligned} 2x + 3y + z &= 9 \\ 4x + 6y + 2z &= 18 \\ -\frac{1}{2}x - \frac{3}{4}y - \frac{1}{4}z &= -\frac{9}{4} \end{aligned}$$

36.
$$\begin{aligned} 3x - 5y - 2z &= -9 \\ -4x + 3y + z &= 11 \\ 8x - 5y + 4z &= 6 \end{aligned}$$

37.
$$\begin{aligned} x + 2y - w &= 3 \\ 2x + 4z + 2w &= -6 \\ x + 2y - z &= 6 \\ 2x - y + z + w &= -3 \end{aligned}$$

38.
$$\begin{aligned} x + 3y - 2z - w &= 9 \\ 2x + 4y + 2w &= 10 \\ -3x - 5y + 2z - w &= -15 \\ x - y - 3z + 2w &= 6 \end{aligned}$$

39.
$$\begin{aligned} x + y - z + 2w &= -20 \\ 2x - y + z + w &= 11 \\ 3x - 2y + z - 2w &= 27 \end{aligned}$$

40.
$$\begin{aligned} 4x - 3y + z + w &= 21 \\ -2x - y + 2z + 7w &= 2 \\ 10x - 5z - 20w &= 15 \end{aligned}$$

41. $10.47x + 3.52y + 2.58z - 6.42w = 218.65$
$8.62x - 4.93y - 1.75z + 2.83w = 157.03$
$4.92x + 6.83y - 2.97z + 2.65w = 462.3$
$2.86x + 19.10y - 6.24z - 8.73w = 398.4$

42. $28.6x + 94.5y + 16.0z - 2.94w = 198.3$
$16.7x + 44.3y - 27.3z + 8.9w = 254.7$
$12.5x - 38.7y + 92.5z + 22.4w = 562.7$
$40.1x - 28.3y + 17.5z - 10.2w = 375.4$

43. On National Public Radio, the "Weekend Edition" program on Sunday, July 29, 2001, posed the following puzzle: Draw a three-by-three square (three boxes across by three boxes down). Put the fraction 3/8 in the first square in the first row. Put the fraction 1/4 in the last square in the second row. The object is to put a fraction in each of the remaining boxes, so the three numbers in each row, each column, and each of the long diagonals add up to 1. Solve this puzzle by letting seven variables represent the seven unknown fractions, writing eight equations for the eight sums, and solving by the Gauss-Jordan method.

▶ **Applications**

BUSINESS AND ECONOMICS

44. *Surveys* The president of Sam's Supermarkets plans to hire two public relations firms to survey 500 customers by phone, 750 by mail, and 250 by in-person interviews. The Garcia firm has personnel to do 10 phone surveys, 30 mail surveys, and 5 interviews per hour. The Wong firm can handle 20 phone surveys, 10 mail surveys, and 10 interviews per hour. For how many hours should each firm be hired to produce the exact number of surveys needed?

45. *Transportation* A knitting shop orders yarn from three suppliers in Toronto, Montreal, and Ottawa. One month the shop ordered a total of 100 units of yarn from these suppliers. The delivery costs were $80, $50, and $65 per unit for the orders from Toronto, Montreal, and Ottawa, respectively, with total delivery costs of $5990. The shop ordered the same amount from Toronto and Ottawa. How many units were ordered from each supplier?

46. *Manufacturing* Fred's Furniture Factory has 1950 machine hours available each week in the cutting department, 1490 hours in the assembly department, and 2160 in the finishing department. Manufacturing a chair requires 0.2 hours of cutting, 0.3 hours of assembly, and 0.1 hours of finishing. A cabinet requires 0.5 hours of cutting, 0.4 hours of assembly, and 0.6 hours of finishing. A buffet requires 0.3 hours of cutting, 0.1 hours of assembly, and 0.4 hours of finishing. How many chairs, cabinets, and buffets should be produced in order to use all the available production capacity?

47. *Manufacturing* Nadir Inc. produces three models of television sets: deluxe, super-deluxe, and ultra. Each deluxe set requires 2 hours of electronics work, 2 hours of assembly time, and 1 hour of finishing time. Each super-deluxe requires 1, 3, and 1 hour of electronics, assembly, and finishing time, respectively. Each ultra requires 3, 2, and 2 hours of the same work, respectively.

a. There are 100 hours available for electronics, 100 hours available for assembly, and 65 hours available for finish-

ing per week. How many of each model should be produced each week if all available time is to be used?

b. Suppose everything is the same as in part a, but an ultra set requires 6, rather than 3, hours of electronics work. How many solutions are there now?

c. Suppose everything is the same as in part b, but the total hours available for electronics changes from 100 hours to 160 hours. Now how many solutions are there?

48. *Transportation* An electronics company produces three models of stereo speakers, models A, B, and C, and can deliver them by truck, van, or station wagon. A truck holds 2 boxes of model A, 2 of model B, and 3 of model C. A van holds 3 boxes of model A, 4 boxes of model B, and 2 boxes of model C. A station wagon holds 3 boxes of model A, 5 boxes of model B, and 1 box of model C.

a. If 25 boxes of model A, 33 boxes of model B, and 22 boxes of model C are to be delivered, how many vehicles of each type should be used so that all operate at full capacity?

b. Model C has been discontinued. If 25 boxes of model A and 33 boxes of model B are to be delivered, how many vehicles of each type should be used so that all operate at full capacity?

49. *Truck Rental* The U-Drive Rent-A-Truck company plans to spend $7 million on 200 new vehicles. Each commercial van will cost $35,000, each small truck $30,000, and each large truck $50,000. Past experience shows that they need twice as many vans as small trucks. How many of each type of vehicle can they buy?

50. *Loans* To get the necessary funds for a planned expansion, a small company took out three loans totaling $25,000. Company owners were able to get interest rates of 8%, 9%, and 10%. They borrowed $1000 more at 9% than they borrowed at 10%. The total annual interest on the loans was $2190.

a. How much did they borrow at each rate?

b. Suppose we drop the condition that they borrowed $1000 more at 9% than at 10%. What can you say about the amount borrowed at 10%? What is the solution if the amount borrowed at 10% is $5000?

c. Suppose the bank sets a maximum of $10,000 at the lowest interest rate of 8%. Is a solution possible that still meets all of the original conditions?

d. Explain why $10,000 at 8%, $8000 at 9%, and $7000 at 10% is not a feasible solution for part c.

51. *Transportation* An auto manufacturer sends cars from two plants, I and II, to dealerships A and B located in a midwestern city. Plant I has a total of 28 cars to send, and plant II has 8. Dealer A needs 20 cars, and dealer B needs 16. Transportation costs per car, based on the distance of each dealership from each plant, are $220 from I to A, $300 from I to B, $400 from II to A, and $180 from II to B. The manufacturer wants to limit transportation costs to $10,640. How many cars should be sent from each plant to each of the two dealerships?

52. *Transportation* A manufacturer purchases a part for use at both of its plants—one at Roseville, California, the other at Akron, Ohio. The part is available in limited quantities from two suppliers. Each supplier has 75 units available. The Roseville plant needs 40 units, and the Akron plant requires 75 units. The first supplier charges $70 per unit delivered to Roseville and $90 per unit delivered to Akron. Corresponding costs from the second supplier are $80 and $120. The manufacturer wants to order a total of 75 units from the first, less expensive supplier, with the remaining 40 units to come from the second supplier. If the company spends $10,750 to purchase the required number of units for the two plants, find the number of units that should be sent from each supplier to each plant.

53. *Packaging* A company produces three combinations of mixed vegetables that sell in 1-kg packages. Italian style combines 0.3 kg of zucchini, 0.3 of broccoli, and 0.4 of carrots. French style combines 0.6 kg of broccoli and 0.4 of carrots. Oriental style combines 0.2 kg of zucchini, 0.5 of broccoli, and 0.3 of carrots. The company has a stock of 16,200 kg of zucchini, 41,400 kg of broccoli, and 29,400 kg of carrots. How many packages of each style should it prepare to use up existing supplies?

54. *Tents* L. L. Bean makes three sizes of Ultra Dome tents: two-person, four-person, and six-person models, which cost $129, $179, and $229, respectively. A two-person tent provides 40 ft^2 of floor space, while a four-person and a six-person model provide 64 ft^2 and 88 ft^2 of floor space, respectively.* A recent order by an organization that takes children camping ordered enough tents to hold 200 people and provide 3200 ft^2 of floor space. The total cost was $8950, and we wish to know how many tents of each size were ordered.

a. How many solutions are there to this problem?

b. What is the solution with the most four-person tents?

c. What is the solution with the most two-person tents?

d. Discuss the company's pricing strategy that led to a system of equations that is dependent. Do you think that this is a coincidence or an example of logical thinking?

LIFE SCIENCES

55. *Animal Breeding* An animal breeder can buy four types of food for Vietnamese pot-bellied pigs. Each case of Brand A contains 25 units of fiber, 30 units of protein, and 30 units of fat. Each case of Brand B contains 50 units of fiber, 30 units of protein, and 20 units of fat. Each case of Brand C contains 75 units of fiber, 30 units of protein, and 20 units of fat. Each case of Brand D contains 100 units of fiber, 60 units of protein, and 30 units of fat. How many cases of each should the breeder mix together to obtain a food that provides 1200 units of fiber, 600 units of protein, and 400 units of fat?

56. *Dietetics* A hospital dietician is planning a special diet for a certain patient. The total amount per meal of food groups A, B, and C must equal 400 grams. The diet should include one-third as much of group A as of group B, and the sum of the amounts of group A and group C should equal twice the amount of group B.

a. How many grams of each food group should be included?

b. Suppose we drop the requirement that the diet include one-third as much of group A as of group B. Describe the set of all possible solutions.

c. Suppose that, in addition to the conditions given in the original problem, foods A and B cost 2 cents per gram and food C costs 3 cents per gram, and that a meal must cost $8. Is a solution possible?

57. *Bacterial Food Requirements* Three species of bacteria are fed three foods, I, II, and III. A bacterium of the first species consumes 1.3 units each of foods I and II and 2.3 units of food III each day. A bacterium of the second species consumes 1.1 units of food I, 2.4 units of food II, and 3.7 units of food III each day. A bacterium of the third species consumes 8.1 units of I, 2.9 units of II, and 5.1 units of III each day. If 16,000 units of I, 28,000 units of II, and 44,000 units of III are supplied each day, how many of each species can be maintained in this environment?

58. *Fish Food Requirements* A lake is stocked each spring with three species of fish, A, B, and C. Three foods, I, II, and III, are available in the lake. Each fish of species A requires an average of 1.32 units of food I, 2.9 units of food II, and 1.75 units of food III each day. Species B fish each require 2.1 units of food I, 0.95 unit of food II, and 0.6 unit of food III daily. Species C fish require 0.86, 1.52, and 2.01 units of I, II, and III per day, respectively. If 490 units of food I, 897 units of food II, and 653 units of food III are available daily, how many of each species should be stocked?

*L. L. Bean, http://www.llbean.com.

59. *Agriculture* According to data from a Texas agricultural report, the amount of nitrogen (in lb/acre), phosphate (in lb/acre), and labor (in hr/acre) needed to grow honeydews, yellow onions, and lettuce is given by the following table.*

	Honeydews	Yellow Onions	Lettuce
Nitrogen	120	150	180
Phosphate	180	80	80
Labor	4.97	4.45	4.65

a. If the farmer has 220 acres, 29,100 lb of nitrogen, 32,600 lb of phosphate, and 480 hours of labor, is it possible to use all resources completely? If so, how many acres should he allot for each crop?

b. Suppose everything is the same as in part a, except that 1061 hours of labor are available. Is it possible to use all resources completely? If so, how many acres should he allot for each crop?

60. *Archimedes' Problem Bovinum* Archimedes is credited with the authorship of a famous problem involving the number of cattle of the sun god. A simplified version of the problem is stated as follows:[†]

> The sun god had a herd of cattle consisting of bulls and cows, one part of which was white, a second black, a third spotted, and a fourth brown.
>
> Among the bulls, the number of white ones was one half plus one third the number of the black greater than the brown; the number of the black, one quarter plus one fifth the number of the spotted greater than the brown; the number of the spotted, one sixth and one seventh the number of the white greater than the brown.
>
> Among the cows, the number of white ones was one third plus one quarter of the total black cattle; the number of the black, one quarter plus one fifth the total of the spotted cattle; the number of the spotted, one fifth plus one sixth the total of the brown cattle; the number of the brown, one sixth plus one seventh the total of the white cattle.
>
> What was the composition of the herd?

The problem can be solved by converting the statements into two systems of equations, using X, Y, Z, and T for the number of white, black, spotted, and brown bulls, respectively, and x, y, z, and t for the number of white, black, spotted, and brown cows, respectively. For example, the first statement can be written as $X = (1/2 + 1/3)Y + T$

and then reduced. The result is the following two systems of equations:

$$6X - 5Y = 6T \qquad 12x - 7y = 7Y$$
$$20Y - 9Z = 20T \quad \text{and} \quad 20y - 9z = 9Z$$
$$42Z - 13X = 42T \qquad 30z - 11t = 11T$$
$$-13x + 42t = 13X$$

a. Show that these two systems of equations represent Archimedes' Problem Bovinum.

b. If it is known that the number of brown bulls, T, is 4,149,387, use the Gauss-Jordan method to first find a solution to the 3×3 system and then use these values and the Gauss-Jordan method to find a solution to the 4×4 system of equations.

61. *Health* The U.S. National Center for Health Statistics tracks the major causes of death in the United States. After a steady increase, the death rate by cancer has decreased since the early 1990s. The table lists the age-adjusted death rate per 1,000,000 people for 4 years.[‡]

Year	Rate
1980	207.9
1990	216.0
2000	199.6
2003	190.1

a. If the relationship between the death rate R and the year t is expressed as $R = at^2 + bt + c$, where $t = 0$ corresponds to 1980, use data from 1980, 1990, and 2000 and a linear system of equations to determine the constants a, b, and c.

b. Use the equation from part a to predict the rate in 2003, and compare the result with the actual data.

c. If the relationship between the death rate R and the year t is expressed as $R = at^3 + bt^2 + ct + d$, where $t = 0$ corresponds to 1980, use all four data points and a linear system of equations to determine the constants a, b, c, and d.

d. Discuss the appropriateness of the functions used in parts a and c to model this data.

SOCIAL SCIENCES

62. *Modeling War* One of the factors that contribute to the success or failure of a particular army during war is its abil-

---

*Paredes, Miguel, Mohammad Fatehi, and Richard Hinthorn, "The Transformation of an Inconsistent Linear System into a Consistent System," *The AMATYC Review*, Vol. 13, No. 2, Spring 1992.

[†]Dorrie, Heinrich, *100 Great Problems of Elementary Mathematics, Their History and Solution*, New York: Dover Publications, 1965, pp. 3–7.

[‡]http://www.cdc.gov/nchs/data, and *Time Almanac 2006*, p. 135.

ity to get new troops ready for service. It is possible to analyze the rate of change in the number of troops of two hypothetical armies with the following simplified model,

$$\text{Rate of increase (RED ARMY)} = 200{,}000 - 0.5r - 0.3b$$

$$\text{Rate of increase (BLUE ARMY)} = 350{,}000 - 0.5r - 0.7b,$$

where r is the number of soldiers in the Red Army at a given time and b is the number of soldiers in the Blue Army at a given time. The factors 0.5 and 0.7 represent each army's efficiency of bringing new soldiers to the fight.*

a. Solve this system of equations to determine the number of soldiers in each army when the rate of increase for each is zero.

b. Describe what might be going on in a war when the rate of increase is zero.

63. *Traffic Control* At rush hours, substantial traffic congestion is encountered at the traffic intersections shown in the figure. (The streets are one-way, as shown by the arrows.)

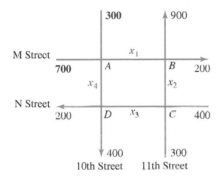

The city wishes to improve the signals at these corners so as to speed the flow of traffic. The traffic engineers first gather data. As the figure shows, 700 cars per hour come down M Street to intersection A, and 300 cars per hour come down 10th Street to intersection A. A total of x_1 of these cars leave A on M Street, and x_4 cars leave A on 10th Street. The number of cars entering A must equal the number leaving, so that

$$x_1 + x_4 = 700 + 300$$

or

$$x_1 + x_4 = 1000.$$

For intersection B, x_1 cars enter on M Street and x_2 on 11th Street. The figure shows that 900 cars leave B on 11th and 200 on M. Thus,

$$x_1 + x_2 = 900 + 200$$

$$x_1 + x_2 = 1100.$$

a. Write two equations representing the traffic entering and leaving intersections C and D.

b. Use the four equations to set up an augmented matrix, and solve the system by the Gauss-Jordan method, using x_4 as the parameter.

c. Based on your solution to part b, what are the largest and smallest possible values for the number of cars leaving intersection A on 10th Street?

d. Answer the question in part c for the other three variables.

e. Verify that you could have discarded any one of the four original equations without changing the solution. What does this tell you about the original problem?

64. *Ice Cream* Researchers have determined that the amount of sugar contained in ice cream helps to determine the overall "degree of like" that a consumer has toward that particular flavor. They have also determined that too much or too little sugar will have the same negative affect on the "degree of like" and that this relationship follows a quadratic function. In an experiment conducted at Pennsylvania State University, the following condensed table was obtained.[†]

Percentage of Sugar	Degree of Like
8	5.4
13	6.3
18	5.6

a. Use this information and the Gauss-Jordan method to determine the coefficients a, b, c, of the quadratic equation

$$y = ax^2 + bx + c,$$

---

*Bellany, Ian, "Modeling War," *Journal of Peace Research*, Vol. 36, No. 6, 1999, pp. 729–739.
[†]Guinard, J., C. Zoumas-Morse, L. Mori, B. Uatoni, D. Panyam, and A. Kilar, "Sugar and Fat Effects on Sensory Properties of Ice Cream," *Journal of Food Science*, Vol. 62, No. 4, Sept./Oct. 1997, pp. 1087–1094.

where y is the "degree of like" and x is the percentage of sugar in the ice cream mix.

b. Repeat part a by using the quadratic regression feature on a graphing calculator. Compare your answers.

65. *Toys* One hundred toys are to be given out to a group of children. A ball costs $2, a doll costs $3, and a car costs $4. A total of $295 was spent on the toys.

a. A ball weighs 12 oz, a doll 16 oz, and a car 18 oz. The total weight of all the toys is 1542 oz. Find how many of each toy there are.

b. Now suppose the weight of a ball, doll, and car are 11, 15, and 19 oz, respectively. If the total weight is still 1542 oz, how many solutions are there now?

c. Keep the weights as in part b, but change the total weight to 1480 oz. How many solutions are there?

d. Give the solution to part c that has the smallest number of cars.

e. Give the solution to part c that has the largest number of cars.

66. *Lights Out* The Tiger Electronics' game, Lights Out, consists of five rows of five lighted buttons. When a button is pushed, it changes the on/off status of it and the status of all of its vertical and horizontal neighbors. For any given situation where some of the lights are on and some are off, the goal of the game is to push buttons until all of the lights are turned off. It turns out that for any given array of lights, solving a system of equations can be used to develop a strategy for turning the lights out.* The follow-

ing system of equations can be used to solve the problem for a simplified version of the game with 2 rows of 2 buttons where all of the lights are initially turned on.

$$x_{11} + x_{12} + x_{21} = 1$$
$$x_{11} + x_{12} + x_{22} = 1$$
$$x_{11} + x_{21} + x_{22} = 1$$
$$x_{12} + x_{21} + x_{22} = 1,$$

where $x_{ij} = 1$ if the light in row i, column j, is on and $x_{ij} = 0$ when it is off. The order in which the buttons are pushed does not matter, so we are only seeking which buttons should be pushed.

a. Solve this system of equations and determine a strategy to turn the lights out. (*Hint:* While doing row operations, if an odd number is found, immediately replace this value with a 1; if an even number is found, then immediately replace that number with a zero. This is called modulo 2 arithmetic, and it is necessary in problems dealing with on/off switches.)

b. Resolve the equation with the right side changed to $(0, 1, 1, 0)$.

67. *Baseball* Ichiro Suzuki holds the American League record for the most hits in a single baseball season. In 2004, Suzuki had a total of 262 hits for the Seattle Mariners. He hit three fewer triples than home runs, and he hit three times as many doubles as home runs. Suzuki also hit 45 times as many singles as triples.[†] Find the number of singles, doubles, triples, and home runs hit by Suzuki during the season.

2.3 Addition and Subtraction of Matrices

 **THINK ABOUT IT**

A company sends monthly shipments to its warehouses in several cities. How might the company keep track of the shipments to each warehouse most efficiently?

In the previous section, matrices were used to store information about systems of linear equations. In this section, we begin a study of matrices and show additional uses of matrix notation that will answer the question posed above. The use of matrices has gained increasing importance in the fields of management, natural science, and social science because matrices provide a convenient way to organize data, as Example 1 demonstrates.

EXAMPLE 1   **Furniture Shipments**

The EZ Life Company manufactures sofas and armchairs in three models, A, B, and C. The company has regional warehouses in New York, Chicago, and San

---

*Anderson, Marlow and Todd Feil, "Turning Lights Out with Linear Algebra," *Mathematics Magazine*, Vol. 71, No. 4, 1998, pp. 300–303.
†http://www.baseball-almanac.com.

Francisco. In its August shipment, the company sends 10 model-A sofas, 12 model-B sofas, 5 model-C sofas, 15 model-A chairs, 20 model-B chairs, and 8 model-C chairs to each warehouse. Use a matrix to organize this information.

▶**Solution** To organize this data, we might first list it as follows.

| Sofas | 10 model-A | 12 model-B | 5 model-C |
| Chairs | 15 model-A | 20 model-B | 8 model-C |

Alternatively, we might tabulate the data in a chart.

		Model		
		A	**B**	**C**
Furniture Type	*Sofas*	10	12	5
	Chairs	15	20	8

With the understanding that the numbers in each row refer to the furniture type (sofa, chair) and the numbers in each column refer to the model (A, B, C), the same information can be given by a matrix, as follows.

$$M = \begin{bmatrix} 10 & 12 & 5 \\ 15 & 20 & 8 \end{bmatrix}$$

Matrices often are named with capital letters, as in Example 1. Matrices are classified by **size**; that is, by the number of rows and columns they contain. For example, matrix M above has two rows and three columns. This matrix is a 2×3 (read "2 by 3") matrix. By definition, a matrix with m rows and n columns is an $m \times n$ matrix. The number of rows is always given first.

EXAMPLE 2 Matrix Size

(a) The matrix $\begin{bmatrix} -3 & 5 \\ 2 & 0 \\ 5 & -1 \end{bmatrix}$ is a 3×2 matrix.

(b) $\begin{bmatrix} 0.5 & 8 & 0.9 \\ 0 & 5.1 & -3 \\ -4 & 0 & 5 \end{bmatrix}$ is a 3×3 matrix.

(c) $\begin{bmatrix} 1 & 6 & 5 & -2 & 5 \end{bmatrix}$ is a 1×5 matrix.

(d) $\begin{bmatrix} 3 \\ -5 \\ 0 \\ 2 \end{bmatrix}$ is a 4×1 matrix.

A matrix with the same number of rows as columns is called a **square matrix**. The matrix in Example 2(b) is a square matrix.

A matrix containing only one row is called a **row matrix** or a **row vector**. The matrix in Example 2(c) is a row matrix, as are

$$[5 \quad 8], \quad [6 \quad -9 \quad 2], \quad \text{and} \quad [-4 \quad 0 \quad 0 \quad 0].$$

A matrix of only one column, as in Example 2(d), is a **column matrix** or a **column vector**.

Equality for matrices is defined as follows.

> **MATRIX EQUALITY**
>
> Two matrices are equal if they are the same size and if each pair of corresponding elements is equal.

By this definition,

$$\begin{bmatrix} 2 & 1 \\ 3 & -5 \end{bmatrix} \quad \text{and} \quad \begin{bmatrix} 1 & 2 \\ -5 & 3 \end{bmatrix}$$

are not equal (even though they contain the same elements and are the same size) since the corresponding elements differ.

EXAMPLE 3   **Matrix Equality**

(a) From the definition of matrix equality given above, the only way that the statement

$$\begin{bmatrix} 2 & 1 \\ p & q \end{bmatrix} = \begin{bmatrix} x & y \\ -1 & 0 \end{bmatrix}$$

can be true is if $2 = x$, $1 = y$, $p = -1$, and $q = 0$.

(b) The statement

$$\begin{bmatrix} x \\ y \end{bmatrix} = \begin{bmatrix} 1 \\ -3 \\ 0 \end{bmatrix}$$

can never be true, since the two matrices are different sizes. (One is 2×1 and the other is 3×1.)

Addition   The matrix given in Example 1,

$$M = \begin{bmatrix} 10 & 12 & 5 \\ 15 & 20 & 8 \end{bmatrix},$$

shows the August shipment from the EZ Life plant to each of its warehouses. If matrix N below gives the September shipment to the New York warehouse, what is the total shipment of each item of furniture to the New York warehouse for these two months?

$$N = \begin{bmatrix} 45 & 35 & 20 \\ 65 & 40 & 35 \end{bmatrix}$$

If 10 model-A sofas were shipped in August and 45 in September, then altogether $10 + 45 = 55$ model-A sofas were shipped in the two months. The other corresponding entries can be added in a similar way to get a new matrix Q, which represents the total shipment for the two months.

$$Q = \begin{bmatrix} 55 & 47 & 25 \\ 80 & 60 & 43 \end{bmatrix}$$

It is convenient to refer to Q as the sum of M and N.

The way these two matrices were added illustrates the following definition of addition of matrices.

> **ADDING MATRICES**
>
> The sum of two $m \times n$ matrices X and Y is the $m \times n$ matrix $X + Y$ in which each element is the sum of the corresponding elements of X and Y.

CAUTION It is important to remember that only matrices that are the same size can be added. ∎

EXAMPLE 4 Adding Matrices

Find each sum, if possible.

▶Solution

(a) $\begin{bmatrix} 5 & -6 \\ 8 & 9 \end{bmatrix} + \begin{bmatrix} 4 & 6 \\ 8 & -3 \end{bmatrix} = \begin{bmatrix} 5 + (-4) & 6 + 6 \\ 8 + 8 & 9 + (-3) \end{bmatrix} = \begin{bmatrix} 1 & 0 \\ 16 & 6 \end{bmatrix}$

(b) The matrices

$$A = \begin{bmatrix} 5 & -8 \\ 6 & 2 \end{bmatrix} \quad \text{and} \quad B = \begin{bmatrix} 3 & -9 & 1 \\ 4 & 2 & -5 \end{bmatrix}$$

are different sizes. Therefore, the sum $A + B$ does not exist. ▬

EXAMPLE 5 Furniture Shipments

The September shipments from the EZ Life Company to the New York, San Francisco, and Chicago warehouses are given in matrices N, S, and C below.

$$N = \begin{bmatrix} 45 & 35 & 20 \\ 65 & 40 & 35 \end{bmatrix} \quad S = \begin{bmatrix} 30 & 32 & 28 \\ 43 & 47 & 30 \end{bmatrix} \quad C = \begin{bmatrix} 22 & 25 & 38 \\ 31 & 34 & 35 \end{bmatrix}$$

What was the total amount shipped to the three warehouses in September?

▶Solution The total of the September shipments is represented by the sum of the three matrices N, S, and C.

$$N + S + C = \begin{bmatrix} 45 & 35 & 20 \\ 65 & 40 & 35 \end{bmatrix} + \begin{bmatrix} 30 & 32 & 28 \\ 43 & 47 & 30 \end{bmatrix} + \begin{bmatrix} 22 & 25 & 38 \\ 31 & 34 & 35 \end{bmatrix}$$

$$= \begin{bmatrix} 97 & 92 & 86 \\ 139 & 121 & 100 \end{bmatrix}$$

For example, this sum shows that the total number of model-C sofas shipped to the three warehouses in September was 86.

The additive inverse of the real number a is $-a$; a similar definition applies to matrices.

ADDITIVE INVERSE

The **additive inverse** (or **negative**) of a matrix X is the matrix $-X$ in which each element is the additive inverse of the corresponding element of X.

If

$$A = \begin{bmatrix} 1 & 2 & 3 \\ 0 & -1 & 5 \end{bmatrix} \quad \text{and} \quad B = \begin{bmatrix} -2 & 3 & 0 \\ 1 & -7 & 2 \end{bmatrix},$$

then by the definition of the additive inverse of a matrix,

$$-A = \begin{bmatrix} -1 & -2 & -3 \\ 0 & 1 & -5 \end{bmatrix} \quad \text{and} \quad -B = \begin{bmatrix} 2 & -3 & 0 \\ -1 & 7 & -2 \end{bmatrix}.$$

By the definition of matrix addition, for each matrix X the sum $X + (-X)$ is a **zero matrix**, O, whose elements are all zeros. For the matrix A above,

$$A + (-A) = \begin{bmatrix} 0 & 0 & 0 \\ 0 & 0 & 0 \end{bmatrix}.$$

► FOR REVIEW

Compare this with the identity property for real numbers: for any real number a, we have $a + 0 = 0 + a = a$. Exercises 34–37 give other properties of matrices that are parallel to the properties of real numbers.

There is an $m \times n$ zero matrix for each pair of values of m and n. Such a matrix serves as an $m \times n$ **additive identity**, similar to the additive identity 0 for any real number. Zero matrices have the following identity property.

ZERO MATRIX

If O is an $m \times n$ zero matrix, and A is any $m \times n$ matrix, then

$$A + O = O + A = A.$$

Subtraction   The subtraction of matrices is defined in a manner comparable to subtraction of real numbers.

SUBTRACTING MATRICES

For two $m \times n$ matrices X and Y, the difference $X - Y$ is the $m \times n$ matrix defined by

$$X - Y = X + (-Y).$$

This definition means that matrix subtraction can be performed by subtracting corresponding elements. For example, with A, B, and $-B$ as defined above,

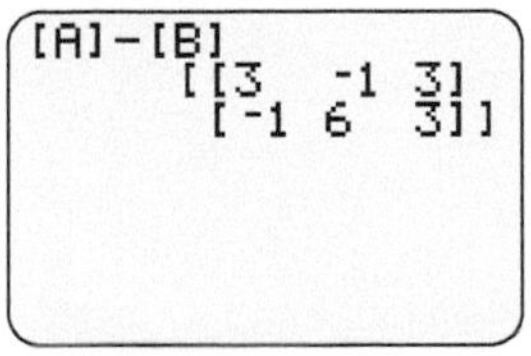

[A]-[B]
 [[3 -1 3]
  [-1 6 3]]

FIGURE 12

$$A - B = A + (-B) = \begin{bmatrix} 1 & 2 & 3 \\ 0 & -1 & 5 \end{bmatrix} + \begin{bmatrix} 2 & -3 & 0 \\ -1 & 7 & -2 \end{bmatrix}$$
$$= \begin{bmatrix} 3 & -1 & 3 \\ -1 & 6 & 3 \end{bmatrix}.$$

Matrix operations are easily performed on a graphing calculator. Figure 12 shows the previous operation; the matrices A and B were already entered into the calculator.

Spreadsheet programs are designed to effectively organize data that can be represented in rows and columns. Accordingly, matrix operations are also easily performed on spreadsheets. See *The Spreadsheet Manual* available with this book for details.

EXAMPLE 6 Subtracting Matrices

(a) $\begin{bmatrix} 8 & 6 & -4 \end{bmatrix} - \begin{bmatrix} 3 & 5 & -8 \end{bmatrix} = \begin{bmatrix} 5 & 1 & 4 \end{bmatrix}$

(b) The matrices

$$\begin{bmatrix} -2 & 5 \\ 0 & 1 \end{bmatrix} \quad \text{and} \quad \begin{bmatrix} 3 \\ 5 \end{bmatrix}$$

are different sizes and cannot be subtracted.

EXAMPLE 7 Furniture Shipments

During September the Chicago warehouse of the EZ Life Company shipped out the following numbers of each model.

$$K = \begin{bmatrix} 5 & 10 & 8 \\ 11 & 14 & 15 \end{bmatrix}$$

What was the Chicago warehouse inventory on October 1, taking into account only the number of items received and sent out during the month?

▶**Solution** The number of each kind of item received during September is given by matrix C from Example 5; the number of each model sent out during September is given by matrix K. The October 1 inventory will be represented by the matrix $C - K$:

$$\begin{bmatrix} 22 & 25 & 38 \\ 31 & 34 & 35 \end{bmatrix} - \begin{bmatrix} 5 & 10 & 8 \\ 11 & 14 & 15 \end{bmatrix} = \begin{bmatrix} 17 & 15 & 30 \\ 20 & 20 & 20 \end{bmatrix}.$$

▶2.3 Exercises

Decide whether each statement is true or false. If false, tell why.

1. $\begin{bmatrix} 1 & 3 \\ 5 & 7 \end{bmatrix} = \begin{bmatrix} 1 & 5 \\ 3 & 7 \end{bmatrix}$

2. $\begin{bmatrix} 1 \\ 2 \\ 3 \end{bmatrix} = \begin{bmatrix} 1 & 2 & 3 \end{bmatrix}$

3. $\begin{bmatrix} x \\ y \end{bmatrix} = \begin{bmatrix} -2 \\ 8 \end{bmatrix}$ if $x = -2$ and $y = 8$.

4. $\begin{bmatrix} 3 & 5 & 2 & 8 \\ 1 & -1 & 4 & 0 \end{bmatrix}$ is a 4 × 2 matrix.

5. $\begin{bmatrix} 1 & 9 & -4 \\ 3 & 7 & 2 \\ -1 & 1 & 0 \end{bmatrix}$ is a square matrix.

6. $\begin{bmatrix} 2 & 4 & -1 \\ 3 & 7 & 5 \\ 0 & 0 & 0 \end{bmatrix} = \begin{bmatrix} 2 & 4 & -1 \\ 3 & 7 & 5 \end{bmatrix}$

Find the size of each matrix. Identify any square, column, or row matrices. Give the additive inverse of each matrix.

7. $\begin{bmatrix} -4 & 8 \\ 2 & 3 \end{bmatrix}$

8. $\begin{bmatrix} 2 & -3 & 7 \\ 1 & 0 & 4 \end{bmatrix}$

9. $\begin{bmatrix} -6 & 8 & 0 & 0 \\ 4 & 1 & 9 & 2 \\ 3 & -5 & 7 & 1 \end{bmatrix}$

10. $\begin{bmatrix} 8 & -2 & 4 & 6 & 3 \end{bmatrix}$

11. $\begin{bmatrix} -7 \\ 5 \end{bmatrix}$

12. $\begin{bmatrix} -9 \end{bmatrix}$

13. The sum of an $n \times m$ matrix and its additive inverse is _____.

14. If A is a 5 × 2 matrix and $A + K = A$, what do you know about K?

Find the values of the variables in each equation.

15. $\begin{bmatrix} 3 & 4 \\ -8 & 1 \end{bmatrix} = \begin{bmatrix} 3 & x \\ y & z \end{bmatrix}$

16. $\begin{bmatrix} -5 \\ y \end{bmatrix} = \begin{bmatrix} -5 \\ 8 \end{bmatrix}$

17. $\begin{bmatrix} s - 4 & t + 2 \\ -5 & 7 \end{bmatrix} = \begin{bmatrix} 6 & 2 \\ -5 & r \end{bmatrix}$

18. $\begin{bmatrix} 9 & 7 \\ r & 0 \end{bmatrix} = \begin{bmatrix} m - 3 & n + 5 \\ 8 & 0 \end{bmatrix}$

19. $\begin{bmatrix} a + 2 & 3b & 4c \\ d & 7f & 8 \end{bmatrix} + \begin{bmatrix} -7 & 2b & 6 \\ -3d & -6 & -2 \end{bmatrix} = \begin{bmatrix} 15 & 25 & 6 \\ -8 & 1 & 6 \end{bmatrix}$

20. $\begin{bmatrix} a + 2 & 3z + 1 & 5m \\ 4k & 0 & 3 \end{bmatrix} + \begin{bmatrix} 3a & 2z & 5m \\ 2k & 5 & 6 \end{bmatrix} = \begin{bmatrix} 10 & -14 & 80 \\ 10 & 5 & 9 \end{bmatrix}$

Perform the indicated operations, where possible.

21. $\begin{bmatrix} 2 & 4 & 5 & -7 \\ 6 & -3 & 12 & 0 \end{bmatrix} + \begin{bmatrix} 8 & 0 & -10 & 1 \\ -2 & 8 & -9 & 11 \end{bmatrix}$

22. $\begin{bmatrix} 1 & 5 \\ 2 & -3 \\ 3 & 7 \end{bmatrix} + \begin{bmatrix} 2 & 3 \\ 8 & 5 \\ -1 & 9 \end{bmatrix}$

23. $\begin{bmatrix} 1 & 3 & -2 \\ 4 & 7 & 1 \end{bmatrix} + \begin{bmatrix} 3 & 0 \\ 6 & 4 \\ -5 & 2 \end{bmatrix}$

24. $\begin{bmatrix} 8 & 0 & -3 \\ 1 & 19 & -5 \end{bmatrix} - \begin{bmatrix} 1 & -5 & 2 \\ 3 & 9 & -8 \end{bmatrix}$

25. $\begin{bmatrix} 2 & 8 & 12 & 0 \\ 7 & 4 & -1 & 5 \\ 1 & 2 & 0 & 10 \end{bmatrix} - \begin{bmatrix} 1 & 3 & 6 & 9 \\ 2 & -3 & -3 & 4 \\ 8 & 0 & -2 & 17 \end{bmatrix}$

26. $\begin{bmatrix} 2 & 1 \\ 5 & -3 \\ -7 & 2 \\ 9 & 0 \end{bmatrix} + \begin{bmatrix} 1 & -8 & 0 \\ 5 & 3 & 2 \\ -6 & 7 & -5 \\ 2 & -1 & 0 \end{bmatrix}$

27. $\begin{bmatrix} 2 & 3 \\ -2 & 4 \end{bmatrix} + \begin{bmatrix} 4 & 3 \\ 7 & 8 \end{bmatrix} - \begin{bmatrix} 3 & 2 \\ 1 & 4 \end{bmatrix}$

28. $\begin{bmatrix} 4 & 3 \\ 1 & 2 \end{bmatrix} - \begin{bmatrix} 1 & 1 \\ 1 & 0 \end{bmatrix} + \begin{bmatrix} 1 & 1 \\ 1 & 4 \end{bmatrix}$

29. $\begin{bmatrix} 2 & -1 \\ 0 & 13 \end{bmatrix} - \begin{bmatrix} 4 & 8 \\ -5 & 7 \end{bmatrix} + \begin{bmatrix} 12 & 7 \\ 5 & 3 \end{bmatrix}$

30. $\begin{bmatrix} 5 & 8 \\ -3 & 1 \end{bmatrix} + \begin{bmatrix} 0 & 1 \\ -2 & -2 \end{bmatrix} + \begin{bmatrix} -5 & -8 \\ 6 & 1 \end{bmatrix}$

31. $\begin{bmatrix} -4x + 2y & -3x + y \\ 6x - 3y & 2x - 5y \end{bmatrix} + \begin{bmatrix} -8x + 6y & 2x \\ 3y - 5x & 6x + 4y \end{bmatrix}$

32. $\begin{bmatrix} 4k - 8y \\ 6z - 3x \\ 2k + 5a \\ -4m + 2n \end{bmatrix} - \begin{bmatrix} 5k + 6y \\ 2z + 5x \\ 4k + 6a \\ 4m - 2n \end{bmatrix}$

33. For matrix $X = \begin{bmatrix} x & y \\ z & w \end{bmatrix}$, find the matrix $-X$.

Using matrices $O = \begin{bmatrix} 0 & 0 \\ 0 & 0 \end{bmatrix}$, $P = \begin{bmatrix} m & n \\ p & q \end{bmatrix}$, $T = \begin{bmatrix} r & s \\ t & u \end{bmatrix}$, and $X = \begin{bmatrix} x & y \\ z & w \end{bmatrix}$, verify the statements in Exercises 34–37.

34. $X + T = T + X$ (commutative property of addition of matrices)

35. $X + (T + P) = (X + T) + P$ (associative property of addition of matrices)

36. $X + (-X) = O$ (inverse property of addition of matrices)

37. $P + O = P$ (identity property of addition of matrices)

38. Which of the above properties are valid for matrices that are not square?

▶ Applications

BUSINESS AND ECONOMICS

39. *Management* A toy company has plants in Boston, Chicago, and Seattle that manufacture toy phones and calculators. The following matrix gives the production costs (in dollars) for each item at the Boston plant:

$$\begin{array}{cc} & \text{Phones} \quad \text{Calculators} \\ \begin{matrix} \text{Material} \\ \text{Labor} \end{matrix} & \begin{bmatrix} 4.27 & 6.94 \\ 3.45 & 3.65 \end{bmatrix} \end{array}$$

a. In Chicago, a phone costs $4.05 for material and $3.27 for labor; a calculator costs $7.01 for material and $3.51 for labor. In Seattle, material costs are $4.40 for a phone and $6.90 for a calculator; labor costs are $3.54 for a phone and $3.76 for a calculator. Write the production cost matrices for Chicago and Seattle.

b. Suppose labor costs increase by $0.11 per item in Chicago and material costs there increase by $0.37 for a phone and $0.42 for a calculator. What is the new production cost matrix for Chicago?

40. *Management* There are three convenience stores in Folsom. This week, store I sold 88 loaves of bread, 48 qt of milk, 16 jars of peanut butter, and 112 lb of cold cuts. Store II sold 105 loaves of bread, 72 qt of milk, 21 jars of peanut butter, and 147 lb of cold cuts. Store III sold 60 loaves of bread, 40 qt of milk, no peanut butter, and 50 lb of cold cuts.

a. Use a 4×3 matrix to express the sales information for the three stores.

b. During the following week, sales on these products at store I increased by 25%; sales at store II increased by 1/3; and sales at store III increased by 10%. Write the sales matrix for that week.

c. Write a matrix that represents total sales over the two-week period.

LIFE SCIENCES

41. *Dietetics* A dietician prepares a diet specifying the amounts a patient should eat of four basic food groups: group I, meats; group II, fruits and vegetables; group III, breads and starches; group IV, milk products. Amounts are given in "exchanges" that represent 1 oz (meat), 1/2 cup (fruits and vegetables), 1 slice (bread), 8 oz (milk), or other suitable measurements.

a. The number of "exchanges" for breakfast for each of the four food groups, respectively, are 2, 1, 2, and 1; for lunch, 3, 2, 2, and 1; and for dinner, 4, 3, 2, and 1. Write a 3×4 matrix using this information.

b. The amounts of fat, carbohydrates, and protein (in appropriate units) in each food group, respectively, are as follows.

Fat: 5, 0, 0, 10

Carbohydrates: 0, 10, 15, 12

Protein: 7, 1, 2, 8

Use this information to write a 4×3 matrix.

c. There are 8 calories per exchange of fat, 4 calories per exchange of carbohydrates, and 5 calories per exchange of protein. Summarize this data in a 3×1 matrix.

42. *Animal Growth* At the beginning of a laboratory experiment, five baby rats measured 5.6, 6.4, 6.9, 7.6, and 6.1 cm in length, and weighed 144, 138, 149, 152, and 146 g, respectively.

a. Write a 2×5 matrix using this information.

b. At the end of two weeks, their lengths (in centimeters) were 10.2, 11.4, 11.4, 12.7, and 10.8 and their weights (in grams) were 196, 196, 225, 250, and 230. Write a 2×5 matrix with this information.

c. Use matrix subtraction and the matrices found in parts a and b to write a matrix that gives the amount of change in length and weight for each rat.

d. During the third week, the rats grew by the amounts shown in the matrix below.

$$\begin{array}{c} \begin{matrix} \text{Length} \\ \text{Weight} \end{matrix} \begin{bmatrix} 1.8 & 1.5 & 2.3 & 1.8 & 2.0 \\ 25 & 22 & 29 & 33 & 20 \end{bmatrix} \end{array}$$

What were their lengths and weights at the end of this week?

43. *Testing Medication* A drug company is testing 200 patients to see if Painfree (a new headache medicine) is effective. Half the patients receive Painfree and half receive a

placebo. The data on the first 50 patients is summarized in this matrix:

Pain Relief Obtained

$$\begin{array}{c} \\ \text{Painfree} \\ \text{Placebo} \end{array} \begin{array}{cc} \text{Yes} & \text{No} \\ \begin{bmatrix} 22 & 3 \\ 8 & 17 \end{bmatrix} \end{array}.$$

a. Of those who took the placebo, how many got relief?

b. Of those who took the new medication, how many got no relief?

c. The test was repeated on three more groups of 50 patients each, with the results summarized by these matrices.

$$\begin{bmatrix} 21 & 4 \\ 6 & 19 \end{bmatrix} \quad \begin{bmatrix} 19 & 6 \\ 10 & 15 \end{bmatrix} \quad \begin{bmatrix} 23 & 2 \\ 3 & 22 \end{bmatrix}$$

Find the total results for all 200 patients.

d. On the basis of these results, does it appear that Painfree is effective?

44. *Driving Habits* The following tables give the percentages of male and female high school students who rarely or never wore a seatbelt, rode with drivers who had been drinking, and drove after drinking for various years from 1997 to 2003.*

Male	1997	1999	2001	2003
Rarely or never wore seatbelt	23.2	20.8	18.1	21.5
Rode with drinking driver	38.3	34.4	31.8	29.2
Drove after drinking	27.9	25.5	24.6	22.4

Female	1997	1999	2001	2003
Rarely or never wore seatbelt	14.5	11.9	10.2	14.6
Rode with drinking driver	34.5	31.7	29.6	31.1
Drove after drinking	16.2	13.3	14.1	12.3

a. Write a matrix for the driving habits of male drivers.

b. Write a matrix for the driving habits of female drivers.

c. Use the matrices from parts a and b to write a matrix showing the difference between the driving habits of males and females.

d. Analyze the results from part c and discuss any noticeable trends.

45. *Life Expectancy* The following table gives the life expectancy of African American males and females and white American males and females at the beginning of each decade since 1970.[†]

| Year | African American | | White American | |
	Male	**Female**	**Male**	**Female**
1970	60.0	68.3	68.0	75.6
1980	63.8	72.5	70.7	78.1
1990	64.5	73.6	72.7	79.4
2000	68.2	74.9	74.8	80.0

a. Write a matrix for the life expectancy of African Americans.

b. Write a matrix for the life expectancy of white Americans.

c. Use the matrices from parts a and b to write a matrix showing the difference between the two groups.

d. Analyze the results from part c and discuss any noticeable trends.

46. *Educational Attainment* The table on the next page gives the educational attainment of the U.S. population 25 years and older since 1960.[‡]

a. Write a matrix for the educational attainment of males.

b. Write a matrix for the educational attainment of females.

c. Use the matrices from parts a and b to write a matrix showing the difference in educational attainment between males and females since 1960.

---

*National Highway Traffic Safety Administration, Traffic Safety Facts 2003 (Table 63, issued January 2005), http:www-nrd.nhtsa.dot.gov.

[†]*The World Almanac and Book of Facts 2006*, p. 181.

[‡]U.S. Department of Commerce, Census Bureau, Current Population Reports, "Educational Attainment in the United States, 2004." March 25, 2005;
http://www.census.gov/population/www/socdemo/education/cps2004.

	Male		Female	
Year	Percentage with 4 Years of High School or More	Percentage with 4 Years of College or More	Percentage with 4 Years of High School or More	Percentage with 4 Years of College or More
1960	39.5	9.7	42.5	5.8
1970	51.9	13.5	52.8	8.1
1980	67.3	20.1	65.8	12.8
1990	77.7	24.4	77.5	18.4
2000	84.2	27.8	84.0	23.6
2004	84.8	29.4	85.4	26.1

47. *Educational Attainment* The following table gives the educational attainment of African Americans and Hispanic Americans 25 years and older since 1980.*

	African American		Hispanic American	
Year	Percentage with 4 Years of High School or More	Percentage with 4 Years of College or More	Percentage with 4 Years of High School or More	Percentage with 4 Years of College or More
1980	51.4	7.9	44.5	7.6
1985	59.9	11.1	47.9	8.5
1990	66.2	11.3	50.8	9.2
1995	73.8	13.3	53.4	9.3
2000	78.9	16.6	57.0	10.6
2004	80.6	17.6	58.4	12.1

a. Write a matrix for the educational attainment of African Americans.

b. Write a matrix for the educational attainment of Hispanic Americans.

c. Use the matrices from parts a and b to write a matrix showing the difference in educational attainment between African and Hispanic Americans.

GENERAL INTEREST

48. *Animal Interactions* When two kittens named Cauchy and Cliché were introduced into a household with Jamie (an older cat) and Musk (a dog), the interactions among animals were complicated. The two kittens liked each other and Jamie, but didn't like Musk. Musk liked everybody, but Jamie didn't like any of the other animals.

a. Write a 4 × 4 matrix in which rows (and columns) 1, 2, 3, and 4 refer to Musk, Jamie, Cauchy, and Cliché. Make an element a 1 if the animal for that row likes the animal for that column, and otherwise make the element a 0. Assume every animal likes herself.

b. Within a few days, Cauchy and Cliché decided that they liked Musk after all. Write a 4 × 4 matrix, as you did in part a, representing the new situation.

*U.S. Department of Commerce, Bureau of the Census, U.S. Census of Population, 1960, Vol. 1, part 1; *Current Population Reports*, Series P-20 and unpublished data; and Folger, John K. and Charles B. Nam, "Education of the American Population," *1960 Census Monograph*, from U.S. Dept. of Education, National Center for Education Statistics, *Digest of Education Statistics 2003*, and U.S. Census Bureau, *Current Population Survey*, March 2005.

2.4 Multiplication of Matrices

? THINK ABOUT IT

What is a contractor's total cost for materials required for various types of model homes?

Matrix multiplication will be used to answer this question in Example 5. We begin by defining the product of a real number and a matrix. In work with matrices, a real number is called a **scalar**.

PRODUCT OF A MATRIX AND A SCALAR

The product of a scalar k and a matrix X is the matrix kX, each of whose elements is k times the corresponding element of X.

For example,

$$(-5)\begin{bmatrix} 3 & 4 \\ 0 & -1 \end{bmatrix} = \begin{bmatrix} -15 & -20 \\ 0 & 5 \end{bmatrix}.$$

Finding the product of two matrices is more involved, but such multiplication is important in solving practical problems. To understand the reasoning behind matrix multiplication, it may be helpful to consider another example concerning EZ Life Company discussed in the previous section. Suppose sofas and chairs of the same model are often sold as sets. Matrix W shows the number of sets of each model in each warehouse.

$$\begin{array}{c} \text{New York} \\ \text{Chicago} \\ \text{San Francisco} \end{array} \begin{array}{ccc} A & B & C \end{array} \\ \begin{bmatrix} 10 & 7 & 3 \\ 5 & 9 & 6 \\ 4 & 8 & 2 \end{bmatrix} = W$$

If the selling price of a model-A set is $1000, of a model-B set $1200, and of a model-C set $1400, the total value of the sets in the New York warehouse is found as follows.

Type	Number of Sets		Price of Set		Total
A	10	×	$1000	=	$10,000
B	7	×	$1200	=	$8400
C	3	×	$1400	=	$4200
		(Total for New York)			$22,600

The total value of the three kinds of sets in New York is $22,600.

The work done in the table above is summarized as follows:

$$10(\$1000) + 7(\$1200) + 3(\$1400) = \$22,600.$$

In the same way, we find that the Chicago sets have a total value of

$$5(\$1000) + 9(\$1200) + 6(\$1400) = \$24{,}200,$$

and in San Francisco, the total value of the sets is

$$4(\$1000) + 8(\$1200) + 2(\$1400) = \$16{,}400.$$

The selling prices can be written as a column matrix P, and the total value in each location as another column matrix, V.

$$\begin{bmatrix} 1000 \\ 1200 \\ 1400 \end{bmatrix} = P \qquad \begin{bmatrix} 22{,}600 \\ 24{,}200 \\ 16{,}400 \end{bmatrix} = V$$

Look at the elements of W and P below; multiplying the first, second, and third elements of the first row of W by the first, second, and third elements, respectively, of the column matrix P and then adding these products gives the first element in V. Doing the same thing with the second row of W gives the second element of V; the third row of W leads to the third element of V, suggesting that it is reasonable to write the product of matrices

$$W = \begin{bmatrix} 10 & 7 & 3 \\ 5 & 9 & 6 \\ 4 & 8 & 2 \end{bmatrix} \quad \text{and} \quad P = \begin{bmatrix} 1000 \\ 1200 \\ 1400 \end{bmatrix}$$

as

$$WP = \begin{bmatrix} 10 & 7 & 3 \\ 5 & 9 & 6 \\ 4 & 8 & 2 \end{bmatrix} \begin{bmatrix} 1000 \\ 1200 \\ 1400 \end{bmatrix} = \begin{bmatrix} 22{,}600 \\ 24{,}200 \\ 16{,}400 \end{bmatrix} = V.$$

The product was found by multiplying the elements of *rows* of the matrix on the left and the corresponding elements of the *column* of the matrix on the right, and then finding the sum of these separate products. Notice that the product of a 3×3 matrix and a 3×1 matrix is a 3×1 matrix.

The product AB of an $m \times n$ matrix A and an $n \times k$ matrix B is found as follows. Multiply each element of the first row of A by the corresponding element of the *first column* of B. The sum of these n products is the *first-row, first-column* element of AB. Similarly, the sum of the products found by multiplying the elements of the *first row* of A by the corresponding elements of the *second column* of B gives the *first-row, second-column* element of AB, and so on.

PRODUCT OF TWO MATRICES

Let A be an $m \times n$ matrix and let B be an $n \times k$ matrix. To find the element in the ith row and jth column of the **product matrix** AB, multiply each element in the ith row of A by the corresponding element in the jth column of B, and then add these products. The product matrix AB is an $m \times k$ matrix.

EXAMPLE 1 **Matrix Product**

Find the product AB of matrices

$$A = \begin{bmatrix} 2 & 3 & -1 \\ 4 & 2 & 2 \end{bmatrix} \quad \text{and} \quad B = \begin{bmatrix} 1 \\ 8 \\ 6 \end{bmatrix}.$$

▶**Solution** Since A is 2×3 and B is 3×1, we can find the product matrix AB.

Step 1 Multiply the elements of the first row of A and the corresponding elements of the column of B.

$$\begin{bmatrix} 2 & 3 & -1 \\ 4 & 2 & 2 \end{bmatrix} \begin{bmatrix} 1 \\ 8 \\ 6 \end{bmatrix} \qquad 2 \cdot 1 + 3 \cdot 8 + (-1) \cdot 6 = 20$$

Thus, 20 is the first-row entry of the product matrix AB.

Step 2 Multiply the elements of the second row of A and the corresponding elements of B.

$$\begin{bmatrix} 2 & 3 & -1 \\ 4 & 2 & 2 \end{bmatrix} \begin{bmatrix} 1 \\ 8 \\ 6 \end{bmatrix} \qquad 4 \cdot 1 + 2 \cdot 8 + 2 \cdot 6 = 32$$

The second-row entry of the product matrix AB is 32.

Step 3 Write the product as a column matrix using the two entries found above.

$$AB = \begin{bmatrix} 2 & 3 & -1 \\ 4 & 2 & 2 \end{bmatrix} \begin{bmatrix} 1 \\ 8 \\ 6 \end{bmatrix} = \begin{bmatrix} 20 \\ 32 \end{bmatrix}$$

Note that the product of a 2×3 matrix and a 3×1 matrix is a 2×1 matrix.

EXAMPLE 2 **Matrix Product**
Find the product CD of matrices

$$C = \begin{bmatrix} -3 & 4 & 2 \\ 5 & 0 & 4 \end{bmatrix} \quad \text{and} \quad D = \begin{bmatrix} -6 & 4 \\ 2 & 3 \\ 3 & -2 \end{bmatrix}.$$

▶**Solution** Since C is 2×3 and D is 3×2, we can find the product matrix CD.

Step 1 $\begin{bmatrix} -3 & 4 & 2 \\ 5 & 0 & 4 \end{bmatrix} \begin{bmatrix} -6 & 4 \\ 2 & 3 \\ 3 & -2 \end{bmatrix} \qquad (-3) \cdot (-6) + 4 \cdot 2 + 2 \cdot 3 = 32$

Step 2 $\begin{bmatrix} -3 & 4 & 2 \\ 5 & 0 & 4 \end{bmatrix} \begin{bmatrix} -6 & 4 \\ 2 & 3 \\ 3 & -2 \end{bmatrix} \qquad (-3) \cdot 4 + 4 \cdot 3 + 2 \cdot (-2) = -4$

Step 3 $\begin{bmatrix} -3 & 4 & 2 \\ 5 & 0 & 4 \end{bmatrix} \begin{bmatrix} -6 & 4 \\ 2 & 3 \\ 3 & -2 \end{bmatrix} \qquad 5 \cdot (-6) + 0 \cdot 2 + 4 \cdot 3 = -18$

Step 4 $\begin{bmatrix} -3 & 4 & 2 \\ 5 & 0 & 4 \end{bmatrix} \begin{bmatrix} -6 & 4 \\ 2 & 3 \\ 3 & -2 \end{bmatrix} \qquad 5 \cdot 4 + 0 \cdot 3 + 4 \cdot (-2) = 12$

Step 5   The product is

$$CD = \begin{bmatrix} -3 & 4 & 2 \\ 5 & 0 & 4 \end{bmatrix} \begin{bmatrix} -6 & 4 \\ 2 & 3 \\ 3 & -2 \end{bmatrix} = \begin{bmatrix} 32 & -4 \\ -18 & 12 \end{bmatrix}.$$

Here the product of a 2 × 3 matrix and a 3 × 2 matrix is a 2 × 2 matrix.

NOTE   One way to avoid errors in matrix multiplication is to lower the first matrix so it is below and to the left of the second matrix, and then write the product in the space between the two matrices. For example, to multiply the matrices in Example 2, we could rewrite the product as shown below.

$$\downarrow$$
$$\begin{bmatrix} -6 & 4 \\ 2 & 3 \\ 3 & -2 \end{bmatrix}$$
$$\rightarrow \begin{bmatrix} -3 & 4 & 2 \\ 5 & 0 & 4 \end{bmatrix} \begin{bmatrix} \\ * \\ \end{bmatrix}$$

To find the entry where the * is, for example, multiply the row and the column indicated by the arrows: $5 \cdot (-6) + 0 \cdot 2 + 4 \cdot 3 = -18$.

As the definition of matrix multiplication shows,

> the product AB of two matrices A and B can be found only if the number of columns of A is the same as the number of rows of B.

The final product will have as many rows as A and as many columns as B.

EXAMPLE 3   Matrix Product
Suppose matrix A is 2 × 2 and matrix B is 2 × 4. Can the products AB and BA be calculated? If so, what is the size of each product?

►Solution   The following diagram helps decide the answers to these questions.

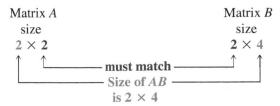

The product of A and B can be found because A has two columns and B has two rows. The size of the product is 2 × 4.

Matrix *B*   Matrix *A*
size   size
2 × 4   2 × 2

└──────── do not match ────────┘

The product BA cannot be found because B has 4 columns and A has 2 rows.

EXAMPLE 4 **Comparing Matrix Products AB and BA**

Find AB and BA, given

$$A = \begin{bmatrix} 1 & -3 \\ 7 & 2 \\ -2 & 5 \end{bmatrix} \quad \text{and} \quad B = \begin{bmatrix} 1 & 0 & -1 \\ 3 & 1 & 4 \end{bmatrix}.$$

▶**Solution**

METHOD 1
Calculating by Hand

$$AB = \begin{bmatrix} 1 & -3 \\ 7 & 2 \\ -2 & 5 \end{bmatrix} \begin{bmatrix} 1 & 0 & -1 \\ 3 & 1 & 4 \end{bmatrix}$$

$$= \begin{bmatrix} -8 & -3 & -13 \\ 13 & 2 & 1 \\ 13 & 5 & 22 \end{bmatrix}$$

$$BA = \begin{bmatrix} 1 & 0 & -1 \\ 3 & 1 & 4 \end{bmatrix} \begin{bmatrix} 1 & -3 \\ 7 & 2 \\ -2 & 5 \end{bmatrix}$$

$$= \begin{bmatrix} 3 & -8 \\ 2 & 13 \end{bmatrix}$$

METHOD 2
Graphing Calculators

Matrix multiplication is easily performed on a graphing calculator. Figure 13 shows the results. The matrices A and B were already entered into the calculator.

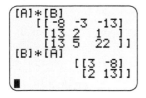

FIGURE 13

Matrix multiplication can also be easily done with a spreadsheet. See *The Spreadsheet Manual* available with this textbook for details.

Notice in Example 4 that $AB \neq BA$; matrices AB and BA aren't even the same size. In Example 3, we showed that they may not both exist. This means that matrix multiplication is *not* commutative. Even if both A and B are square matrices, in general, matrices AB and BA are not equal. (See Exercise 31.) Of course, there may be special cases in which they are equal, but this is not true in general.

CAUTION Since matrix multiplication is not commutative, always be careful to multiply matrices in the correct order. ∎

Matrix multiplication *is* associative, however. For example, if

$$C = \begin{bmatrix} 3 & 2 \\ 0 & -4 \\ -1 & 1 \end{bmatrix},$$

then $(AB)C = A(BC)$, where A and B are the matrices given in Example 4. (Verify this.) Also, there is a distributive property of matrices such that, for appropriate matrices A, B, and C,

$$A(B + C) = AB + AC.$$

(See Exercises 32 and 33.) Other properties of matrix multiplication involving scalars are included in the exercises. Multiplicative inverses and multiplicative identities are defined in the next section.

EXAMPLE 5 **Home Construction**

A contractor builds three kinds of houses, models A, B, and C, with a choice of two styles, Spanish and contemporary. Matrix P shows the number of each kind of house planned for a new 100-home subdivision. The amounts for each of the exterior materials depend primarily on the style of the house. These amounts are shown in matrix Q. (Concrete is in cubic yards, lumber in units of 1000 board feet, brick in 1000s, and shingles in units of 100 ft^2.) Matrix R gives the cost in dollars for each kind of material.

$$
\begin{array}{c}
\begin{array}{cc} \text{Spanish} & \text{Contemporary} \end{array} \\
\begin{array}{c} \text{Model A} \\ \text{Model B} \\ \text{Model C} \end{array}
\left[\begin{array}{cc} 0 & 30 \\ 10 & 20 \\ 20 & 20 \end{array} \right] = P
\end{array}
$$

$$
\begin{array}{c}
\begin{array}{cccc} \text{Concrete} & \text{Lumber} & \text{Brick} & \text{Shingles} \end{array} \\
\begin{array}{c} \text{Spanish} \\ \text{Contemporary} \end{array}
\left[\begin{array}{cccc} 10 & 2 & 0 & 2 \\ 50 & 1 & 20 & 2 \end{array} \right] = Q
\end{array}
$$

$$
\begin{array}{c}
\begin{array}{c} \text{Cost per Unit} \end{array} \\
\begin{array}{c} \text{Concrete} \\ \text{Lumber} \\ \text{Brick} \\ \text{Shingles} \end{array}
\left[\begin{array}{c} 20 \\ 180 \\ 60 \\ 25 \end{array} \right] = R
\end{array}
$$

 (a) What is the total cost of these materials for each model?

▶**Solution** To find the cost for each model, first find PQ, which shows the amount of each material needed for each model.

$$
PQ = \left[\begin{array}{cc} 0 & 30 \\ 10 & 20 \\ 20 & 20 \end{array} \right] \left[\begin{array}{cccc} 10 & 2 & 0 & 2 \\ 50 & 1 & 20 & 2 \end{array} \right]
$$

$$
= \begin{array}{c}
\begin{array}{cccc} \text{Concrete} & \text{Lumber} & \text{Brick} & \text{Shingles} \end{array} \\
\left[\begin{array}{cccc} 1500 & 30 & 600 & 60 \\ 1100 & 40 & 400 & 60 \\ 1200 & 60 & 400 & 80 \end{array} \right]
\begin{array}{c} \text{Model A} \\ \text{Model B} \\ \text{Model C} \end{array}
\end{array}
$$

Now multiply PQ and R, the cost matrix, to get the total cost of the exterior materials for each model.

$$
\left[\begin{array}{cccc} 1500 & 30 & 600 & 60 \\ 1100 & 40 & 400 & 60 \\ 1200 & 60 & 400 & 80 \end{array} \right] \left[\begin{array}{c} 20 \\ 180 \\ 60 \\ 25 \end{array} \right] =
\begin{array}{c}
\begin{array}{c} \text{Cost} \end{array} \\
\left[\begin{array}{c} 72{,}900 \\ 54{,}700 \\ 60{,}800 \end{array} \right]
\begin{array}{c} \text{Model A} \\ \text{Model B} \\ \text{Model C} \end{array}
\end{array}
$$

The total cost of materials is $72,900 for model A, $54,700 for model B, and $60,800 for model C.

(b) How much of each of the four kinds of material must be ordered?

▶**Solution** The totals of the columns of matrix PQ will give a matrix whose elements represent the total amounts of each material needed for the subdivision. Call this matrix T, and write it as a row matrix.

$$T = \begin{bmatrix} 3800 & 130 & 1400 & 200 \end{bmatrix}$$

Thus, 3800 yd^3 of concrete, 130,000 board feet of lumber, 1,400,000 bricks, and 20,000 ft^2 of shingles are needed.

(c) What is the total cost for exterior materials?

▶**Solution** For the total cost of all the exterior materials, find the product of matrix T, the matrix showing the total amount of each material, and matrix R, the cost matrix. (To multiply these and get a 1×1 matrix representing total cost, we need a 1×4 matrix multiplied by a 4×1 matrix. This is why T was written as a row matrix in (b) above.)

$$TR = \begin{bmatrix} 3800 & 130 & 1400 & 200 \end{bmatrix} \begin{bmatrix} 20 \\ 180 \\ 60 \\ 25 \end{bmatrix} = \begin{bmatrix} 188,400 \end{bmatrix}$$

The total cost for exterior materials is $188,400.

(d) Suppose the contractor builds the same number of homes in five subdivisions. Calculate the total amount of each exterior material for each model for all five subdivisions.

▶**Solution** Multiply PQ by the scalar 5, as follows.

$$5(PQ) = 5 \begin{bmatrix} 1500 & 30 & 600 & 60 \\ 1100 & 40 & 400 & 60 \\ 1200 & 60 & 400 & 80 \end{bmatrix} = \begin{bmatrix} 7500 & 150 & 3000 & 300 \\ 5500 & 200 & 2000 & 300 \\ 6000 & 300 & 2000 & 400 \end{bmatrix}$$

The total amount of concrete needed for model A homes, for example, is 7500 yd^3.

Choosing Matrix Notation   It is helpful to use a notation that keeps track of the quantities a matrix represents. We will use the notation

meaning of the rows/meaning of the columns,

that is, writing the meaning of the rows first, followed by the meaning of the columns. In Example 5, we would use the notation models/styles for matrix P, styles/materials for matrix Q, and materials/cost for matrix R. In multiplying PQ, we are multiplying models/styles by styles/materials. The result is models/materials. Notice that styles, the common quantity in both P and Q, was eliminated in the product PQ. By this method, the product $(PQ)R$ represents models/cost.

In practical problems this notation helps us decide in which order to multiply matrices so that the results are meaningful. In Example 5(c) either RT or TR can be calculated. Since T represents subdivisions/materials and R represents materials/cost, the product TR gives subdivisions/cost, while the product RT is meaningless.

▶ 2.4 Exercises

Let $A = \begin{bmatrix} -2 & 4 \\ 0 & 3 \end{bmatrix}$ and $B = \begin{bmatrix} -6 & 2 \\ 4 & 0 \end{bmatrix}$. Find each value.

1. $2A$

2. $-3B$

3. $-6A$

4. $5B$

5. $-4A + 5B$

6. $7B - 3A$

In Exercises 7–12, the sizes of two matrices A and B are given. Find the sizes of the product AB and the product BA, whenever these products exist.

7. A is 2×2, and B is 2×2.

8. A is 3×3, and B is 3×3.

9. A is 3×4, and B is 4×4.

10. A is 4×3, and B is 3×6.

11. A is 4×2, and B is 3×4.

12. A is 3×2, and B is 1×3.

13. To find the product matrix AB, the number of _____ of A must be the same as the number of _____ of B.

14. The product matrix AB has the same number of _____ as A and the same number of _____ as B.

Find each matrix product, if possible.

15. $\begin{bmatrix} 2 & -1 \\ 5 & 8 \end{bmatrix} \begin{bmatrix} 3 \\ -2 \end{bmatrix}$

16. $\begin{bmatrix} -1 & 5 \\ 7 & 0 \end{bmatrix} \begin{bmatrix} 6 \\ 2 \end{bmatrix}$

17. $\begin{bmatrix} 2 & -1 & 7 \\ -3 & 0 & -4 \end{bmatrix} \begin{bmatrix} 5 \\ 10 \\ 2 \end{bmatrix}$

18. $\begin{bmatrix} 5 & 2 \\ 7 & 6 \\ 1 & 0 \end{bmatrix} \begin{bmatrix} 1 & 4 & 0 \\ 2 & -1 & 2 \end{bmatrix}$

19. $\begin{bmatrix} 2 & -1 \\ 3 & 6 \end{bmatrix} \begin{bmatrix} -1 & 0 & 4 \\ 5 & -2 & 0 \end{bmatrix}$

20. $\begin{bmatrix} 6 & 0 & -4 \\ 1 & 2 & 5 \\ 10 & -1 & 3 \end{bmatrix} \begin{bmatrix} 1 \\ 2 \\ 0 \end{bmatrix}$

21. $\begin{bmatrix} 2 & 2 & -1 \\ 3 & 0 & 1 \end{bmatrix} \begin{bmatrix} 0 & 2 \\ -1 & 4 \\ 0 & 2 \end{bmatrix}$

22. $\begin{bmatrix} -3 & 1 & 0 \\ 6 & 0 & 8 \end{bmatrix} \begin{bmatrix} 3 \\ -1 \\ -2 \end{bmatrix}$

23. $\begin{bmatrix} 1 & 2 \\ 3 & 4 \end{bmatrix} \begin{bmatrix} -1 & 5 \\ 7 & 0 \end{bmatrix}$

24. $\begin{bmatrix} 2 & 8 \\ -7 & 5 \end{bmatrix} \begin{bmatrix} 1 & 0 \\ 0 & 1 \end{bmatrix}$

25. $\begin{bmatrix} -2 & -3 & 7 \\ 1 & 5 & 6 \end{bmatrix} \begin{bmatrix} 1 \\ 2 \\ 3 \end{bmatrix}$

26. $\begin{bmatrix} 2 \\ -9 \\ 12 \end{bmatrix} \begin{bmatrix} 1 & 0 & -1 \end{bmatrix}$

27. $\left(\begin{bmatrix} 2 & 1 \\ -3 & -6 \\ 4 & 0 \end{bmatrix} \begin{bmatrix} 1 & -2 \\ 2 & -1 \end{bmatrix} \right) \begin{bmatrix} 3 \\ 1 \end{bmatrix}$

28. $\begin{bmatrix} 2 & 1 \\ -3 & -6 \\ 4 & 0 \end{bmatrix} \left(\begin{bmatrix} 1 & -2 \\ 2 & -1 \end{bmatrix} \begin{bmatrix} 3 \\ 1 \end{bmatrix} \right)$

29. $\begin{bmatrix} 2 & -2 \\ 1 & -1 \end{bmatrix} \left(\begin{bmatrix} 4 & 3 \\ 1 & 2 \end{bmatrix} + \begin{bmatrix} 7 & 0 \\ -1 & 5 \end{bmatrix} \right)$

30. $\begin{bmatrix} 2 & -2 \\ 1 & -1 \end{bmatrix} \begin{bmatrix} 4 & 3 \\ 1 & 2 \end{bmatrix} + \begin{bmatrix} 2 & -2 \\ 1 & -1 \end{bmatrix} \begin{bmatrix} 7 & 0 \\ -1 & 5 \end{bmatrix}$

31. Let $A = \begin{bmatrix} -2 & 4 \\ 1 & 3 \end{bmatrix}$ and $B = \begin{bmatrix} -2 & 1 \\ 3 & 6 \end{bmatrix}$.

a. Find AB.

b. Find BA.

c. Did you get the same answer in parts a and b?

d. In general, for matrices A and B such that AB and BA both exist, does AB always equal BA?

Given matrices $P = \begin{bmatrix} m & n \\ p & q \end{bmatrix}$, $X = \begin{bmatrix} x & y \\ z & w \end{bmatrix}$, and $T = \begin{bmatrix} r & s \\ t & u \end{bmatrix}$, *verify that the statements in Exercises 32–35 are true. The statements are valid for any matrices whenever matrix multiplication and addition can be carried out. This, of course, depends on the size of the matrices.*

32. $(PX)T = P(XT)$ (associative property: see Exercises 27 and 28)

33. $P(X + T) = PX + PT$ (distributive property: see Exercises 29 and 30)

34. $k(X + T) = kX + kT$ for any real number k.

35. $(k + h)P = kP + hP$ for any real numbers k and h.

36. Let I be the matrix $I = \begin{bmatrix} 1 & 0 \\ 0 & 1 \end{bmatrix}$, and let matrices P, X, and T be defined as for Exercises 32–35.

    a. Find IP, PI, and IX.

    b. Without calculating, guess what the matrix IT might be.

    c. Suggest a reason for naming a matrix such as I an *identity matrix*.

37. Show that the system of linear equations

$$2x_1 + 3x_2 + x_3 = 5$$
$$x_1 - 4x_2 + 5x_3 = 8$$

can be written as the matrix equation

$$\begin{bmatrix} 2 & 3 & 1 \\ 1 & -4 & 5 \end{bmatrix} \begin{bmatrix} x_1 \\ x_2 \\ x_3 \end{bmatrix} = \begin{bmatrix} 5 \\ 8 \end{bmatrix}.$$

38. Let $A = \begin{bmatrix} 1 & 2 \\ -3 & 5 \end{bmatrix}$, $X = \begin{bmatrix} x_1 \\ x_2 \end{bmatrix}$, and $B = \begin{bmatrix} -4 \\ 12 \end{bmatrix}$. Show that the equation $AX = B$ represents a linear system of two equations in two unknowns. Solve the system and substitute into the matrix equation to check your results.

Use a computer or graphing calculator and the following matrices to find the matrix products and sums in Exercises 39–41.

$$A = \begin{bmatrix} 2 & 3 & -1 & 5 & 10 \\ 2 & 8 & 7 & 4 & 3 \\ -1 & -4 & -12 & 6 & 8 \\ 2 & 5 & 7 & 1 & 4 \end{bmatrix} \qquad B = \begin{bmatrix} 9 & 3 & 7 & -6 \\ -1 & 0 & 4 & 2 \\ -10 & -7 & 6 & 9 \\ 8 & 4 & 2 & -1 \\ 2 & -5 & 3 & 7 \end{bmatrix}$$

$$C = \begin{bmatrix} -6 & 8 & 2 & 4 & -3 \\ 1 & 9 & 7 & -12 & 5 \\ 15 & 2 & -8 & 10 & 11 \\ 4 & 7 & 9 & 6 & -2 \\ 1 & 3 & 8 & 23 & 4 \end{bmatrix} \qquad D = \begin{bmatrix} 5 & -3 & 7 & 9 & 2 \\ 6 & 8 & -5 & 2 & 1 \\ 3 & 7 & -4 & 2 & 11 \\ 5 & -3 & 9 & 4 & -1 \\ 0 & 3 & 2 & 5 & 1 \end{bmatrix}$$

39. a. Find AC.   **b.** Find CA.   **c.** Does $AC = CA$?

40. a. Find CD.   **b.** Find DC.   **c.** Does $CD = DC$?

41. a. Find $C + D$.   **b.** Find $(C + D)B$.   **c.** Find CB.

    d. Find DB.   **e.** Find $CB + DB$.   **f.** Does $(C + D)B = CB + DB$?

42. Which property of matrices does Exercise 41 illustrate?

► **Applications**

43. *Cost Analysis* The four departments of Spangler Enterprises need to order the following amounts of the same products.

	Paper	Tape	Binders	Memo Pads	Pens
Department 1	10	4	3	5	6
Department 2	7	2	2	3	8
Department 3	4	5	1	0	10
Department 4	0	3	4	5	5

The unit price (in dollars) of each product is given in the next column for two suppliers.

	Supplier A	Supplier B
Paper	2	3
Tape	1	1
Binders	4	3
Memo Pads	3	3
Pens	1	2

a. Use matrix multiplication to get a matrix showing the comparative costs for each department for the products from the two suppliers.

b. Find the total cost over all departments to buy products from each supplier. From which supplier should the company make the purchase?

44. *Cost Analysis* The Mundo Candy Company makes three types of chocolate candy: Cheery Cherry, Mucho Mocha, and Almond Delight. The company produces its products in San Diego, Mexico City, and Managua using two main ingredients: chocolate and sugar.

a. Each kilogram of Cheery Cherry requires 0.5 kg of sugar and 0.2 kg of chocolate; each kilogram of Mucho Mocha requires 0.4 kg of sugar and 0.3 kg of chocolate; and each kilogram of Almond Delight requires 0.3 kg of sugar and 0.3 kg of chocolate. Put this information into a 2×3 matrix, labeling the rows and columns.

b. The cost of 1 kg of sugar is $4 in San Diego, $2 in Mexico City, and $1 in Managua. The cost of 1 kg of chocolate is $3 in San Diego, $5 in Mexico City, and $7 in Managua. Put this information into a matrix in such a way that when you multiply it with your matrix from part a, you get a matrix representing the ingredient cost of producing each type of candy in each city.

c. Multiply the matrices in parts a and b, labeling the product matrix.

d. From part c, what is the combined sugar-and-chocolate cost to produce 1 kg of Mucho Mocha in Managua?

e. Mundo Candy needs to quickly produce a special shipment of 100 kg of Cheery Cherry, 200 kg of Mucho Mocha, and 500 kg of Almond Delight, and it decides to select one factory to fill the entire order. Use matrix multiplication to determine in which city the total sugar-and-chocolate cost to produce the order is the smallest.

45. *Management* In Exercise 39 from Section 2.3, consider the matrices $\begin{bmatrix} 4.27 & 6.94 \\ 3.45 & 3.65 \end{bmatrix}$, $\begin{bmatrix} 4.05 & 7.01 \\ 3.27 & 3.51 \end{bmatrix}$, and $\begin{bmatrix} 4.40 & 6.90 \\ 3.54 & 3.76 \end{bmatrix}$ for the production costs at the Boston, Chicago, and Seattle plants, respectively.

a. Assume each plant makes the same number of each item. Write a matrix that expresses the average production costs for all three plants.

b. In part b of Exercise 39 in Section 2.3, cost increases for the Chicago plant resulted in a new production cost matrix $\begin{bmatrix} 4.42 & 7.43 \\ 3.38 & 3.62 \end{bmatrix}$. Following these cost increases the Boston plant was closed and production divided evenly between the Chicago and Seattle plants. What is the matrix that now expresses the average production cost for the entire country?

46. *House Construction* Consider the matrices P, Q, and R given in Example 5.

a. Find and interpret the matrix product QR.

b. Verify that $P(QR)$ is equal to $(PQ)R$ calculated in Example 5.

47. *Shoe Sales* Sal's Shoes and Fred's Footwear both have outlets in California and Arizona. Sal's sells shoes for $80, sandals for $40, and boots for $120. Fred's prices are $60, $30, and $150 for shoes, sandals, and boots, respectively. Half of all sales in California stores are shoes, 1/4 are sandals, and 1/4 are boots. In Arizona the fractions are 1/5 shoes, 1/5 sandals, and 3/5 boots.

a. Write a 2×3 matrix called P representing prices for the two stores and three types of footwear.

b. Write a 3×2 matrix called F representing the fraction of each type of footwear sold in each state.

c. Only one of the two products PF and FP is meaningful. Determine which one it is, calculate the product, and describe what the entries represent.

48. *Management* In Exercise 40 from Section 2.3, consider the matrix

$$\begin{bmatrix} 88 & 105 & 60 \\ 48 & 72 & 40 \\ 16 & 21 & 0 \\ 112 & 147 & 50 \end{bmatrix}$$

expressing the sales information for the three stores.

a. Write a 3×1 matrix expressing the factors by which sales in each store should be multiplied to reflect the fact that sales increased during the following week by 25%, 1/3, and 10% in stores I, II, and III, respectively, as described in part b of Exercise 40 from Section 2.3.

b. Multiply the matrix expressing sales information by the matrix found in part a of this exercise to find the sales for all three stores in the second week.

LIFE SCIENCES

49. *Dietetics* In Exercise 41 from Section 2.3, label the matrices

$$\begin{bmatrix} 2 & 1 & 2 & 1 \\ 3 & 2 & 2 & 1 \\ 4 & 3 & 2 & 1 \end{bmatrix}, \quad \begin{bmatrix} 5 & 0 & 7 \\ 0 & 10 & 1 \\ 0 & 15 & 2 \\ 10 & 12 & 8 \end{bmatrix}, \text{ and } \begin{bmatrix} 8 \\ 4 \\ 5 \end{bmatrix}$$

found in parts a, b, and c, respectively, X, Y, and Z.

a. Find the product matrix XY. What do the entries of this matrix represent?

b. Find the product matrix YZ. What do the entries represent?

c. Find the products $(XY)Z$ and $X(YZ)$ and verify that they are equal. What do the entries represent?

50. *Driving Habits* In Exercise 44 from Section 2.3, you constructed matrices that represent percentages for various years of male and female high school students who rarely or never wore a seatbelt, rode with drivers who had been drinking, and drove after drinking. Use matrix operations to combine these two matrices to form one matrix that represents the combined percentages of driving habits for males and females. Assume males and females represented are equal in number. (*Hint:* Add the two matrices together and then multiply the resulting matrix by the scalar 1/2.)

51. *Life Expectancy* In Exercise 45 from Section 2.3, you constructed matrices that represent the life expectancy of African American and white American males and females. Use matrix operations to combine these two matrices to form one matrix that represents the combined life expectancy of both races at the beginning of each decade since 1970. Use the fact that of the combined African and white American population, African Americans are about one-sixth of the total and white Americans about five-sixths. (*Hint:* Multiply the matrix for African Americans by 1/6 and the matrix for the white Americans by 5/6, and then add the results.)

52. *Northern Spotted Owl Population** In an attempt to save the endangered northern spotted owl, the U.S. Fish and Wildlife Service imposed strict guidelines for the use of 12 million acres of Pacific Northwest forest. This decision led to a national debate between the logging industry and environmentalists. Mathematical ecologists have created a mathematical model to analyze population dynamics of the northern spotted owl by dividing the female owl population into three categories: juvenile (up to 1 year old), subadult (1 to 2 years), and adult (over 2 years old). By analyzing these three subgroups, it is possible to use the number of females in each subgroup at time n to estimate the number of females in each group at any time $n + 1$ with the following matrix equation:

$$\begin{bmatrix} j_{n+1} \\ s_{n+1} \\ a_{n+1} \end{bmatrix} = \begin{bmatrix} 0 & 0 & 0.33 \\ 0.18 & 0 & 0 \\ 0 & 0.71 & 0.94 \end{bmatrix} \begin{bmatrix} j_n \\ s_n \\ a_n \end{bmatrix},$$

where j_n is the number of juveniles, s_n is the number of subadults, and a_n is the number of adults at time n.[†]

a. If there are currently 4000 female northern spotted owls made up of 900 juveniles, 500 subadults, and 2600 adults, use a graphing calculator or spreadsheet and matrix operations to determine the total number of female owls for each of the next 5 years. (*Hint:* Round each answer to the nearest whole number after each matrix multiplication.)

b. With advanced techniques from linear algebra, it is possible to show that in the long run, the following holds.

$$\begin{bmatrix} j_{n+1} \\ s_{n+1} \\ a_{n+1} \end{bmatrix} \approx 0.98359 \begin{bmatrix} j_n \\ s_n \\ a_n \end{bmatrix}$$

What can we conclude about the long-term survival of the northern spotted owl?

---

*This problem was created by David I. Schneider, University of Maryland.
[†]Lamberson, R., R. McKelvey, B. Noon, and C. Voss, "A Dynamic Analysis of Northern Spotted Owl Viability in a Fragmented Forest Landscape," *Conservation Biology*, Vol. 6, No. 4, Dec. 1992, pp. 505–512.

	Births	Deaths
Africa	0.036	0.014
Asia	0.019	0.008
Latin America	0.021	0.006
North America	0.014	0.008
Europe	0.011	0.011

Year	Africa	Asia	Latin America	North America	Europe
1960	283	1628	218	199	425
1970	361	2038	286	227	460
1980	473	2494	362	252	484
1990	627	2978	443	278	499
2002	839	3518	539	320	513

c. Notice that only 18 percent of the juveniles become subadults. Assuming that, through better habitat management, this number could be increased to 40 percent, rework part a. Discuss possible reasons why only 18 percent of the juveniles become subadults. Under the new assumption, what can you conclude about the long-term survival of the northern spotted owl?

SOCIAL SCIENCES

53. *World Population* The 2002 birth and death rates per million for several regions and the world population (in millions) by region are given in the following tables.*

a. Write the information in each table as a matrix.

b. Use the matrices from part a to find the total number (in millions) of births and deaths in each year.

c. Using the results of part b, compare the number of births in 1960 and in 2002. Also compare the birth rates from part a. Which gives better information?

d. Using the results of part b, compare the number of deaths in 1980 and in 2002. Discuss how this comparison differs from a comparison of death rates from part a.

2.5 Matrix Inverses

? THINK ABOUT IT

One top leader needs to get an important message to one of her agents. How can she encrypt the message to ensure secrecy?

This question is answered in Example 6. In this section, we introduce the idea of a matrix inverse, which is comparable to the reciprocal of a real number. This will allow us to solve a matrix equation.

Earlier, we defined a zero matrix as an additive identity matrix with properties similar to those of the real number 0, the additive identity for real numbers. The real number 1 is the *multiplicative* identity for real numbers: for any real number a, we have $a \cdot 1 = 1 \cdot a = a$. In this section, we define a *multiplicative identity matrix I* that has properties similar to those of the number 1. We then use

---

*"World Population by Region and Development Category, 1950–2050," from U.S. Bureau of the Census, World Population Profile: 2002 (Issued March 2004).

the definition of matrix I to find the *multiplicative inverse* of any square matrix that has an inverse.

If I is to be the identity matrix, both of the products AI and IA must equal A. This means that an identity matrix exists only for square matrices. The 2×2 **identity matrix** that satisfies these conditions is

$$I = \begin{bmatrix} 1 & 0 \\ 0 & 1 \end{bmatrix}.$$

To check that I, as defined above, is really the 2×2 identity, let

$$A = \begin{bmatrix} a & b \\ c & d \end{bmatrix}.$$

Then AI and IA should both equal A.

$$AI = \begin{bmatrix} a & b \\ c & d \end{bmatrix}\begin{bmatrix} 1 & 0 \\ 0 & 1 \end{bmatrix} = \begin{bmatrix} a(1) + b(0) & a(0) + b(1) \\ c(1) + d(0) & c(0) + d(1) \end{bmatrix} = \begin{bmatrix} a & b \\ c & d \end{bmatrix} = A$$

$$IA = \begin{bmatrix} 1 & 0 \\ 0 & 1 \end{bmatrix}\begin{bmatrix} a & b \\ c & d \end{bmatrix} = \begin{bmatrix} 1(a) + 0(c) & 1(b) + 0(d) \\ 0(a) + 1(c) & 0(b) + 1(d) \end{bmatrix} = \begin{bmatrix} a & b \\ c & d \end{bmatrix} = A$$

This verifies that I has been defined correctly.

It is easy to verify that the identity matrix I is unique. Suppose there is another identity; call it J. Then IJ must equal I, because J is an identity, and IJ must also equal J, because I is an identity. Thus $I = J$.

The identity matrices for 3×3 matrices and 4×4 matrices, respectively, are

$$I = \begin{bmatrix} 1 & 0 & 0 \\ 0 & 1 & 0 \\ 0 & 0 & 1 \end{bmatrix} \quad \text{and} \quad I = \begin{bmatrix} 1 & 0 & 0 & 0 \\ 0 & 1 & 0 & 0 \\ 0 & 0 & 1 & 0 \\ 0 & 0 & 0 & 1 \end{bmatrix}.$$

By generalizing, we can find an $n \times n$ identity matrix for any value of n.

Recall that the multiplicative inverse of the nonzero real number a is $1/a$. The product of a and its multiplicative inverse $1/a$ is 1. Given a matrix A, can a **multiplicative inverse matrix A^{-1}** (read "A-inverse") that will satisfy both

$$AA^{-1} = I \quad \text{and} \quad A^{-1}A = I$$

be found? For a given matrix, we often can find an inverse matrix by using the row operations of Section 2.2.

$\boxed{\text{NOTE}}$ A^{-1} does not mean $1/A$; here, A^{-1} is just the notation for the multiplicative inverse of matrix A. Also, only square matrices can have inverses because both $A^{-1}A$ and AA^{-1} must exist and be equal to an identity matrix of the same size. ▪

If an inverse exists, it is unique. That is, any given square matrix has no more than one inverse. The proof of this is left to Exercise 50 in this section.

As an example, let us find the inverse of

$$A = \begin{bmatrix} 1 & 3 \\ -1 & 2 \end{bmatrix}.$$

Let the unknown inverse matrix be

$$A^{-1} = \begin{bmatrix} x & y \\ z & w \end{bmatrix}.$$

By the definition of matrix inverse, $AA^{-1} = I$, or

$$AA^{-1} = \begin{bmatrix} 1 & 3 \\ -1 & 2 \end{bmatrix} \begin{bmatrix} x & y \\ z & w \end{bmatrix} = \begin{bmatrix} 1 & 0 \\ 0 & 1 \end{bmatrix}.$$

By matrix multiplication,

$$\begin{bmatrix} x + 3z & y + 3w \\ -x + 2z & -y + 2w \end{bmatrix} = \begin{bmatrix} 1 & 0 \\ 0 & 1 \end{bmatrix}.$$

Setting corresponding elements equal gives the system of equations

$$x + 3z = 1 \tag{1}$$
$$y + 3w = 0 \tag{2}$$
$$-x + 2z = 0 \tag{3}$$
$$-y + 2w = 1. \tag{4}$$

Since equations (1) and (3) involve only x and z, while equations (2) and (4) involve only y and w, these four equations lead to two systems of equations,

$$\begin{array}{cc} x + 3z = 1 \\ -x + 2z = 0 \end{array} \quad \text{and} \quad \begin{array}{cc} y + 3w = 0 \\ -y + 2w = 1. \end{array}$$

Writing the two systems as augmented matrices gives

$$\begin{bmatrix} 1 & 3 & | & 1 \\ -1 & 2 & | & 0 \end{bmatrix} \quad \text{and} \quad \begin{bmatrix} 1 & 3 & | & 0 \\ -1 & 2 & | & 1 \end{bmatrix}.$$

Each of these systems can be solved by the Gauss-Jordan method. Notice, however, that the elements to the left of the vertical bar are identical. The two systems can be combined into the single matrix

$$\begin{bmatrix} 1 & 3 & | & 1 & 0 \\ -1 & 2 & | & 0 & 1 \end{bmatrix}.$$

This is of the form $[A\,|\,I]$. It is solved simultaneously as follows.

$$R_1 + R_2 \to R_2 \qquad \begin{bmatrix} 1 & 3 & | & 1 & 0 \\ 0 & 5 & | & 1 & 1 \end{bmatrix} \quad \begin{array}{l} \text{Get 0 in the second-row,} \\ \text{first-column position.} \end{array}$$

$$-3R_2 + 5R_1 \to R_1 \qquad \begin{bmatrix} 5 & 0 & | & 2 & -3 \\ 0 & 5 & | & 1 & 1 \end{bmatrix} \quad \begin{array}{l} \text{Get 0 in the first-row,} \\ \text{second-column position.} \end{array}$$

$$\begin{array}{l} \tfrac{1}{5}R_1 \to R_1 \\ \tfrac{1}{5}R_2 \to R_2 \end{array} \qquad \begin{bmatrix} 1 & 0 & | & \tfrac{2}{5} & -\tfrac{3}{5} \\ 0 & 1 & | & \tfrac{1}{5} & \tfrac{1}{5} \end{bmatrix} \quad \begin{array}{l} \text{Get 1's down the} \\ \text{diagonal.} \end{array}$$

The numbers in the first column to the right of the vertical bar give the values of x and z. The second column gives the values of y and w. That is,

$$\begin{bmatrix} 1 & 0 & | & x & y \\ 0 & 1 & | & z & w \end{bmatrix} = \begin{bmatrix} 1 & 0 & | & \tfrac{2}{5} & -\tfrac{3}{5} \\ 0 & 1 & | & \tfrac{1}{5} & \tfrac{1}{5} \end{bmatrix}$$

so that

$$A^{-1} = \begin{bmatrix} x & y \\ z & w \end{bmatrix} = \begin{bmatrix} \frac{2}{5} & -\frac{3}{5} \\ \frac{1}{5} & \frac{1}{5} \end{bmatrix}.$$

To check, multiply A by A^{-1}. The result should be I.

$$AA^{-1} = \begin{bmatrix} 1 & 3 \\ -1 & 2 \end{bmatrix} \begin{bmatrix} \frac{2}{5} & -\frac{3}{5} \\ \frac{1}{5} & \frac{1}{5} \end{bmatrix} = \begin{bmatrix} \frac{2}{5} + \frac{3}{5} & -\frac{3}{5} + \frac{3}{5} \\ -\frac{2}{5} + \frac{2}{5} & \frac{3}{5} + \frac{2}{5} \end{bmatrix} = \begin{bmatrix} 1 & 0 \\ 0 & 1 \end{bmatrix} = I$$

Verify that $A^{-1}A = I$, also.

FINDING A MULTIPLICATIVE INVERSE MATRIX

To obtain A^{-1} for any $n \times n$ matrix A for which A^{-1} exists, follow these steps.

1. Form the augmented matrix $[A|I]$, where I is the $n \times n$ identity matrix.
2. Perform row operations on $[A|I]$ to get a matrix of the form $[I|B]$, if this is possible.
3. Matrix B is A^{-1}.

EXAMPLE 1 **Inverse Matrix**

Find A^{-1} if $A = \begin{bmatrix} 1 & 0 & 1 \\ 2 & -2 & -1 \\ 3 & 0 & 0 \end{bmatrix}$.

METHOD 1
Calculating by Hand

▶**Solution** Write the augmented matrix $[A \mid I]$.

$$[A|I] = \begin{bmatrix} 1 & 0 & 1 & | & 1 & 0 & 0 \\ 2 & -2 & -1 & | & 0 & 1 & 0 \\ 3 & 0 & 0 & | & 0 & 0 & 1 \end{bmatrix}$$

Begin by selecting the row operation that produces a zero for the first element in row 2.

$$\begin{array}{c} \\ -2R_1 + R_2 \to R_2 \\ -3R_1 + R_3 \to R_3 \end{array} \begin{bmatrix} 1 & 0 & 1 & | & 1 & 0 & 0 \\ 0 & -2 & -3 & | & -2 & 1 & 0 \\ 0 & 0 & -3 & | & -3 & 0 & 1 \end{bmatrix} \quad \text{Get 0's in the first column.}$$

Column 2 already has zeros in the required positions, so work on column 3.

$$\begin{array}{c} R_3 + 3R_1 \to R_1 \\ R_3 + (-1)R_2 \to R_2 \\ \\ \end{array} \begin{bmatrix} 3 & 0 & 0 & | & 0 & 0 & 1 \\ 0 & 2 & 0 & | & -1 & -1 & 1 \\ 0 & 0 & -3 & | & -3 & 0 & 1 \end{bmatrix} \quad \text{Get 0's in the third column.}$$

Now get 1's down the main diagonal.

$$\begin{array}{c} \frac{1}{3}R_1 \to R_1 \\ \frac{1}{2}R_2 \to R_2 \\ -\frac{1}{3}R_3 \to R_3 \end{array} \begin{bmatrix} 1 & 0 & 0 & | & 0 & 0 & \frac{1}{3} \\ 0 & 1 & 0 & | & -\frac{1}{2} & -\frac{1}{2} & \frac{1}{2} \\ 0 & 0 & 1 & | & 1 & 0 & -\frac{1}{3} \end{bmatrix} \quad \text{Get 1's down the diagonal.}$$

From the last transformation, the desired inverse is

$$A^{-1} = \begin{bmatrix} 0 & 0 & \frac{1}{3} \\ -\frac{1}{2} & -\frac{1}{2} & \frac{1}{2} \\ 1 & 0 & -\frac{1}{3} \end{bmatrix}.$$

Confirm this by forming the products $A^{-1}A$ and AA^{-1}, both of which should equal I.

METHOD 2
Graphing Calculators

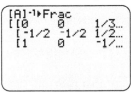

FIGURE 14

The inverse of A can also be found with a graphing calculator, as shown in Figure 14. (The matrix A had previously been entered into the calculator.) The entire answer can be viewed by pressing the right and left arrow keys on the calculator.

Spreadsheets also have the capability of calculating the inverse of a matrix with a simple command. See *The Spreadsheet Manual* available with this book for details.

EXAMPLE 2 **Inverse Matrix**

Find A^{-1} if $A = \begin{bmatrix} 2 & -4 \\ 1 & 2 \end{bmatrix}$.

▶**Solution** Using row operations to transform the first column of the augmented matrix

$$\begin{bmatrix} 2 & -4 & | & 1 & 0 \\ 1 & 2 & | & 0 & 1 \end{bmatrix}$$

gives the following results.

$$R_1 + (\ 2)R_2 \rightarrow R_2 \quad \begin{bmatrix} 2 & -4 & | & 1 & 0 \\ 0 & 0 & | & 1 & -2 \end{bmatrix}$$

Because the last row has all zeros to the left of the vertical bar, there is no way to complete the process of finding the inverse matrix. What is wrong? Just as the real number 0 has no multiplicative inverse, some matrices do not have inverses. Matrix A is an example of a matrix that has no inverse: there is no matrix A^{-1} such that $AA^{-1} = A^{-1}A = I$.

Solving Systems of Equations with Inverses

We used matrices to solve systems of linear equations by the Gauss-Jordan method in Section 2.2. Another way to use matrices to solve linear systems is to write the system as a matrix equation $AX = B$, where A is the matrix of the coefficients of the variables of the system, X is the matrix of the variables, and B is the matrix of the constants. Matrix A is called the **coefficient matrix**.

To solve the matrix equation $AX = B$, first see if A^{-1} exists. Assuming A^{-1} exists and using the facts that $A^{-1}A = I$ and $IX = X$ gives

$$AX = B$$
$$A^{-1}(AX) = A^{-1}B \qquad \text{Multiply both sides by } A^{-1}.$$
$$(A^{-1}A)X = A^{-1}B \qquad \text{Associative property}$$
$$IX = A^{-1}B \qquad \text{Multiplicative inverse property}$$
$$X = A^{-1}B. \qquad \text{Identity property}$$

CAUTION When multiplying by matrices on both sides of a matrix equation, be careful to multiply in the same order on both sides of the equation, since multiplication of matrices is not commutative (unlike multiplication of real numbers). ∎

The work above leads to the following method of solving a system of equations written as a matrix equation.

SOLVING A SYSTEM   USING MATRIX INVERSES

To solve a system of equations $AX = B$, where A is the matrix of coefficients, X is the matrix of variables, and B is the matrix of constants, first find A^{-1}. Then $X = A^{-1}B$.

This method is most practical in solving several systems that have the same coefficient matrix but different constants, as in Example 4 in this section. Then just one inverse matrix must be found.

EXAMPLE 3 **Inverse Matrices and Systems of Equations**
Use the inverse of the coefficient matrix to solve the linear system

$$2x - 3y = 4$$
$$x + 5y = 2.$$

▶**Solution** To represent the system as a matrix equation, use the coefficient matrix of the system together with the matrix of variables and the matrix of constants:

$$A = \begin{bmatrix} 2 & -3 \\ 1 & 5 \end{bmatrix}, \quad X = \begin{bmatrix} x \\ y \end{bmatrix}, \quad \text{and} \quad B = \begin{bmatrix} 4 \\ 2 \end{bmatrix}.$$

The system can now be written in matrix form as the equation $AX = B$ since

$$AX = \begin{bmatrix} 2 & -3 \\ 1 & 5 \end{bmatrix} \begin{bmatrix} x \\ y \end{bmatrix} = \begin{bmatrix} 2x - 3y \\ x + 5y \end{bmatrix} = \begin{bmatrix} 4 \\ 2 \end{bmatrix} = B.$$

To solve the system, first find A^{-1}. Do this by using row operations on matrix $[A|I]$ to get

$$\begin{bmatrix} 1 & 0 & | & \frac{5}{13} & \frac{3}{13} \\ 0 & 1 & | & -\frac{1}{13} & \frac{2}{13} \end{bmatrix}.$$

From this result,

$$A^{-1} = \begin{bmatrix} \frac{5}{13} & \frac{3}{13} \\ -\frac{1}{13} & \frac{2}{13} \end{bmatrix}.$$

Next, find the product $A^{-1}B$.

$$A^{-1}B = \begin{bmatrix} \frac{5}{13} & \frac{3}{13} \\ -\frac{1}{13} & \frac{2}{13} \end{bmatrix} \begin{bmatrix} 4 \\ 2 \end{bmatrix} = \begin{bmatrix} 2 \\ 0 \end{bmatrix}.$$

Since $X = A^{-1}B$,

$$X = \begin{bmatrix} x \\ y \end{bmatrix} = \begin{bmatrix} 2 \\ 0 \end{bmatrix}.$$

The solution of the system is $(2, 0)$.

EXAMPLE 4   Fertilizer

Three brands of fertilizer are available that provide nitrogen, phosphoric acid, and soluble potash to the soil. One bag of each brand provides the following units of each nutrient.

		Fertifun	Big Grow	Soakem
		Brand		
		Fertifun	**Big Grow**	**Soakem**
Nutrient	*Nitrogen*	1	2	3
	Phosphoric Acid	3	1	2
	Potash	2	0	1

For ideal growth, the soil on a Michigan farm needs 18 units of nitrogen, 23 units of phosphoric acid, and 13 units of potash per acre. The corresponding numbers for a California farm are 31, 24, and 11, and for a Kansas farm are 20, 19, and 15. How many bags of each brand of fertilizer should be used per acre for ideal growth on each farm?

▶**Solution**   Rather than solve three separate systems, we consider the single system

$$x + 2y + 3z = a$$
$$3x + y + 2z = b$$
$$2x + z = c,$$

where a, b, and c represent the units of nitrogen, phosphoric acid, and potash needed for the different farms. The system of equations is then of the form $AX = B$, where

$$A = \begin{bmatrix} 1 & 2 & 3 \\ 3 & 1 & 2 \\ 2 & 0 & 1 \end{bmatrix} \quad \text{and} \quad X = \begin{bmatrix} x \\ y \\ z \end{bmatrix}.$$

B has different values for the different farms. We find A^{-1} first, then use it to solve all three systems.

To find A^{-1}, we start with the matrix

$$[A|I] = \begin{bmatrix} 1 & 2 & 3 & | & 1 & 0 & 0 \\ 3 & 1 & 2 & | & 0 & 1 & 0 \\ 2 & 0 & 1 & | & 0 & 0 & 1 \end{bmatrix}$$

and use row operations to get $[I|A^{-1}]$. The result is

$$A^{-1} = \begin{bmatrix} -\frac{1}{3} & \frac{2}{3} & -\frac{1}{3} \\ -\frac{1}{3} & \frac{5}{3} & -\frac{7}{3} \\ \frac{2}{3} & -\frac{4}{3} & \frac{5}{3} \end{bmatrix}.$$

Now we can solve each of the three systems by using $X = A^{-1}B$.

For the Michigan farm, $B = \begin{bmatrix} 18 \\ 23 \\ 13 \end{bmatrix}$, and

$$X = \begin{bmatrix} -\frac{1}{3} & \frac{2}{3} & -\frac{1}{3} \\ -\frac{1}{3} & \frac{5}{3} & -\frac{7}{3} \\ \frac{2}{3} & -\frac{4}{3} & \frac{5}{3} \end{bmatrix} \begin{bmatrix} 18 \\ 23 \\ 13 \end{bmatrix} = \begin{bmatrix} 5 \\ 2 \\ 3 \end{bmatrix}.$$

Therefore, $x = 5$, $y = 2$, and $z = 3$. Buy 5 bags of Fertifun, 2 bags of Big Grow, and 3 bags of Soakem.

For the California farm, $B = \begin{bmatrix} 31 \\ 24 \\ 11 \end{bmatrix}$, and

$$X = \begin{bmatrix} -\frac{1}{3} & \frac{2}{3} & -\frac{1}{3} \\ -\frac{1}{3} & \frac{5}{3} & -\frac{7}{3} \\ \frac{2}{3} & -\frac{4}{3} & \frac{5}{3} \end{bmatrix} \begin{bmatrix} 31 \\ 24 \\ 11 \end{bmatrix} = \begin{bmatrix} 2 \\ 4 \\ 7 \end{bmatrix}.$$

Buy 2 bags of Fertifun, 4 bags of Big Grow, and 7 bags of Soakem.

For the Kansas farm, $B = \begin{bmatrix} 20 \\ 19 \\ 15 \end{bmatrix}$. Verify that this leads to $x = 1$, $y = -10$, and $z = 13$. We cannot have a negative number of bags, so this solution is impossible. In buying enough bags to meet all of the nutrient requirements, the farmer must purchase an excess of some nutrients. In the next two chapters, we will study a method of solving such problems at a minimum cost.   ▬

In Example 4, using the matrix inverse method of solving the systems involved considerably less work than using row operations for each of the three systems.

EXAMPLE 5   **Solving an Inconsistent System of Equations**
Use the inverse of the coefficient matrix to solve the system

$$2x - 4y = 13$$
$$x - 2y = 1.$$

▶**Solution** We saw in Example 2 that the coefficient matrix $\begin{bmatrix} 2 & -4 \\ 1 & -2 \end{bmatrix}$ does not have an inverse. This means that the given system either has no solution or has an infinite number of solutions. Verify that this system is inconsistent and has no solution.   ▬

EXAMPLE 6   **Cryptography**
Throughout the Cold War and as the Internet has grown and developed, the need for sophisticated methods of coding and decoding messages has increased. Although there are many methods of encrypting messages, one fairly sophisti-

cated method uses matrix operations. This method first assigns a number to each letter of the alphabet. The simplest way to do this is to assign the number 1 to A, 2 to B, and so on, with the number 27 used to represent a space between words.

For example, the message *math is cool* can be divided into groups of three letters each and then converted into numbers as follows

$$\begin{bmatrix} m \\ a \\ t \end{bmatrix} = \begin{bmatrix} 13 \\ 1 \\ 20 \end{bmatrix}.$$

The entire message would then consist of four 3×1 columns of numbers:

$$\begin{bmatrix} 13 \\ 1 \\ 20 \end{bmatrix}, \begin{bmatrix} 8 \\ 27 \\ 9 \end{bmatrix}, \begin{bmatrix} 19 \\ 27 \\ 3 \end{bmatrix}, \begin{bmatrix} 15 \\ 15 \\ 12 \end{bmatrix}.$$

This code is easy to break, so we further complicate the code by choosing a matrix that has an inverse (in this case a 3×3 matrix) and calculate the products of the matrix and each of the column vectors above.

If we choose the coding matrix

$$A = \begin{bmatrix} 1 & 3 & 4 \\ 2 & 1 & 3 \\ 4 & 2 & 1 \end{bmatrix},$$

then the products of A with each of the column vectors above produce a new set of vectors

$$\begin{bmatrix} 96 \\ 87 \\ 74 \end{bmatrix}, \begin{bmatrix} 125 \\ 70 \\ 95 \end{bmatrix}, \begin{bmatrix} 112 \\ 74 \\ 133 \end{bmatrix}, \begin{bmatrix} 108 \\ 81 \\ 102 \end{bmatrix}.$$

This set of vectors represents our coded message and it will be transmitted as 96, 87, 74, 125 and so on.

When the intended person receives the message, it is divided into groups of three numbers, and each group is formed into a column matrix. The message is easily decoded if the receiver knows the inverse of the original matrix. The inverse of matrix A is

$$A^{-1} = \begin{bmatrix} -0.2 & 0.2 & 0.2 \\ 0.4 & -0.6 & 0.2 \\ 0 & 0.4 & -0.2 \end{bmatrix}.$$

Thus, the message is decoded by taking the product of the inverse matrix with each column vector of the received message. For example,

$$A^{-1} \begin{bmatrix} 96 \\ 87 \\ 74 \end{bmatrix} = \begin{bmatrix} 13 \\ 1 \\ 20 \end{bmatrix}.$$

Unless the original matrix or its inverse is known, this type of code can be difficult to break. In fact, very large matrices can be used to encrypt data. It is interesting to note that many mathematicians are employed by the National Security Agency to develop encryption methods that are virtually unbreakable.

▶ **2.5 Exercises**

Decide whether the given matrices are inverses of each other. (Check to see if their product is the identity matrix I.)

1. $\begin{bmatrix} 2 & 1 \\ 5 & 3 \end{bmatrix}$ and $\begin{bmatrix} 3 & -1 \\ -5 & 2 \end{bmatrix}$

2. $\begin{bmatrix} 1 & -4 \\ 2 & -7 \end{bmatrix}$ and $\begin{bmatrix} -7 & 4 \\ -2 & 1 \end{bmatrix}$

3. $\begin{bmatrix} 2 & 6 \\ 2 & 4 \end{bmatrix}$ and $\begin{bmatrix} -1 & 2 \\ 2 & -4 \end{bmatrix}$

4. $\begin{bmatrix} -1 & 2 \\ 3 & -5 \end{bmatrix}$ and $\begin{bmatrix} -5 & -2 \\ -3 & -1 \end{bmatrix}$

5. $\begin{bmatrix} 2 & 0 & 1 \\ 1 & 1 & 2 \\ 0 & 1 & 0 \end{bmatrix}$ and $\begin{bmatrix} 1 & 1 & -1 \\ 0 & 1 & 0 \\ -1 & -2 & 2 \end{bmatrix}$

6. $\begin{bmatrix} 0 & 1 & 0 \\ 0 & 0 & -2 \\ 1 & -1 & 0 \end{bmatrix}$ and $\begin{bmatrix} 1 & 0 & 1 \\ 1 & 0 & 0 \\ 0 & -1 & 0 \end{bmatrix}$

7. $\begin{bmatrix} 1 & 3 & 3 \\ 1 & 4 & 3 \\ 1 & 3 & 4 \end{bmatrix}$ and $\begin{bmatrix} 7 & -3 & -3 \\ -1 & 1 & 0 \\ -1 & 0 & 1 \end{bmatrix}$

8. $\begin{bmatrix} 1 & 0 & 0 \\ -1 & -2 & 3 \\ 0 & 1 & 0 \end{bmatrix}$ and $\begin{bmatrix} 1 & 0 & 0 \\ 0 & 0 & 1 \\ \frac{1}{3} & \frac{1}{3} & \frac{2}{3} \end{bmatrix}$

9. Does a matrix with a row of all zeros have an inverse? Why?

10. Matrix A has A^{-1} as its inverse. What does $(A^{-1})^{-1}$ equal? (*Hint:* Experiment with a few matrices to see what you get.)

Find the inverse, if it exists, for each matrix.

11. $\begin{bmatrix} 1 & -1 \\ 2 & 0 \end{bmatrix}$

12. $\begin{bmatrix} 1 & 1 \\ 2 & 3 \end{bmatrix}$

13. $\begin{bmatrix} 3 & -1 \\ -5 & 2 \end{bmatrix}$

14. $\begin{bmatrix} -3 & -8 \\ 1 & 3 \end{bmatrix}$

15. $\begin{bmatrix} 1 & -3 \\ -2 & 6 \end{bmatrix}$

16. $\begin{bmatrix} 5 & 10 \\ -3 & -6 \end{bmatrix}$

17. $\begin{bmatrix} 1 & 0 & 0 \\ 0 & -1 & 0 \\ 1 & 0 & 1 \end{bmatrix}$

18. $\begin{bmatrix} 1 & 3 & 0 \\ 0 & 2 & -1 \\ 1 & 0 & 2 \end{bmatrix}$

19. $\begin{bmatrix} -1 & -1 & -1 \\ 4 & 5 & 0 \\ 0 & 1 & -3 \end{bmatrix}$

20. $\begin{bmatrix} 2 & 1 & 0 \\ 0 & 3 & 1 \\ 4 & -1 & -3 \end{bmatrix}$

21. $\begin{bmatrix} 1 & 2 & 3 \\ -3 & -2 & -1 \\ -1 & 0 & 1 \end{bmatrix}$

22. $\begin{bmatrix} 2 & 0 & 4 \\ 1 & 0 & -1 \\ 3 & 0 & -2 \end{bmatrix}$

23. $\begin{bmatrix} 1 & 3 & -2 \\ 2 & 7 & -3 \\ 3 & 8 & -5 \end{bmatrix}$

24. $\begin{bmatrix} 4 & 1 & -4 \\ 2 & 1 & -1 \\ -2 & -4 & 5 \end{bmatrix}$

25. $\begin{bmatrix} 1 & -2 & 3 & 0 \\ 0 & 1 & -1 & 1 \\ -2 & 2 & -2 & 4 \\ 0 & 2 & -3 & 1 \end{bmatrix}$

26. $\begin{bmatrix} 1 & 1 & 0 & 2 \\ 2 & -1 & 1 & -1 \\ 3 & 3 & 2 & -2 \\ 1 & 2 & 1 & 0 \end{bmatrix}$

Solve each system of equations by using the inverse of the coefficient matrix.

27. $2x + 5y = 15$
$\qquad x + 4y = 9$

28. $-x + 2y = 15$
$\qquad -2x - y = 20$

29. $2x + y = 5$
$\qquad 5x + 3y = 13$

30. $-x - 2y = 8$
$\qquad 3x + 4y = 24$

31. $3x - 2y = 3$
$\qquad 7x - 5y = 0$

32. $3x - 6y = 1$
$\qquad -5x + 9y = -1$

33. $-x - 8y = 12$
$\qquad 3x + 24y = -36$

34. $2x + 7y = 14$
$\qquad 3x + 4y = 8$

Solve each system of equations by using the inverse of the coefficient matrix. (The inverses for the first four problems were found in Exercises 19, 20, 23, and 24.)

35. $-x - y - z = 1$
$\quad\quad 4x + 5y = -2$
$\quad\quad\quad y - 3z = 3$

36. $2x + y = 1$
$\quad\quad\quad 3y + z = 8$
$\quad 4x - y - 3z = 8$

37. $x + 3y - 2z = 4$
$\quad 2x + 7y - 3z = 8$
$\quad 3x + 8y - 5z = -4$

38. $4x + y - 4z = 17$
$\quad 2x + y - z = 12$
$\quad -2x - 4y + 5z = 17$

39. $2x - 2y = 5$
$\quad\quad 4y + 8z = 7$
$\quad\quad x + 2z = 1$

40. $x + 2z = -1$
$\quad\quad y - z = 5$
$\quad -x - y = -8$

Solve each system of equations by using the inverse of the coefficient matrix. (The inverses were found in Exercises 25 and 26.)

41. $x - 2y + 3z = 4$
$\quad\quad y - z + w = -8$
$\quad -2x + 2y - 2z + 4w = 12$
$\quad\quad 2y - 3z + w = -4$

42. $x + y + 2w = 3$
$\quad 2x - y + z - w = 3$
$\quad 3x + 3y + 2z - 2w = 5$
$\quad x + 2y + z = 3$

Let $A = \begin{bmatrix} a & b \\ c & d \end{bmatrix}$ *in Exercises 43–48.*

43. Show that $IA = A$.

44. Show that $AI = A$.

45. Show that $A \cdot O = O$.

46. Find A^{-1}.
(Assume $ad - bc \neq 0$.)

47. Show that $A^{-1}A = I$.

48. Show that $AA^{-1} = I$.

49. Using the definition and properties listed in this section, show that for square matrices A and B of the same size, if $AB = O$ and if A^{-1} exists, then $B = O$.

50. Prove that, if it exists, the inverse of a matrix is unique. (*Hint:* Assume there are two inverses B and C for some matrix A, so that $AB = BA = I$ and $AC = CA = I$. Multiply the first equation by C and the second by B.)

Use matrices C and D in Exercises 51–55.

$$C = \begin{bmatrix} -6 & 8 & 2 & 4 & -3 \\ 1 & 9 & 7 & -12 & 5 \\ 15 & 2 & -8 & 10 & 11 \\ 4 & 7 & 9 & 6 & -2 \\ 1 & 3 & 8 & 23 & 4 \end{bmatrix}, \quad D = \begin{bmatrix} 5 & 3 & 7 & 9 & 2 \\ 6 & 8 & -5 & 2 & 1 \\ 3 & 7 & -4 & 2 & 11 \\ 5 & -3 & 9 & 4 & -1 \\ 0 & 3 & 2 & 5 & 1 \end{bmatrix}$$

51. Find C^{-1}.
52. Find $(CD)^{-1}$.
53. Find D^{-1}.
54. Is $C^{-1}D^{-1} = (CD)^{-1}$?
55. Is $D^{-1}C^{-1} = (CD)^{-1}$?

Solve the matrix equation $AX = B$ for X by finding A^{-1}, given A and B as follows.

56. $A = \begin{bmatrix} 2 & -5 & 7 \\ 4 & -3 & 2 \\ 15 & 2 & 6 \end{bmatrix}$, $B = \begin{bmatrix} -2 \\ 5 \\ 8 \end{bmatrix}$

57. $A = \begin{bmatrix} 2 & 5 & 7 & 9 \\ 1 & 3 & -4 & 6 \\ -1 & 0 & 5 & 8 \\ 2 & -2 & 4 & 10 \end{bmatrix}$, $B = \begin{bmatrix} 3 \\ 7 \\ -1 \\ 5 \end{bmatrix}$

58. $A = \begin{bmatrix} 3 & 2 & -1 & -2 & 6 \\ -5 & 17 & 4 & 3 & 15 \\ 7 & 9 & -3 & -7 & 12 \\ 9 & -2 & 1 & 4 & 8 \\ 1 & 21 & 9 & -7 & 25 \end{bmatrix}$, $B = \begin{bmatrix} -2 \\ 5 \\ 3 \\ -8 \\ 25 \end{bmatrix}$

▶ **Applications**

BUSINESS AND ECONOMICS

Solve each exercise by using the inverse of the coefficient matrix to solve a system of equations.

59. *Analysis of Orders* The Bread Box Bakery sells three types of cakes, each requiring the amounts of the basic ingredients shown in the following matrix.

$$
\begin{array}{cc}
 & \begin{array}{ccc} \text{Type of Cake} \\ \text{I} & \text{II} & \text{III} \end{array} \\
\begin{array}{l} \text{Flour (in cups)} \\ \text{Ingredient} \quad \text{Sugar (in cups)} \\ \text{Eggs} \end{array} &
\begin{bmatrix} 2 & 4 & 2 \\ 2 & 1 & 2 \\ 2 & 1 & 3 \end{bmatrix}
\end{array}
$$

To fill its daily orders for these three kinds of cake, the bakery uses 72 cups of flour, 48 cups of sugar, and 60 eggs.

a. Write a 3×1 matrix for the amounts used daily.

b. Let the number of daily orders for cakes be a 3×1 matrix X with entries x_1, x_2, and x_3. Write a matrix equation that can be solved for X, using the given matrix and the matrix from part a.

c. Solve the equation from part b to find the number of daily orders for each type of cake.

60. *Production Requirements* An electronics company produces transistors, resistors, and computer chips. Each transistor requires 3 units of copper, 1 unit of zinc, and 2 units of glass. Each resistor requires 3, 2, and 1 units of the three materials, and each computer chip requires 2, 1, and 2 units of these materials, respectively. How many of each product can be made with the following amounts of materials?

a. 810 units of copper, 410 units of zinc, and 490 units of glass

b. 765 units of copper, 385 units of zinc, and 470 units of glass

c. 1010 units of copper, 500 units of zinc, and 610 units of glass

61. *Investments* An investment firm recommends that a client invest in AAA-, A-, and B-rated bonds. The average yield on AAA bonds is 6%, on A bonds 6.5%, and on B bonds 8%. The client wants to invest twice as much in AAA bonds as in B bonds. How much should be invested in each type of bond under the following conditions?

a. The total investment is $25,000, and the investor wants an annual return of $1650 on the three investments.

b. The values in part a are changed to $30,000 and $1985, respectively.

c. The values in part a are changed to $40,000 and $2660, respectively.

62. *Production* Pretzels cost $4 per lb, dried fruit $5 per lb, and nuts $9 per lb. The three ingredients are to be combined in a trail mix containing twice the weight of pretzels as dried fruit. How many pounds of each should be used to produce the following amounts at the given cost?

a. 140 lb at $6 per lb

b. 100 lb at $7.60 per lb

c. 125 lb at $6.20 per lb

LIFE SCIENCES

63. *Vitamins* Greg Tobin mixes together three types of vitamin tablets. Each Super Vim tablet contains, among other things, 15 mg of niacin and 12 I.U. of vitamin E. The figures for a Multitab tablet are 20 mg and 15 I.U., and for a Mighty Mix are 25 mg and 35 I.U. How many of each tablet are there if the total number of tablets, total amount of niacin, and total amount of vitamin E are as follows?

a. 225 tablets, 4750 mg of niacin, and 5225 I.U. of vitamin E

b. 185 tablets, 3625 mg of niacin, and 3750 I.U. of vitamin E

c. 230 tablets, 4450 mg of niacin, and 4210 I.U. of vitamin E

GENERAL INTEREST

64. *Encryption* Use the matrices presented in Example 6 of this section to do the following:

a. Encode the message, "All is fair in love and war."

b. Decode the message 138, 81, 102, 101, 67, 109, 162, 124, 173, 210, 150, 165.

65. *Encryption* Use the methods presented in Example 6 along with the given matrix B to do the following.

$$
B = \begin{bmatrix} 2 & 4 & 6 \\ -1 & -4 & -3 \\ 0 & 1 & -1 \end{bmatrix}
$$

a. Encode the message, "To be or not to be."

b. Find the inverse of B.

c. Use the inverse of B to decode the message 116, -60, -15, 294, -197, -2, 148, -92, -9, 96, -64, 4, 264, -182, -2.

66. *Music* During a marching band's half-time show, the band members generally line up in such a way that a common shape is recognized by the fans. For example, as illustrated in the figure, a band might form a letter T, where an x represents a member of the band. As the music is played, the band will either create a new shape or rotate the original shape. In doing this, each member of the band will need to move from one point on the field to another. For larger bands, keeping track of who goes where can be a daunting task. However, it is possible to use matrix inverses to make the process a bit easier.* The entire process is calculated by knowing how three band members, all of whom cannot be in a straight line, will move from the current position to a new position. For example, in the figure, we can see that there are band members at $(50, 0)$, $(50, 15)$, and $(45, 20)$. We will assume that these three band members move to $(40, 10)$, $(55, 10)$, and $(60, 15)$, respectively.

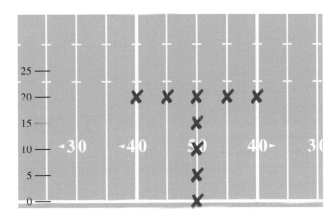

a. Find the inverse of $B = \begin{bmatrix} 50 & 50 & 45 \\ 0 & 15 & 20 \\ 1 & 1 & 1 \end{bmatrix}$.

b. Find $A = \begin{bmatrix} 40 & 55 & 60 \\ 10 & 10 & 15 \\ 1 & 1 & 1 \end{bmatrix} B^{-1}$.

c. Use the result of part b to find the new position of the other band members. What is the shape of the new position? (*Hint:* Multiply the matrix A by a 3×1 column vector with the first two components equal to the original position of each band member and the third component equal to 1. The new position of the band member is in the first two components of the product.)

2.6 Input-Output Models

What production levels are needed to keep an economy going and to supply demands from outside the economy?

A method for solving such questions is developed in this section.

Wassily Leontief (1906–1999) developed an interesting and powerful application of matrix theory to economics and was recognized for this contribution with the Nobel prize in economics in 1973. His matrix models for studying the interdependencies in an economy are called *input-output* models. In practice these models are very complicated, with many variables. Only simple examples with a few variables are discussed here.

Input-output models are concerned with the production and flow of goods (and perhaps services). In an economy with n basic commodities, or sectors, the production of each commodity uses some (perhaps all) of the commodities in the economy as inputs. The amounts of each commodity used in the production of

*Isaksen, Daniel, "Linear Algebra on the Gridiron," *The College Mathematics Journal*, Vol. 26, No. 5, Nov. 1995, pp. 358–360.

one unit of each commodity can be written as an $n \times n$ matrix A, called the **technological matrix** or **input-output matrix** of the economy.

EXAMPLE 1 Input-Output Matrix

Suppose a simplified economy involves just three commodity categories: agriculture, manufacturing, and transportation, all in appropriate units. Production of 1 unit of agriculture requires 1/2 unit of manufacturing and 1/4 unit of transportation; production of 1 unit of manufacturing requires 1/4 unit of agriculture and 1/4 unit of transportation; and production of 1 unit of transportation requires 1/3 unit of agriculture and 1/4 unit of manufacturing. Give the input-output matrix for this economy.

▶Solution

$$
\begin{array}{c}
\quad \text{Agriculture} \quad \text{Manufacturing} \quad \text{Transportation} \\
\begin{array}{c}
\text{Agriculture} \\
\text{Manufacturing} \\
\text{Transportation}
\end{array}
\begin{bmatrix}
0 & \frac{1}{4} & \frac{1}{3} \\
\frac{1}{2} & 0 & \frac{1}{4} \\
\frac{1}{4} & \frac{1}{4} & 0
\end{bmatrix} = A
\end{array}
$$

The first column of the input-output matrix represents the amount of each of the three commodities consumed in the production of 1 unit of agriculture. The second column gives the amounts required to produce 1 unit of manufacturing, and the last column gives the amounts required to produce 1 unit of transportation. (Although it is perhaps unrealistic that production of a unit of each commodity requires none of that commodity, the simpler matrix involved is useful for our purposes.)

NOTE Notice that for each commodity produced, the various units needed are put in a column. Each column corresponds to a commodity produced, and the rows correspond to what is needed to produce the commodity.

Another matrix used with the input-output matrix is the matrix giving the amount of each commodity produced, called the **production matrix**, or the matrix of gross output. In an economy producing n commodities, the production matrix can be represented by a column matrix X with entries $x_1, x_2, x_3, \ldots, x_n$.

EXAMPLE 2 Production Matrix

In Example 1, suppose the production matrix is

$$
X = \begin{bmatrix} 60 \\ 52 \\ 48 \end{bmatrix}.
$$

Then 60 units of agriculture, 52 units of manufacturing, and 48 units of transportation are produced. Because 1/4 unit of agriculture is used for each unit of manufacturing produced, $1/4 \times 52 = 13$ units of agriculture must be used in the "production" of manufacturing. Similarly, $1/3 \times 48 = 16$ units of agriculture will be used in the "production" of transportation. Thus, $13 + 16 = 29$ units of agriculture are used for production in the economy. Look again at the matrices A and X. Since X gives the number of units of each commodity produced and A gives the amount (in units) of each commodity used to produce 1 unit of each of the various commodities, the matrix product AX gives the amount of each commodity used in the production process.

$$AX = \begin{bmatrix} 0 & \frac{1}{4} & \frac{1}{3} \\ \frac{1}{2} & 0 & \frac{1}{4} \\ \frac{1}{4} & \frac{1}{4} & 0 \end{bmatrix} \begin{bmatrix} 60 \\ 52 \\ 48 \end{bmatrix} = \begin{bmatrix} 29 \\ 42 \\ 28 \end{bmatrix}$$

From this result, 29 units of agriculture, 42 units of manufacturing, and 28 units of transportation are used to produce 60 units of agriculture, 52 units of manufacturing, and 48 units of transportation.

The matrix product AX represents the amount of each commodity used in the production process. The remainder (if any) must be enough to satisfy the demand for the various commodities from outside the production system. In an n-commodity economy, this demand can be represented by a **demand matrix** D with entries $d_1, d_2, \ldots, d_n$. If no production is to remain unused, the difference between the production matrix X and the amount AX used in the production process must equal the demand D, or

$$D = X - AX.$$

In Example 2,

$$D = \begin{bmatrix} 60 \\ 52 \\ 48 \end{bmatrix} - \begin{bmatrix} 29 \\ 42 \\ 28 \end{bmatrix} - \begin{bmatrix} 31 \\ 10 \\ 20 \end{bmatrix},$$

so production of 60 units of agriculture, 52 units of manufacturing, and 48 units of transportation would satisfy a demand of 31, 10, and 20 units of each commodity, respectively.

In practice, A and D usually are known and X must be found. That is, we need to decide what amounts of production are needed to satisfy the required demands. Matrix algebra can be used to solve the equation $D = X - AX$ for X.

$D = X - AX$	
$D = IX - AX$	Identity property
$D = (I - A)X$	Distributive property

If the matrix $I - A$ has an inverse, then

$$X = (I - A)^{-1}D.$$

> **FOR REVIEW**
>
> Recall that I is the identity matrix, a square matrix in which each element on the main diagonal is 1 and all other elements are 0.

If the production matrix is large or complicated, we could use a graphing calculator. On the TI-83/84 Plus, for example, we would enter the command `(identity(3) - [A])`$^{-1}$`*[D]` for a 3 × 3 matrix A. It is also practical to do these calculations on a spreadsheet.

EXAMPLE 3   **Demand Matrix**

Suppose, in the three-commodity economy from Examples 1 and 2, there is a demand for 516 units of agriculture, 258 units of manufacturing, and 129 units of transportation. What should production of each commodity be?

▶**Solution** The demand matrix is

$$D = \begin{bmatrix} 516 \\ 258 \\ 129 \end{bmatrix}.$$

To find the production matrix X, first calculate $I - A$.

$$I - A = \begin{bmatrix} 1 & 0 & 0 \\ 0 & 1 & 0 \\ 0 & 0 & 1 \end{bmatrix} - \begin{bmatrix} 0 & \frac{1}{4} & \frac{1}{3} \\ \frac{1}{2} & 0 & \frac{1}{4} \\ \frac{1}{4} & \frac{1}{4} & 0 \end{bmatrix} = \begin{bmatrix} 1 & -\frac{1}{4} & -\frac{1}{3} \\ -\frac{1}{2} & 1 & -\frac{1}{4} \\ -\frac{1}{4} & -\frac{1}{4} & 1 \end{bmatrix}$$

Use row operations to find the inverse of $I - A$ (the entries are rounded to two decimal places).

$$(I - A)^{-1} = \begin{bmatrix} 1.40 & 0.50 & 0.59 \\ 0.84 & 1.36 & 0.62 \\ 0.56 & 0.47 & 1.30 \end{bmatrix}$$

Since $X = (I - A)^{-1}D$,

$$X = \begin{bmatrix} 1.40 & 0.50 & 0.59 \\ 0.84 & 1.36 & 0.62 \\ 0.56 & 0.47 & 1.30 \end{bmatrix} \begin{bmatrix} 516 \\ 258 \\ 129 \end{bmatrix} = \begin{bmatrix} 928 \\ 864 \\ 578 \end{bmatrix}.$$

(Each entry in X has been rounded to the nearest whole number.)

The last result shows that production of 928 units of agriculture, 864 units of manufacturing, and 578 units of transportation are required to satisfy demands of 516, 258, and 129 units, respectively.

The entries in the matrix $(I - A)^{-1}$ are often called *multipliers*, and they have important economic interpretations. For example, every \$1 increase in total agricultural demand will result in an increase in agricultural production by \$1.40, an increase in manufacturing production by \$0.84, and an increase in transportation production by \$0.56. Similarly, every \$3 increase in total manufacturing demand will result in an increase of $3(0.50) = 1.50$, $3(1.36) = 4.08$, and $3(0.47) = 1.41$ dollars in agricultural production, manufacturing production, and transportation production, respectively.

EXAMPLE 4 **Wheat and Oil Production**

An economy depends on two basic products, wheat and oil. To produce 1 metric ton of wheat requires 0.25 metric tons of wheat and 0.33 metric tons of oil. Production of 1 metric ton of oil consumes 0.08 metric tons of wheat and 0.11 metric tons of oil.

(a) Find the production that will satisfy a demand for 500 metric tons of wheat and 1000 metric tons of oil.

▶Solution The input-output matrix is

$$A = \begin{bmatrix} 0.25 & 0.08 \\ 0.33 & 0.11 \end{bmatrix}.$$

Also,

$$I - A = \begin{bmatrix} 0.75 & -0.08 \\ -0.33 & 0.89 \end{bmatrix}.$$

Next, calculate $(I - A)^{-1}$.

$$(I - A)^{-1} = \begin{bmatrix} 1.3882 & 0.1248 \\ 0.5147 & 1.1699 \end{bmatrix} \quad \text{(rounded)}$$

To find the production matrix X, use the equation $X = (I - A)^{-1}D$, with

$$D = \begin{bmatrix} 500 \\ 1000 \end{bmatrix}.$$

The production matrix is

$$X = \begin{bmatrix} 1.3882 & 0.1248 \\ 0.5147 & 1.1699 \end{bmatrix} \begin{bmatrix} 500 \\ 1000 \end{bmatrix} \approx \begin{bmatrix} 819 \\ 1427 \end{bmatrix}.$$

Production of 819 metric tons of wheat and 1427 metric tons of oil is required to satisfy the indicated demand.

(b) Suppose the demand for wheat goes up from 500 to 600 metric tons. Find the increased production in wheat and oil that will be required to meet the new demand.

▶**Solution** One way to solve this problem is using the multipliers for wheat, found in the first column of $(I - A)^{-1}$ from part (a). The element in the first row, 1.3882, is used to find the increased production in wheat, while the item in the second row, 0.5147, is used to find the increased production in oil. Since the increase in demand for wheat is 100 metric tons, the increased production in wheat must be $100(1.3882) \approx 139$ metric tons. Similarly, the increased production in oil is $100(0.5147) \approx 51$ metric tons.

Alternatively, we could have found the new production in wheat and oil with the equation $X = (I - A)^{-1}D$, giving

$$X = \begin{bmatrix} 1.3882 & 0.1248 \\ 0.5147 & 1.1699 \end{bmatrix} \begin{bmatrix} 600 \\ 1000 \end{bmatrix} \approx \begin{bmatrix} 958 \\ 1479 \end{bmatrix}.$$

We find the increased production by subtracting the answers found in part (a) from these answers. The increased production in wheat is $958 - 819 = 139$ metric tons, and the increased production in oil is $1479 - 1427 = 52$ metric tons. The slight difference here from the previous answer of 51 metric tons is due to rounding.

Closed Models

The input-output model discussed above is referred to as an **open model**, since it allows for a surplus from the production equal to D. In the **closed model**, all the production is consumed internally in the production process, so that $X = AX$. There is nothing left over to satisfy any outside demands from other parts of the economy or from other economies. In this case, the sum of each column in the input-output matrix equals 1.

To solve the closed model, set $D = O$ in the equation derived earlier.

$$(I - A)X = D = O$$

The system of equations that corresponds to $(I - A)X = O$ does not have a single unique solution, but it can be solved in terms of a parameter. (It can be shown that if the columns of a matrix A sum to 1, then the equation $(I - A)X = O$ has an infinite number of solutions.)

➡ **FOR REVIEW**

Parameters were discussed in the first section of this chapter. As mentioned there, parameters are required when a system has infinitely many solutions.

EXAMPLE 5

Closed Input-Output Model

Use matrix A below to find the production of each commodity in a closed model.

$$A = \begin{bmatrix} \frac{1}{2} & \frac{1}{4} & \frac{1}{3} \\ 0 & \frac{1}{4} & \frac{1}{3} \\ \frac{1}{2} & \frac{1}{2} & \frac{1}{3} \end{bmatrix}$$

►**Solution** Find the value of $I - A$, then set $(I - A)X = O$ to find X.

$$I - A = \begin{bmatrix} \frac{1}{2} & -\frac{1}{4} & -\frac{1}{3} \\ 0 & \frac{3}{4} & -\frac{1}{3} \\ -\frac{1}{2} & -\frac{1}{2} & \frac{2}{3} \end{bmatrix}$$

$$(I - A)X = \begin{bmatrix} \frac{1}{2} & -\frac{1}{4} & -\frac{1}{3} \\ 0 & \frac{3}{4} & -\frac{1}{3} \\ -\frac{1}{2} & -\frac{1}{2} & \frac{2}{3} \end{bmatrix} \begin{bmatrix} x_1 \\ x_2 \\ x_3 \end{bmatrix} = \begin{bmatrix} 0 \\ 0 \\ 0 \end{bmatrix}$$

Multiply to get

$$\begin{bmatrix} \frac{1}{2}x_1 - \frac{1}{4}x_2 - \frac{1}{3}x_3 \\ 0x_1 + \frac{3}{4}x_2 - \frac{1}{3}x_3 \\ -\frac{1}{2}x_1 - \frac{1}{2}x_2 + \frac{2}{3}x_3 \end{bmatrix} = \begin{bmatrix} 0 \\ 0 \\ 0 \end{bmatrix}.$$

The last matrix equation corresponds to the following system.

$$\frac{1}{2}x_1 - \frac{1}{4}x_2 - \frac{1}{3}x_3 = 0$$
$$\frac{3}{4}x_2 - \frac{1}{3}x_3 = 0$$
$$-\frac{1}{2}x_1 - \frac{1}{2}x_2 + \frac{2}{3}x_3 = 0$$

Solving the system with x_3 as the parameter gives the solution of the system

$$\left(\frac{8}{9}x_3, \frac{4}{9}x_3, x_3\right).$$

For example, if $x_3 = 9$ (a choice that eliminates fractions in the answer), then $x_1 = 8$ and $x_2 = 4$, so the production of the three commodities should be in the ratio 8:4:9.

Production matrices for actual economies are much larger than those shown in this section. An analysis of the U.S. economy in 1997 has close to 500 commodity categories.* Such matrices require large human and computer resources for their analysis. Some of the exercises at the end of this section use actual data in which categories have been combined to simplify the work.

*U.S. Bureau of Economic Analysis, http://www.bea.gov/bea/an2.htm.

FINDING A PRODUCTION MATRIX

To obtain the production matrix, X, for an open input-output model, follow these steps:

1. Form the $n \times n$ input-output matrix, A, by placing in each column the amount of the various commodities required to produce 1 unit of a particular commodity.
2. Calculate $I - A$, where I is the $n \times n$ identity matrix.
3. Find the inverse, $(I - A)^{-1}$.
4. Multiply the inverse on the right by the demand matrix, D, to obtain $X = (I - A)^{-1}D$.

To obtain a production matrix, X, for a closed input-output model, solve the system $(I - A)X = O$.

▶ **2.6 Exercises**

Find the production matrix for the following input-output and demand matrices using the open model.

1. $A = \begin{bmatrix} 0.8 & 0.2 \\ 0.2 & 0.7 \end{bmatrix}$, $D = \begin{bmatrix} 2 \\ 3 \end{bmatrix}$

2. $A = \begin{bmatrix} 0.2 & 0.04 \\ 0.6 & 0.05 \end{bmatrix}$, $D = \begin{bmatrix} 3 \\ 10 \end{bmatrix}$

3. $A = \begin{bmatrix} 0.1 & 0.03 \\ 0.07 & 0.6 \end{bmatrix}$, $D = \begin{bmatrix} 5 \\ 10 \end{bmatrix}$

4. $A = \begin{bmatrix} 0.02 & 0.03 \\ 0.06 & 0.08 \end{bmatrix}$, $D = \begin{bmatrix} 100 \\ 200 \end{bmatrix}$

5. $A = \begin{bmatrix} 0.8 & 0 & 0.1 \\ 0.1 & 0.5 & 0.2 \\ 0 & 0 & 0.7 \end{bmatrix}$, $D = \begin{bmatrix} 1 \\ 6 \\ 3 \end{bmatrix}$

6. $A = \begin{bmatrix} 0.1 & 0.5 & 0 \\ 0 & 0.3 & 0.4 \\ 0.1 & 0.2 & 0.1 \end{bmatrix}$, $D = \begin{bmatrix} 10 \\ 4 \\ 2 \end{bmatrix}$

Find the ratios of products A, B, *and* C *using a closed model.*

7.
$\begin{array}{c} \\ A \\ B \\ C \end{array}$
$\begin{array}{ccc} A & B & C \end{array}$
$\begin{bmatrix} 0.3 & 0.1 & 0.8 \\ 0.5 & 0.6 & 0.1 \\ 0.2 & 0.3 & 0.1 \end{bmatrix}$

8.
$\begin{array}{c} \\ A \\ B \\ C \end{array}$
$\begin{array}{ccc} A & B & C \end{array}$
$\begin{bmatrix} 0.3 & 0.2 & 0.3 \\ 0.1 & 0.5 & 0.4 \\ 0.6 & 0.3 & 0.3 \end{bmatrix}$

✎ *Use a graphing calculator or computer to find the production matrix X, given the following input-output and demand matrices.*

9. $A = \begin{bmatrix} 0.25 & 0.25 & 0.25 & 0.05 \\ 0.01 & 0.02 & 0.01 & 0.1 \\ 0.3 & 0.3 & 0.01 & 0.1 \\ 0.2 & 0.01 & 0.3 & 0.01 \end{bmatrix}$, $D = \begin{bmatrix} 2930 \\ 3570 \\ 2300 \\ 580 \end{bmatrix}$

10. $A = \begin{bmatrix} 0.01 & 0.2 & 0.01 & 0.2 \\ 0.5 & 0.02 & 0.03 & 0.02 \\ 0.09 & 0.05 & 0.02 & 0.03 \\ 0.3 & 0.2 & 0.2 & 0.01 \end{bmatrix}$, $D = \begin{bmatrix} 5000 \\ 1000 \\ 4000 \\ 500 \end{bmatrix}$

► Applications

BUSINESS AND ECONOMICS

Input-Output Open Model In Exercises 11 and 12, refer to Example 4.

11. If the demand is changed to 925 metric tons of wheat and 1250 metric tons of oil, how many units of each commodity should be produced?

12. Change the technological matrix so that production of 1 metric ton of wheat requires 1/5 metric ton of oil (and no wheat), and production of 1 metric ton of oil requires 1/3 metric ton of wheat (and no oil). To satisfy the same demand matrix, how many units of each commodity should be produced?

Input-Output Open Model In Exercises 13–16, refer to Example 3.

13. If the demand is changed to 607 units of each commodity, how many units of each commodity should be produced?

14. Suppose 1/3 unit of manufacturing (no agriculture or transportation) is required to produce 1 unit of agriculture, 1/4 unit of transportation is required to produce 1 unit of manufacturing, and 1/2 unit of agriculture is required to produce 1 unit of transportation. How many units of each commodity should be produced to satisfy a demand of 1000 units of each commodity?

15. Suppose 1/4 unit of manufacturing and 1/2 unit of transportation are required to produce 1 unit of agriculture, 1/2 unit of agriculture and 1/4 unit of transportation to produce 1 unit of manufacturing, and 1/4 unit of agriculture and 1/4 unit of manufacturing to produce 1 unit of transportation. How many units of each commodity should be produced to satisfy a demand of 1000 units for each commodity?

16. If the input-output matrix is changed so that 1/4 unit of manufacturing and 1/2 unit of transportation are required to produce 1 unit of agriculture, 1/2 unit of agriculture and 1/4 unit of transportation are required to produce 1 unit of manufacturing, and 1/4 unit each of agriculture and manufacturing are required to produce 1 unit of transportation, find the number of units of each commodity that should be produced to satisfy a demand for 500 units of each commodity.

Input-Output Open Model

17. A primitive economy depends on two basic goods, yams and pork. Production of 1 bushel of yams requires 1/4 bushel of

yams and 1/2 of a pig. To produce 1 pig requires 1/6 bushel of yams. Find the amount of each commodity that should be produced to get the following.

a. 1 bushel of yams and 1 pig

b. 100 bushels of yams and 70 pigs

18. A simple economy depends on three commodities: oil, corn, and coffee. Production of 1 unit of oil requires 0.2 unit of oil, 0.4 unit of corn, and no units of coffee. To produce 1 unit of corn requires 0.4 unit of oil, 0.2 unit of corn, and 0.1 unit of coffee. To produce 1 unit of coffee requires 0.2 unit of oil, 0.1 unit of corn, and 0.2 unit of coffee. Find the production required to meet a demand of 1000 units each of oil, corn, and coffee.

19. In his work *Input-Output Economics*, Leontief provides an example of a simplified economy with just three sectors: agriculture, manufacturing, and households (i.e., the sector of the economy that produces labor).* It has the following input-output matrix:

	Agriculture	Manufacturing	Households
Agriculture	0.25	0.40	0.133
Manufacturing	0.14	0.12	0.100
Households	0.80	3.60	0.133

He also gives the demand matrix

$$D = \begin{bmatrix} 35 \\ 38 \\ 40 \end{bmatrix}.$$

Find the amount of each commodity that should be produced.

20. A much-simplified version of Leontief's 42-sector analysis of the 1947 American economy has the following input-output matrix.[†]

	Agriculture	Manufacturing	Households
Agriculture	0.245	0.102	0.051
Manufacturing	0.099	0.291	0.279
Households	0.433	0.372	0.011

The demand matrix (in billions of dollars) is

$$D = \begin{bmatrix} 2.88 \\ 31.45 \\ 30.91 \end{bmatrix}.$$

Find the amount of each commodity that should be produced.

*Leontief, Wassily, *Input-Output Economics*, 2nd ed., Oxford University Press, 1966, pp. 20–27.
†Ibid, pp. 6–9.

21. An analysis of the 1958 Israeli economy is simplified here by grouping the economy into three sectors, with the following input-output matrix:*

	Agriculture	Manufacturing	Energy
Agriculture	0.293	0	0
Manufacturing	0.014	0.207	0.017
Energy	0.044	0.010	0.216

The demand (in thousands of Israeli pounds) as measured by exports is

$$D = \begin{bmatrix} 138{,}213 \\ 17{,}597 \\ 1786 \end{bmatrix}.$$

Find the amount of each commodity that should be produced.

22. The 1981 Chinese economy can be simplified to three sectors: agriculture, industry and construction, and transportation and commerce.[†] The input-output matrix is given below.

	Agriculture	Industry/ Constr.	Trans./ Commerce
Agriculture	0.158	0.156	0.009
Industry/Constr.	0.136	0.432	0.071
Trans./Commerce	0.013	0.041	0.011

The demand (in 100,000 RMB, the unit of money in China) is

$$D = \begin{bmatrix} 106{,}674 \\ 144{,}739 \\ 26{,}725 \end{bmatrix}.$$

a. Find the amount of each commodity that should be produced.

b. Interpret the economic value of an increase in demand of 1 RMB in agricultural exports.

23. *Washington* The 1987 economy of the state of Washington has been simplified to four sectors: natural resources, manufacturing, trade and services, and personal consumption. The input-output matrix is given below.[‡]

	Natural Resources	Manufacturing	Trade & Services	Personal Consumption
Natural Resources	0.1045	0.0428	0.0029	0.0031
Manufacturing	0.0826	0.1087	0.0584	0.0321
Trade & Services	0.0867	0.1019	0.2032	0.3555
Personal Consumption	0.6253	0.3448	0.6106	0.0798

Suppose the demand (in millions of dollars) is

$$D = \begin{bmatrix} 450 \\ 300 \\ 125 \\ 100 \end{bmatrix}.$$

Find the amount of each commodity that should be produced.

24. *Washington* In addition to solving the previous input-output model, most models of this nature also include an employment equation. For the previous model, the employment equation is added and a new system of equations is obtained as follows.[‡]

$$\begin{bmatrix} x_1 \\ x_2 \\ x_3 \\ x_4 \\ N \end{bmatrix} = (I - B)^{-1}C,$$

where x_1, x_2, x_3, x_4 represent the amount, in millions of dollars, that must be produced to satisfy internal and external demands of the four sectors; N is the total workforce required for a particular set of demands; and

$$B = \begin{bmatrix} 0.1045 & 0.0428 & 0.0029 & 0.0031 & 0 \\ 0.0826 & 0.1087 & 0.0584 & 0.0321 & 0 \\ 0.0867 & 0.1019 & 0.2032 & 0.3555 & 0 \\ 0.6253 & 0.3448 & 0.6106 & 0.0798 & 0 \\ 21.6 & 6.6 & 20.2 & 0 & 0 \end{bmatrix}.$$

a. Suppose that a $50 million change in manufacturing occurs. How will this increase in demand affect the economy? (*Hint:* Find $(I - B)^{-1}C$, where $C = \begin{bmatrix} 0 \\ 50 \\ 0 \\ 0 \\ 0 \end{bmatrix}$.)

b. Interpret the meaning of the bottom row in the matrix $(I - B)^{-1}$.

25. *Community Links* The use of input-output analysis can also be used to model how changes in one city can affect cities that are connected with it in some way.[§] For example, if a large manufacturing company shuts down in one city, it is very likely that the economic welfare of all of

*Ibid., pp. 174–177.

[†]*Input-Output Tables of China, 1981*, China Statistical Information and Consultancy Service Centre, 1987, pp. 17–19.

[‡]Chase, Robert, Philip Bourque, and Richard Conway Jr., "The 1987 Washington State Input-Output Study," Report to the Graduate School of Business Administration, University of Washington, Sept. 1993.

[§]The idea for this problem came from an example created by Thayer Watkins, Department of Economics, San Jose State University, www.sjsu/faculty/watkins/inputoutput.htm.

the cities around it will suffer. Consider three Pennsylvania communities: Sharon, Farrell, and Hermitage. Due to their proximity to each other, residents of these three communities regularly spend time and money in the other communities. Suppose that we have gathered information in the form of an input-output matrix.

$$A = \begin{array}{c} \\ \text{S} \\ \text{F} \\ \text{H} \end{array} \begin{array}{ccc} \text{S} & \text{F} & \text{H} \\ \begin{bmatrix} 0.2 & 0.1 & 0.1 \\ 0.1 & 0.1 & 0 \\ 0.5 & 0.6 & 0.7 \end{bmatrix} \end{array}$$

This matrix can be thought of as the likelihood that a person from a particular community will spend money in each of the communities.

a. Treat this matrix like an input-output matrix and calculate $(I - A)^{-1}$.

b. Interpret the entries of this inverse matrix.

Input-Output Closed Model

26. Use the input-output matrix

$$\begin{array}{c} \\ \text{Yams} \\ \text{Pigs} \end{array} \begin{array}{cc} \text{Yams} & \text{Pigs} \\ \begin{bmatrix} \frac{1}{4} & \frac{1}{2} \\ \frac{3}{4} & \frac{1}{2} \end{bmatrix} \end{array}$$

and the closed model to find the ratio of yams to pigs produced.

27. Use the input-output matrix

$$\begin{array}{c} \\ \text{Steel} \\ \text{Coal} \end{array} \begin{array}{cc} \text{Steel} & \text{Coal} \\ \begin{bmatrix} \frac{3}{4} & \frac{1}{3} \\ \frac{1}{4} & \frac{2}{3} \end{bmatrix} \end{array}$$

and the closed model to find the ratio of coal to steel produced.

28. Suppose that production of 1 unit of agriculture requires 1/3 unit of agriculture, 1/3 unit of manufacturing, and 1/3 unit of transportation. To produce 1 unit of manufacturing requires 1/2 unit of agriculture, 1/4 unit of manufacturing, and 1/4 unit of transportation. To produce 1 unit of transportation requires 0 units of agriculture, 1/4 unit of manufacturing, and 3/4 unit of transportation. Find the ratio of the three commodities in the closed model.

29. Suppose that production of 1 unit of mining requires 1/5 unit of mining, 2/5 unit of manufacturing, and 2/5 unit of communication. To produce 1 unit of manufacturing requires 3/5 unit of mining, 1/5 unit of manufacturing, and 1/5 unit of communication. To produce 1 unit of communication requires 0 units of mining, 4/5 unit of manufacturing, and 1/5 unit of communication. Find the ratio of the three commodities in the closed model.

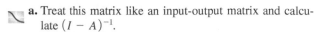

Chapter 2 Review

► *Chapter Summary*

In this chapter we extended our study of linear functions to include finding solutions of systems of linear equations. Techniques such as the echelon method and the Gauss-Jordan method were developed and used to solve systems of linear equations. We introduced matrices, which are used to store mathematical information. We saw that matrices can be combined using addition, subtraction, scalar multiplication, and matrix multiplication. Two special matrices, the zero matrix and the identity matrix, were also introduced.

- The zero matrix O is a matrix whose elements are all zero.
- The identity matrix I is an $n \times n$ matrix consisting of 1's along the diagonal and 0's elsewhere.

We then developed the concept of a multiplicative inverse of a matrix and used such inverses to solve systems of equations. We concluded the chapter by introducing the Leontief input-output models, which are used to study interdependencies in an economy.

SYSTEMS OF LINEAR EQUATIONS AND MATRICES SUMMARY

Row Operations   For any augmented matrix of a system of equations, the following operations produce the augmented matrix of an equivalent system:

1. interchanging any two rows;
2. multiplying the elements of a row by a nonzero real number;
3. adding a nonzero multiple of the elements of one row to the corresponding elements of a nonzero multiple of some other row.

The Gauss-Jordan Method

1. Write each equation so that variable terms are in the same order on the left side of the equals sign and constants are on the right.
2. Write the augmented matrix that corresponds to the system.
3. Use row operations to transform the first column so that all elements except the element in the first row are zero.
4. Use row operations to transform the second column so that all elements except the element in the second row are zero.
5. Use row operations to transform the third column so that all elements except the element in the third row are zero.
6. Continue in this way, when possible, until the last row is written in the form

$$[0\ 0\ 0\ \cdots\ 0\ j\ |\ k],$$

where j and k are constants with $j \neq 0$. When this is not possible, continue until every row has more zeros on the left than the previous row (except possibly for any rows of all zero at the bottom of the matrix), and the first nonzero entry in each row is the only nonzero entry in its column.
7. Multiply each row by the reciprocal of the nonzero element in that row.

Adding Matrices   The sum of two $m \times n$ matrices X and Y is the $m \times n$ matrix $X + Y$ in which each element is the sum of the corresponding elements of X and Y.

Subtracting Matrices   For two $m \times n$ matrices X and Y, the difference $X - Y$ is the $m \times n$ matrix defined by

$$X - Y = X + (-Y).$$

Product of a Matrix and a Scalar   The product of a scalar k and a matrix X is the matrix kX, each of whose elements is k times the corresponding element of X.

Product of Two Matrices   Let A be an $m \times n$ matrix and let B be an $n \times k$ matrix. To find the element in the ith row and jth column of the product AB, multiply each element in the ith row of A by the corresponding element in the jth column of B, and then add these products. The product matrix AB is an $m \times k$ matrix.

Solving a System $AX = B$ Using Matrix Inverses   To solve a system of equations $AX = B$, where A is a square matrix of coefficients, X is the matrix of variables, and B is the matrix of constants, first find A^{-1}. Then, $X = A^{-1}B$.

Finding a Production Matrix

1. Form the input-output matrix, A.
2. Calculate $I - A$, where I is the $n \times n$ identity matrix.
3. Find the inverse, $(I - A)^{-1}$.
4. Multiply the inverse on the right by the demand matrix, D, to obtain
$$X = (I - A)^{-1}D.$$

To obtain a production matrix, X, for a closed input-output model, solve the system $(I - A)X = O$.

▶ Key Terms

To understand the concepts presented in this chapter, you should know the meaning and use of the following terms. For easy reference, the section in the chapter where a word (or expression) was first used is provided.

	system of equations	parameter	column matrix (column	multiplicative inverse
2.1	first-degree equation in	2.2 matrix (matrices)	vector)	matrix
	n unknowns	element (entry)	additive inverse	coefficient matrix
	unique solution	augmented matrix	(negative) of a matrix	2.6 input-output
	inconsistent system	row operations	zero matrix	(technological) matrix
	dependent equations	Gauss-Jordan method	additive identity	production matrix
	equivalent system	2.3 size	2.4 scalar	demand matrix
	echelon method	square matrix	product matrix	open model
	back-substitution	row matrix (row vector)	2.5 identity matrix	closed model

▶ Concept Check

Determine whether each of the following statements is true or false, and explain why.

1. If a system of equations has three equations and four unknowns, then it could have a unique solution.

2. If $A = \begin{bmatrix} 2 & 3 \\ 1 & -1 \end{bmatrix}$ and $B = \begin{bmatrix} 3 & 4 \\ 7 & 4 \\ 1 & 0 \end{bmatrix}$, then $A + B = \begin{bmatrix} 5 & 7 \\ 8 & 3 \\ 1 & 0 \end{bmatrix}$.

3. If a system of equations has three equations and three unknowns, then it may have a unique solution, an infinite number of solutions, or no solutions.

4. The only solution to the system of equations

$$2x + 3y = 7$$
$$5x - 4y = 6$$

is $x = 2$ and $y = 1$.

5. If A is a 2×3 matrix and B is a 3×4 matrix, then $A + B$ is a 2×4 matrix.

6. If A is an $n \times k$ matrix and B is a $k \times m$ matrix, then AB is an $n \times m$ matrix.

7. If A is a 4×4 matrix and B is a 4×4 matrix, then $AB = BA$.

8. A 3×4 matrix could have an inverse.

9. It is not possible to find a matrix A such that $OA = AO = I$, where O is a 5×5 zero matrix and I is a 5×5 identity matrix.

10. When solving a system of equations by the Gauss-Jordan method, we can add a nonzero multiple of the elements of one column to the corresponding elements of some nonzero multiple of some other column.

11. Every square matrix has an inverse.

12. If A, B, and C are matrices such that $AB = C$, then $B = \dfrac{C}{A}$.

13. A system of three equations in three unknowns might have exactly five positive integer solutions.

14. If A and B are matrices such that $A = B^{-1}$, then $AB = BA$.

15. If A, B, and C are matrices such that $AB = CB$, then $A = C$.

16. The difference between an open and a closed input-output model is that in a closed model, the demand matrix D is a zero matrix.

→ *Chapter 2 Review Exercises*

1. What is true about the number of solutions to a system of m linear equations in n unknowns if $m = n$? If $m < n$? If $m > n$?

2. Suppose someone says that a more reasonable way to multiply two matrices than the method presented in the text is to multiply corresponding elements. For example, the result of

$$\begin{bmatrix} 1 & 2 \\ 3 & 4 \end{bmatrix} \cdot \begin{bmatrix} 3 & 5 \\ 7 & 11 \end{bmatrix} \text{ should be } \begin{bmatrix} 3 & 10 \\ 21 & 44 \end{bmatrix},$$

according to this person. How would you respond?

Solve each system by the echelon method.

3. $2x - 3y = 14$
       $3x + 2y = -5$

4. $\dfrac{x}{2} + \dfrac{y}{4} = 3$
       $\dfrac{x}{4} - \dfrac{y}{2} = 4$

5. $2x - 3y + z = -5$
       $x + 4y + 2z = 13$
       $5x + 5y + 3z = 14$

6. $x + 2y + 3z = 9$
       $x - 2y = 4$
       $3x + 2z = 12$

Solve each system by the Gauss-Jordan method.

7. $2x + 4y = -6$
       $-3x - 5y = 12$

8. $x - 4y = 10$
       $5x + 3y = 119$

9. $x - y + 3z = 13$
       $4x + y + 2z = 17$
       $3x + 2y + 2z = 1$

10. $x - 2z = 5$
        $3x + 2y = 8$
        $-x + 2z = 10$

11. $3x - 6y + 9z = 12$
        $x + 2y - 3z = -4$
        $x + y + 2z = 7$

Find the size of each matrix, find the values of any variables, and identify any square, row, or column matrices.

12. $\begin{bmatrix} 2 & 3 \\ 5 & q \end{bmatrix} - \begin{bmatrix} a & b \\ c & 9 \end{bmatrix}$

13. $\begin{bmatrix} 2 & x \\ y & 6 \\ 5 & z \end{bmatrix} = \begin{bmatrix} a & -1 \\ 4 & 6 \\ p & 7 \end{bmatrix}$

14. $\begin{bmatrix} 2m & 4 & 3z & -12 \end{bmatrix} = \begin{bmatrix} 12 & k+1 & -9 & r-3 \end{bmatrix}$

15. $\begin{bmatrix} a+5 & 3b & 6 \\ 4c & 2+d & -3 \\ -1 & 4p & q-1 \end{bmatrix} = \begin{bmatrix} -7 & b+2 & 2k-3 \\ 3 & 2d-1 & 4l \\ m & 12 & 8 \end{bmatrix}$

Given the matrices

$$A = \begin{bmatrix} 4 & 10 \\ -2 & -3 \\ 6 & 9 \end{bmatrix}, \quad B = \begin{bmatrix} 2 & 3 & -2 \\ 2 & 4 & 0 \\ 0 & 1 & 2 \end{bmatrix}, \quad C = \begin{bmatrix} 5 & 0 \\ -1 & 3 \\ 4 & 7 \end{bmatrix},$$

$$D = \begin{bmatrix} 6 \\ 1 \\ 0 \end{bmatrix}, \quad E = \begin{bmatrix} 1 & 3 & -4 \end{bmatrix}, \quad F = \begin{bmatrix} -1 & 4 \\ 3 & 7 \end{bmatrix}, \quad G = \begin{bmatrix} -2 & 0 \\ 1 & 5 \end{bmatrix},$$

find each of the following, if it exists.

16. $A + C$

17. $2G - 4F$

18. $3C + 2A$

19. $B - C$

20. $2A - 5C$

21. AG

22. AC

23. DE

24. ED

25. BD

26. EC

27. F^{-1}

28. B^{-1}

29. $(A + C)^{-1}$

Find the inverse of each matrix that has an inverse.

30. $\begin{bmatrix} 1 & 3 \\ 2 & 7 \end{bmatrix}$

31. $\begin{bmatrix} -4 & 2 \\ 0 & 3 \end{bmatrix}$

32. $\begin{bmatrix} 3 & -6 \\ -4 & 8 \end{bmatrix}$

33. $\begin{bmatrix} 6 & 4 \\ 3 & 2 \end{bmatrix}$

34. $\begin{bmatrix} 2 & -1 & 0 \\ 1 & 0 & 1 \\ 1 & -2 & 0 \end{bmatrix}$

35. $\begin{bmatrix} 2 & 0 & 4 \\ 1 & -1 & 0 \\ 0 & 1 & -2 \end{bmatrix}$

36. $\begin{bmatrix} 1 & 3 & 6 \\ 4 & 0 & 9 \\ 5 & 15 & 30 \end{bmatrix}$

37. $\begin{bmatrix} 2 & -3 & 4 \\ 1 & 5 & 7 \\ -4 & 6 & -8 \end{bmatrix}$

Solve the matrix equation $AX = B$ for X using the given matrices.

38. $A = \begin{bmatrix} 5 & 1 \\ -2 & -2 \end{bmatrix}$, $B = \begin{bmatrix} -8 \\ 24 \end{bmatrix}$

39. $A = \begin{bmatrix} 1 & 2 \\ 2 & 4 \end{bmatrix}$, $B = \begin{bmatrix} 5 \\ 10 \end{bmatrix}$

40. $A = \begin{bmatrix} 1 & 0 & 2 \\ -1 & 1 & 0 \\ 3 & 0 & 4 \end{bmatrix}$, $B = \begin{bmatrix} 8 \\ 4 \\ -6 \end{bmatrix}$

41. $A = \begin{bmatrix} 2 & 4 & 0 \\ 1 & -2 & 0 \\ 0 & 0 & 3 \end{bmatrix}$, $B = \begin{bmatrix} 72 \\ -24 \\ 48 \end{bmatrix}$

Solve each system of equations by inverses.

42. $x + 2y = 4$

    $2x - 3y = 1$

43. $5x + 10y = 80$

    $3x - 2y = 120$

44. $x + y + z = 1$

    $2x + y = -2$

    $3y + z = 2$

45. $x - 4y + 2z = -1$

    $-2x + y - 3z = -9$

    $3x + 5y - 2z = 7$

Find each production matrix, given the following input-output and demand matrices.

46. $A = \begin{bmatrix} 0.01 & 0.05 \\ 0.04 & 0.03 \end{bmatrix}$, $D = \begin{bmatrix} 200 \\ 300 \end{bmatrix}$

47. $A = \begin{bmatrix} 0.2 & 0.1 & 0.3 \\ 0.1 & 0 & 0.2 \\ 0 & 0 & 0.4 \end{bmatrix}$, $D = \begin{bmatrix} 500 \\ 200 \\ 100 \end{bmatrix}$

 48. The following system of equations is given.

$$x + 2y + z = 7$$
$$2x - y - z = 2$$
$$3x - 3y + 2z = -5$$

a. Solve by the echelon method.

b. Solve by the Gauss-Jordan method. Compare with the echelon method.

c. Write the system as a matrix equation, $AX = B$.

d. Find the inverse of matrix A from part c.

e. Solve the system using A^{-1} from part d.

▶ Applications

In Exercises 49–52, write a system of equations and solve.

49. *Scheduling Production* An office supply manufacturer makes two kinds of paper clips, standard and extra large. To make 1000 standard paper clips requires 1/4 hour on a cutting machine and 1/2 hour on a machine that shapes the clips. One thousand extra large paper clips require 1/3 hour on each machine. The manager of paper clip production has 4 hours per day available on the cutting machine and 6 hours per day on the shaping machine. How many of each kind of clip can he make?

50. *Production Requirements* The Waputi Indians make woven blankets, rugs, and skirts. Each blanket requires 24 hours for spinning the yarn, 4 hours for dyeing the yarn, and 15 hours for weaving. Rugs require 30, 5, and 18 hours and skirts 12, 3, and 9 hours, respectively. If there are 306, 59, and 201 hours available for spinning, dyeing, and weaving, respectively, how many of each item can be made? (*Hint:* Simplify the equations you write, if possible, before solving the system.)

51. *Distribution* An oil refinery in Tulsa sells 50% of its production to a Chicago distributor, 20% to a Dallas distributor, and 30% to an Atlanta distributor. Another refinery in New Orleans sells 40% of its production to the Chicago distributor, 40% to the Dallas distributor, and 20% to the Atlanta distributor. A third refinery in Ardmore sells the same distributors 30%, 40%, and 30% of its production. The three distributors received 219,000, 192,000, and 144,000 gal of oil, respectively. How many gallons of oil were produced at each of the three plants?

52. *Stock Reports* The New York Stock Exchange reports in daily newspapers give the dividend, price-to-earnings ratio, sales (in hundreds of shares), last price, and change in price for each company. Write the following stock reports as a 4 × 5 matrix: American Telephone & Telegraph: 1.33, 17.6, 152,000, 26.75, +1.88; General Electric: 1.00, 20.0, 238,200, 32.36, −1.50; Sara Lee: 0.79, 25.4, 39,110, 16.51, −0.89; Walt Disney Company: 0.27, 21.2, 122,500, 28.60, +0.75.

53. *Filling Orders* A printer has three orders for pamphlets that require three kinds of paper, as shown in the following matrix.

	Order		
	I	II	III
High-grade	10	5	8
Paper Medium-grade	12	0	4
Coated	0	10	5

The printer has on hand 3170 sheets of high-grade paper, 2360 sheets of medium-grade paper, and 1800 sheets of coated paper. All the paper must be used in preparing the order.

a. Write a 3 × 1 matrix for the amounts of paper on hand.

b. Write a matrix of variables to represent the number of pamphlets that must be printed in each of the three orders.

c. Write a matrix equation using the given matrix and your matrices from parts a and b.

d. Solve the equation from part c.

54. *Input-Output* An economy depends on two commodities, goats and cheese. It takes 2/3 of a unit of goats to produce 1 unit of cheese and 1/2 unit of cheese to produce 1 unit of goats.

a. Write the input-output matrix for this economy.

b. Find the production required to satisfy a demand of 400 units of cheese and 800 units of goats.

55. *Nebraska* The 1970 economy of the state of Nebraska has been condensed to six sectors: livestock, crops, food products, mining and manufacturing, households, and other. The input-output matrix is given below.[*]

$$\begin{bmatrix} 0.178 & 0.018 & 0.411 & 0 & 0.005 & 0 \\ 0.143 & 0.018 & 0.088 & 0 & 0.001 & 0 \\ 0.089 & 0 & 0.035 & 0 & 0.060 & 0.003 \\ 0.001 & 0.010 & 0.012 & 0.063 & 0.007 & 0.014 \\ 0.141 & 0.252 & 0.088 & 0.089 & 0.402 & 0.124 \\ 0.188 & 0.156 & 0.103 & 0.255 & 0.008 & 0.474 \end{bmatrix}$$

a. Find the matrix $(I - A)^{-1}$ and interpret the value in row 2, column 1 of this matrix.

b. Suppose the demand (in millions of dollars) is

$$D = \begin{bmatrix} 1980 \\ 650 \\ 1750 \\ 1000 \\ 2500 \\ 3750 \end{bmatrix}.$$

Find the dollar amount of each commodity that should be produced.

*Lamphear, F. Charles and Theodore Roesler, "1970 Nebraska Input-Output Tables," Nebraska Economic and Business Report No. 10, Bureau of Business Research, University of Nebraska-Lincoln, 1971.

LIFE SCIENCES

56. *Animal Activity* The activities of a grazing animal can be classified roughly into three categories: grazing, moving, and resting. Suppose horses spend 8 hours grazing, 8 moving, and 8 resting; cattle spend 10 grazing, 5 moving, and 9 resting; sheep spend 7 grazing, 10 moving, and 7 resting; and goats spend 8 grazing, 9 moving, and 7 resting. Write this information as a 4×3 matrix.

57. *CAT Scans* Computer Aided Tomography (CAT) scanners take X-rays of a part of the body from different directions, and put the information together to create a picture of a cross section of the body.* The amount by which the energy of the X-ray decreases, measured in linear-attenuation units, tells whether the X-ray has passed through healthy tissue, tumorous tissue, or bone, based on the following table.

Type of Tissue	Linear-Attenuation Values
Healthy tissue	0.1625–0.2977
Tumorous tissue	0.2679–0.3930
Bone	0.3857–0.5108

The part of the body to be scanned is divided into cells. If an X-ray passes through more than one cell, the total linear-attenuation value is the sum of the values for the cells. For example, in the figure, let a, b, and c be the values for cells A, B, and C. The attenuation value for beam 1 is $a + b$ and for beam 2 is $a + c$.

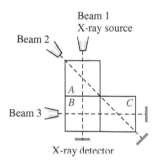

Beam 1
X-ray source

Beam 2

Beam 3

X-ray detector

a. Find the attenuation value for beam 3.

b. Suppose that the attenuation values are 0.8, 0.55, and 0.65 for beams 1, 2, and 3, respectively. Set up and solve the system of three equations for a, b, and c. What can you conclude about cells A, B, and C?

c. Find the inverse of the coefficient matrix from part b to find a, b, and c for the following three cases, and make conclusions about cells A, B, and C for each.

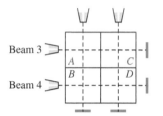

Patient	Linear-Attenuation Values		
	Beam 1	**Beam 2**	**Beam 3**
X	0.54	0.40	0.52
Y	0.65	0.80	0.75
Z	0.51	0.49	0.44

58. *CAT Scans* (Refer to Exercise 57.)* Four X-ray beams are aimed at four cells, as shown in the following figure.

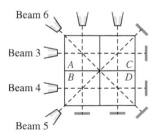

Beam 1 Beam 2

Beam 3

Beam 4

a. Suppose the attenuation values for beams 1, 2, 3, and 4 are 0.60, 0.75, 0.65, and 0.70, respectively. Do we have enough information to determine the values of a, b, c, and d? Explain.

b. Suppose we have the data from part a, as well as the following values for d. Find the values for a, b, and c, and draw conclusions about cells A, B, C, and D in each case.

(i) 0.33 **(ii)** 0.43

c. Two X-ray beams are added, as shown in the figure. In addition to the data in part a, we now have attenuation values for beams 5 and 6 of 0.85 and 0.50. Find the values for a, b, c, and d, and make conclusions about cells A, B, C, and D.

Beam 1 Beam 2

Beam 6

Beam 3

Beam 4

Beam 5

*Exercises 57 and 58 are based on the article "Medical Applications of Linear Equations" by David Jabon, Gail Nord, Bryce W. Wilson, and Penny Coffman, *The Mathematics Teacher*, Vol. 89, No. 5, May 1996, p. 398.

d. Six X-ray beams are not necessary because four appropriately chosen beams are sufficient. Give two examples of four beams (chosen from beams 1–6 in part c) that will give the solution. (*Note:* There are 12 possible solutions.)

e. Discuss what properties the four beams selected in part d must have in order to provide a unique solution.

59. *Hockey* In a recent study, the number of head and neck injuries among hockey players wearing full face shields and half face shields were compared. The following table provides the rates per 1000 athlete-exposures for specific injuries that caused a player wearing either shield to miss one or more events.*

	Half Shield	**Full Shield**
Head and Face Injuries (Excluding Concussions)	3.54	1.41
Concussions	1.53	1.57
Neck Injuries	0.34	0.29
Other	7.53	6.21

If an equal number of players in a large league wear each type of shield and the total number of athlete-exposures for the league in a season is 8000, use matrix operations to estimate the total number of injuries of each type.

PHYSICAL SCIENCES

60. *Roof Trusses* Linear systems occur in the design of roof trusses for new homes and buildings. The simplest type of roof truss is a triangle. The truss shown in the figure below is used to frame roofs of small buildings. If a 100-lb force is applied at the peak of the truss, then the forces or weights W_1 and W_2 exerted parallel to each rafter of the truss are determined by the following linear system of equations.

$$\frac{\sqrt{3}}{2}(W_1 + W_2) = 100$$

$$W_1 - W_2 = 0$$

Solve the system to find W_1 and W_2.[†]

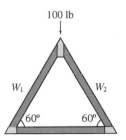

61. *Roof Trusses* (Refer to Exercise 60.) Use the following system of equations to determine the force or weights W_1 and W_2 exerted on each rafter for the truss shown in the figure.

$$\frac{1}{2}W_1 + \frac{\sqrt{2}}{2}W_2 = 150$$

$$\frac{\sqrt{3}}{2}W_1 - \frac{\sqrt{2}}{2}W_2 = 0$$

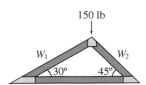

---

*Benson, Brian, Nicholas Nohtadi, Sarah Rose, and Willem Meeuwisse, "Head and Neck Injuries Among Ice Hockey Players Wearing Full Face Shields vs. Half Face Shields," *JAMA*, Vol. 282, No. 24, Dec. 22/29, 1999, pp. 2328–2332.
[†]Hibbeler, R., *Structural Analysis,* Prentice-Hall, 1995.

62. *Carbon Dioxide* Determining the amount of carbon dioxide in the atmosphere is important because carbon dioxide is known to be a greenhouse gas. Carbon dioxide concentrations (in parts per million) have been measured at Mauna Loa, Hawaii, for more than 40 years. The concentrations have increased quadratically.* The table lists readings for 3 years.

Year	CO_2
1960	317
1980	339
2004	377

a. If the relationship between the carbon dioxide concentration C and the year t is expressed as $C = at^2 + bt + c$, where $t = 0$ corresponds to 1960, use a linear system of equations to determine the constants a, b, and c.

b. Predict the year when the amount of carbon dioxide in the atmosphere will double from its 1960 level. (*Hint:* This requires solving a quadratic equation.)

63. *Chemistry* When carbon monoxide (CO) reacts with oxygen (O_2), carbon dioxide (CO_2) is formed. This can be written as $CO + (1/2)O_2 = CO_2$ and as a matrix equation.[†] If we form a 2×1 column matrix by letting the first element be the number of carbon atoms and the second element be the number of oxygen atoms, then CO would have the column matrix

$$\begin{bmatrix} 1 \\ 1 \end{bmatrix}.$$

Similarly, O_2 and CO_2 would have the column matrices $\begin{bmatrix} 0 \\ 2 \end{bmatrix}$ and $\begin{bmatrix} 1 \\ 2 \end{bmatrix}$, respectively.

a. Use the Gauss-Jordan method to find numbers x and y (known as *stoichiometric numbers*) that solve the system of equations

$$\begin{bmatrix} 1 \\ 1 \end{bmatrix} x + \begin{bmatrix} 0 \\ 2 \end{bmatrix} y = \begin{bmatrix} 1 \\ 2 \end{bmatrix}.$$

Compare your answers to the equation written above.

b. Repeat the process for $xCO_2 + yH_2 + zCO = H_2O$, where H_2 is hydrogen, and H_2O is water. In words, what does this mean?

GENERAL INTEREST

64. *Students* Suppose 20% of the boys and 30% of the girls in a high school like tennis, and 60% of the boys and 90% of the girls like math. If 500 students like tennis and 1500 like math, how many boys and girls are in the school? Find all possible solutions.

65. *Baseball* In the 2004 Major League Baseball season, slugger Barry Bonds had a total of 135 hits. Bonds hit 15 times as many home runs as triples, and he hit 50% more home runs than doubles and triples. He also hit twice as many singles as doubles and triples.[‡] Find the number of singles, doubles, triples, and home runs that Bonds hit during the season.

66. *Cookies* Regular Nabisco Oreo cookies are made of two chocolate cookie wafers surrounding a single layer of vanilla cream. The claim on the package states that a single serving is 34 g, which is three cookies. Nabisco Double Stuf cookies are made of the same two chocolate cookie wafers surrounding a double layer of vanilla cream. The claim on this package states that a single serving is 29 g, which is two Double Stuf cookies. If the Double Stuf cookies truly have a double layer of vanilla cream, find the weight of a single chocolate wafer and the weight of a single layer of vanilla cream.

---

*Atmospheric Carbon Dioxide Record from Mauna Loa, University of California, La Jolla, http://cdiac.esd.ornl.gov/ftp/trends/co2/maunaloa.co2.
[†] Alberty, Robert, "Chemical Equations Are Actually Matrix Equations," *Journal of Chemical Education*, Vol. 68, No. 12, Dec. 1991, p. 984.
[‡] http://www.baseball-reference.com.

Contagion

Suppose that three people have contracted a contagious disease.* A second group of five people may have been in contact with the three infected persons. A third group of six people may have been in contact with the second group. We can form a 3×5 matrix P with rows representing the first group of three and columns representing the second group of five. We enter a one in the corresponding position if a person in the first group has contact with a person in the second group. These direct contacts are called *first-order contacts*. Similarly, we form a 5×6 matrix Q representing the first-order contacts between the second and third group. For example, suppose

$$P = \begin{bmatrix} 1 & 0 & 0 & 1 & 0 \\ 0 & 0 & 1 & 1 & 0 \\ 1 & 1 & 0 & 0 & 0 \end{bmatrix} \text{ and}$$

$$Q = \begin{bmatrix} 1 & 1 & 0 & 1 & 1 & 1 \\ 0 & 0 & 0 & 0 & 1 & 0 \\ 0 & 0 & 0 & 0 & 0 & 0 \\ 0 & 1 & 0 & 1 & 0 & 0 \\ 1 & 0 & 0 & 0 & 1 & 0 \end{bmatrix}.$$

From matrix P we see that the first person in the first group had contact with the first and fourth persons in the second group. Also, none of the first group had contact with the last person in the second group.

A *second-order contact* is an indirect contact between persons in the first and third groups through some person in the second group. The product matrix PQ indicates these contacts. Verify that the second-row, fourth-column entry of PQ is 1. That is, there is one second-order contact between the second person in group one and the fourth person in group three. Let a_{ij} denote the element in the ith row and jth column of the matrix PQ. By looking at the products that form a_{24} below, we see that the common contact was with the fourth individual in group two. (The p_{ij} are entries in P, and the q_{ij} are entries in Q.)

$$a_{24} = p_{21}q_{14} + p_{22}q_{24} + p_{23}q_{34} + p_{24}q_{44} + p_{25}q_{54}$$
$$= 0 \cdot 1 + 0 \cdot 0 + 1 \cdot 0 + 1 \cdot 1 + 0 \cdot 0$$
$$= 1$$

The second person in group 1 and the fourth person in group 3 both had contact with the fourth person in group 2.

This idea could be extended to third-, fourth-, and larger-order contacts. It indicates a way to use matrices to trace the spread of a contagious disease. It could also pertain to the dispersal of ideas or anything that might pass from one individual to another.

EXERCISES

1. Find the second-order contact matrix PQ mentioned in the text.

2. How many second-order contacts were there between the second contagious person and the third person in the third group?

3. Is there anyone in the third group who has had no contacts at all with the first group?

4. The totals of the columns in PQ give the total number of second-order contacts per person, while the column totals in P and Q give the total number of first-order contacts per person. Which person(s) in the third group had the most contacts, counting first- and second-order contacts?

DIRECTIONS FOR GROUP PROJECT

Assume that your group (3–5 students) is trying to map the spread of a new disease. Suppose also that the information given above has been obtained from interviews with the first three people that were hospitalized with symptoms of the disease and their contacts. Using the questions above as a guide, prepare a presentation for a public meeting that describes the method of obtaining the data, the data itself, and addresses the spirit of each question. Formulate a strategy for how to handle the spread of this disease to other people. The presentation should be mathematically sound, grammatically correct, and professionally crafted. Use presentation software, such as Microsoft PowerPoint, to present your findings.

---

*Grossman, Stanley, "First and Second Order Contact to a Contagious Disease." *Finite Mathematics with Applications to Business, Life Sciences, and Social Sciences*, WCB/McGraw-Hill, 1993.

3

Linear Programming:
The Graphical
Method

▶ An oil refinery turns crude oil into many different products, including gasoline and fuel oil. Efficient management requires matching the output of each product to the demand and the available shipping capacity. In an exercise in Section 3, we explore the use of linear programming to allocate refinery production for maximum profit.

Many realistic problems involve inequalities—a factory can manufacture *no more* than 12 items on a shift, or a medical researcher must interview *at least* a hundred patients to be sure that a new treatment for a disease is better than the old treatment. *Linear inequalities* of the form $ax + by \leq c$ (or with $\geq$, $<$, or $>$ instead of $\leq$) can be used in a process called *linear programming* to *optimize* (find the maximum or minimum value of a quantity) for a given situation.

In this chapter we introduce some *linear programming* problems that can be solved by graphical methods. Then, in Chapter 4, we discuss the simplex method, a general method for solving linear programming problems with many variables.

3.1 Graphing Linear Inequalities

? THINK ABOUT IT

How can a company determine the feasible number of units of each product to manufacture in order to meet all production requirements?

We can answer this question by graphing a set of inequalities.

As mentioned above, a linear inequality is defined as follows.

LINEAR INEQUALITY

A **linear inequality** in two variables has the form

$$ax + by \leq c$$
$$ax + by < c,$$
$$ax + by \geq c,$$

or $\quad ax + by > c,$

for real numbers a, b, and c, with a and b not both 0.

EXAMPLE 1

Graphing an Inequality

Graph the linear inequality $2x - 3y \leq 12$.

▶Solution   Because of the "=" portion of $\leq$, the points of the line $2x - 3y = 12$ satisfy the linear inequality $2x - 3y \leq 12$ and are part of its graph. As in Chapter 1, find the intercepts by first letting $x = 0$ and then letting $y = 0$; use these points to get the graph of $2x - 3y = 12$ shown in Figure 1.

▶FOR REVIEW

Recall from Chapter 1 that one way to sketch a line is to first let $x = 0$ to find the y-intercept, then let $y = 0$ to find the x-intercept. For example, given $2x - 3y = 12$, letting $x = 0$ yields $-3y = 12$, so $y = -4$, and the corresponding point is $(0, -4)$. Letting $y = 0$ yields $2x = 12$, so $x = 6$ and the point is $(6, 0)$. Plot these two points, as in Figure 1, then use a straightedge to draw a line through them.

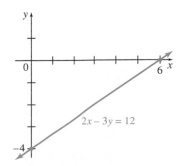

FIGURE 1

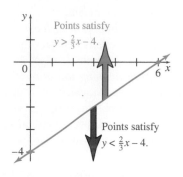

FIGURE 2

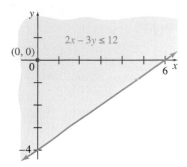

FIGURE 3

The points on the line satisfy "$2x - 3y$ *equals* 12." To locate the points satisfying "$2x - 3y$ *is less than* or equal to 12," first solve $2x - 3y \leq 12$ for y.

$$2x - 3y \leq 12$$
$$-3y \leq -2x + 12 \qquad \text{Subtract } 2x.$$
$$y \geq \frac{2}{3}x - 4 \qquad \text{Multiply by } -\frac{1}{3}.$$

(Recall that multiplying both sides of an inequality by a negative number reverses the direction of the inequality symbol.)

As shown in Figure 2, the points *above* the line $2x - 3y = 12$ satisfy

$$y > \frac{2}{3}x - 4,$$

while those below the line satisfy

$$y < \frac{2}{3}x - 4.$$

In summary, the inequality $2x - 3y \leq 12$ is satisfied by all points *on or above* the line $2x - 3y = 12$. Indicate the points above the line by shading, as in Figure 3. The line and shaded region in Figure 3 make up the graph of the linear inequality $2x - 3y \leq 12$.

CAUTION   In this chapter, be sure to use a straightedge to draw lines, and to plot the points with care. A sloppily drawn line could give a deceptive picture of the region being considered.   ■

In Example 1, the line $2x - 3y = 12$, which separates the points in the solution from the points that are not in the solution, is called the **boundary**.

There is an alternative way to find the correct region to shade, or to check the method shown above. Choose as a test point any point not on the boundary line. For example, in Example 1 we could choose the point $(0, 0)$, which is not on the line $2x - 3y = 12$. Substitute 0 for x and 0 for y in the given inequality.

$$2x - 3y \leq 12$$
$$2(0) - 3(0) \leq 12$$
$$0 \leq 12 \qquad \text{True}$$

Since the result $0 \leq 12$ is true, the test point $(0, 0)$ belongs on the side of the boundary where all points satisfy $2x - 3y < 12$. For this reason, we shade the side containing $(0, 0)$, as in Figure 3. Choosing a point on the other side of the line, such as $(4, -3)$, would produce a false result when the values $x = 4$ and $y = -3$ were substituted into the given inequality. In such a case, we would shade the side of the line *not including* the test point.

EXAMPLE 2   **Graphing an Inequality**
Graph $x - 4y > 4$.

▶**Solution**   The boundary here is the line $x - 4y = 4$. Since the points on this line do not satisfy $x - 4y > 4$, the line is drawn dashed, as in Figure 4. To

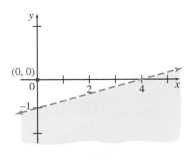

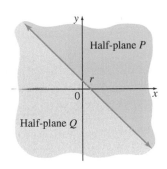

FIGURE 4

decide whether to shade the region above the line or the region below the line, we will choose a test point not on the boundary line. Choosing $(0, 0)$, we replace x with 0 and y with 0:

$$x - 4y > 4$$
$$0 - 4(0) > 4$$
$$0 > 4. \quad \text{False}$$

The correct half-plane is the one that does *not* contain $(0, 0)$; the region below the boundary line is shaded, as shown in Figure 4.

> **CAUTION** Be careful. If the point $(0, 0)$ is on the boundary line, it cannot be used as a test point. ∎

As the examples above suggest, the graph of a linear inequality is represented by a shaded region in the plane, perhaps including the line that is the boundary of the region. Each shaded region is an example of a **half-plane**, a region on one side of a line. For example, in Figure 5 line r divides the plane into half-planes P and Q. The points on r belong neither to P nor to Q. Line r is the boundary of each half-plane.

Graphing calculators can shade regions on the plane. Casio has an inequality mode that offers options for $y >$, $y <$, $y \geq$, or $y \leq$. Refer to your instruction book for details.

TI calculators have a DRAW menu that includes an option to shade above or below a line. For instance, to graph the inequality in Example 2, first solve the equation for y, then use your calculator to graph the line $y = (1/4)x - 1$. Select the DRAW feature, then the Shade option, which requires an upper and a lower boundary for the region to be shaded. To match Figure 5, choose for the lower boundary a horizontal line that lies below the bottom of the graphing calculator screen. We will use a standard window with $-10 \leq y \leq 10$, and so we let $y = -20$ be the lower boundary. For the upper boundary, use $y = (1/4)x - 1$. Then the command Shade(-20, (1/4)X - 1) produces Figure 6(a).

The TI-83/84 Plus calculator offers another way to graph the region above or below a line. Press the y= key. Note the slanted line to the right of Y_1, Y_2, and so on. Use the left arrow key to move the cursor to that position for Y_1. Press ENTER until you see the symbol ◤. This indicates that the calculator will shade below the line whose equation is entered in Y_1. (The symbol ◥ operates similarly to shade above a line.) We used this method to get the graph in Figure 6(b).

FIGURE 5

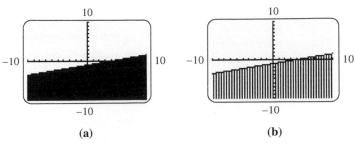

(a)   **(b)**

FIGURE 6

Notice that you cannot tell from the calculator graph whether the boundary line is solid or dashed. It is important to understand the concepts in order to interpret the graph correctly. In this case, the points on the line are not part of the solution, because of the strict inequality, $<$.

See *The Spreadsheet Manual* available with this book for information on graphing linear inequalities with a spreadsheet.

The steps in graphing a linear inequality are summarized below.

GRAPHING A LINEAR INEQUALITY

1. Draw the graph of the boundary line. Make the line solid if the inequality involves $\leq$ or $\geq$; make the line dashed if the inequality involves $<$ or $>$.
2. Decide which half-plane to shade. Use either of the following methods.

   a. Solve the inequality for y; shade the region above the line if the inequality is of the form $y >$ or $y \geq$; shade the region below the line if the inequality is of the form $y <$ or $y \leq$.

   b. Choose any point not on the line as a test point. Shade the half-plane that includes the test point if the test point satisfies the original inequality; otherwise, shade the half-plane on the other side of the boundary line.

Systems of Inequalities   Realistic problems often involve many inequalities. For example, a manufacturing problem might produce inequalities resulting from production requirements as well as inequalities about cost requirements. A collection of at least two inequalities is called a **system of inequalities**. The solution of a system of inequalities is made up of all those points that satisfy all the inequalities of the system at the same time. To graph the solution of a system of inequalities, graph all the inequalities on the same axes and identify, by heavy shading, the region common to all graphs. The next example shows how this is done.

NOTE   When shading regions by hand, it may be difficult to tell what is shaded heavily and what is shaded only lightly, particularly when more than two inequalities are involved. In such cases, an alternative technique is to shade the region *opposite* that of the inequality. In other words, the region that is *not* wanted can be shaded. Then, when the various regions are shaded, whatever is not shaded is the desired region. We will not use this technique in this text, but you may wish to try it on your own.

EXAMPLE 3   Graphing a System of Inequalities
Graph the system

$$y < -3x + 12$$
$$x < 2y.$$

▶**Solution**   The graph of the first inequality has the line $y = -3x + 12$ as its boundary. Because of the $<$ symbol, we use a dotted line and shade *below* the line. The second inequality should first be solved for y to get $y > (1/2)x$ to see that the graph is the region *above* the dotted boundary line $y = (1/2)x$.

The heavily shaded region in Figure 7(a) shows all the points that satisfy both inequalities of the system. Since the points on the boundary lines are not in the solution, the boundary lines are dashed.

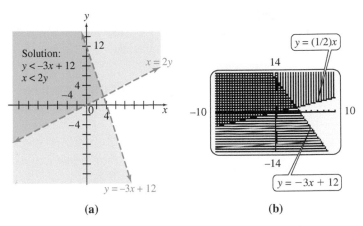

FIGURE 7

A calculator graph of the system in Example 3 is shown in Figure 7(b). You can also graph this system on your calculator using Shade(Y_2, Y_1).

A region consisting of the overlapping parts of two or more graphs of inequalities in a system, such as the heavily shaded region in Figure 7, is sometimes called the **region of feasible solutions** or the **feasible region**, since it is made up of all the points that satisfy (are feasible for) all inequalities of the system.

EXAMPLE 4 | **Graphing a Feasible Region**

Graph the feasible region for the system

$$y \leq -2x + 8$$
$$-2 \leq x \leq 1.$$

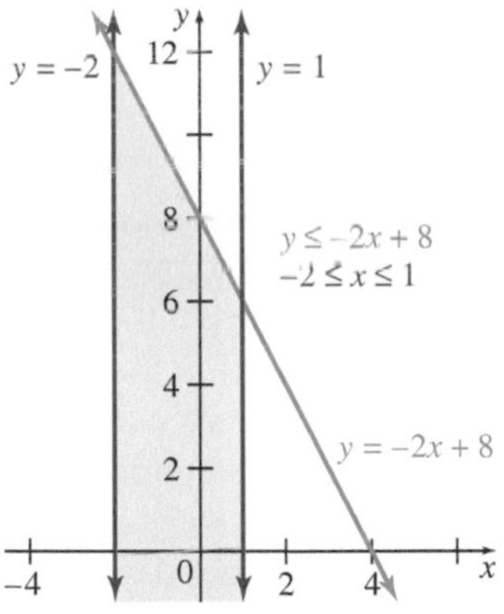

▶**Solution** The boundary line of the first inequality is $y = -2x + 8$. Because of the $\leq$ symbol, we use a solid line and shade *below* the line.

The second inequality is a compound inequality, indicating $-2 \leq x$ *and* $x \leq 1$. Recall that the graph $x = -2$ is the vertical line through $(-2, 0)$, and the graph $x = 1$ is the vertical line through $(1, 0)$. For $-2 \leq x$ we draw a vertical line and shade the region to the right. For $x \leq 1$, we draw a vertical line and shade the region to the left.

The shaded region in Figure 8 shows all the points that satisfy the system of inequalities.

FIGURE 8

EXAMPLE 5 | **Graphing a Feasible Region**

Graph the feasible region for the system

$$2x - 5y \leq 10$$
$$x + 2y \leq 8$$
$$x \geq 0$$
$$y \geq 0.$$

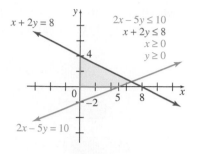

$x + 2y = 8$

$2x - 5y = 10$

$$\begin{array}{l} 2x - 5y \leq 10 \\ x + 2y \leq 8 \\ x \geq 0 \\ y \geq 0 \end{array}$$

FIGURE 9

▶**Solution** On the same axes, graph each inequality by graphing the boundary and choosing the appropriate half-plane. Then find the feasible region by locating the overlap of all the half-planes. This feasible region is shaded in Figure 9.

NOTE   The inequalities $x \geq 0$ and $y \geq 0$ restrict the feasible region to the first quadrant.

Applications   As shown in the rest of this chapter, many realistic problems lead to systems of linear inequalities. The next example is typical of such problems.

EXAMPLE 6   Manufacturing

Happy Ice Cream Cone Company makes cake cones and sugar cones, both of which must be processed in the mixing department and the baking department. Manufacturing one batch of cake cones requires 1 hour in the mixing department and 2 hours in the baking department, and producing one batch of sugar cones requires 2 hours in the mixing department and 1 hour in the baking department. Each department is operated for at most 12 hours per day.

   (a) Write a system of inequalities that expresses these restrictions.

▶**Solution** Let x represent the number of batches of cake cones made and y represent the number of batches of sugar cones made. Then, make a table that summarizes the given information.

	Cake	Sugar		Total
Number of Units Made	x	y		
Hours in Mixing Dept.	1	2	$\leq$	12
Hours in Baking Dept.	2	1	$\leq$	12

Since the departments operate at most 12 hours per day, we put the total number of hours as ≤ 12. Putting the inequality ($\leq$ or $\geq$) next to the number in the chart may help you remember which way to write the inequality.

In the mixing department, x batches of cake cones require a total of $1 \cdot x = x$ hours, and y batches of sugar cones require $2 \cdot y = 2y$ hours. Since the mixing department can operate no more than 12 hours per day,

$$x + 2y \leq 12. \quad \text{Mixing department}$$

We translated "no more than" as "less than or equal to." Notice how this inequality corresponds to the row in the table for the mixing department. Similarly, the row corresponding to the baking department gives

$$2x + y \leq 12. \quad \text{Baking department}$$

Since it is not possible to produce a negative number of cake cones or sugar cones,

$$x \geq 0 \quad \text{and} \quad y \geq 0.$$

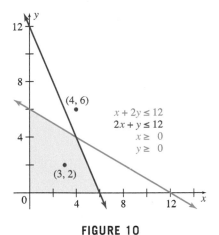

FIGURE 10

The inequalities shown on the graph:
$x + 2y \leq 12$
$2x + y \leq 12$
$x \geq 0$
$y \geq 0$

(b) Graph the feasible region.

▶**Solution** The feasible region for this system of inequalities is shown in Figure 10.

(c) Using the graph from part (b), can 3 batches of cake cones and 2 batches of sugar cones be manufactured in one day? Can 4 batches of cake cones and 6 batches of sugar cones be manufactured in one day?

▶**Solution** Three batches of cake cones and two batches of sugar cones correspond to the point $(3, 2)$. Since $(3, 2)$ is in the feasible region in Figure 10, it is possible to manufacture these quantities in one day. However, since $(4, 6)$ is *not* in the feasible region in Figure 10, it is *not* possible to manufacture 4 batches of cake cones and 6 batches of sugar cones in one day.

The following steps summarize the process of finding the feasible region.

1. Form a table that summarizes the information.

2. Convert the table into a set of linear inequalities.

3. Graph each linear inequality.

4. Graph the region that is common to all the regions graphed in step 3.

▶ 3.1 Exercises

Graph each linear inequality.

1. $x + y \leq 2$

2. $y \leq x + 1$

3. $x \geq 2 - y$

4. $y > x - 3$

5. $4x - y < 6$

6. $4y + x > 6$

7. $4x + y < 8$

8. $2x - y > 2$

9. $x + 3y \geq -2$

10. $2x + 3y \leq 6$

11. $x \leq 3y$

12. $2x \geq y$

13. $x + y \leq 0$

14. $3x + 2y \geq 0$

15. $y < x$

16. $y > 5x$

17. $x < 4$

18. $y > 5$

19. $y \leq -2$

20. $x \geq -4$

Graph the feasible region for each system of inequalities.

21. $x + y \leq 1$
$x - y \geq 2$

22. $4x - y < 6$
$3x + y < 9$

23. $x + 3y \leq 6$
$2x + 4y \geq 7$

24. $-x - y < 5$
$2x - y < 4$

25. $x + y \leq 7$
$x - y \leq -4$
$4x + y \geq 0$

26. $3x - 2y \geq 6$
$x + y \leq -5$
$y \leq 4$

27. $-2 < x < 3$
$-1 \leq y \leq 5$
$2x + y < 6$

28. $1 < x < 4$
$y > 2$
$x > y$

29. $y - 2x \leq 4$
$y \geq 2 - x$
$x \geq 0$
$y \geq 0$

30. $2x + 3y \leq 12$
$2x + 3y > -6$
$3x + y < 4$
$x \geq 0$
$y \geq 0$

31. $3x + 4y > 12$
$2x - 3y < 6$
$0 \leq y \leq 2$
$x \geq 0$

32. $0 \leq x \leq 9$
$x - 2y \geq 4$
$3x + 5y \leq 30$
$y \geq 0$

Use a graphing calculator to graph the following.

33. $2x - 6y > 12$

34. $4x - 3y < 12$

35. $3x - 4y < 6$
$2x + 5y > 15$

36. $6x - 4y > 8$
$2x + 5y < 5$

37. The regions A through G in the figure can be described by the inequalities

$$x + 3y \; ? \; 6$$

$$x + y \; ? \; 3$$

$$x - 2y \; ? \; 2$$

$$x \geq 0$$

$$y \geq 0,$$

where ? can be either $\leq$ or $\geq$. For each region, tell what the ? should be in the three inequalities. For example, for region A, the ? should be $\geq$, $\leq$, and $\leq$, because region A is described by the inequalities

$$x + 3y \geq 6$$

$$x + y \leq 3$$

$$x - 2y \leq 2$$

$$x \geq 0$$

$$y \geq 0.$$

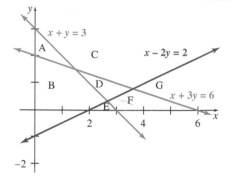

▶ Applications

BUSINESS AND ECONOMICS

38. *Production Scheduling* A small pottery shop makes two kinds of planters, glazed and unglazed. The glazed type requires 1/2 hour to throw on the wheel and 1 hour in the kiln. The unglazed type takes 1 hour to throw on the wheel and 6 hours in the kiln. The wheel is available for at most 8 hours per day, and the kiln for at most 20 hours per day.

a. Complete the following table.

	Glazed	Unglazed	Total
Number Made	*x*	*y*	
Time on Wheel			
Time in Kiln			

b. Set up a system of inequalities and graph the feasible region.

c. Using your graph from part b, can 5 glazed and 2 unglazed planters be made? Can 10 glazed and 2 unglazed planters be made?

39. *Time Management* Carmella and Walt produce handmade shawls and afghans. They spin the yarn, dye it, and then weave it. A shawl requires 1 hour of spinning, 1 hour of dyeing, and 1 hour of weaving. An afghan needs 2 hours of spinning, 1 hour of dyeing, and 4 hours of weaving. Together, they spend at most 8 hours spinning, 6 hours dyeing, and 14 hours weaving.

a. Complete the following table.

	Shawls	Afghans	Total
Number Made	*x*	*y*	
Spinning Time			
Dyeing Time			
Weaving Time			

b. Set up a system of inequalities and graph the feasible region.

c. Using your graph from part b, can 3 shawls and 2 afghans be made? Can 4 shawls and 3 afghans be made?

For Exercises 40–45, perform the following steps.

    a. *Write a system of inequalities to express the conditions of the problem.*

    b. *Graph the feasible region of the system.*

40. *Transportation* Southwestern Oil supplies two distributors located in the Northwest. One distributor needs at least 3000 barrels of oil, and the other needs at least 5000 barrels. Southwestern can send out at most 10,000 barrels. Let x = the number of barrels of oil sent to distributor 1 and y = the number sent to distributor 2.

41. *Finance* The loan department in a bank will use at most $30 million for commercial and home loans. The bank's policy is to allocate at least four times as much money to home loans as to commercial loans. The bank's return is 6% on a home loan and 8% on a commercial loan. The manager of the loan department wants to earn a return of at least $1.6 million on these loans. Let x = the amount (in millions) for home loans and y = the amount (in millions) for commercial loans.

42. *Transportation* The California Almond Growers have at most 2400 boxes of almonds to be shipped from their plant in Sacramento to Des Moines and San Antonio. The Des Moines market needs at least 1000 boxes, while the San Antonio market must have at least 800 boxes. Let x = the number of boxes to be shipped to Des Moines and y = the number of boxes to be shipped to San Antonio.

43. *Management* The Gillette Company produces two popular battery-operated razors, the M3Power™ and the Fusion Power™. Because of demand, the number of M3Power™ razors is never more than one-half the number of Fusion Power™ razors. The factory's production cannot exceed 800 razors per day. Let x = the number of M3Power™ razors and y = the number of Fusion Power™ razors produced per day.

44. *Production Scheduling* A cement manufacturer produces at least 3.2 million barrels of cement annually. He is told by the Environmental Protection Agency (EPA) that his operation emits 2.5 lb of dust for each barrel produced. The EPA has ruled that annual emissions must be reduced to no more than 1.8 million lb. To do this, the manufacturer plans to replace the present dust collectors with two types of electronic precipitators. One type would reduce emissions to 0.5 lb per barrel and operating costs would be 16¢ per barrel. The other would reduce the dust to 0.3 lb per barrel and operating costs would be 20¢ per barrel. The manufacturer does not want to spend more than 0.8 million dollars in operating costs on the precipitators. He needs to know how many barrels he could produce with each type. Let x = the number of barrels (in millions) produced with the first type and y = the number of barrels (in millions) produced with the second type.

LIFE SCIENCES

45. *Nutrition* A dietician is planning a snack package of fruit and nuts. Each ounce of fruit will supply 1 unit of protein, 2 units of carbohydrates, and 1 unit of fat. Each ounce of nuts will supply 1 unit of protein, 1 unit of carbohydrates, and 1 unit of fat. Every package must provide at least 7 units of protein, at least 10 units of carbohydrates, and no more than 9 units of fat. Let x = the ounces of fruit and y = the ounces of nuts to be used in each package.

3.2 Solving Linear Programming Problems Graphically

Many mathematical models designed to solve problems in business, biology, and economics involve finding an optimum value (maximum or minimum) of a function, subject to certain restrictions. In a **linear programming** problem, we must find the maximum or minimum value of a function, called the **objective function**, and also satisfy a set of restrictions, or **constraints**, given by linear inequalities. When only two variables are involved, the solution to a linear programming problem can be found by first graphing the set of constraints, then finding the feasible region as discussed in the previous section. This method is explained in the following example.

Maximization

Find the maximum value of the objective function $z = 3x + 4y$, subject to the following constraints.

$$2x + y \leq 4$$
$$-x + 2y \leq 4$$
$$x \geq 0$$
$$y \geq 0$$

▶**Solution** The feasible region is graphed in Figure 11. We can find the coordinates of point A, $(4/5, 12/5)$, by solving the system

$$2x + y = 4$$
$$-x + 2y = 4.$$

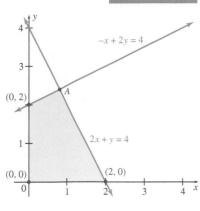

FIGURE 11

Every point in the feasible region satisfies all the constraints; however, we want to find those points that produce the maximum possible value of the objective function. To see how to find this maximum value, change the graph of Figure 11 by adding lines that represent the objective function $z = 3x + 4y$ for various sample values of z. By choosing the values 0, 5, 10, and 15 for z, the objective function becomes (in turn)

$$0 = 3x + 4y, \quad 5 = 3x + 4y, \quad 10 = 3x + 4y, \quad \text{and} \quad 15 = 3x + 4y.$$

These four lines are graphed in Figure 12. (Why are the lines parallel?) The figure shows that z cannot take on the value 15 because the graph for $z = 15$ is entirely outside the feasible region. The maximum possible value of z will be obtained from a line parallel to the others and between the lines representing the objective function when $z = 10$ and $z = 15$. The value of z will be as large as possible and all constraints will be satisfied if this line just touches the feasible region. This occurs at point A. We find that A has coordinates $(4/5, 12/5)$. (See the review in the margin.) The value of z at this point is

$$z = 3x + 4y = 3\left(\frac{4}{5}\right) + 4\left(\frac{12}{5}\right) = \frac{60}{5} = 12.$$

▶ FOR REVIEW

Recall from Chapter 2 that two equations in two unknowns can be solved by using row operations to eliminate one variable. For example, to solve the system

$$2x + y = 4$$
$$-x + 2y = 4,$$

we could take the first equation plus 2 times the second to eliminate x. (This is equivalent to $R_1 + 2R_2 \rightarrow R_2$ in the Gauss-Jordan method.) The result is $5y = 12$, so $y = 12/5$. We can then substitute this value of y into either equation and solve for x. For example, substitution into the first equation yields

$$2x + \frac{12}{5} = 4$$
$$2x = \frac{8}{5}$$
$$x = \frac{4}{5}.$$

We instead could have subtracted the two original equations to eliminate y, yielding $5x = 4$, or $x = 4/5$.

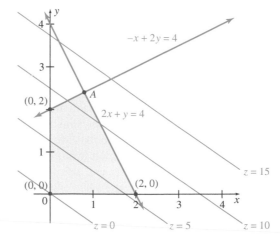

FIGURE 12

The maximum possible value of z is 12. Of all the points in the feasible region, A leads to the largest possible value of z.

A graphing calculator is particularly useful for finding the coordinates of intersection points such as point A. We do this by solving each equation for y, graphing each line, and then using the capability of the calculator to find the coordinates of the point of intersection.

Points such as A in Example 1 are called corner points. A **corner point** is a point in the feasible region where the boundary lines of two constraints cross. Since corner points occur where two straight lines cross, the coordinates of a corner point are the solution of a system of two linear equations. As we saw in Example 1, corner points play a key role in the solution of linear programming problems. We will make this explicit after the following example.

EXAMPLE 2   **Minimization**
Solve the following linear programming problem.

$$\text{Minimize} \quad z = 2x + 4y$$
$$\text{subject to:} \quad x + 2y \geq 10$$
$$3x + y \geq 10$$
$$x \geq 0$$
$$y \geq 0.$$

▶**Solution** Figure 13 shows the feasible region and the lines that result when z in the objective function is replaced by 0, 10, 20, 40, and 50. The line representing the objective function touches the region of feasible solutions when $z = 20$. Two corner points, $(2, 4)$ and $(10, 0)$, lie on this line; both $(2, 4)$ and $(10, 0)$, as well as all the points on the boundary line between them, give the same optimum value of z. There are infinitely many equally good values of x and y that will give the same minimum value of the objective function $z = 2x + 4y$. This minimum value is 20.

The feasible region in Example 1 is **bounded**, since the region is enclosed by boundary lines on all sides. Linear programming problems with bounded regions

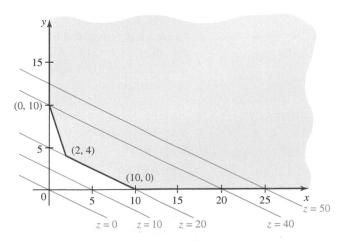

FIGURE 13

always have solutions. On the other hand, the feasible region in Example 2 is **unbounded**, and no solution will *maximize* the value of the objective function.

Some general conclusions can be drawn from the method of solution used in Examples 1 and 2. Figure 14 shows various feasible regions and the lines that result from various values of z. (We assume the lines are in order from left to right as z increases.) In Figure 14(a), the objective function takes on its minimum value at corner point Q and its maximum value at P. The minimum is again at Q in part (b), but the maximum occurs at P_1 or P_2, or any point on the line segment connecting them. Finally, in part (c), the minimum value occurs at Q, but the objective function has no maximum value because the feasible region is unbounded. As long as the objective function increases as x and y increase, the objective function will have no maximum over an unbounded region.

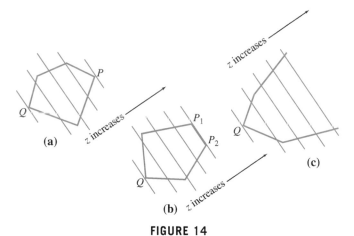

FIGURE 14

The preceding discussion suggests the truth of the **corner point theorem**.

CORNER POINT THEOREM

If an optimum value (either a maximum or a minimum) of the objective function exists, it will occur at one or more of the corner points of the feasible region.

This theorem simplifies the job of finding an optimum value. First, we graph the feasible region and find all corner points. Then we test each corner point in the objective function. Finally, we identify the corner point producing the optimum solution. For unbounded regions, we must decide whether the required optimum can be found (see Example 2).

NOTE As the corner point theorem states and Example 2 illustrates, the optimal value of a linear programming problem may occur at more than one corner point. When the optimal solution occurs at two corner points, every point on the line segment between the two points is also an optimal solution. ■

With the theorem, we can solve the problem in Example 1 by first identifying the four corner points in Figure 11: $(0, 0)$, $(0, 2)$, $(4/5, 12/5)$, and $(2, 0)$. Then we substitute each of the four points into the objective function $z = 3x + 4y$ to identify the corner point that produces the maximum value of z.

Corner Point	Value of $z = 3x + 4y$	
$(0, 0)$	$3(0) + 4(0) = 0$	
$(0, 2)$	$3(0) + 4(2) = 8$	
$\left(\frac{4}{5}, \frac{12}{5}\right)$	$3\left(\frac{4}{5}\right) + 4\left(\frac{12}{5}\right) = 12$	Maximum
$(2, 0)$	$3(2) + 4(0) = 6$	

From these results, the corner point $(4/5, 12/5)$ yields the maximum value of 12. This is the same as the result found earlier.

The following summary gives the steps to use in solving a linear programming problem by the graphical method.

SOLVING A LINEAR PROGRAMMING PROBLEM

1. Write the objective function and all necessary constraints.
2. Graph the feasible region.
3. Identify all corner points.
4. Find the value of the objective function at each corner point.
5. For a bounded region, the solution is given by the corner point producing the optimum value of the objective function.
6. For an unbounded region, check that a solution actually exists. If it does, it will occur at a corner point.

EXAMPLE 3 Maximization and Minimization

Sketch the feasible region for the following set of constraints, and then find the maximum and minimum values of the objective function $z = x + 10y$.

$$x + 4y \geq 12$$
$$x - 2y \leq 0$$
$$2y - x \leq 6$$
$$x \leq 6$$

▶**Solution** The graph in Figure 15 shows that the feasible region is bounded. Use the corner points from the graph to find the maximum and minimum values of the objective function.

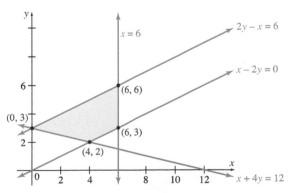

FIGURE 15

Corner Point	Value of $z = x + 10y$	
$(0, 3)$	$0 + 10(3) = 30$	
$(4, 2)$	$4 + 10(2) = 24$	Minimum
$(6, 3)$	$6 + 10(3) = 36$	
$(6, 6)$	$6 + 10(6) = 66$	Maximum

The minimum value of $z = x + 10y$ is 24 at the corner point $(4, 2)$. The maximum value is 66 at $(6, 6)$.

   To verify that the minimum or maximum is correct in a linear programming problem, you might want to add the graph of the line $z = 0$ to the graph of the feasible region. For instance, in Example 3, the result of adding the line $x + 10y = 0$ is shown in Figure 16. Now imagine moving a straightedge through the feasible region parallel to this line. It appears that the first place the line touches the feasible region is at $(4, 2)$, where we found the minimum. Similarly, the last place the line touches is at $(6, 6)$, where we found the maximum. In Figure 16, these parallel lines, labeled $z = 24$ and $z = 66$, are also shown.

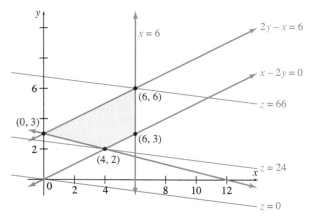

FIGURE 16

▶ 3.2 Exercises

The following graphs show regions of feasible solutions. Use these regions to find maximum and minimum values of the given objective functions.

1. a. $z = 3x + 2y$
  b. $z = x + 4y$

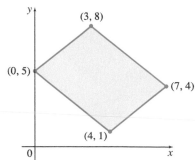

2. a. $z = x + 4y$
  b. $z = 5x + 2y$

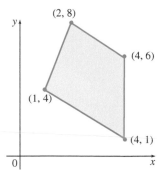

3. a. $z = 0.40x + 0.75y$
   b. $z = 1.50x + 0.25y$

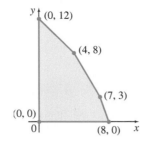

4. a. $z = 0.35x + 1.25y$
   b. $z = 1.5x + 0.5y$

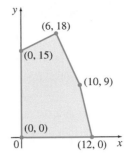

5. a. $z = 4x + 2y$
   b. $z = 2x + 3y$
   c. $z = 2x + 4y$
   d. $z = x + 4y$

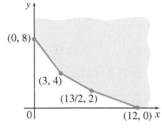

6. a. $z = 4x + y$
   b. $z = 5x + 6y$
   c. $z = x + 2y$
   d. $z = x + 6y$

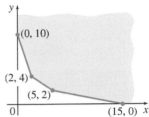

Use graphical methods to solve each linear programming problem.

7. Minimize $z = 4x + 7y$
   subject to:
   $$x - y \geq 1$$
   $$3x + 2y \geq 18$$
   $$x \geq 0$$
   $$y \geq 0.$$

8. Minimize $z = x + 3y$
   subject to:
   $$x + y \leq 10$$
   $$5x + 2y \geq 20$$
   $$-x + 2y \geq 0$$
   $$x \geq 0$$
   $$y \geq 0.$$

9. Maximize $z = 5x + 2y$
   subject to:
   $$4x - y \leq 16$$
   $$2x + y \geq 11$$
   $$x \geq 3$$
   $$y \leq 8.$$

10. Maximize $z = 10x + 8y$
   subject to:
   $$2x + 3y \leq 100$$
   $$5x + 4y \leq 200$$
   $$x \geq 10$$
   $$0 \leq y \leq 20.$$

11. Maximize $z = 10x + 10y$
   subject to:
   $$5x + 8y \geq 200$$
   $$25x - 10y \geq 250$$
   $$x + y \leq 150$$
   $$x \geq 0$$
   $$y \geq 0.$$

12. Maximize $z = 4x + 5y$
   subject to:
   $$10x - 5y \leq 100$$
   $$20x + 10y \geq 150$$
   $$x + y \geq 12$$
   $$x \geq 0$$
   $$y \geq 0.$$

13. Maximize $z = 3x + 6y$
   subject to:
   $$2x - 3y \leq 12$$
   $$x + y \leq 5$$
   $$3x + 4y \geq 24$$
   $$x \geq 0$$
   $$y \geq 0.$$

14. Maximize $z = 4x + 6y$
   subject to:
   $$3 \leq x + y \leq 10$$
   $$x - y \geq 3$$
   $$x \geq 0$$
   $$y \geq 0.$$

15. Find values of $x \geq 0$ and $y \geq 0$ that maximize $z = 10x + 12y$ subject to each set of constraints.

   a. $x + y \leq 20$
   $x + 3y \leq 24$

   b. $3x + y \leq 15$
   $x + 2y \leq 18$

   c. $2x + 5y \geq 22$
   $4x + 3y \leq 28$
   $2x + 2y \leq 17$

16. Find values of $x \geq 0$ and $y \geq 0$ that minimize $z = 3x + 2y$ subject to each set of constraints.

   a. $10x + 7y \leq 42$
   $4x + 10y \geq 35$

   b. $6x + 5y \geq 25$
   $2x + 6y \geq 15$

   c. $x + 2y \geq 10$
   $2x + y \geq 12$
   $x - y \leq 8$

17. You are given the following linear programming problem:*

Maximize $z = c_1 x_1 + c_2 x_2$

subject to: $2x_1 + x_2 \leq 11$

$-x_1 + 2x_2 \leq 2$

$x_1 \geq 0, x_2 \geq 0.$

If $c_2 > 0$, determine the range of c_1/c_2 for which $(x_1, x_2) = (4, 3)$ is an optimal solution. (Choose one of the following.)

a. $[-2, 1/2]$ **b.** $[-1/2, 2]$ **c.** $[-11, -1]$ **d.** $[1, 11]$ **e.** $[-11, 11]$

 Applications of Linear Programming

 THINK ABOUT IT   **How many canoes and kayaks should a business purchase, given a limited budget and limited storage?**

We will use linear programming to answer this question in Example 1.

EXAMPLE 1   **Canoe Rentals**

Mr. Trenga plans to start a new business called River Explorers, which will rent canoes and kayaks to people to travel 10 miles down the Clarion River in Cook Forest State Park. He has $45,000 to purchase new boats. He can buy the canoes for $600 each and the kayaks for $750 each. His facility can hold up to 65 boats. The canoes will rent for $25 a day, and the kayaks will rent for $30 a day. How many canoes and how many kayaks should he buy to earn the most revenue?

▶**Solution**   Let x represent the number of canoes and let y represent the number of kayaks. Summarize the given information in a table.

	Canoes	Kayaks		Total
Number of Boats	x	y	$\leq$	65
Cost of Each	$600	$750	$\leq$	$45,000
Revenue	$25	$30		

The constraints, imposed by the number of boats and the cost, correspond to the rows in the table as follows.

$$x + y \leq 65$$

$$600x + 750y \leq 45,000$$

Dividing both sides of the second constraint by 150 gives the equivalent inequality

$$4x + 5y \leq 300.$$

Since the number of boats cannot be negative, $x \geq 0$ and $y \geq 0$. The objective function to be maximized gives the amount of revenue. If the variable z represents

---

*Problem 5 from "November 1989 Course 130 Examination Operations Research" of the *Education and Examination Committee of The Society of Actuaries*. Reprinted by permission of The Society of Actuaries.

the total revenue, the objective function is

$$z = 25x + 30y.$$

In summary, the mathematical model for the given linear programming problem is as follows:

Maximize	$z = 25x + 30y$		**(1)**
subject to:	$x + y \leq 65$		**(2)**
	$4x + 5y \leq 300$		**(3)**
	$x \geq 0$		**(4)**
	$y \geq 0.$		**(5)**

Using the methods described in the previous section, graph the feasible region for the system of inequalities (2)–(5), as in Figure 17. Three of the corner points can be identified from the graph as (0, 0), (65, 0), and (0, 60). The fourth corner point, labeled Q in the figure, can be found by solving the system of equations

$$x + y = 65$$
$$4x + 5y = 300.$$

Solve this system to find that Q is the point (25, 40). Now test these four points in the objective function to determine the maximum value of z. The results are shown in the table.

Corner Point	Value of $z = 25x + 30y$	
$(0, 0)$	$25(0) + 30(0) = 0$	
$(65, 0)$	$25(65) + 30(0) = 1625$	
$(0, 60)$	$25(0) + 30(60) = 1800$	
$(25, 40)$	$25(25) + 30(40) = 1825$	Maximum

The objective function, which represents revenue, is maximized when $x = 25$ and $y = 40$. He should buy 25 canoes and 40 kayaks.

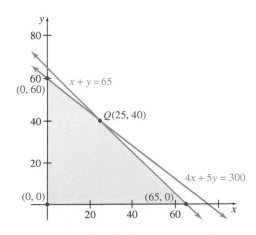

FIGURE 17

Fortunately, the answer to the linear programming problem in Example 1 is a point with integer coordinates, as the number of each type of boat must be an integer. Unfortunately, there is no guarantee that this will always happen. When the solution to a linear programming problem is restricted to integers, it is an *integer programming* problem, which is more difficult to solve than a linear programming problem. In this text, all problems in which fractional solutions are meaningless are contrived to have integer solutions.

EXAMPLE 2

Farm Animals

A 4-H member raises only goats and pigs. She wants to raise no more than 16 animals, including no more than 10 goats. She spends $25 to raise a goat and $75 to raise a pig, and she has $900 available for this project. The 4-H member wishes to maximize her profits. Each goat produces $12 in profit and each pig $40 in profit.

▶**Solution** First, set up a table that shows the information given in the problem.

	Goats	**Pigs**		**Total**
Number Raised	x	y	≤	16
Goat Limit	x		≤	10
Cost to Raise	$25	$75	≤	$900
Profit (each)	$12	$40		

Use the table to write the necessary constraints. Since the total number of animals cannot exceed 16, the first constraint is

$$x + y \leq 16.$$

"No more than 10 goats" means

$$x \leq 10.$$

The cost to raise x goats at $25 per goat is $25x$ dollars, while the cost for y pigs at $75 each is $75y$ dollars. Since only $900 is available,

$$25x + 75y \leq 900.$$

Dividing both sides by 25 gives the equivalent inequality

$$x + 3y \leq 36.$$

The number of goats and pigs cannot be negative, so

$$x \geq 0 \quad \text{and} \quad y \geq 0.$$

The 4-H member wants to know how many goats and pigs to raise in order to produce maximum profit. Each goat yields $12 profit and each pig $40. If z represents total profit, then

$$z = 12x + 40y.$$

In summary, we have the following linear programming problem:

$$\text{Maximize} \quad z = 12x + 40y$$
$$\text{subject to:} \quad x + y \le 16$$
$$x + 3y \le 36$$
$$x \le 10$$
$$x \ge 0$$
$$y \ge 0.$$

A graph of the feasible region is shown in Figure 18. The corner points $(0, 12)$, $(0, 0)$, and $(10, 0)$ can be read directly from the graph. The coordinates of each of the other corner points can be found by solving a system of linear equations.

Test each corner point in the objective function to find the maximum profit.

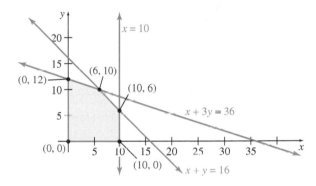

FIGURE 18

Corner Point	Value of $z = 12x + 40y$	
$(0, 12)$	$12(0) + 40(12) = 480$	Maximum
$(6, 10)$	$12(6) + 40(10) = 472$	
$(10, 6)$	$12(10) + 40(6) = 360$	
$(10, 0)$	$12(10) + 40(0) = 120$	
$(0, 0)$	$12(0) + 40(0) = 0$	

The maximum of 480 occurs at $(0, 12)$. Thus, 12 pigs and no goats will produce a maximum profit of $480.

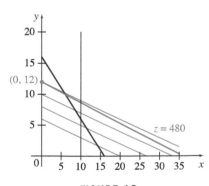

FIGURE 19

In the maximization problem in Example 2, since the profit for a single pig is $40 and the profit for a single goat is only $12, it is more profitable to raise only pigs and no goats. However, if the profit from raising pigs begins to decrease (or the profit from goats begins to increase), it will eventually be more profitable to raise both goats and pigs. In fact, if the profit from raising pigs decreases to a number below $36, then the previous solution is no longer optimal.

To see why this is true, in Figure 19 we have graphed the original objective function $(z = 12x + 40y)$ for various values of z, as we did in Example 1 of the previous section. Notice that each of these objective lines has slope

$m = -12/40 = -3/10$. When $z = 480$, the line touches only one feasible point, $(0, 12)$, which is where the maximum profit occurs.

If the profit from raising pigs decreases from \$40 to \$$p$, where p is a value slightly below 40, the objective function lines will have the equation $z = 12x + py$ for various values of z, and the slope of the lines becomes $m = -12/p$. Eventually, as p becomes smaller, the slope of these objective lines will be equal to the slope of the line $x + 3y = 36$ (that is, $-1/3$), corresponding to the second constraint. This occurs when $-12/p = -1/3$, or $p = 36$, as illustrated by the overlapping blue and dotted lines in Figure 20. In this case, the optimal solution occurs at every point on the line segment that joins $(0, 12)$ and $(6, 10)$.

Once the profit from raising pigs decreases to below \$36, the slopes of the sample objective function lines become more negative (steeper) and the optimal solution changes, as indicated in Figure 21. As z increases, the last feasible point that the lines touch is $(6, 10)$. For profits from raising pigs that are slightly below \$36, the optimal solution will occur when $x = 6$ and $y = 10$. In other words, the maximum profit will occur when she raises both goats and pigs.

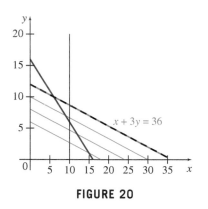

FIGURE 20

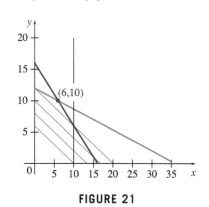

FIGURE 21

EXAMPLE 3 **Nutrition**

Certain animals in a rescue shelter must have at least 30 g of protein and at least 20 g of fat per feeding period. These nutrients come from food A, which costs 18 cents per unit and supplies 2 g of protein and 4 g of fat; and food B, which costs 12 cents per unit and has 6 g of protein and 2 g of fat. Food B is bought under a long-term contract requiring that at least 2 units of B be used per serving.

(a) How much of each food must be bought to produce the minimum cost per serving?

▶**Solution** Let x represent the required amount of food A and y the amount of food B. Use the given information to prepare the following table.

	Food A	Food B		Total
Number of Units	x	y		
Grams of Protein	2	6	$\geq$	30
Grams of Fat	4	2	$\geq$	20
Long-Term Contract		y	$\geq$	2
Cost	18¢	12¢		

Since the animals must have *at least* 30 g of protein and 20 g of fat, we use $\geq$ in the inequality. If the animals needed *at most* a certain amount of some nutrient, we would use $\leq$. The long-term contract requires that $y \geq 2$.

The linear programming problem can be stated as follows.

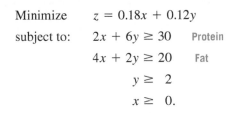

(The usual constraint $y \geq 0$ is redundant because of the constraint $y \geq 2$.) A graph of the feasible region is shown in Figure 22. The corner points are $(0, 10), (3, 4),$ and $(9, 2)$.

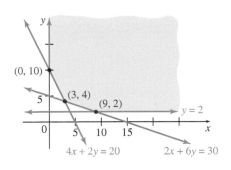

FIGURE 22

Test each corner point in the objective function to find the minimum cost.

Corner Point	Value of $z = 0.18x + 0.12y$	
$(0, 10)$	$0.18(0) + 0.12(10) = 1.20$	
$(3, 4)$	$0.18(3) + 0.12(4) = 1.02$	Minimum
$(9, 2)$	$0.18(9) + 0.12(2) = 1.86$	

The minimum of 1.02 occurs at $(3, 4)$. Thus, 3 units of food A and 4 units of food B will produce a minimum cost of $1.02 per serving.

(b) The rescue shelter manager notices that although the long-term contract states that at least 2 units of food B be used per serving, the solution uses 4 units of food B, which is 2 units more than the minimum amount required. Can a more economical solution be found that only uses 2 units of food B?

▶**Solution** The solution found in part (a) is the most economical solution, even though it exceeds the requirement for using at least 2 units of food B. Notice from Figure 22 that the three lines representing the three constraints do not meet at a single point, so any solution in the feasible region will have to exceed at least one constraint. The rescue shelter manager might use this information to negotiate a better deal with the distributor of food B by making a guarantee to use at least 4 units of food B per serving in the future.

The notion that some constraints are not met exactly is related to the concepts of *surplus* and *slack variables*, which will be explored in the next chapter.

The feasible region in Figure 22 is an *unbounded* feasible region—the region extends indefinitely to the upper right. With this region it would not be possible to *maximize* the objective function, because the total cost of the food could always be increased by encouraging the animals to eat more.

▶ 3.3 Exercises

Write Exercises 1–6 as linear inequalities. Identify all variables used. (Note: Not all of the given information is used in Exercises 5 and 6.)

1. Product A requires 3 hours on machine I, while product B needs 5 hours on the same machine. The machine is available for at most 60 hours per week.

2. A cow requires a third of an acre of pasture and a sheep needs a quarter acre. A rancher wants to use at least 120 acres of pasture.

3. Jessica Corpo needs at least 1500 units of calcium supplements per day. Her calcium carbonate supplement provides 600 units, and her calcium citrate supplement supplies 250 units.

4. Pauline Wong spends 3 hours selling a small computer and 5 hours selling a larger model. She works no more than 45 hours per week.

5. Coffee costing $8 per lb is to be mixed with coffee costing $10 per lb to get at least 40 lb of a blended coffee.

6. A tank in an oil refinery holds 120 gal. The tank contains a mixture of light oil worth $1.25 per gal and heavy oil worth $0.80 per gal.

▶ Applications

BUSINESS AND ECONOMICS

7. *Transportation* The Miers Company produces small engines for several manufacturers. The company receives orders from two assembly plants for their Top-flight engine. Plant I needs at least 45 engines, and plant II needs at least 32 engines. The company can send at most 90 engines to these two assembly plants. It costs $30 per engine to ship to plant I and $40 per engine to ship to plant II. Plant I gives Miers $20 in rebates toward its products for each engine they buy, while plant II gives similar $15 rebates. Miers estimates that they need at least $1200 in rebates to cover products they plan to buy from the two plants. How many engines should be shipped to each plant to minimize shipping costs? What is the minimum cost?

8. *Transportation* A manufacturer of refrigerators must ship at least 100 refrigerators to its two West Coast warehouses. Each warehouse holds a maximum of 100 refrigerators. Warehouse A holds 25 refrigerators already, and warehouse B has 20 on hand. It costs $12 to ship a refrigerator to warehouse A and $10 to ship one to warehouse B. Union rules require that at least 300 workers be hired. Shipping a refrigerator to warehouse A requires 4 workers, while shipping a refrigerator to warehouse B requires 2 workers. How many refrigerators should be shipped to each warehouse to minimize costs? What is the minimum cost?

9. *Insurance Premiums* A company is considering two insurance plans with the types of coverage and premiums shown in the following table.

	Policy A	Policy B
Fire/Theft	$10,000	$15,000
Liability	$180,000	$120,000
Premium	$50	$40

(For example, this means that $50 buys one unit of plan A, consisting of $10,000 fire and theft insurance and $180,000 of liability insurance.)

a. The company wants at least $300,000 fire/theft insurance and at least $3,000,000 liability insurance from these plans. How many units should be purchased from each plan to minimize the cost of the premiums? What is the minimum premium?

b. Suppose the premium for policy A is reduced to $25. Now how many units should be purchased from each plan to minimize the cost of the premiums? What is the minimum premium?

10. *Profit* The Muro Manufacturing Company makes two kinds of plasma screen television sets. It produces the Flexscan set that sells for $350 profit and the Panoramic I that sells for $500 profit. On the assembly line, the Flexscan requires 5 hours, and the Panoramic I takes 7 hours. The cabinet shop spends 1 hour on the cabinet for the Flexscan and 2 hours on the cabinet for the Panoramic I. Both sets require 4 hours for testing and packing. On a particular production run, the Muro Company has available 3600 work-hours on the

assembly line, 900 work-hours in the cabinet shop, and 2600 work-hours in the testing and packing department.

a. How many sets of each type should it produce to make a maximum profit? What is the maximum profit?

b. Suppose the profit on the Flexscan goes up to $450. Now how many sets of each type should it produce to make a maximum profit. What is the maximum profit?

c. The solutions from parts a and b leave some unused time in either the assembly line, the cabinet shop, or the testing and packing department. Identify any unused time in each solution. Is it possible to have a solution that leaves no excess time? Explain.

11. *Revenue* A machine shop manufactures two types of bolts. The bolts require time on each of the three groups of machines, but the time required on each group differs, as shown in the table below.

	Type I	**Type II**
Machine 1	0.2 min	0.2 min
Machine 2	0.6 min	0.2 min
Machine 3	0.04 min	0.08 min

Production schedules are made up one day at a time. In a day, 300, 720, and 100 minutes are available, respectively, on these machines. Type I bolts sell for 15¢ and type II bolts for 20¢.

a. How many of each type of bolt should be manufactured per day to maximize revenue?

b. What is the maximum revenue?

c. Suppose the selling price of type I bolts began to increase. How much would this price have to increase before a different number of each type of bolts should be produced to maximize revenue?

12. *Revenue* The manufacturing process requires that oil refineries must manufacture at least 2 gal of gasoline for every gallon of fuel oil. To meet the winter demand for fuel oil, at least 3 million gal a day must be produced. The demand for gasoline is no more than 6.4 million gal per day. It takes 0.25 hour to ship each million gal of gasoline and 1 hour to ship each million gal of fuel oil out of the warehouse. No more than 4.65 hours are available for shipping. If the refinery sells gasoline for $2.50 per gal and fuel oil for $2 per gal, how much of each should be produced to maximize revenue? Find the maximum revenue.

13. *Revenue* A candy company has 150 kg of chocolate-covered nuts and 90 kg of chocolate-covered raisins to be sold as two different mixes. One mix will contain half nuts and half raisins and will sell for $7 per kg. The other mix will contain 3/4 nuts and 1/4 raisins and will sell for $9.50 per kg.

a. How many kilograms of each mix should the company prepare for the maximum revenue? Find the maximum revenue.

b. The company raises the price of the second mix to $11 per kg. Now how many kilograms of each mix should the company prepare for the maximum revenue? Find the maximum revenue.

14. *Profit* A small country can grow only two crops for export, coffee and cocoa. The country has 500,000 hectares of land available for the crops. Long-term contracts require that at least 100,000 hectares be devoted to coffee and at least 200,000 hectares to cocoa. Cocoa must be processed locally, and production bottlenecks limit cocoa to 270,000 hectares. Coffee requires two workers per hectare, with cocoa requiring five. No more than 1,750,000 people are available for working with these crops. Coffee produces a profit of $220 per hectare and cocoa a profit of $550 per hectare. How many hectares should the country devote to each crop in order to maximize profit? Find the maximum profit.

15. *Blending* The Mostpure Milk Company gets milk from two dairies and then blends the milk to get the desired amount of butterfat for the company's premier product. Milk from dairy I costs $2.40 per gal, and milk from dairy II costs $0.80 per gal. At most $144 is available for purchasing milk. Dairy I can supply at most 50 gal of milk averaging 3.7% butterfat. Dairy II can supply at most 80 gal of milk averaging 3.2% butterfat.

a. How much milk from each supplier should Mostpure use to get at most 100 gal of milk with the maximum total percent of butterfat? What is the maximum percent of butterfat?

b. The solution from part a leaves both dairy I and dairy II with excess capacity. Calculate the amount of additional milk each dairy could produce. Is there any way all this capacity could be used while still meeting the other constraints? Explain.

16. *Transportation* A greeting card manufacturer has 370 boxes of a particular card in warehouse I and 290 boxes of the same card in warehouse II. A greeting card shop in San Jose orders 350 boxes of the card, and another shop in Memphis orders 300 boxes. The shipping costs per box to these shops from the two warehouses are shown in the following table.

		Destination	
		San Jose	*Memphis*
Warehouse	*I*	$0.25	$0.22
	II	$0.23	$0.21

How many boxes should be shipped to each city from each warehouse to minimize shipping costs? What is the minimum cost? (*Hint:* Use x, $350 - x$, y, and $300 - y$ as the variables.)

17. *Finance* A pension fund manager decides to invest a total of at most $30 million in U.S. Treasury bonds paying 4% annual interest and in mutual funds paying 8% annual interest. He plans to invest at least $5 million in bonds and at least $10 million in mutual funds. Bonds have an initial fee of $100 per million dollars, while the fee for mutual funds is $200 per million. The fund manager is allowed to spend no more than $5000 on fees. How much should be invested in each to maximize annual interest? What is the maximum annual interest?

Manufacturing (*Note: Exercises 18–20 are from qualification examinations for Certified Public Accountants.**) *The Random Company manufactures two products, Zeta and Beta. Each product must pass through two processing operations. All materials are introduced at the start of Process No. 1. There are no work-in-process inventories. Random may produce either one product exclusively or various combinations of both products subject to the following constraints:*

	Process No. 1	Process No. 2	Contribution Margin (per unit)
Hours Required to Produce One Unit:			
Zeta	1 hr	1 hr	$4.00
Beta	2 hr	3 hr	$5.25
Total Capacity (in hours per day)	1000 hr	1275 hr	

A shortage of technical labor has limited Beta production to 400 units per day. There are no constraints on the production of Zeta other than the hour constraints in the above schedule. Assume that all relationships between capacity and production are linear.

18. Given the objective to maximize total contribution margin, what is the production constraint for Process No. 1? (Choose one of the following.)

a. Zeta + Beta $\leq$ 1000   **b.** Zeta + 2 Beta $\leq$ 1000

c. Zeta + Beta $\geq$ 1000   **d.** Zeta + 2 Beta $\geq$ 1000

19. Given the objective to maximize total contribution margin, what is the labor constraint for production of Beta? (Choose one of the following.)

a. Beta $\leq$ 400   **b.** Beta $\geq$ 400

c. Beta $\leq$ 425   **d.** Beta $\geq$ 425

20. What is the objective function of the data presented? (Choose one of the following.)

a. Zeta + 2 Beta = $9.25

b. $4.00 Zeta + 3($5.25)Beta = Total Contribution Margin

c. $4.00 Zeta + $5.25 Beta = Total Contribution Margin

d. 2($4.00) Zeta + 3($5.25) Beta = Total Contribution Margin

LIFE SCIENCES

21. *Health Care* Mark, who is ill, takes vitamin pills. Each day he must have at least 16 units of vitamin A, 5 units of vitamin B_1, and 20 units of vitamin C. He can choose between pill 1, which contains 8 units of A, 1 of B_1, and 2 of C; and pill 2, which contains 2 units of A, 1 of B_1, and 7 of C. Pill 1 costs 15¢, and pill 2 costs 30¢.

  a. How many of each pill should he buy in order to minimize his cost? What is the minimum cost?

  b. For the solution in part a, Mark is receiving more than he needs of at least one vitamin. Identify that vitamin, and tell how much surplus he is receiving. Is there any way he can avoid receiving that surplus while still meeting the other constraints and minimizing the cost? Explain.

22. *Predator Food Requirements* A certain predator requires at least 10 units of protein and 8 units of fat per day. One prey of species I provides 5 units of protein and 2 units of fat; one prey of species II provides 3 units of protein and 4 units of fat. Capturing and digesting each species-II prey requires 3 units of energy, and capturing and digesting each species-I prey requires 2 units of energy. How many of each prey would meet the predator's daily food requirements with the least expenditure of energy? Are the answers reasonable? How could they be interpreted?

23. *Nutrition* A dietician is planning a snack package of fruit and nuts. Each ounce of fruit will supply zero units of protein, 2 units of carbohydrates, and 1 unit of fat, and will contain 20 calories. Each ounce of nuts will supply 3 units of protein, 1 unit of carbohydrate, and 2 units of fat, and will contain 30 calories. Every package must provide at least 6 units of protein, at least 10 units of carbohydrates, and no more than 9 units of fat. Find the number of ounces of fruit and number of ounces of nuts that will meet the requirement with the least number of calories. What is the least number of calories?

24. *Health Care* Ms. Oliveras was given the following advice. She should supplement her daily diet with at least 6000 USP units of vitamin A, at least 195 mg of vitamin C, and at least 600 USP units of vitamin D. Ms. Oliveras finds that

*Material from *Uniform CPA Examinations and Unofficial Answers*, copyright © 1973, 1974, 1975 by the American Institute of Certified Public Accountants, Inc., is reprinted with permission.

Mason's Pharmacy carries Brand X vitamin pills at 5¢ each and Brand Y vitamins at 4¢ each. Each Brand X pill contains 3000 USP units of A, 45 mg of C, and 75 USP units of D, while Brand Y pills contain 1000 USP units of A, 50 mg of C, and 200 USP units of D.

a. What combination of vitamin pills should she buy to obtain the least possible cost? What is the least possible cost per day?

b. For the solution in part a, Ms. Oliveras is receiving more than she needs of at least one vitamin. Identify that vitamin, and tell how much surplus she is receiving. Is there any way she can avoid receiving that surplus while still meeting the other constraints and minimizing the cost? Explain.

SOCIAL SCIENCES

25. *Anthropology* An anthropology article presents a hypothetical situation that could be described by a linear programming model.* Suppose a population gathers plants and animals for survival. They need at least 360 units of energy, 300 units of protein, and 8 hides during some time period. One unit of plants provides 30 units of energy, 10 units of protein, and no hides. One animal provides 20 units of energy, 25 units of protein, and 1 hide.

Only 25 units of plants and 25 animals are available. It costs the population 30 hours of labor to gather one unit of a plant and 15 hours for an animal. Find how many units of plants and how many animals should be gathered to meet the requirements with a minimum number of hours of labor.

GENERAL INTEREST

26. *Construction* In a small town in South Carolina, zoning rules require that the window space (in square feet) in a house be at least one-sixth of the space used up by solid walls. The cost to build windows is $10 per ft^2, while the cost to build solid walls is $20 per ft^2. The total amount available for building walls and windows is no more than $12,000. The estimated monthly cost to heat the house is $0.32 for each square foot of windows and $0.20 for each square foot of solid walls. Find the maximum total area (windows plus walls) if no more than $160 per month is available to pay for heat.

27. *Farming* An agricultural advisor looks at the results of Example 2 and claims that it cannot possibly be correct. After all, the 4-H member is able to raise 16 animals, and she is only raising 12 animals. Surely she can earn more profit by raising all 16 animals. How would you respond?

Chapter 3 Review

► Chapter Summary

In this chapter, we introduced linear programming, which attempts to solve maximization and minimization problems with linear constraints. Linear programming models can be used to analyze a wide range of applications from many disciplines. The corner point theorem assures us that the optimal solution to a linear program, if it exists, must occur at one or more of the corner points of the feasible region. Linear programs can be solved using the graphical method, which graphs the region described by the linear constraints and then locates the corner point corresponding to the optimal solution value. The graphical method, however, is restricted to problems with two or three variables. In the next chapter, we will study a method that does not have this restriction.

LINEAR PROGRAMMING: THE GRAPHICAL METHOD SUMMARY

Graphing a Linear Inequality   **1.** Draw the graph of the boundary line. Make the line solid if the inequality involves ≤ or ≥; make the line dashed if the inequality involves < or >.

*Reidhead, Van A., "Linear Programming Models in Archaeology," *Annual Review of Anthropology*, Vol. 8, 1979, pp. 543–578.

2. Decide which half-plane to shade. Use either of the following methods.

   a. Solve the inequality for y; shade the region above the line if the inequality is of the form of $y > $ or $y \geq$; shade the region below the line if the inequality is of the form of $y <$ or $y \leq$.

   b. Choose any point not on the line as a test point. Shade the half-plane that includes the test point if the test point satisfies the original inequality; otherwise, shade the half-plane on the other side of the boundary line.

Corner Point Theorem If an optimum value (either a maximum or a minimum) of the objective function exists, it will occur at one or more of the corner points of the feasible region.

Solving a Linear Programming Problem

1. Write the objective function and all necessary constraints.

2. Graph the feasible region.

3. Identify all corner points.

4. Find the value of the objective function at each corner point.

5. For a bounded region, the solution is given by the corner point(s) producing the optimum value of the objective function.

6. For an unbounded region, check that a solution actually exists. If it does, it will occur at one or more corner points.

Key Terms

To understand the concepts presented in this chapter, you should know the meaning and use of the following terms.

3.1 linear inequality	system of inequalities	**3.2** linear programming	corner point
boundary	region of feasible	objective function	bounded
half-plane	solutions	constraints	unbounded

Concept Check

Determine whether each of the following statements is true or false, and explain why.

1. The graphical method can be used to solve a linear programming problem with four variables.

2. For the inequality $5x + 4y \geq 20$, the test point $(3, 4)$ suggests that the correct half-plane to shade includes this point.

3. Let x represent the number of acres of wheat planted and y represent the number of acres of corn planted. The inequality $x \leq 2y$ implies that the number of acres of wheat planted will be at least twice the number of acres of corn planted.

4. For the variables in Exercise 3, assume that we have a total of 60 hours to plant the wheat and corn and that it takes 2 hours per acre to prepare a wheat field and 1 hour per acre to prepare a corn field. The inequality $2x + y \geq 60$ represents the constraint on the amount of time available for planting.

5. For the variables in Exercise 3, assume that we make a profit of $14 for each acre of corn and $10 for each acre of wheat. The objective function that can be used to maximize profit is $14x + 10y$.

6. The point $(2, 3)$ is a corner point of the linear programming problem

$$\begin{aligned} \text{Maximize} \quad & z = 7x + 4y \\ \text{subject to:} \quad & 3x + 8y \leq 30 \\ & 4x + 2y \leq 15 \\ & x \geq 0, y \geq 0. \end{aligned}$$

7. The point $(2, 3)$ is a feasible point of the linear programming problem in Exercise 6.

8. The optimal solution to the linear programming problem in Exercise 6 occurs at point $(2, 3)$.

9. It is possible to find a point that lies on both sides of a linear inequality.

10. Every linear programming problem either has a solution or is unbounded.

11. Solutions to linear programming problems may include fractions.

12. The inequality $4^2x + 5^2y \leq 7^2$ is a linear constraint.

13. The optimal solution to a linear programming problem can occur at a point that is not a corner point.

▶ *Chapter 3 Review Exercises*

1. Why doesn't the graphical method work for more than three variables?

2. How many constraints are we limited to in the graphical method?

Graph each linear inequality.

3. $y \geq 2x + 3$

4. $5x - 2y \leq 10$

5. $2x + 6y \leq 8$

6. $2x \quad 6y \geq 18$

7. $y \geq x$

8. $y \geq -2$

Graph the solution of each system of inequalities. Find all corner points.

9. $x + y \leq 6$
  $2x - y \geq 3$

10. $3x + 2y \geq 12$
  $4x - 5y \leq 20$

11. $-4 \leq x \leq 2$
  $-1 \leq y \leq 3$
  $x + y \leq 4$

12. $2 \leq x \leq 5$
  $1 \leq y \leq 7$
  $x - y \leq 3$

13. $x + 2y \leq 4$
  $5x - 6y \leq 12$
  $x \geq 0$
  $y \geq 0$

14. $x + 2y \leq 4$
  $2x - 3y \leq 6$
  $x \geq 0$
  $y \geq 0$

Use the given regions to find the maximum and minimum values of the objective function $z = 2x + 4y$.

15.

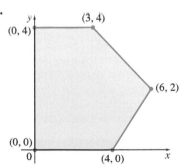

16.

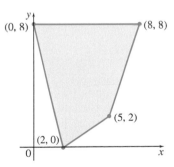

Use the graphical method to solve each linear programming problem.

17. Maximize $z = 2x + 4y$
  subject to: $3x + 2y \leq 12$
      $5x + y \geq 5$
      $x \geq 0$
      $y \geq 0.$

18. Minimize $z = 5x + 3y$
  subject to: $8x + 5y \geq 40$
      $4x + 10y \geq 40$
      $x \geq 0$
      $y \geq 0.$

19. Minimize $\quad z = 4x + 2y$

subject to: $\quad x + y \leq 50$

$\quad\quad\quad 2x + y \geq 20$

$\quad\quad\quad x + 2y \geq 30$

$\quad\quad\quad\quad x \geq 0$

$\quad\quad\quad\quad y \geq 0.$

20. Maximize $\quad z = 8x + 4y$

subject to: $\quad 3x + 12y \leq 36$

$\quad\quad\quad x + y \leq 4$

$\quad\quad\quad\quad x \geq 0$

$\quad\quad\quad\quad y \geq 0.$

21. Why must the solution to a linear programming problem always occur at a corner point of the feasible region?

22. Is there necessarily a unique point in the feasible region where the maximum or minimum occurs? Why or why not?

23. It is not necessary to check all corner points in a linear programming problem. This exercise illustrates an alternative procedure, which is essentially an expansion of the ideas illustrated in Example 1 of Section 3.2.

$$\text{Maximize} \quad z = 3x + 4y$$

$$\text{subject to:} \quad 2x + y \leq 4$$

$$-x + 2y \leq 4$$

$$x \geq 0$$

$$y \geq 0.$$

a. Sketch the feasible region, and add the line $z = 8$. (*Note:* 8 is chosen because the numbers work out simply, but the chosen value of z is arbitrary.)

b. Draw a line parallel to the line $z = 8$ that is as far from the origin as possible but still touches the feasible region.

c. The line you drew in part b should go through the point $(4/5, 12/5)$. Explain how you know the maximum must be located at this point.

24. Use the method described in the previous exercise to solve Exercise 20.

▶ Applications

BUSINESS AND ECONOMICS

25. *Time Management* A bakery makes both cakes and cookies. Each batch of cakes requires 2 hours in the oven and 3 hours in the decorating room. Each batch of cookies needs $1\frac{1}{2}$ hours in the oven and $\frac{2}{3}$ hour in the decorating room. The oven is available no more than 15 hours per day, and the decorating room can be used no more than 13 hours per day. Set up a system of inequalities, and then graph the solution of the system.

26. *Cost Analysis* DeMarco's pizza shop makes two specialty pizzas, the Mighty Meaty and the Very Veggie. The Mighty Meaty is topped with 5 different meat toppings and 2 different cheeses. The Very Veggie has 6 different vegetable toppings and 4 different cheeses. The shop sells at least 4 Mighty Meaty and 6 Very Veggie pizzas every day. The cost of the toppings for each Mighty Meaty is $3, and the cost of the vegetable toppings is $2 for each Very Veggie. No more than $60 per day can be spent on these toppings. The cheese used for the Mighty Meaty is $2 per pizza, and the cheese for the Very Veggie is $4 per pizza. No more than $80 per day can be spent on cheese. Set up a system of inequalities, and then graph the solution of the system.

27. *Profit* Refer to Exercise 25.

   a. How many batches of cakes and cookies should the bakery in Exercise 25 make in order to maximize profits if cookies produce a profit of $20 per batch and cakes produce a profit of $30 per batch?

   b. How much would the profit from selling cookies have to increase before it becomes more profitable to sell only cookies?

28. *Revenue* How many pizzas of each kind should the pizza shop in Exercise 26 make in order to maximize revenue if the Mighty Meaty sells for $15 and the Very Veggie sells for $12?

29. *Planting* In Karla's garden shop, she makes two kinds of mixtures for planting. A package of gardening mixture requires 2 lb of soil, 1 lb of peat moss, and 1 lb of fertilizer. A package of potting mixture requires 1 lb of soil, 2 lb of peat moss, and 3 lb of fertilizer. She has 16 lb of soil, 11 lb of peat moss, and 15 lb of fertilizer. If a package of gardening mixture sells for $3 and a package of potting mixture for $5, how many of each should she make in order to maximize her income? What is the maximum income?

30. *Construction* A contractor builds boathouses in two basic models, the Atlantic and the Pacific. Each Atlantic model requires 1000 ft of framing lumber, 3000 ft^3 of concrete, and $2000 for advertising. Each Pacific model requires 2000 ft of framing lumber, 3000 ft^3 of concrete, and $3000 for advertising. Contracts call for using at least 8000 ft of framing lumber, 18,000 ft^3 of concrete, and $15,000 worth of advertising. If the construction cost for each Atlantic model is $30,000 and the construction cost for each Pacific model is $40,000, how many of each model should be built to minimize construction costs?

31. *Steel* A steel company produces two types of alloys. A run of type I requires 3000 lb of molybdenum and 2000 tons of iron ore pellets as well as $2000 in advertising. A run of

type II requires 3000 lb of molybdenum and 1000 tons of iron ore pellets as well as $3000 in advertising. Total costs are $15,000 on a run of type I and $6000 on a run of type II. Because of various contracts, the company must use at least 18,000 lb of molybdenum and 7000 tons of iron ore pellets and spend at least $14,000 on advertising. How much of each type should be produced to minimize costs?

LIFE SCIENCES

32. *Nutrition* A dietician in a hospital is to arrange a special diet containing two foods, Health Trough and Power Gunk. Each ounce of Health Trough contains 30 mg of calcium, 10 mg of iron, 10 IU of vitamin A, and 8 mg of cholesterol. Each ounce of Power Gunk contains 10 mg of calcium, 10 mg of iron, 30 IU of vitamin A, and 4 mg of cholesterol. If the minimum daily requirements are 360 mg of calcium, 160 mg of iron, and 240 IU of vitamin A, how many ounces of each food should be used to meet the minimum requirements and at the same time minimize the cholesterol intake? Also, what is the minimum cholesterol intake?

SOCIAL SCIENCES

33. *Anthropology* A simplified model of the Mountain Fur economy of central Africa has been proposed.[*] In this model, two crops can be grown, millet and wheat, which produce 400 lb and 800 lb per acre, respectively. Millet requires 36 days to harvest one acre, while wheat requires only 8 days. There are 2 acres of land and 48 days of harvest labor available. How many acres should be devoted to each crop to maximize the pounds of grain harvested?

GENERAL INTEREST

34. *Studying* Ron Hampton is trying to allocate his study time this weekend. He can spend time working with either his math tutor or his accounting tutor to prepare for exams in both classes the following Monday. His math tutor charges $20 per hour, and his accounting tutor charges $40 per hour. He has $220 to spend on tutoring. Each hour that he spends working with his math tutor requires 1 aspirin and 1 hour of sleep to recover, while each hour he spends with his accounting tutor requires 1/2 aspirin and 3 hours of sleep. The maximum dosage of aspirin that he can safely take during his study time is 8 tablets, and he can only afford 15 hours of sleep this weekend. He expects that each hour with his math tutor will increase his score on the math exam by 3 points, while each hour with his accounting tutor will increase his score on the accounting exam by 5 points. How many hours should he spend with each tutor in order to maximize the number of points he will get on the two tests combined?

[*]Joy, Leonard, "Barth's Presentation of Economic Spheres in Darfur," in *Themes in Economic Anthropology*, edited by Raymond Firth, Tavistock Publications, 1967, pp. 175–189.

4

Linear Programming: The Simplex Method

Each type of beer has its own recipe and an associated cost per unit, and brings in a specific revenue per unit. The brewery manager must meet a revenue target with minimum production costs. An exercise in Section 3 formulates the manager's goal as a linear programming problem and solves for the optimum production schedule when there are two beer varieties.

In the previous chapter we discussed solving linear programming problems by the graphical method. This method illustrates the basic ideas of linear programming, but it is practical only for problems with two variables. For problems with more than two variables, or problems with two variables and many constraints, the *simplex method* is used. This method grew out of a practical problem faced by George B. Dantzig in 1947. Dantzig was concerned with finding the least expensive way to allocate supplies for the United States Air Force.

The **simplex method** starts with the selection of one corner point (often the origin) from the feasible region. Then, in a systematic way, another corner point is found that attempts to improve the value of the objective function. Finally, an optimum solution is reached, or it can be seen that no such solution exists.

The simplex method requires a number of steps. In this chapter we divide the presentation of these steps into two parts. First, a problem is set up in Section 4.1 and the method started; then, in Section 4.2, the method is completed. Special situations are discussed in the remainder of the chapter.

4.1 Slack Variables and the Pivot

Because the simplex method is used for problems with many variables, it usually is not convenient to use letters such as x, y, z, or w as variable names. Instead, the symbols x_1 (read "x-sub-one"), x_2, x_3, and so on, are used. These variable names lend themselves easily to use on the computer. In the simplex method, all constraints must be expressed in the linear form

$$a_1 x_1 + a_2 x_2 + a_3 x_3 + \cdots \leq b,$$

where $x_1, x_2, x_3, \ldots$ are variables and $a_1, a_2, \ldots,$ and b are constants.

In this section we will use the simplex method only for problems such as the following:

$$\begin{aligned} \text{Maximize} \quad & z = 2x_1 - 3x_2 \\ \text{subject to:} \quad & 2x_1 + x_2 \leq 10 \\ & x_1 - 3x_2 \leq 5 \\ \text{with} \quad & x_1 \geq 0, \quad x_2 \geq 0. \end{aligned}$$

This type of problem is said to be in *standard maximum form*.

STANDARD MAXIMUM FORM

A linear programming problem is in **standard maximum form** if the following conditions are satisfied.

1. The objective function is to be maximized.
2. All variables are nonnegative $(x_i \geq 0)$.
3. All remaining constraints are stated in the form

$$a_1 x_1 + a_2 x_2 + \cdots + a_n x_n \leq b \quad \text{with } b \geq 0.$$

(Problems that do not meet all of these conditions are discussed in Sections 4.3 and 4.4.)

To use the simplex method, we start by converting the constraints, which are linear inequalities, into linear equations. We do this by adding a nonnegative variable, called a **slack variable**, to each constraint. For example, the inequality $x_1 + x_2 \leq 10$ is converted into an equation by adding the slack variable s_1 to get

$$x_1 + x_2 + s_1 = 10, \quad \text{where } s_1 \geq 0.$$

The inequality $x_1 + x_2 \leq 10$ says that the sum $x_1 + x_2$ is less than or perhaps equal to 10. The variable s_1 "takes up any slack" and represents the amount by which $x_1 + x_2$ fails to equal 10. For example, if $x_1 + x_2$ equals 8, then s_1 is 2. If $x_1 + x_2 = 10$, then s_1 is 0.

| CAUTION | A different slack variable must be used for each constraint. ■

EXAMPLE 1

Slack Variables

Restate the following linear programming problem by introducing slack variables.

$$\text{Maximize} \quad z = 3x_1 + 2x_2 + x_3$$
$$\text{subject to:} \quad 2x_1 + x_2 + x_3 \leq 150$$
$$2x_1 + 2x_2 + 8x_3 \leq 200$$
$$2x_1 + 3x_2 + x_3 \leq 320$$
$$\text{with} \quad x_1 \geq 0, \quad x_2 \geq 0, \quad x_3 \geq 0.$$

►**Solution** Rewrite the three constraints as equations by adding slack variables s_1, s_2, and s_3, one for each constraint. Then the problem can be restated as follows.

$$\text{Maximize} \quad z = 3x_1 + 2x_2 + x_3$$
$$\text{subject to:} \quad 2x_1 + x_2 + x_3 + s_1 = 150$$
$$2x_1 + 2x_2 + 8x_3 + s_2 = 200$$
$$2x_1 + 3x_2 + x_3 + s_3 = 320$$
$$\text{with} \quad x_1 \geq 0, \quad x_2 \geq 0, \quad x_3 \geq 0, \quad s_1 \geq 0, \quad s_2 \geq 0, \quad s_3 \geq 0.$$

Adding slack variables to the constraints converts a linear programming problem into a system of linear equations. In each of these equations, all variables should be on the left side of the equals sign and all constants on the right. All the equations in Example 1 satisfy this condition except for the objective function, $z = 3x_1 + 2x_2 + x_3$, which may be written with all variables on the left as

$$-3x_1 - 2x_2 - x_3 + z = 0.$$

Now the equations in Example 1 can be written as the following augmented matrix.

x_1	x_2	x_3	s_1	s_2	s_3	z	
2	1	1	1	0	0	0	50
2	2	8	0	1	0	0	200
2	3	1	0	0	1	0	320
−3	−2	−1	0	0	0	1	0

Indicators

This matrix is called the initial **simplex tableau**. The numbers in the bottom row, which are from the objective function, are called **indicators** (except for the 1 and 0 at the far right).

EXAMPLE 2 Initial Simplex Tableau

Set up the initial simplex tableau for the following problem.

A farmer has 100 acres of available land on which he wishes to plant a mixture of potatoes, corn, and cabbage. It costs him $400 to produce an acre of potatoes, $160 to produce an acre of corn, and $280 to produce an acre of cabbage. He has a maximum of $20,000 to spend. He makes a profit of $120 per acre of potatoes, $40 per acre of corn, and $60 per acre of cabbage. How many acres of each crop should he plant to maximize his profit?

▶**Solution** Begin by summarizing the given information as follows.

	Potatoes	Corn	Cabbage		Total
Number of Acres	x_1	x_2	x_3	$\leq$	100
Cost (per acre)	$400	$160	$280	$\leq$	$20,000
Profit (per acre)	$120	$40	$60		

If the number of acres allotted to each of the three crops is represented by x_1, x_2, and x_3, respectively, then the constraint pertaining to the number of acres can be expressed as

$$x_1 + x_2 + x_3 \leq 100 \quad \text{Number of acres}$$

where x_1, x_2, and x_3 are all nonnegative. This constraint says that $x_1 + x_2 + x_3$ is less than or perhaps equal to 100. Use s_1 as the slack variable, giving the equation

$$x_1 + x_2 + x_3 + s_1 = 100.$$

Here s_1 represents the amount of the farmer's 100 acres that will not be used (s_1 may be 0 or any value up to 100).

The constraint pertaining to the production cost can be expressed as

$$400x_1 + 160x_2 + 280x_3 \leq 20,000, \quad \text{Production costs}$$

or if we divide both sides by 40, as

$$10x_1 + 4x_2 + 7x_3 \leq 500.$$

This inequality can also be converted into an equation by adding a slack variable, s_2.

$$10x_1 + 4x_2 + 7x_3 + s_2 = 500$$

If we had not divided by 40, the slack variable would have represented any unused portion of the farmer's $20,000 capital. Instead, the slack variable represents $1/40$ of that unused portion. (Note that s_2 may be any value from 0 to 500.)

The objective function represents the profit. The farmer wants to maximize

$$z = 120x_1 + 40x_2 + 60x_3.$$

The linear programming problem can now be stated as follows:

Maximize $\quad z = 120x_1 + 40x_2 + 60x_3$

subject to: $\quad x_1 + x_2 + x_3 + s_1 \qquad\quad = 100$

$\qquad\qquad\quad 10x_1 + 4x_2 + 7x_3 \qquad + s_2 = 500$

with $\qquad\quad x_1 \geq 0, \quad x_2 \geq 0, \quad x_3 \geq 0, \quad s_1 \geq 0, \quad s_2 \geq 0.$

Rewrite the objective function as $-120x_1 - 40x_2 - 60x_3 + z = 0$, and complete the initial simplex tableau as follows.

$$
\begin{array}{cccccc}
x_1 & x_2 & x_3 & s_1 & s_2 & z \\
\end{array}
$$

$$
\left[
\begin{array}{cccccc|c}
1 & 1 & 1 & 1 & 0 & 0 & 100 \\
10 & 4 & 7 & 0 & 1 & 0 & 500 \\
\hline
-120 & -40 & -60 & 0 & 0 & 1 & 0 \\
\end{array}
\right]
$$

The maximization problem in Example 2 consists of a system of two equations (describing the constraints) in five variables, together with the objective function. As with the graphical method, it is necessary to solve this system to find corner points of the region of feasible solutions. Since there are more variables than equations, the system will have an infinite number of solutions.

To see this, solve the system for s_1 and s_2.

$$
\begin{array}{l}
s_1 = 100 - x_1 - x_2 - x_3 \\
s_2 = 500 - 10x_1 - 4x_2 - 7x_3
\end{array}
$$

Each choice of values for x_1, x_2, and x_3 gives corresponding values for s_1 and s_2 that produce a solution of the system. But only some of these solutions are feasible.

In a feasible solution, all variables must be nonnegative. To get a unique feasible solution, we set three of the five variables equal to 0. In general, if there are m equations, then m variables can be nonzero. These m nonzero variables are called **basic variables**, and the corresponding solutions are called **basic feasible solutions**. Each basic feasible solution corresponds to a corner point. In particular, if we choose the solution with $x_1 = 0$, $x_2 = 0$, and $x_3 = 0$, then $s_1 = 100$ and $s_2 = 500$ are the basic variables. This solution, which corresponds to the corner point at the origin, is hardly optimal. It produces a profit of $0 for the farmer, since the equation that corresponds to the objective function becomes

$$
-120(0) - 40(0) - 60(0) + 0s_1 + 0s_2 + z = 0.
$$

In the next section we will use the simplex method to start with this solution and improve it to find the maximum possible profit.

Each step of the simplex method produces a solution that corresponds to a corner point of the region of feasible solutions. These solutions can be read directly from the matrix, as shown in the next example.

EXAMPLE 3 **Basic Variables**

Read a solution from the following simplex tableau.

$$
\begin{array}{cccccc}
x_1 & x_2 & x_3 & s_1 & s_2 & z \\
\end{array}
$$

$$
\left[
\begin{array}{cccccc|c}
2 & 0 & 8 & 5 & 2 & 0 & 17 \\
9 & 5 & 3 & 12 & 0 & 0 & 45 \\
\hline
-2 & 0 & -4 & 0 & 0 & 3 & 90 \\
\end{array}
\right]
$$

▶**Solution** In this solution, the variables x_2 and s_2 are basic variables. They can be identified quickly because the columns for these variables have all zeros except for one nonzero entry. All variables that are not basic variables have the value 0. This means that in the tableau just shown, x_2 and s_2 are the basic variables, while x_1, x_3, and s_1 have the value 0. The nonzero entry for x_2 is 5 in the second row. Since x_1, x_3, and s_1 are zero, the second row of the tableau represents the equation $5x_2 = 45$, so $x_2 = 9$. Similarly, from the top row, $2s_2 = 17$, so $s_2 = 17/2$. From the bottom row, $3z = 90$, so $z = 30$. The solution is thus $x_1 = 0$, $x_2 = 9$, $x_3 = 0$, $s_1 = 0$, and $s_2 = 17/2$, with $z = 30$. ∎

▶ FOR REVIEW

We discussed three row operations in Chapter 2:

1. interchanging any two rows;

2. multiplying the elements of a row by any nonzero real number; and

3. adding a multiple of the elements of one row to the corresponding elements of a multiple of any other row.

In this chapter we will only use operation 2 and a restricted version of operation 3; we will never interchange two rows.

Pivots   Solutions read directly from the initial simplex tableau are seldom optimal. It is necessary to proceed to other solutions (corresponding to other corner points of the feasible region) until an optimum solution is found. To get these other solutions, we use restricted versions of the row operations from Chapter 2 to change the tableau by using one of the nonzero entries of the tableau as a **pivot**. The row operations are performed to change to 0 all entries in the column containing the pivot (except for the pivot itself, which remains unchanged). Pivoting, explained in the next example, produces a new tableau leading to another solution of the system of equations obtained from the original problem.

CAUTION   In this chapter, when adding a multiple of one row to a multiple of another, we will never take a negative multiple of the row being changed. For example, when changing row 2, we might use $-2R_1 + 3R_2 \rightarrow R_2$, but we will never use $2R_1 - 3R_2 \rightarrow R_2$. If you get a negative number in the rightmost column, you will know immediately that you have made an error. The reason for this restriction is that violating it turns negative numbers into positive, and vice versa. This is disastrous in the bottom row, where we will seek negative numbers when we choose our pivot column. It will also cause problems with choosing pivots, particularly in the algorithm for solving nonstandard problems in Section 4.4. ∎

When we are performing row operations by hand, as we did in Chapter 2, we will postpone getting a 1 in each basic variable column until the final step. This will avoid fractions and decimals, which can make the operations more difficult and more prone to error. When using a graphing calculator, however, we must change the pivot to a 1 before performing row operations. The next example illustrates both of these methods.

EXAMPLE 4   **Pivot**

Pivot about the indicated 2 of the following initial simplex tableau.

$$
\begin{array}{ccccccc}
x_1 & x_2 & x_3 & s_1 & s_2 & s_3 & z \\
\end{array}
$$

$$
\left[
\begin{array}{ccccccc|c}
\mathbf{2} & 1 & 1 & 1 & 0 & 0 & 0 & 150 \\
1 & 2 & 8 & 0 & 1 & 0 & 0 & 200 \\
2 & 3 & 1 & 0 & 0 & 1 & 0 & 320 \\
\hline
-3 & -2 & -1 & 0 & 0 & 0 & 1 & 0
\end{array}
\right]
$$

METHOD 1
Calculating by Hand

▶**Solution**

Using the row operations indicated in color to get zeros in the column with the pivot, we arrive at the following tableau.

$$
\begin{array}{cc}
 & \begin{array}{ccccccc} x_1 & x_2 & x_3 & s_1 & s_2 & s_3 & z \end{array} \\
\begin{array}{c} \\ -R_1 + 2R_2 \rightarrow R_2 \\ -R_1 + R_3 \rightarrow R_3 \\ 3R_1 + 2R_4 \rightarrow R_4 \end{array} &
\left[\begin{array}{ccccccc|c}
2 & 1 & 1 & 1 & 0 & 0 & 0 & 150 \\
0 & 3 & 15 & -1 & 2 & 0 & 0 & 250 \\
0 & 2 & 0 & -1 & 0 & 1 & 0 & 170 \\
0 & -1 & 1 & 3 & 0 & 0 & 2 & 450
\end{array} \right]
\end{array}
$$

In this simplex tableau, the variables x_1, s_2, and s_3 are basic variables. The solution is $x_1 = 75$, $x_2 = 0$, $x_3 = 0$, $s_1 = 0$, $s_2 = 125$, and $s_3 = 170$. Substituting these results into the objective function gives

$$0(75) - 1(0) + 1(0) + 3(0) + 0(125) + 0(170) + 2z = 450,$$

or $z = 225$. (This shows that the value of z can always be found using the number in the bottom row of the z column and the number in the lower right-hand corner.)

Finally, to be able to read the solution directly from the tableau, we multiply rows 1, 2, and 4 by $1/2$, getting the following tableau.

$$
\begin{array}{cc}
 & \begin{array}{ccccccc} x_1 & x_2 & x_3 & s_1 & s_2 & s_3 & z \end{array} \\
\begin{array}{c} \frac{1}{2}R_1 \rightarrow R_1 \\ \frac{1}{2}R_2 \rightarrow R_2 \\ \\ \frac{1}{2}R_4 \rightarrow R_4 \end{array} &
\left[\begin{array}{ccccccc|c}
1 & \frac{1}{2} & \frac{1}{2} & \frac{1}{2} & 0 & 0 & 0 & 75 \\
0 & \frac{3}{2} & \frac{15}{2} & -\frac{1}{2} & 1 & 0 & 0 & 125 \\
0 & 2 & 0 & -1 & 0 & 1 & 0 & 170 \\
0 & -\frac{1}{2} & \frac{1}{2} & \frac{3}{2} & 0 & 0 & 1 & 225
\end{array} \right]
\end{array}
$$

METHOD 2
Graphing Calculator

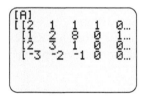

FIGURE 1

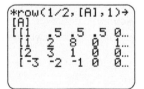

FIGURE 2

The row operations of the simplex method can also be done on a graphing calculator, as we saw in Chapter 2. Figure 1 shows the result when the tableau in this example is entered into a TI-83/84 Plus. The right side of the tableau is not visible but can be seen by pressing the right arrow key.

Recall that we must change the pivot to 1 before performing row operations with a graphing calculator. Figure 2 shows the result of multiplying row 1 of matrix A by $1/2$. In Figure 3 we show the same result with the decimal numbers changed to fractions.

We can now modify column 1, using the commands described in Chapter 2, to agree with the tableau under Method 1. The result is shown in Figure 4.

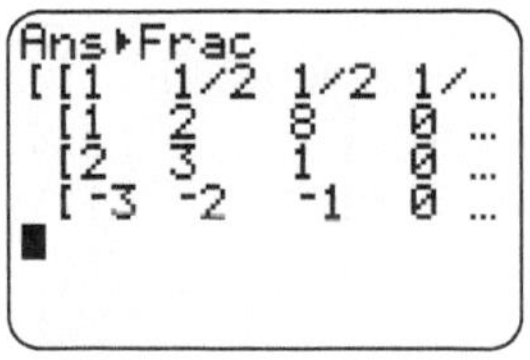

FIGURE 3

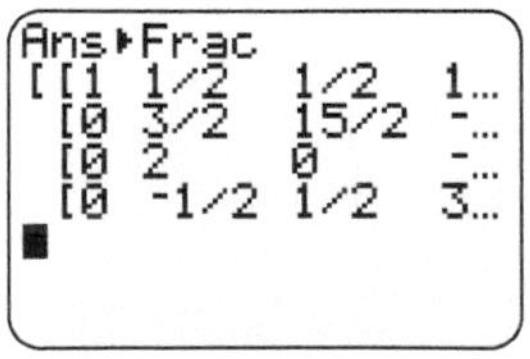

FIGURE 4

In the simplex method, the pivoting process (without the final step of getting a 1 in each basic variable column when using Method 1) is repeated until an optimum solution is found, if one exists. In the next section we will see how to decide where to pivot to improve the value of the objective function and how to tell when an optimum solution either has been reached or does not exist.

➤ 4.1 Exercises

Convert each inequality into an equation by adding a slack variable.

1. $x_1 + 2x_2 \leq 6$ 　　　　**2.** $6x_1 + 2x_2 \leq 50$ 　　**3.** $2.3x_1 + 5.7x_2 + 1.8x_3 \leq 17$ 　　**4.** $8x_1 + 6x_2 + 5x_3 \leq 250$

For Exercises 5–8, (a) determine the number of slack variables needed, (b) name them, and (c) use slack variables to convert each constraint into a linear equation.

5. Maximize 　$z = 5x_1 + 7x_2$
　subject to: 　$2x_1 + 3x_2 \leq 15$
　　　　　　$4x_1 + 5x_2 \leq 35$
　　　　　　$x_1 + 6x_2 \leq 20$
　with 　　$x_1 \geq 0, \quad x_2 \geq 0.$

6. Maximize 　$z = 1.2x_1 + 3.5x_2$
　subject to: 　$2.4x_1 + 1.5x_2 \leq 10$
　　　　　　$1.7x_1 + 1.9x_2 \leq 15$
　with 　　$x_1 \geq 0, \quad x_2 \geq 0.$

7. Maximize 　$z = 8x_1 + 3x_2 + x_3$
　subject to: 　$7x_1 + 6x_2 + 8x_3 \leq 118$
　　　　　　$4x_1 + 5x_2 + 10x_3 \leq 220$
　with 　　$x_1 \geq 0, \quad x_2 > 0, \quad x_3 \geq 0.$

8. Maximize 　$z = 12x_1 + 15x_2 + 10x_3$
　subject to: 　$2x_1 + 2x_2 + x_3 \leq 8$
　　　　　　$x_1 + 4x_2 + 3x_3 \leq 12$
　with 　　$x_1 \geq 0, \quad x_2 \geq 0, \quad x_3 \geq 0.$

Write the solutions that can be read from each simplex tableau.

9.
$$\begin{array}{cccccc|c}
x_1 & x_2 & x_3 & s_1 & s_2 & z & \\
1 & 0 & 4 & 5 & 1 & 0 & 8 \\
3 & 1 & 1 & 2 & 0 & 0 & 4 \\
\hline
-2 & 0 & 2 & 3 & 0 & 1 & 28
\end{array}$$

10.
$$\begin{array}{cccccc|c}
x_1 & x_2 & x_3 & s_1 & s_2 & z & \\
1 & 5 & 0 & 1 & 2 & 0 & 6 \\
0 & 2 & 1 & 2 & 3 & 0 & 15 \\
\hline
0 & 4 & 0 & 1 & -2 & 1 & 64
\end{array}$$

11.
$$\begin{array}{ccccccc|c}
x_1 & x_2 & x_3 & s_1 & s_2 & s_3 & z & \\
6 & 2 & 2 & 3 & 0 & 0 & 0 & 16 \\
2 & 2 & 0 & 1 & 0 & 5 & 0 & 35 \\
2 & 1 & 0 & 3 & 1 & 0 & 0 & 6 \\
\hline
-3 & -2 & 0 & 2 & 0 & 0 & 3 & 36
\end{array}$$

12.
$$\begin{array}{ccccccc|c}
x_1 & x_2 & x_3 & s_1 & s_2 & s_3 & z & \\
0 & 2 & 0 & 5 & 2 & 2 & 0 & 15 \\
0 & 3 & 1 & 0 & 1 & 2 & 0 & 2 \\
7 & 4 & 0 & 0 & 3 & 5 & 0 & 35 \\
\hline
0 & -4 & 0 & 0 & 4 & 3 & 2 & 40
\end{array}$$

Pivot once as indicated in each simplex tableau. Read the solution from the result.

13.
$$\begin{array}{cccccc|c}
x_1 & x_2 & x_3 & s_1 & s_2 & z & \\
1 & 2 & 4 & 1 & 0 & 0 & 56 \\
2 & \boxed{2} & 1 & 0 & 1 & 0 & 40 \\
\hline
-1 & -3 & -2 & 0 & 0 & 1 & 0
\end{array}$$

14.
$$\begin{array}{cccccc|c}
x_1 & x_2 & x_3 & s_1 & s_2 & z & \\
2 & 3 & 4 & 1 & 0 & 0 & 18 \\
6 & \boxed{3} & 2 & 0 & 1 & 0 & 15 \\
\hline
-1 & -6 & -2 & 0 & 0 & 1 & 0
\end{array}$$

15.
$$\begin{array}{ccccccc|c}
x_1 & x_2 & x_3 & s_1 & s_2 & s_3 & z & \\
2 & 2 & \boxed{1} & 1 & 0 & 0 & 0 & 12 \\
1 & 2 & 3 & 0 & 1 & 0 & 0 & 45 \\
3 & 1 & 1 & 0 & 0 & 1 & 0 & 20 \\
\hline
-2 & -1 & -3 & 0 & 0 & 0 & 1 & 0
\end{array}$$

16.
$$\begin{array}{ccccccc|c}
x_1 & x_2 & x_3 & s_1 & s_2 & s_3 & z & \\
4 & 2 & 3 & 1 & 0 & 0 & 0 & 22 \\
2 & 2 & \boxed{5} & 0 & 1 & 0 & 0 & 28 \\
1 & 3 & 2 & 0 & 0 & 1 & 0 & 45 \\
\hline
-3 & -2 & -4 & 0 & 0 & 0 & 1 & 0
\end{array}$$

17.
$$\begin{array}{ccccccc|c}
x_1 & x_2 & x_3 & s_1 & s_2 & s_3 & z & \\
2 & \boxed{2} & 3 & 1 & 0 & 0 & 0 & 500 \\
4 & 1 & 1 & 0 & 1 & 0 & 0 & 300 \\
7 & 2 & 4 & 0 & 0 & 1 & 0 & 700 \\
\hline
-3 & -4 & -2 & 0 & 0 & 0 & 1 & 0
\end{array}$$

18.
$$\begin{array}{cccccccc|c}
x_1 & x_2 & x_3 & x_4 & s_1 & s_2 & s_3 & z & \\
1 & 2 & 3 & 1 & 1 & 0 & 0 & 0 & 115 \\
2 & 1 & 8 & 5 & 0 & 1 & 0 & 0 & 200 \\
\boxed{1} & 0 & 1 & 0 & 0 & 0 & 1 & 0 & 50 \\
\hline
-2 & -1 & -1 & -1 & 0 & 0 & 0 & 1 & 0
\end{array}$$

Introduce slack variables as necessary, then write the initial simplex tableau for each linear programming problem.

19. Find $x_1 \geq 0$ and $x_2 \geq 0$ such that
$$4x_1 + 2x_2 \leq 5$$
$$x_1 + 2x_2 \leq 4$$
and $z = 7x_1 + x_2$ is maximized.

20. Find $x_1 \geq 0$ and $x_2 \geq 0$ such that
$$2x_1 + 3x_2 \leq 100$$
$$5x_1 + 4x_2 \leq 200$$
and $z = x_1 + 3x_2$ is maximized.

21. Find $x_1 \geq 0$ and $x_2 \geq 0$ such that
$$x_1 + x_2 \leq 10$$
$$5x_1 + 2x_2 \leq 20$$
$$x_1 + 2x_2 \leq 36$$
and $z = x_1 + 3x_2$ is maximized.

22. Find $x_1 \geq 0$ and $x_2 \geq 0$ such that
$$x_1 + x_2 \leq 25$$
$$4x_1 + 3x_2 \leq 48$$
and $z = 5x_1 + 3x_2$ is maximized.

23. Find $x_1 \geq 0$ and $x_2 \geq 0$ such that
$$3x_1 + x_2 \leq 12$$
$$x_1 + x_2 \leq 15$$
and $z = 2x_1 + x_2$ is maximized.

24. Find $x_1 \geq 0$ and $x_2 \geq 0$ such that
$$10x_1 + 4x_2 \leq 100$$
$$20x_1 + 10x_2 \leq 150$$
and $z = 4x_1 + 5x_2$ is maximized.

▶ Applications

Set up Exercises 25–29 for solution by the simplex method. First express the linear constraints and objective function, then add slack variables, and then set up the initial simplex tableau. The solutions of some of these problems will be completed in the exercises for the next section.

BUSINESS AND ECONOMICS

25. *Royalties* The authors of a best-selling textbook in finite mathematics are told that, for the next edition of their book, each simple figure would cost the project $20, each figure with additions would cost $35, and each computer-drawn sketch would cost $60. They are limited to 400 figures, for which they are allowed to spend up to $2200. The number of computer-drawn sketches must be no more than the number of the other two types combined, and there must be at least twice as many simple figures as there are figures with additions. If each simple figure increases the royalties by $95, each figure with additions increases royalties by $200, and each computer-drawn figure increases royalties by $325, how many of each type of figure should be included to maximize royalties, assuming that all art costs are borne by the publisher?

26. *Manufacturing Bicycles* A manufacturer of bicycles builds racing, touring, and mountain models. The bicycles are made of both aluminum and steel. The company has available 91,800 units of steel and 42,000 units of aluminum. The racing, touring, and mountain models need 17, 27, and 34 units of steel, and 12, 21, and 15 units of alu-

minum, respectively. How many of each type of bicycle should be made in order to maximize profit if the company makes $8 per racing bike, $12 per touring bike, and $22 per mountain bike? What is the maximum possible profit?

27. *Production—Picnic Tables* The manager of a large park has received many complaints about the insufficient number of picnic tables available. At the end of the park season, she has surplus cash and labor resources available and decides to make as many tables as possible. She considers three possible models: redwood, stained Douglas fir, and stained white spruce (all of which last equally well). She has carpenters available for assembly work for a maximum of 90 eight-hour days, while laborers for staining work are available for no more than 60 eight-hour days. Each redwood table requires 8 hours to assemble but no staining, and it costs $159 (including all labor and materials). Each Douglas fir table requires 7 hours to assemble and 2 hours to stain, and it costs $138.85. Each white spruce table requires 8 hours to assemble and 2 hours to stain, and it costs $129.35. If no more than $15,000 is available for this project, what is the maximum number of tables which can be made, and how many of each type should be made?*

28. *Production—Knives* The Cut-Right Company sells sets of kitchen knives. The Basic Set consists of 2 utility knives and 1 chef's knife. The Regular Set consists of 2 utility knives, 1 chef's knife, and 1 slicer. The Deluxe Set consists of 3 utility knives, 1 chef's knife, and 1 slicer. Their profit is $30 on a Basic Set, $40 on a Regular Set, and $60 on a Deluxe Set.

The factory has on hand 800 utility knives, 400 chef's knives, and 200 slicers. Assuming that all sets will be sold, how many of each type should be produced in order to maximize profit? What is the maximum profit?

29. *Advertising* The Fancy Fashions, an independent, local boutique, has $8000 available each month for advertising. Newspaper ads cost $400 each, and no more than 30 can run per month. Internet banner ads cost $20 each, and no more than 60 can run per month. TV ads cost $2000 each, with a maximum of 10 available each month. Approximately 4000 women will see each newspaper ad, 3000 will see each Internet banner, and 10,000 will see each TV ad. How much of each type of advertising should be used if the store wants to maximize its ad exposure?

4.2 Maximization Problems

 **THINK ABOUT IT**

How many racing, touring, and mountain bicycles should a bicycle manufacturer make to maximize profit?

We will answer this question in Exercise 25 of this section using an algorithm called the simplex method.

In the previous section we showed how to prepare a linear programming problem for solution. First, we converted the constraints to linear equations with slack variables; then we used the coefficients of the variables from the linear equation to write an augmented matrix. Finally, we used the pivot to go from one corner point to another corner point in the region of feasible solutions.

Now we are ready to put all this together and produce an optimum value for the objective function. To see how this is done, let us complete Example 2 from Section 4.1. In this example, we were trying to determine, under certain constraints, the number of acres of potatoes (x_1), corn (x_2), and cabbage (x_3) the farmer should plant in order to optimize his profit (z). In the previous section, we set up the following simplex tableau.

$$
\begin{array}{cccccc}
x_1 & x_2 & x_3 & s_1 & s_2 & z \\
\left[\begin{array}{cccccc|c}
1 & 1 & 1 & 1 & 0 & 0 & 100 \\
10 & 4 & 7 & 0 & 1 & 0 & 500 \\
\hline
-120 & -40 & -60 & 0 & 0 & 1 & 0
\end{array}\right]
\end{array}
$$

This tableau leads to the solution $x_1 = 0$, $x_2 = 0$, $x_3 = 0$, $s_1 = 100$, and $s_2 = 500$, with s_1 and s_2 as the basic variables. These values produce a value of 0 for z. In this solution, the farmer is planting 0 acres and earning $0 profit. We can easily see that there are other combinations of potatoes, corn, and cabbage that

---

*This exercise was provided by Professor Karl K. Norton, Husson College.

produce a nonzero profit, and thus we know that the farmer has better alternatives than planting nothing.

To decide which crops he should plant, we look at the original objective function representing profit,

$$z = 120x_1 + 40x_2 + 60x_3.$$

The coefficient of x_1 is the largest, which indicates that he will make the most profit per acre planting potatoes. It makes sense, then, to first try increasing x_1 to improve the profit.

To determine how much we can increase x_1, we look at the constraint equations:

$$x_1 + x_2 + x_3 + s_1 \qquad\quad = 100$$
$$10x_1 + 4x_2 + 7x_3 + \qquad + s_2 = 500.$$

Because there are two equations, only two of the five variables can be basic (and nonzero). If x_1 is nonzero in the solution, then x_1 will be a basic variable. This means that either s_1 or s_2 no longer will be a basic variable. To decide which variable will no longer be basic, solve the equations for s_1 and s_2, respectively:

$$s_1 = 100 - \quad x_1 - \quad x_2 - \quad x_3$$
$$s_2 = 500 - 10x_1 - 4x_2 - 7x_3.$$

Only x_1 is being changed to a nonzero value; both x_2 and x_3 keep the value 0. Replacing x_2 and x_3 with 0 gives

$$s_1 = 100 - \quad x_1$$
$$s_2 = 500 - 10x_1.$$

Since both s_1 and s_2 must remain nonnegative, there is a limit to how much the value of x_1 can be increased. The equation $s_1 = 100 - x_1$ (or $s_1 = 100 - 1x_1$) shows that x_1 cannot exceed $100/1$, or 100. The second equation, $s_2 = 500 - 10x_1$, shows that x_1 cannot exceed $500/10$, or 50. To satisfy both these conditions, x_1 cannot exceed 50, the smaller of 50 and 100. If we let x_1 take the value of 50, then $x_1 = 50$, $x_2 = 0$, $x_3 = 0$, and $s_2 = 0$. Since $s_1 = 100 - x_1$, then

$$s_1 = 100 - 50 = 50.$$

Therefore, s_1 is still a basic variable, while s_2 is no longer a basic variable, having been replaced in the set of basic variables by x_1. This solution gives a profit of

$$z = 120x_1 + 40x_2 + 60x_3 + 0s_1 + 0s_2$$
$$= 120(50) + 40(0) + 60(0) + 0(50) + 0(0) = 6000,$$

or $6000, when 50 acres of potatoes are planted.

The same result could have been found from the initial simplex tableau given on the next page. Recall that the indicators are the numbers in the bottom row in the columns labeled with real or slack variables. To use the tableau, we select the variable with the most negative indicator. (If no indicator is negative, then the value of the objective function cannot be improved.) In this example, the variable with the most negative indicator is x_1.

Basic variables

$$\begin{array}{c} \downarrow \quad \downarrow \\ \begin{array}{cccccc} x_1 & x_2 & x_3 & s_1 & s_2 & z \end{array} \\ \left[\begin{array}{cccccc|c} 1 & 1 & 1 & 1 & 0 & 0 & 100 \\ 10 & 4 & 7 & 0 & 1 & 0 & 500 \\ \hline -120 & -40 & -60 & 0 & 0 & 1 & 0 \end{array}\right] \end{array}$$

↑
Most negative indicator

The most negative indicator identifies the variable whose value is to be made nonzero, if possible. To find the variable that is now basic and will become nonbasic, calculate the quotients that were found above. Do this by dividing each number from the right side of the tableau by the corresponding number from the column with the most negative indicator.

Basic variables

$$\begin{array}{cc} & \begin{array}{c} \downarrow \quad \downarrow \\ \text{Quotients} \quad \begin{array}{cccccc} x_1 & x_2 & x_3 & s_1 & s_2 & z \end{array} \end{array} \\ \begin{array}{c} 100/1 = 100 \\ \text{Smaller} \ > 500/10 = 50 \end{array} \left[\begin{array}{cccccc|c} 1 & 1 & 1 & 1 & 0 & 0 & 100 \\ \mathbf{10} & 4 & 7 & 0 & 1 & 0 & 500 \\ \hline -120 & -40 & -60 & 0 & 0 & 1 & 0 \end{array}\right] \end{array}$$

Notice that we do not form a quotient for the bottom row. Of the two quotients found, the smallest is 50 (from the second row), so 10 is the pivot. Using 10 as the pivot, perform the appropriate row operations to get zeros in the rest of the column. We will use Method 1 from Section 4.1 (calculating by hand) to perform the pivoting, but Method 2 (graphing calculator) could be used just as well. The new tableau is as follows.

Basic variables

$$\begin{array}{cc} & \begin{array}{c} \downarrow \downarrow \\ \begin{array}{cccccc} x_1 & x_2 & x_3 & s_1 & s_2 & z \end{array} \end{array} \\ \begin{array}{c} -R_2 + 10R_1 \rightarrow R_1 \\ \\ 12R_2 + R_3 \rightarrow R_3 \end{array} \left[\begin{array}{cccccc|c} 0 & 6 & 3 & 10 & -1 & 0 & 500 \\ 10 & 4 & 7 & 0 & 1 & 0 & 500 \\ \hline 0 & 8 & 24 & 0 & 12 & 1 & 6000 \end{array}\right] \end{array}$$

The solution read from this tableau is

$$x_1 = 50, \quad x_2 = 0, \quad x_3 = 0, \quad s_1 = 50, \quad s_2 = 0,$$

with $z = 6000$, the same as the result found above.

None of the indicators in the final simplex tableau are negative, which means that the value of z cannot be improved beyond \$6000. To see why, recall that the last row gives the coefficients of the objective function so that

$$0x_1 + 8x_2 + 24x_3 + 0s_1 + 12s_2 + z = 6000,$$

or $\qquad z = 6000 - 0x_1 - 8x_2 - 24x_3 - 0s_1 - 12s_2.$

Since x_2, x_3, and s_2 are zero, $z = 6000$, but if any of these three variables were to increase, z would decrease.

This result suggests that the optimal solution has been found as soon as no indicators are negative. As long as an indicator is negative, the value of the objective function may be improved. If any indicators are negative, we just find a new pivot and use row operations, repeating the process until no negative indicators remain.

Once there are no longer any negative numbers in the final row, create a 1 in the columns corresponding to the basic variables and z. In the previous example, this is accomplished by dividing rows 1 and 2 by 10.

$$
\begin{array}{c}
\\
R_1/10 \rightarrow R_1 \\
R_2/10 \rightarrow R_2 \\
\\
\end{array}
\begin{array}{c}
\begin{array}{cccccc}
x_1 & x_2 & x_3 & s_1 & s_2 & z
\end{array} \\
\left[
\begin{array}{cccccc|c}
0 & \frac{6}{10} & \frac{3}{10} & 1 & -\frac{1}{10} & 0 & 50 \\
1 & \frac{4}{10} & \frac{7}{10} & 0 & \frac{1}{10} & 0 & 50 \\
\hline
0 & 8 & 24 & 0 & 12 & 1 & 6000
\end{array}
\right]
\end{array}
$$

It is now easy to read the solution from this tableau:

$$x_1 = 50, \quad x_2 = 0, \quad x_3 = 0, \quad s_1 = 50, \quad s_2 = 0,$$

with $z = 6000$.

We can finally state the solution to the problem about the farmer. The farmer will make a maximum profit of $6000 by planting 50 acres of potatoes, no acres of corn, and no acres of cabbage. The value $s_1 = 50$ indicates that of the 100 acres of land available, 50 acres should be left unplanted. It may seem strange that leaving assets unused can produce a maximum profit, but such results actually occur often.

Note that since each variable can be increased by a different amount, the most negative indicator is not always the best choice. On average, though, it has been found that the most negative indicator is the best choice.

In summary, the following steps are involved in solving a standard maximum linear programming problem by the simplex method.

SIMPLEX METHOD

1. Determine the objective function.

2. Write all the necessary constraints.

3. Convert each constraint into an equation by adding a slack variable in each.

4. Set up the initial simplex tableau.

5. Locate the most negative indicator. If there are two such indicators, choose the one farther to the left.

6. Form the necessary quotients to find the pivot. Disregard any quotients with 0 or a negative number in the denominator. The smallest nonnegative quotient gives the location of the pivot. If all quotients must be disregarded, no maximum solution exists. If two quotients are both equal and smallest, choose the pivot in the row nearest the top of the matrix.

7. Use row operations to change all other numbers in the pivot column to zero by adding a suitable multiple of the pivot row to a positive multiple of each row.

8. If the indicators are all positive or 0, this is the final tableau. If not, go back to Step 5 and repeat the process until a tableau with no negative indicators is obtained.

9. Read the solution from the final tableau.

In Steps 5 and 6, the choice of the column farthest to the left or the row closest to the top is arbitrary. You may choose another row or column in case of a tie, and you will get the same final answer, but your intermediate results will be different.

CAUTION In performing the simplex method, a negative number in the right-hand column signals that a mistake has been made. One possible error is using a negative value for c_2 in the operation $c_1R_i + c_2R_j \rightarrow R_j$. ∎

EXAMPLE 1 Using the Simplex Method

To compare the simplex method with the graphical method, we use the simplex method to solve the problem in Example 1, Section 3.3. The graph is shown again in Figure 5. The objective function to be maximized was

$$z = 25x_1 + 30x_2. \quad \text{Revenue}$$

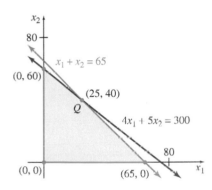

FIGURE 5

(Since we are using the simplex method, we use x_1 and x_2 instead of x and y as variables.) The constraints were as follows:

$$x_1 + x_2 \leq 65 \quad \text{Number}$$
$$4x_1 + 5x_2 \leq 300 \quad \text{Cost}$$

with

$$x_1 \geq 0, \quad x_2 \geq 0.$$

Add a slack variable to each constraint:

$$x_1 + x_2 + s_1 \quad = 65$$
$$4x_1 + 5x_2 \quad + s_2 = 300$$

with

$$x_1 \geq 0, \quad x_2 \geq 0, \quad s_1 \geq 0, \quad s_2 \geq 0.$$

Write the initial tableau.

$$
\begin{array}{ccccc|c}
x_1 & x_2 & s_1 & s_2 & z & \\
\hline
1 & 1 & 1 & 0 & 0 & 65 \\
4 & 5 & 0 & 1 & 0 & 300 \\
\hline
-25 & -30 & 0 & 0 & 1 & 0
\end{array}
$$

This tableau leads to the solution $x_1 = 0$, $x_2 = 0$, $s_1 = 65$, and $s_2 = 300$, with $z = 0$, which corresponds to the origin in Figure 5. The most negative indicator is -30, which is in column 2 of row 3. The quotients of the numbers in the right-hand column and in column 2 are

$$\frac{65}{1} = 65 \quad \text{and} \quad \frac{300}{5} = 60.$$

The smaller quotient is 60, giving 5 as the pivot. Use row operations to get the new tableau. For clarity, we will continue to label the columns with x_1, x_2, and so on, although this is not necessary in practice.

$$
\begin{array}{c}
 \\
-R_2 + 5R_1 \rightarrow R_1 \\
 \\
6R_2 + R_3 \rightarrow R_3
\end{array}
\begin{array}{cccccc}
x_1 & x_2 & s_1 & s_2 & z & \\
\left[\begin{array}{ccccc|c}
1 & 0 & 5 & -1 & 0 & 25 \\
4 & 5 & 0 & 1 & 0 & 300 \\
-1 & 0 & 0 & 6 & 1 & 1800
\end{array}\right]
\end{array}
$$

The solution from this tableau is $x_1 = 0$ and $x_2 = 60$, with $z = 1800$. (From now on, we will list only the original variables when giving the solution.) This corresponds to the corner point $(0, 60)$ in Figure 5. Because of the indicator -1, the value of z might be improved. We compare quotients and choose the 1 in row 1, column 1, as pivot to get the final tableau.

$$
\begin{array}{c}
 \\
-4R_1 + R_2 \rightarrow R_2 \\
R_1 + R_3 \rightarrow R_3
\end{array}
\begin{array}{cccccc}
x_1 & x_2 & s_1 & s_2 & z & \\
\left[\begin{array}{ccccc|c}
1 & 0 & 5 & -1 & 0 & 25 \\
0 & 5 & -20 & 5 & 0 & 200 \\
0 & 0 & 5 & 5 & 1 & 1825
\end{array}\right]
\end{array}
$$

There are no more negative indicators, so the optimum solution has been achieved. Create a 1 in column 2 by multiplying row 2 by $1/5$.

$$
\begin{array}{c}
 \\
(1/5)R_2 \rightarrow R_2 \\
 \\
\end{array}
\begin{array}{cccccc}
x_1 & x_2 & s_1 & s_2 & z & \\
\left[\begin{array}{ccccc|c}
1 & 0 & 5 & -1 & 0 & 25 \\
0 & 1 & -4 & 1 & 0 & 40 \\
0 & 0 & 5 & 5 & 1 & 1825
\end{array}\right]
\end{array}
$$

Here the solution is $x_1 = 25$ and $x_2 = 40$, with $z = 1825$. This solution, which corresponds to the corner point $(25, 40)$ in Figure 5, is the same as the solution found earlier.

Each simplex tableau above gave a solution corresponding to one of the corner points of the feasible region. As shown in Figure 6, the first solution corresponded to the origin, with $z = 0$. By choosing the appropriate pivot, we moved systematically to a new corner point, $(0, 60)$, which improved the value of z to 1800. The next tableau took us to $(25, 40)$, producing the optimum value of $z = 1825$. There was no reason to test the last corner point, $(65, 0)$, since the optimum value z was found before that point was reached.

It is good practice to verify your intermediate answers after each new tableau is calculated. You can check your answers by substituting these values for the original variables and the slack variables in the constraint equations and in the objective function.

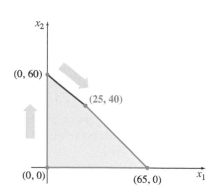

FIGURE 6

CAUTION Never choose a zero or a negative number as the pivot. The reason for this is explained in the next example. ■

EXAMPLE 2 Finding the Pivot

Find the pivot for the following initial simplex tableau.

$$\begin{array}{cccccc} x_1 & x_2 & s_1 & s_2 & s_3 & z \\ \left[\begin{array}{cccccc|c} 1 & -2 & 1 & 0 & 0 & 0 & 100 \\ 3 & 4 & 0 & 1 & 0 & 0 & 200 \\ 5 & 0 & 0 & 0 & 1 & 0 & 150 \\ \hline -10 & -25 & 0 & 0 & 0 & 1 & 0 \end{array}\right] \end{array}$$

▶**Solution** The most negative indicator is -25. To find the pivot, we find the quotients formed by the entries in the rightmost column and in the x_2 column: $100/(-2)$, $200/4$, and $150/0$. The quotients predict the value of a variable in the solution. Thus, since we want all variables to be nonnegative, we must reject a negative quotient. Furthermore, we cannot choose 0 as the pivot, because no multiple of the row with 0, when added to the other rows, will cause the other entries in the x_2 column to become 0.

The only usable quotient is $200/4 = 50$, making 4 the pivot. If all the quotients either are negative or have zero denominators, no unique optimum solution will be found. Such a situation indicates an unbounded feasible region. The quotients, then, determine whether an optimum solution exists. ▬▬

CAUTION If there is a 0 in the right-hand column, do not disregard that row, unless the corresponding number in the pivot column is negative or zero. In fact, such a row gives a quotient of 0, so it will automatically have the smallest ratio. It will not cause an increase in z, but it may lead to another tableau in which z can be further increased. ■

We saw earlier that graphing calculators can be used to perform row operations. A program to solve a linear programming problem with a graphing calculator is given in *The Graphing Calculator Manual* available with this book. Spreadsheets often have such a program built in. Figure 7 on the next page shows the Solver feature of Microsoft Excel (under the Tools menu) for Example 1.

In addition, Solver provides a **sensitivity analysis**, which allows us to see how much the constraints could be varied without changing the solution. Figure 8 on the next page shows a sensitivity analysis for Example 1. Notice that the value of the first coefficient in the objective function is 25, with an allowable increase of 5 and an allowable decrease of 1. This means that, while keeping the second coefficient at 30, the first coefficient of 25 could be increased by 5 (to 30) or decreased by 1 (to 24), and (25, 40) would still be a solution to the maximization problem. Similarly, for the second coefficient of 30, increasing it by 1.25 (to 31.25) or decreasing it by 5 (to 25) would still leave (25, 40) as a solution to the maximization problem. This would be useful to the owner who decides on the

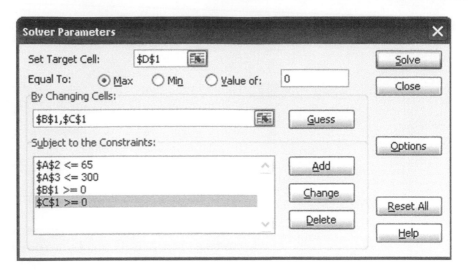

FIGURE 7

solution of (25, 40) (25 canoes and 40 kayaks) and wonders how much the objective function would have to change before the solution would no longer be optimal. The original revenue for a canoe was $25, which is the source of the first coefficient in the objective function. Assuming that everything else stays the same, the revenue could change to anything from $24 to $30, and the original decision would still be optimal.

Notice, however, that any change in one of the revenues will change the total revenue in the optimal solution. For example, if the first coefficient of 25 is increased by 5 to 30, then the optimal objective value will increase by $5 \times 25 = 125$. One can perform similar changes to other parameters of the problem, but that is beyond the scope of this text.

Adjusted Cells

Cell	Name	Final Value	Reduced Cost	Objective Coefficient	Allowable Increase	Allowable Decrease
B1		25	0	25	5	1
C1		40	0	30	1.25	5

Constraints

Cell	Name	Final Value	Shadow Price	Constraint R.H. Side	Allowable Increase	Allowable Decrease
A2		65	5	65	10	5
A3		300	5	300	25	40

FIGURE 8

In many real-life problems, the number of variables and constraints may be in the hundreds, if not the thousands, in which case a computer is used to implement the simplex algorithm. Computer programs for the simplex algorithm differ in some ways from the algorithm we have shown. For example, it is not necessary for a computer to divide common factors out of inequalities to simplify the arithmetic. In fact, computer versions of the algorithm do not necessarily keep all the numbers as integers. As we saw in the previous section, dividing a row by a number may introduce decimals, which makes the arithmetic more difficult to do by hand, but creates no problem for a computer other than round-off error.

If you use a graphing calculator to perform the simplex algorithm, we suggest that you review the pivoting procedure described in Method 2 of the previous section. It differs slightly from Method 1, because it converts each pivot element into a 1, but it works nicely with a calculator to keep track of the arithmetic details.

On the other hand, if you carry out the steps of the simplex method by hand, we suggest that you first eliminate fractions and decimals when setting up the initial tableau. For example, we would rewrite the constraint

$$\frac{2}{3}x_1 + \frac{5}{2}x_2 \le 7$$

as
$$4x_1 + 15x_2 \le 42,$$

by multiplying both sides of the equation by 6. Similarly, we would write

$$5.2x_1 + 4.4x_2 \le 8.5$$

as
$$52x_1 + 44x_2 \le 85$$

by multiplying both sides of the equation by 10. We must be cautious, however, in remembering that the value of the slack and surplus variables in the optimal solution must be adjusted by this factor to represent the original constraint.

NOTE Sometimes the simplex method cycles and returns to a previously visited solution, rather than making progress. Methods are available for handling cycling. In this text, we will avoid examples with this behavior. For more details, see Alan Sultan's *Linear Programming: An Introduction with Applications*, Academic Press, 1993. In real applications, cycling is rare and tends not to come up because of computer rounding.

▶ 4.2 Exercises

In Exercises 1–6, the initial tableau of a linear programming problem is given. Use the simplex method to solve each problem.

1.

x_1	x_2	x_3	s_1	s_2	z	
1	4	4	1	0	0	16
2	1	5	0	1	0	20
−3	−1	−2	0	0	1	0

2.

x_1	x_2	x_3	s_1	s_2	z	
3	3	2	1	0	0	18
2	2	3	0	1	0	16
−4	−6	−2	0	0	1	0

3.

$$
\begin{array}{ccccccc}
x_1 & x_2 & s_1 & s_2 & s_3 & z \\
\end{array}
$$

$$
\left[\begin{array}{cccccc|c}
1 & 3 & 1 & 0 & 0 & 0 & 12 \\
2 & 1 & 0 & 1 & 0 & 0 & 10 \\
1 & 1 & 0 & 0 & 1 & 0 & 4 \\
\hline
-2 & -1 & 0 & 0 & 0 & 1 & 0
\end{array}\right]
$$

4.

$$
\begin{array}{ccccccc}
x_1 & x_2 & x_3 & s_1 & s_2 & s_3 & z \\
\end{array}
$$

$$
\left[\begin{array}{ccccccc|c}
2 & 1 & 2 & 1 & 0 & 0 & 0 & 25 \\
4 & 3 & 2 & 0 & 1 & 0 & 0 & 40 \\
3 & 1 & 6 & 0 & 0 & 1 & 0 & 60 \\
\hline
-4 & -2 & -3 & 0 & 0 & 0 & 1 & 0
\end{array}\right]
$$

5.

$$
\begin{array}{ccccccc}
x_1 & x_2 & x_3 & s_1 & s_2 & s_3 & z \\
\end{array}
$$

$$
\left[\begin{array}{ccccccc|c}
2 & 2 & 8 & 1 & 0 & 0 & 0 & 40 \\
4 & -5 & 6 & 0 & 1 & 0 & 0 & 60 \\
2 & -2 & 6 & 0 & 0 & 1 & 0 & 24 \\
\hline
-14 & -10 & -12 & 0 & 0 & 0 & 1 & 0
\end{array}\right]
$$

6.

$$
\begin{array}{cccccc}
x_1 & x_2 & x_3 & s_1 & s_2 & z \\
\end{array}
$$

$$
\left[\begin{array}{cccccc|c}
3 & 2 & 4 & 1 & 0 & 0 & 18 \\
2 & 1 & 5 & 0 & 1 & 0 & 8 \\
\hline
-1 & -4 & -2 & 0 & 0 & 1 & 0
\end{array}\right]
$$

Use the simplex method to solve each linear programming problem.

7. Maximize $z = 3x_1 + 5x_2$

subject to: $4x_1 + x_2 \leq 25$

$2x_1 + 3x_2 \leq 15$

with $x_1 \geq 0, \ x_2 \geq 0$.

8. Maximize $z = 5x_1 + 2x_2$

subject to: $2x_1 + 4x_2 \leq 15$

$3x_1 + x_2 \leq 10$

with $x_1 \geq 0, \ x_2 \geq 0$.

9. Maximize $z = 10x_1 + 12x_2$

subject to: $4x_1 + 2x_2 \leq 20$

$5x_1 + x_2 \leq 50$

$2x_1 + 2x_2 \leq 24$

with $x_1 \geq 0, \ x_2 \geq 0$.

10. Maximize $z = 1.5x_1 + 4.2x_2$

subject to: $2.8x_1 + 3.4x_2 \leq 21$

$1.4x_1 + 2.2x_2 \leq 11$

with $x_1 \geq 0, \ x_2 \geq 0$.

11. Maximize $z = 8x_1 + 3x_2 + x_3$

subject to: $x_1 + 6x_2 + 8x_3 \leq 118$

$x_1 + 5x_2 + 10x_3 \leq 220$

with $x_1 \geq 0, \ x_2 \geq 0, \ x_3 \geq 0$.

12. Maximize $z = 8x_1 + 10x_2 + 7x_3$

subject to: $x_1 + 3x_2 + 2x_3 \leq 10$

$x_1 + 5x_2 + x_3 \leq 8$

with $x_1 \geq 0, \ x_2 \geq 0, \ x_3 \geq 0$.

13. Maximize $z = 10x_1 + 15x_2 + 10x_3 + 5x_4$

subject to: $x_1 + x_2 + x_3 + x_4 \leq 300$

$x_1 + 2x_2 + 3x_3 + x_4 \leq 360$

with $x_1 \geq 0, \ x_2 \geq 0, \ x_3 \geq 0, \ x_4 \geq 0$.

14. Maximize $z = x_1 + x_2 + 4x_3 + 5x_4$

subject to: $x_1 + 2x_2 + 3x_3 + x_4 \leq 115$

$2x_1 + x_2 + 8x_3 + 5x_4 \leq 200$

$x_1 + x_3 \leq 50$

with $x_1 \geq 0, \ x_2 \geq 0, \ x_3 \geq 0, \ x_4 \geq 0$.

15. Maximize $z = 4x_1 + 6x_2$

subject to: $x_1 - 5x_2 \leq 25$

$4x_1 - 3x_2 \leq 12$

with $x_1 \geq 0, \ x_2 \geq 0$.

16. Maximize $z = 2x_1 + 5x_2 + x_3$

subject to: $x_1 - 5x_2 + 2x_3 \leq 30$

$4x_1 - 3x_2 + 6x_3 \leq 72$

with $x_1 > 0, \ x_2 \geq 0, \ x_3 \geq 0$.

Use a graphing calculator, Excel, or other technology to solve the following linear programming problems.

17. Maximize $z = 37x_1 + 34x_2 + 36x_3 + 30x_4 + 35x_5$

subject to: $16x_1 + 19x_2 + 23x_3 + 15x_4 + 21x_5 \leq 42{,}000$

$15x_1 + 10x_2 + 19x_3 + 23x_4 + 10x_5 \leq 25{,}000$

$9x_1 + 16x_2 + 14x_3 + 12x_4 + 11x_5 \leq 23{,}000$

$18x_1 + 20x_2 + 15x_3 + 17x_4 + 19x_5 \leq 36{,}000$

with $x_1 \geq 0, \ x_2 \geq 0, \ x_3 \geq 0, \ x_4 \geq 0, \ x_5 \geq 0$.

18. Maximize $z = 2.0x_1 + 1.7x_2 + 2.1x_3 + 2.4x_4 + 2.2x_5$

   subject to: $12x_1 + 10x_2 + 11x_3 + 12x_4 + 13x_5 \leq 4250$

$8x_1 + 8x_2 + 7x_3 + 18x_4 + 5x_5 \leq 4130$

$9x_1 + 10x_2 + 12x_3 + 11x_4 + 8x_5 \leq 3500$

$5x_1 + 3x_2 + 4x_3 + 5x_4 + 4x_5 \leq 1600$

   with $x_1 \geq 0,\ x_2 \geq 0,\ x_3 \geq 0,\ x_4 \geq 0,\ x_5 \geq 0.$

19. The simplex algorithm still works if an indicator other than the most negative one is chosen. (Try it!) List the disadvantages that might occur if this is done.

20. What goes wrong if a quotient other than the smallest nonnegative quotient is chosen in the simplex algorithm? (Try it!)

▶ Applications

Set up and solve Exercises 21–27 by the simplex method.

BUSINESS AND ECONOMICS

21. *Charitable Contributions* Carrie Green is working to raise money for the homeless by sending information letters and making follow-up calls to local labor organizations and church groups. She discovers that each church group requires 2 hours of letter writing and 1 hour of follow-up, while for each labor union she needs 2 hours of letter writing and 3 hours of follow-up. Carrie can raise $100 from each church group and $200 from each union local, and she has a maximum of 16 hours of letter-writing time and a maximum of 12 hours of follow-up time available per month. Determine the most profitable mixture of groups she should contact and the most money she can raise in a month.

22. *Profit* The Muro Manufacturing Company makes two kinds of plasma screen television sets. It produces the Flexscan set that sells for $350 profit and the Panoramic I that sells for $500 profit. On the assembly line, the Flexscan requires 5 hours, and the Panoramic I takes 7 hours. The cabinet shop spends 1 hour on the cabinet for the Flexscan and 2 hours on the cabinet for the Panoramic I. Both sets require 4 hours for testing and packing. On a particular production run, the Muro Company has available 3600 work-hours on the assembly line, 900 work-hours in the cabinet shop, and 2600 work-hours in the testing and packing department. (See Exercise 10 in Section 3.3.)

   a. How many sets of each type should it produce to make a maximum profit? What is the maximum profit?

   b. Find the values of any nonzero slack variables and describe what they tell you about any unused time.

23. *Poker* The Texas Poker Company assembles three different poker sets. Each Royal Flush poker set contains 1000 poker chips, 4 decks of cards, 10 dice, and 2 dealer buttons. Each Deluxe Diamond poker set contains 600 poker chips, 2 decks of cards, 5 dice, and one dealer button. The Full House poker set contains 300 poker chips, 2 decks of cards, 5 dice, and one dealer button. The Texas Poker Company has 2,800,000 poker chips, 10,000 decks of cards, 25,000 dice, and 6000 dealer buttons in stock. They earn a profit of $38 for each Royal Flush poker set, $22 for each Deluxe Diamond poker set, and $12 for each Full House poker set.

   a. How many of each type of poker set should they assemble to maximize profit? What is the maximum profit?

   b. Find the values of any nonzero slack variables and describe what they tell you about any unused components.

24. *Income* A baker has 150 units of flour, 90 of sugar, and 150 of raisins. A loaf of raisin bread requires 1 unit of flour, 1 of sugar, and 2 of raisins, while a raisin cake needs 5, 2, and 1 units, respectively.

   a. If raisin bread sells for $1.75 a loaf and raisin cake for $4.00 each, how many of each should be baked so that gross income is maximized?

   b. What is the maximum gross income?

   c. Does it require all of the available units of flour, sugar, and raisins to produce the number of loaves of raisin bread and raisin cakes that produce the maximum profit? If not, how much of each ingredient is left over? Compare any leftover to the value of the relevant slack variable.

25. *Manufacturing Bicycles* A manufacturer of bicycles builds racing, touring, and mountain models. The bicycles are made of both aluminum and steel. The company has available 91,800 units of steel and 42,000 units of aluminum. The racing, touring, and mountain models need 17, 27, and 34 units of steel, and 12, 21, and 15 units of aluminum, respectively. (See Exercise 26 in Section 4.1.)

a. How many of each type of bicycle should be made in order to maximize profit if the company makes $8 per racing bike, $12 per touring bike, and $22 per mountain bike?

b. What is the maximum possible profit?

c. Does it require all of the available units of steel and aluminum to build the bicycles that produce the maximum profit? If not, how much of each material is left over? Compare any leftover to the value of the relevant slack variable.

d. There are many unstated assumptions in the problem given above. Even if the mathematical solution is to make only one or two types of the bicycles, there may be demand for the type(s) not being made, which would create problems for the company. Discuss this and other difficulties that would arise in a real situation.

26. *Production* The Cut-Right Company sells sets of kitchen knives. The Basic Set consists of 2 utility knives and 1 chef's knife. The Regular Set consists of 2 utility knives, 1 chef's knife, and 1 slicer. The Deluxe Set consists of 3 utility knives, 1 chef's knife, and 1 slicer. Their profit is $30 on a Basic Set, $40 on a Regular Set, and $60 on a Deluxe Set. The factory has on hand 800 utility knives, 400 chef's knives, and 200 slicers. (See Exercise 28 in Section 4.1.)

a. Assuming that all sets will be sold, how many of each type should be made up in order to maximize profit? What is the maximum profit?

b. A consultant for the Cut-Right Company notes that more profit is made on a Regular Set of knives than on a Basic Set, yet the result from part a recommends making up 100 Basic Sets but no Regular Sets. She is puzzled how this can be the best solution. How would you respond?

27. *Advertising* The Fancy Fashions, an independent, local boutique, has $8000 available each month for advertising. Newspaper ads cost $400 each, and no more than 30 can run per month. Internet banner ads cost $20 each, and no more than 60 can run per month. TV ads cost $2000 each, with a maximum of 10 available each month. Approximately 4000 women will see each newspaper ad, 3000 will see each Internet banner, and 10,000 will see each TV ad. (See Exercise 29 in Section 4.1.)

a. How much of each type of advertising should be used if the store wants to maximize its ad exposure?

b. A marketing analyst is puzzled by the results of part a. More women see each TV ad than each newspaper ad or Internet banner, he reasons, so it makes no sense to use the newspaper ads and Internet banners and no TV ads. How would you respond?

28. *Profit* A manufacturer makes two products, toy trucks and toy fire engines. Both are processed in four different departments, each of which has a limited capacity. The sheet metal department can handle at least $1\frac{1}{2}$ times as many trucks as fire engines; the truck assembly department can handle at most 6700 trucks per week; and the fire engine assembly department assembles at most 5500 fire engines weekly. The painting department, which finishes both toys, has a maximum capacity of 12,000 per week.

a. If the profit is $8.50 for a toy truck and $12.10 for a toy fire engine, how many of each item should the company produce to maximize profit?

b. Find a value for the profit for a toy truck and a value for the profit for a toy fire engine that would result in no fire engines being manufactured to maximize profit, given the constraints in part a.

c. Find a value for the profit for a toy truck and a value for the profit for a toy fire engine that would result in no toy trucks being manufactured to maximize the profit, given the constraints in part a.

Exercises 29 and 30 come from past CPA examinations.*
Select the appropriate answer for each question.

29. *Profit* The Ball Company manufactures three types of lamps, labeled A, B, and C. Each lamp is processed in two departments, I and II. Total available work-hours per day for departments I and II are 400 and 600, respectively. No additional labor is available. Time requirements and profit per unit for each lamp type are as follows:

	A	B	C
Work-hours in I	2	3	1
Work-hours in II	4	2	3
Profit per Unit	$5	$4	$3

The company has assigned you as the accounting member of its profit planning committee to determine the numbers of types of A, B, and C lamps that it should produce in order to maximize its total profit from the sale of lamps.

The following questions relate to a linear programming model that your group has developed.

a. The coefficients of the objective function would be

(**1**) 4, 2, 3.   (**2**) 2, 3, 1.

(**3**) 5, 4, 3.   (**4**) 400, 600.

b. The constraints in the model would be

(**1**) 2, 3, 1.   (**2**) 5, 4, 3.

(**3**) 4, 2, 3.   (**4**) 400, 600.

c. The constraint imposed by the available work-hours in department I could be expressed as

(**1**) $4X_1 + 2X_2 + 3X_3 \le 400$.

(**2**) $4X_1 + 2X_2 + 3X_3 \ge 400$.

(**3**) $2X_1 + 3X_2 + 1X_3 \le 400$.

(**4**) $2X_1 + 3X_2 + 1X_3 \ge 400$.

30. *Profit* The Golden Hawk Manufacturing Company wants to maximize the profits on products A, B, and C. The contribution margin for each product follows:

Product	Contribution Margin
A	$2
B	$5
C	$4

The production requirements and departmental capacities, by departments, are as follows:

Department	Production Requirements by Product (hours)			Departmental Capacity (total hours)
	A	*B*	*C*	
Assembling	2	3	2	30,000
Painting	1	2	2	38,000
Finishing	2	3	1	28,000

a. What is the profit-maximization formula for the Golden Hawk Company? (Choose one of the following.)

(**1**) $\$2A + \$5B + \$4C = X$ (where X = profit)

(**2**) $5A + 8B + 5C \le 96{,}000$

(**3**) $\$2A + \$5B + \$4C \le X$

(**4**) $\$2A + \$5B + \$4C = 96{,}000$

b. What is the constraint for the painting department of the Golden Hawk Company? (Choose one of the following.)

(**1**) $1A + 2B + 2C \ge 38{,}000$

(**2**) $\$2A + \$5B + \$4C \ge 38{,}000$

(**3**) $1A + 2B + 2C \le 38{,}000$

(**4**) $2A + 3B + 2C \le 30{,}000$

31. *Sensitivity Analysis* Using a computer spreadsheet, perform a sensitivity analysis for the objective function in Exercise 21. What are the highest and lowest possible values for the amount raised from each church group that would yield the same solution as the original problem? Answer the same question for the amount raised from each union local.

32. *Sensitivity Analysis* Using a computer spreadsheet, perform a sensitivity analysis for the objective function in Exercise 22. What are the highest and lowest possible values for profit on a Flexscan set that would yield the same solution as the original problem? Answer the same question for a Panoramic I set.

Set up and solve Exercises 33–38 by the simplex method.

LIFE SCIENCES

33. *Calorie Expenditure* Rachel Reeve, a fitness trainer, has an exercise regimen that includes running, biking, and walking. She has no more than 15 hours per week to devote to exercise, including at most 3 hours running. She wants to walk at least twice as many hours as she bikes. According to a Web site,* a 130-pound person like Rachel will burn on average 531 calories per hour running, 472 calories per hour biking, and 354 calories per hour walking. How many hours per week should Rachel spend on each exercise to maximize the number of calories she burns? What is the maximum number of calories she will burn? (*Hint:* Write the constraint involving walking and biking in the form ≤ 0.)

34. *Calorie Expenditure* Joe Vetere's exercise regimen includes light calisthenics, swimming, and playing the drums. He has at most 10 hours per week to devote to these activities. He wants the total time he does calisthenics and plays the drums to be at least twice as long as he swims. His neighbors, however, will tolerate no more than 4 hours per week on the drums. According to a Web site,* a 190-pound person like Joe will burn an average of 388 calories per hour doing calisthenics, 518 calories per hour swimming, and 345 calories per hour playing the drums.

a. How many hours per week should Joe spend on each exercise to maximize the number of calories he burns? What is the maximum number of calories he will burn?

*http://www.nutristrategy.com/activitylist4.htm.

b. What conclusions can you draw about Joe's selection of activities?

35. *Blending Nutrients* A biologist has 500 kg of nutrient A, 600 kg of nutrient B, and 300 kg of nutrient C. These nutrients will be used to make four types of food, whose contents (in percent of nutrient per kilogram of food) and whose "growth values" are as shown in the table.

a. How many kilograms of each food should be produced in order to maximize total growth value?

b. Find the maximum growth value.

	P	Q	R	S
A	0	0	37.5	62.5
B	0	75	50	37.5
C	100	25	12.5	0
Growth Value	90	70	60	50

c. Does it require all of the available nutrients to produce the four types of food that maximizes the total growth value? If not, how much of each nutrient is left over?

36. *Resource Management* The average weights of the three species stocked in the lake referred to in Section 2.2, Exercise 58, are 1.62, 2.14, and 3.01 kg for species A, B, and C, respectively.

a. If the largest amounts of food that can be supplied each day are as given in Exercise 58, how should the lake be stocked to maximize the weight of the fish supported by the lake?

b. Does it require all of the available food to produce the maximum weight of fish? If not, how much of each type of food is left over?

c. Find a value for each of the average weights of the three species that would result in none of species B or C being stocked to maximize the weight of the fish supported by the lake, given the constraints in part a.

d. Find a value for each of the average weights of the three species that would result in none of species A or B being stocked to maximize the weight of the fish supported by the lake, given the constraints in part a.

SOCIAL SCIENCES

37. *Politics* A political party is planning a half-hour television show. The show will have at least 3 minutes of direct requests for money from viewers. Three of the party's politicians will be on the show—a senator, a congresswoman, and a governor. The senator, a party "elder statesman," demands that he be on screen at least twice as long as the governor. The total time taken by the senator and the governor must be at least twice the time taken by the congresswoman. Based on a pre-show survey, it is believed that 35, 40, and 45 (in thousands) viewers will watch the program for each minute the senator, congresswoman, and governor, respectively, are on the air. Find the time that should be allotted to each politician in order to get the maximum number of viewers. Find the maximum number of viewers.

38. *Fund Raising* The political party in Exercise 37 is planning its fund-raising activities for a coming election. It plans to raise money through large fund-raising parties, letters requesting funds, and dinner parties where people can meet the candidate personally. Each large fund-raising party costs $3000, each mailing costs $1000, and each dinner party costs $12,000. The party can spend up to $102,000 for these activities. From experience, the planners know that each large party will raise $200,000, each letter campaign will raise $100,000, and each dinner party will raise $600,000. They are able to carry out a total of 25 of these activities.

a. How many of each should the party plan in order to raise the maximum amount of money? What is the maximum amount?

b. Dinner parties are more expensive than letter campaigns, yet the optimum solution found in part a includes dinner parties but no letter campaigns. Explain how this is possible.

4.3 Minimization Problems; Duality

? THINK ABOUT IT

How many units of different types of feed should a dog breeder purchase to meet the nutrient requirements of her beagles at a minimum cost?

Using the method of duals, we will learn to answer this and other questions.

Minimization Problems   The definition of a problem in standard maximum form was given earlier in this chapter. Now we can define a linear programming problem in *standard minimum form*, as follows.

STANDARD MINIMUM FORM

A linear programming problem is in **standard minimum form** if the following conditions are satisfied.

1. The objective function is to be minimized.
2. All variables are nonnegative.
3. All remaining constraints are stated in the form

$$a_1y_1 + a_2y_2 + \cdots + a_ny_n \geq b, \quad \text{with } b \geq 0.$$

The difference between maximization and minimization problems is in conditions 1 and 3: In problems stated in standard minimum form, the objective function is to be *minimized*, rather than maximized, and all constraints must have $\geq$ instead of $\leq$.

We use y_1, y_2, etc., for the variables and w for the objective function as a reminder that these are minimizing problems. Thus, $w = c_1y_1 + c_2y_2 + \cdots + c_ny_n$.

NOTE   In this section, we require that all coefficients in the objective function be positive, so $c_1 \geq 0, c_2 \geq 0, \ldots, c_n \geq 0$.

Duality   An interesting connection exists between standard maximization and standard minimization problems: any solution of a standard maximization problem produces the solution of an associated standard minimization problem, and vice versa. Each of these associated problems is called the **dual** of the other. One advantage of duals is that standard minimization problems can be solved by the simplex method discussed in the first two sections of this chapter. Let us explain the idea of a dual with an example.

EXAMPLE 1   **Duality**

Minimize $w = 8y_1 + 16y_2$

subject to: $y_1 + 5y_2 \geq 9$

                       $2y_1 + 2y_2 \geq 10$

with $y_1 \geq 0, \quad y_2 \geq 0.$

▶**Solution** Without considering slack variables just yet, write the augmented matrix of the system of inequalities, and include the coefficients of the objective function (not their negatives) as the last row in the matrix.

Constants

$$\begin{bmatrix} 1 & 5 & 9 \\ 2 & 2 & 10 \\ 8 & 16 & 0 \end{bmatrix}$$

Objective function ⟶

Now look at the following matrix, which we obtain from the one above by interchanging rows and columns.

Constants

$$\begin{bmatrix} 1 & 2 & 8 \\ 5 & 2 & 16 \\ 9 & 10 & 0 \end{bmatrix}$$

Objective function ⟶

The *rows* of the first matrix (for the minimization problem) are the *columns* of the second matrix.

The entries in this second matrix could be used to write the following maximization problem in standard form (again ignoring the fact that the numbers in the last row are not negative):

$$\text{Maximize} \qquad z = 9x_1 + 10x_2$$
$$\text{subject to:} \qquad x_1 + 2x_2 \le 8$$
$$5x_1 + 2x_2 \le 16$$

with all variables nonnegative.

Figure 9(a) shows the region of feasible solutions for the minimization problem just given, while Figure 9(b) shows the region of feasible solutions for the maximization problem produced by exchanging rows and columns. The solutions of the two problems are given on the next page.

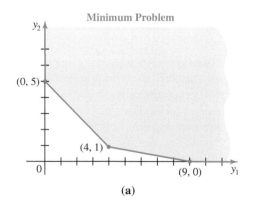

(a)

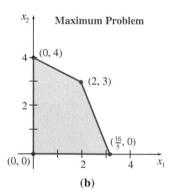

(b)

FIGURE 9

Corner Point	$w = 8y_1 + 16y_2$	
$(0, 5)$	80	
$(4, 1)$	48	Minimum
$(9, 0)$	72	

The minimum is 48 when $y_1 = 4$ and $y_2 = 1$.

Corner Point	$z = 9x_1 + 10x_2$	
$(0, 0)$	0	
$(0, 4)$	40	
$(2, 3)$	48	Maximum
$(16/5, 0)$	28.8	

The maximum is 48 when $x_1 = 2$ and $x_2 = 3$.

The two feasible regions in Figure 9 are different and the corner points are different, but the values of the objective functions are equal—both are 48. An even closer connection between the two problems is shown by using the simplex method to solve this maximization problem.

Maximization Problem

$$\begin{array}{ccccc} x_1 & x_2 & s_1 & s_2 & z \end{array}$$
$$\left[\begin{array}{ccccc|c} 1 & \mathbf{2} & 1 & 0 & 0 & 8 \\ 5 & 2 & 0 & 1 & 0 & 16 \\ \hline -9 & -10 & 0 & 0 & 1 & 0 \end{array}\right]$$

$$\begin{array}{ccccc} x_1 & x_2 & s_1 & s_2 & z \end{array}$$
$$\begin{array}{c} \\ -R_1 + R_2 \to R_2 \\ 5R_1 + R_3 \to R_3 \end{array} \left[\begin{array}{ccccc|c} 1 & 2 & 1 & 0 & 0 & 8 \\ \mathbf{4} & 0 & -1 & 1 & 0 & 8 \\ \hline -4 & 0 & 5 & 0 & 1 & 40 \end{array}\right]$$

$$\begin{array}{ccccc} x_1 & x_2 & s_1 & s_2 & z \end{array}$$
$$\begin{array}{c} -R_2 + 4R_1 \to R_1 \\ \\ R_2 + R_3 \to R_3 \end{array} \left[\begin{array}{ccccc|c} 0 & 8 & 5 & -1 & 0 & 24 \\ 4 & 0 & -1 & 1 & 0 & 8 \\ \hline 0 & 0 & 4 & 1 & 1 & 48 \end{array}\right]$$

$$\begin{array}{ccccc} x_1 & x_2 & s_1 & s_2 & z \end{array}$$
$$\begin{array}{c} R_1/8 \to R_1 \\ R_2/4 \to R_2 \\ \\ \end{array} \left[\begin{array}{ccccc|c} 0 & 1 & \frac{5}{8} & -\frac{1}{8} & 0 & 3 \\ 1 & 0 & -\frac{1}{4} & \frac{1}{4} & 0 & 2 \\ \hline 0 & 0 & \mathbf{4} & \mathbf{1} & 1 & 48 \end{array}\right]$$

The maximum is 48 when
$x_1 = 2$ and $x_2 = 3$.

Notice that the solution to the *minimization problem* is found in the bottom row and slack variable columns of the final simplex tableau for the maximization problem. This result suggests that standard minimization problems can be solved by forming the dual standard maximization problem, solving it by the simplex method, and then reading the solution for the minimization problem from the bottom row of the final simplex tableau.

Before using this method to actually solve a minimization problem, let us find the duals of some typical linear programming problems. The process of exchanging the rows and columns of a matrix, which is used to find the dual, is called *transposing* the matrix, and each of the two matrices is the **transpose** of the other. The transpose of an $m \times n$ matrix A, written A^T, is an $n \times m$ matrix.

EXAMPLE 2 **Transposes**

Find the transpose of each matrix.

(a) $A = \begin{bmatrix} 2 & -1 & 5 \\ 6 & 8 & 0 \\ -3 & 7 & -1 \end{bmatrix}$

▶**Solution** Both matrix A and its transpose are 3×3 matrices. Write the rows of matrix A as the columns of the transpose.

$$A^T = \begin{bmatrix} 2 & 6 & -3 \\ -1 & 8 & 7 \\ 5 & 0 & -1 \end{bmatrix}$$

(b) $B = \begin{bmatrix} 1 & 2 & 4 & 0 \\ 2 & 1 & 7 & 6 \end{bmatrix}$

▶**Solution** The matrix B is 2×4, so B^T is the 4×2 matrix

$$B^T = \begin{bmatrix} 1 & 2 \\ 2 & 1 \\ 4 & 7 \\ 0 & 6 \end{bmatrix}.$$

EXAMPLE 3 **Duals**

Write the dual of each standard linear programming problem.

(a) Maximize $\quad z = 2x_1 + 5x_2$

  subject to: $\quad x_1 + x_2 \le 10$

  $\quad\quad\quad\quad 2x_1 + x_2 \le 8$

  with $\quad\quad x_1 \ge 0, \quad x_2 \ge 0.$

▶**Solution** Begin by writing the augmented matrix for the given problem.

$$\begin{bmatrix} 1 & 1 & | & 10 \\ 2 & 1 & | & 8 \\ \hline 2 & 5 & | & 0 \end{bmatrix}$$

Form the transpose of the matrix as follows:

$$\begin{bmatrix} 1 & 2 & | & 2 \\ 1 & 1 & | & 5 \\ \hline 10 & 8 & | & 0 \end{bmatrix}.$$

The dual problem is stated from this second matrix as follows (using y instead of x):

  Minimize $\quad w = 10y_1 + 8y_2$

  subject to: $\quad y_1 + 2y_2 \ge 2$

  $\quad\quad\quad\quad y_1 + y_2 \ge 5$

  with $\quad\quad y_1 \ge 0, \quad y_2 \ge 0.$

(b) Minimize $\quad w = 7y_1 + 5y_2 + 8y_3$

subject to: $\quad 3y_1 + 2y_2 + y_3 \geq 10$

$$4y_1 + 5y_2 \quad\;\; \geq 25$$

with $\quad y_1 \geq 0, \;\; y_2 \geq 0, \;\; y_3 \geq 0.$

▶**Solution** The dual problem is stated as follows.

$$\text{Maximize} \quad z = 10x_1 + 25x_2$$

$$\text{subject to:} \quad 3x_1 + 4x_2 \leq 7$$

$$2x_1 + 5x_2 \leq 5$$

$$x_1 \quad\;\; \leq 8$$

$$\text{with} \quad x_1 \geq 0, \;\; x_2 \geq 0.$$

In Example 3, all the constraints of the given standard maximization problems were $\leq$ inequalities, while all those in the dual minimization problems were $\geq$ inequalities. This is generally the case; inequalities are reversed when the dual problem is stated.

The following table shows the close connection between a problem and its dual.

Given Problem	Dual Problem
m variables	n variables
n constraints	m constraints
Coefficients from objective function	Constraint constants
Constraint constants	Coefficients from objective function

NOTE To solve a minimization problem with duals, all of the coefficients in the objective function must be positive. Otherwise, negative numbers will appear on the right side of the constraints in the dual problem, which we do not allow. For a method that does not have this restriction, see the next section.

The next theorem, whose proof requires advanced methods, guarantees that a standard minimization problem can be solved by forming a dual standard maximization problem.

THEOREM OF DUALITY

The objective function w of a minimization linear programming problem takes on a minimum value if and only if the objective function z of the corresponding dual maximization problem takes on a maximum value. The maximum value of z equals the minimum value of w.

This method is illustrated in the following example.

EXAMPLE 4

Duality

Minimize $\quad w = 3y_1 + 2y_2$

subject to: $\quad y_1 + 3y_2 \geq 6$

$\qquad\qquad 2y_1 + y_2 \geq 3$

with $\qquad\quad y_1 \geq 0, \quad y_2 \geq 0.$

▶**Solution** Use the given information to write the matrix.

$$\begin{bmatrix} 1 & 3 & 6 \\ 2 & 1 & 3 \\ \hline 3 & 2 & 0 \end{bmatrix}$$

Transpose to get the following matrix for the dual problem.

$$\begin{bmatrix} 1 & 2 & 3 \\ 3 & 1 & 2 \\ \hline 6 & 3 & 0 \end{bmatrix}$$

Write the dual problem from this matrix, as follows.

Maximize $\quad z = 6x_1 + 3x_2$

subject to: $\quad x_1 + 2x_2 \leq 3$

$\qquad\qquad 3x_1 + x_2 \leq 2$

with $\qquad\quad x_1 \geq 0, \quad x_2 \geq 0.$

Solve this standard maximization problem using the simplex method. Start by introducing slack variables to give the system

$$x_1 + 2x_2 + s_1 \qquad\qquad = 3$$
$$3x_1 + x_2 \qquad + s_2 \qquad = 2$$
$$-6x_1 - 3x_2 \qquad\qquad + z = 0$$

with $\qquad x_1 \geq 0, \quad x_2 \geq 0, \quad s_1 \geq 0, \quad s_2 \geq 0.$

The first tableau for this system is given below, with the pivot as indicated.

Quotients	x_1	x_2	s_1	s_2	z	
$3/1 = 3$	1	2	1	0	0	3
$2/3$	**3**	1	0	1	0	2
	-6	-3	0	0	1	0

The simplex method gives the following as the final tableau.

x_1	x_2	s_1	s_2	z	
0	1	$\frac{3}{5}$	$-\frac{1}{5}$	0	$\frac{7}{5}$
1	0	$-\frac{1}{5}$	$\frac{2}{5}$	0	$\frac{1}{5}$
0	0	$\frac{3}{5}$	$\frac{9}{5}$	1	$\frac{27}{5}$

Since a 1 has been created in the z column, the last row of this final tableau gives the solution to the minimization problem. The minimum value of

$w = 3y_1 + 2y_2$, subject to the given constraints, is 27/5 and occurs when $y_1 = 3/5$ and $y_2 = 9/5$. The minimum value of w, 27/5, is the same as the maximum value of z.

Let us summarize the steps in solving a standard minimization linear programming problem by the method of duals.

SOLVING A STANDARD MINIMUM PROBLEM WITH DUALS

1. Find the dual standard maximization problem.
2. Solve the maximization problem using the simplex method.
3. The minimum value of the objective function w is the maximum value of the objective function z.
4. The optimum solution to the minimization problem is given by the entries in the bottom row of the columns corresponding to the slack variables, so long as the entry in the z column is equal to 1.

CAUTION (1) If the final entry in the z column is a value other than 1, divide the bottom row through by that value so that it will become 1. Only then can the solution of the minimization problem be found in the bottom row of the columns corresponding to the slack variables.

(2) Do not simplify an inequality in the dual by dividing out a common factor. For example, if an inequality in the dual is $3x_1 + 3x_2 \le 6$, do not simplify to $x_1 + x_2 \le 2$ by dividing out the 3. Doing so will give an incorrect solution to the original problem. ∎

NOTE If the objective function is written below the constraints (except those stating that each variable must be greater than or equal to 0), and the variables are lined up vertically, it is easy to go from the original problem to the dual: The coefficients in any column of the original problem become the coefficients of the corresponding row in the dual. In Example 4, for instance, if the objective function is written below the constraints, the coefficients in the first column are 1, 2, 3, leading to the first row of the dual: $x_1 + 2x_2 \le 3$. The last column is 6, 3, so the last row of the dual is this: Maximize $z = 6x_1 + 3x_2$.

? **Further Uses of the Dual** The dual is useful not only in solving minimization problems, but also in seeing how small changes in one variable will affect the value of the objective function. For example, suppose a dog breeder needs at least 6 units per day of nutrient A and at least 3 units of nutrient B for her beagles, and that the breeder can choose between two different feeds, feed 1 and feed 2. Find the minimum cost for the breeder if each bag of feed 1 costs $3 and provides 1 unit of nutrient A and 2 units of B, while each bag of feed 2 costs $2 and provides 3 units of nutrient A and 1 of B.

If y_1 represents the number of bags of feed 1 and y_2 represents the number of bags of feed 2, the given information leads to the following problem.

$$\text{Minimize} \quad w = 3y_1 + 2y_2$$
$$\text{subject to:} \quad y_1 + 3y_2 \geq 6$$
$$2y_1 + y_2 \geq 3$$
$$\text{with} \quad y_1 \geq 0, \quad y_2 \geq 0.$$

This standard minimization linear programming problem is the one solved in Example 4 of this section. In that example, the dual was formed and the following tableau was found.

$$
\begin{array}{ccccc}
x_1 & x_2 & s_1 & s_2 & z \\
\left[\begin{array}{ccccc|c}
0 & 1 & \frac{3}{5} & -\frac{1}{5} & 0 & \frac{7}{5} \\
1 & 0 & -\frac{1}{5} & \frac{2}{5} & 0 & \frac{1}{5} \\
\hline
0 & 0 & \frac{3}{5} & \frac{9}{5} & 1 & \frac{27}{5}
\end{array}\right]
\end{array}
$$

This final tableau shows that the breeder will obtain minimum feed costs by using 3/5 bag of feed 1 and 9/5 bags of feed 2 per day, for a daily cost of $27/5 = \$5.40$.

Now look at the data from the problem shown in the following table.

	Unit of Nutrient (per bag):		Cost (per bag)
	A	B	
Feed 1	1	2	$3
Feed 2	3	1	$2
Requirement	6	3	

If x_1 and x_2 are the costs per unit of nutrients A and B, the constraints of the dual problem can be stated as follows.

$$\text{Cost of feed 1:} \quad x_1 + 2x_2 \leq 3$$
$$\text{Cost of feed 2:} \quad 3x_1 + x_2 \leq 2$$

The solution of the dual problem, which maximizes nutrients, can be read from the final tableau:

$$x_1 = \frac{1}{5} = 0.20 \quad \text{and} \quad x_2 = \frac{7}{5} = 1.40,$$

which means that a unit of nutrient A costs $0.20, while a unit of nutrient B costs $1.40. The minimum daily cost, $5.40, is found by the following procedure.

$$(\$0.20 \text{ per unit of A}) \times (6 \text{ units of A}) = \$1.20$$
$$\underline{+ \ (\$1.40 \text{ per unit of B}) \times (3 \text{ units of B}) = \$4.20}$$
$$\text{Minimum daily cost} = \$5.40$$

The numbers 0.20 and 1.40 are called the **shadow costs** of the nutrients. These two numbers from the dual, $0.20 and $1.40, also allow the breeder to calculate feed costs for small changes in nutrient requirements. For example, an increase of one unit in the requirement for each nutrient would produce a total cost of $7.00:

$5.40	6 units of A, 3 of B
0.20	1 extra unit of A
+ 1.40	1 extra unit of B
$7.00	Total cost per day

Shadow costs only give the exact answer for a limited range. Unfortunately, finding that range is somewhat complicated. In the dog feed example, we can add up to 3 units or delete up to 4 units of A, and shadow costs will give the exact answer. If, however, we add 4 units of A, shadow costs give an answer of $6.20, while the true cost is $6.67.

CAUTION If you wish to use shadow costs, do not simplify an inequality in the original problem by dividing out a common factor. For example, if an inequality in the original problem is $3y_1 + 3y_2 \geq 6$, do not simplify to $y_1 + y_2 > 2$ by dividing out the 3. Doing so will give incorrect shadow costs. ■

NOTE Shadow costs become shadow profits in maximization problems. For example, see Exercises 18 and 19. ▨

The Solver in Microsoft Excel provides the values of the dual variables. See *The Spreadsheet Manual* available with this book for more details.

▶ 4.3 Exercises

Find the transpose of each matrix.

1. $\begin{bmatrix} 1 & 2 & 3 \\ 3 & 2 & 1 \\ 1 & 10 & 0 \end{bmatrix}$

2. $\begin{bmatrix} 3 & 4 & -2 & 0 & 1 \\ 2 & 0 & 11 & 5 & 7 \end{bmatrix}$

3. $\begin{bmatrix} 4 & 5 & -3 & 15 \\ 7 & 14 & 20 & -8 \\ 5 & 0 & -2 & 23 \end{bmatrix}$

4. $\begin{bmatrix} 1 & 11 & 15 \\ 0 & 10 & -6 \\ 4 & 12 & -2 \\ 1 & -1 & 13 \\ 2 & 25 & -1 \end{bmatrix}$

State the dual problem for each linear programming problem.

5. Maximize $\quad z = 4x_1 + 3x_2 + 2x_3$

subject to: $\quad x_1 + x_2 + x_3 \leq 5$

$\qquad\qquad x_1 + x_2 \qquad\; \leq 4$

$\qquad\qquad 2x_1 + x_2 + 3x_3 \leq 15$

with $\qquad x_1 \geq 0,\; x_2 \geq 0,\; x_3 \geq 0.$

6. Maximize $\quad z = 2x_1 + 7x_2 + 4x_3$

subject to: $\quad 4x_1 + 2x_2 + x_3 \leq 26$

$\qquad\qquad x_1 + 7x_2 + 8x_3 \leq 33$

with $\qquad x_1 \geq 0,\; x_2 \geq 0,\; x_3 \geq 0.$

7. Minimize $\quad w = 3y_1 + 6y_2 + 4y_3 + y_4$

subject to: $\quad y_1 + y_2 + y_3 + y_4 \geq 150$

$\qquad\qquad 2y_1 + 2y_2 + 3y_3 + 4y_4 \geq 275$

with $\qquad y_1 \geq 0,\; y_2 \geq 0,\; y_3 \geq 0,\; y_4 \geq 0.$

8. Minimize $\quad w = y_1 + y_2 + 4y_3$

subject to: $\quad y_1 + 2y_2 + 3y_3 \geq 115$

$\qquad\qquad 2y_1 + y_2 + 8y_3 \geq 200$

$\qquad\qquad y_1 \qquad\; + y_3 \geq 50$

with $\qquad y_1 \geq 0,\; y_2 \geq 0,\; y_3 \geq 0.$

Use the simplex method to solve.

9. Find $y_1 \geq 0$ and $y_2 \geq 0$ such that
$$2y_1 + 3y_2 \geq 6$$
$$2y_1 + y_2 \geq 7$$
and $w = 5y_1 + 2y_2$ is minimized.

10. Find $y_1 \geq 0$ and $y_2 \geq 0$ such that
$$2y_1 + 3y_2 \geq 15$$
$$5y_1 + 6y_2 \geq 35$$
and $w = 2y_1 + 3y_2$ is minimized.

11. Find $y_1 \geq 0$ and $y_2 \geq 0$ such that
$$10y_1 + 5y_2 \geq 100$$
$$20y_1 + 10y_2 \geq 150$$
and $w = 4y_1 + 5y_2$ is minimized.

12. Minimize $w = 29y_1 + 10y_2$
subject to: $3y_1 + 2y_2 \geq 2$
$5y_1 + y_2 \geq 3$
with $y_1 \geq 0, \ y_2 \geq 0.$

13. Minimize $w = 2y_1 + y_2 + 3y_3$
subject to: $y_1 + y_2 + y_3 \geq 100$
$2y_1 + y_2 \geq 50$
with $y_1 \geq 0, \ y_2 \geq 0, \ y_3 \geq 0.$

14. Minimize $w = 3y_1 + 2y_2$
subject to: $y_1 + 2y_2 \geq 10$
$y_1 + y_2 \geq 8$
$2y_1 + y_2 \geq 12$
with $y_1 \geq 0, \ y_2 \geq 0.$

15. You are given the following linear programming problem (P):*
Minimize $z = x_1 + 2x_2$
subject to: $-2x_1 + x_2 \geq 1$
$x_1 - 2x_2 \geq 1$
$x_1 \geq 0, \ x_2 \geq 0.$

The dual of (P) is (D). Which of the statements below is true?

a. (P) has no feasible solution and the objective function of (D) is unbounded.

b. (D) has no feasible solution and the objective function of (P) is unbounded.

c. The objective functions of both (P) and (D) are unbounded.

d. Both (P) and (D) have optimal solutions.

e. Neither (P) nor (D) has feasible solutions.

▶ Applications

BUSINESS AND ECONOMICS

16. *Production Costs* A brewery produces regular beer and a lower-carbohydrate "light" beer. Steady customers of the brewery buy 10 units of regular beer and 15 units of light beer monthly. While setting up the brewery to produce the beers, the management decides to produce extra beer, beyond that needed to satisfy customers. The cost per unit of regular beer is $32,000 and the cost per unit of light beer is $50,000. Every unit of regular beer brings in $120,000 in revenue, while every unit of light beer brings in $300,000

in revenue. The brewery wants at least $9,000,000 in revenue. At least 20 additional units of beer can be sold.

a. How much of each type of beer should be made so as to minimize total production costs?

b. Suppose the minimum revenue is increased to $9,500,000. Use shadow costs to calculate the total production costs.

17. *Supply Costs* The chemistry department at a local college decides to stock at least 900 small test tubes and 600 large test tubes. It wants to buy at least 2700 test tubes to take

*Problem 2 from "November 1989 Course 130 Examination Operations Research" of the *Education and Examination Committee of The Society of Actuaries*. Reprinted by permission of The Society of Actuaries.

advantage of a special price. Since the small test tubes are broken twice as often as the large, the department will order at least twice as many small tubes as large.

a. If the small test tubes cost 18 cents each and the large ones, made of a cheaper glass, cost 15 cents each, how many of each size should be ordered to minimize cost?

b. Suppose the minimum number of test tubes is increased to 3000. Use shadow costs to calculate the total cost in this case.

In most examples of this section, the original problem is a minimization problem and the dual is a maximization problem whose solution gives shadow costs. The reverse is true in Exercises 18 and 19. The dual here is a minimization problem whose solution can be interpreted as shadow profits.

18. *Agriculture* Refer to the original information in Example 2, Section 4.1.

a. Give the dual problem.

b. Use the shadow profits to estimate the farmer's profit if land is cut to 90 acres but capital increases to $21,000.

c. Suppose the farmer has 110 acres but only $19,000. Find the optimum profit and the planting strategy that will produce this profit.

19. *Toy Manufacturing* A small toy manufacturing firm has 200 squares of felt, 600 oz of stuffing, and 90 ft of trim available to make two types of toys, a small bear and a monkey. The bear requires 1 square of felt and 4 oz of stuffing. The monkey requires 2 squares of felt, 3 oz of stuffing, and 1 ft of trim. The firm makes $1 profit on each bear and $1.50 profit on each monkey.

a. Set up the linear programming problem to maximize profit.

b. Solve the linear programming problem in part a.

c. What is the corresponding dual problem?

d. What is the optimal solution to the dual problem?

e. Use the shadow profits to calculate the profit the firm will make if its supply of felt increases to 210 squares.

f. How much profit will the firm make if its supply of stuffing is cut to 590 oz and its supply of trim is cut to 80 ft?

g. Explain why it makes sense that the shadow profit for trim is 0.

20. *Interview Time* Joan McKee has a part-time job conducting public opinion interviews. She has found that a political interview takes 45 min and a market interview takes 55 min. She needs to minimize the time she spends doing interviews to allow more time for her full-time job. Unfortunately, to keep her part-time job, she must complete at least 8 interviews each week. Also, she must earn at least $60 per week at this job; she earns $8 for each political interview and $10 for each market interview. Finally, to

stay in good standing with her supervisor, she must earn at least 40 bonus points per week; she receives 6 bonus points for each political interview and 5 points for each market interview. How many of each interview should she do each week to minimize the time spent?

21. *Animal Food* An animal food must provide at least 54 units of vitamins and 60 calories per serving. One gram of soybean meal provides 2.5 units of vitamins and 5 calories. One gram of meat byproducts provides 4.5 units of vitamins and 3 calories. One gram of grain provides 5 units of vitamins and 10 calories. A gram of soybean meal costs 8¢, a gram of meat byproducts 9¢, and a gram of grain 10¢.

a. What mixture of these three ingredients will provide the required vitamins and calories at minimum cost?

b. What is the minimum cost?

c. There is more than one optimal basic solution to this problem. The answer found in part a depends on whether the tie in the minimum ratio rule was broken by pivoting on the second row or third row of the dual. Find the other solution.

22. *Feed Costs* Refer to the example at the end of this section on minimizing the daily cost of feeds.

a. Find a combination of feeds that will cost $7 and give 7 units of A and 4 units of B.

b. Use the dual variables to predict the daily cost of feed if the requirements change to 5 units of A and 4 units of B. Find a combination of feeds to meet these requirements at the predicted price.

23. *Pottery* Karla Harby makes three items in her pottery shop: large bowls, small bowls, and pots for plants. A large bowl requires 3 lb of clay and 6 fl oz of glaze. A small bowl requires 2 lb of clay, and 6 fl oz of glaze. A pot requires 4 lb of clay and 2 fl oz of glaze. She must use up 72 lb of old clay and 108 fl oz of old glaze; she can order more if necessary. If Karla can make a large bowl in 5 hours, a small bowl in 6 hours, and a pot in 4 hours, how many of each should she make to minimize her time? What is the minimum time?

LIFE SCIENCES

24. *Calorie Expenditure* Francesca wants to start exercising to burn at least 1500 extra calories per week, but she does not have much spare time for exercise. According to a Web site,* she can burn an average of 3.5 calories per minute walking, 4 calories per minute cycling, and 8 calories per minute swimming. She would like her total time walking and cycling to be at least 3 times as long as she spends swimming. She would also like to walk at least 30 minutes per week. How much time should she spend on each activity to meet her goals but to also minimize her total exercise time per week? What is her minimum exercise time per week?

25. *Health Care* Mark, who is ill, takes vitamin pills. Each day he must have at least 16 units of vitamin A, 5 units of vitamin B_1, and 20 units of vitamin C. He can choose between pill 1, which costs 10¢ and contains 8 units of A, 1 of B_1, and 2 of C; and pill 2, which costs 20¢ and contains 2 units of A, 1 of B_1, and 7 of C. How many of each pill should he buy in order to minimize his cost?

26. *Blending Nutrients* A biologist must make a nutrient of her algae. The nutrient must contain the three basic elements D, E, and F, and must contain at least 10 kg of D, 12 kg of E, and 20 kg of F. The nutrient is made from three ingredients, I, II, and III. The quantity of D, E, and F in one unit of each of the ingredients is as given in the following chart.

		Ingredient		
		I	*II*	*III*
Kilograms of	D	4	1	10
Elements (per	E	3	2	1
unit of ingredient)	F	0	4	5
Cost per unit (in $)		4	7	5

How many units of each ingredient are required to meet the biologist's needs at minimum cost?

4.4 Nonstandard Problems

? THINK ABOUT IT

How many cars should an auto manufacturer send from each of its two plants to each of two dealerships in order to minimize the cost while meeting each dealership's needs?

We will learn techniques in this section for answering questions like the one above.

So far we have used the simplex method to solve linear programming problems in standard maximum or minimum form only. Now, this work is extended to include linear programming problems with mixed $\leq$ and $\geq$ constraints.

For example, suppose a new constraint is added to the farmer problem in Example 2 of Section 4.1: To satisfy orders from regular buyers, the farmer must plant a total of at least 60 acres of the three crops. This constraint introduces the new inequality

$$x_1 + x_2 + x_3 \geq 60.$$

As before, this inequality must be rewritten as an equation in which the variables all represent nonnegative numbers. The inequality $x_1 + x_2 + x_3 \geq 60$ means that

$$x_1 + x_2 + x_3 - s_3 = 60$$

for some nonnegative variable s_3. (Remember that s_1 and s_2 are the slack variables in the problem.)

*http://www.brianmac.demon.co.uk/energyexp.htm.

The new variable, s_3, is called a **surplus variable**. The value of this variable represents the excess number of acres (over 60) that may be planted. Since the total number of acres planted is to be no more than 100 but at least 60, the value of s_3 can vary from 0 to 40.

We must now solve the system of equations

$$
\begin{aligned}
x_1 + \quad x_2 + \quad x_3 + s_1 \qquad\qquad\qquad &= 100 \\
10x_1 + \quad 4x_2 + \quad 7x_3 \qquad + s_2 \qquad\qquad &= 500 \\
x_1 + \quad x_2 + \quad x_3 \qquad\qquad - s_3 \quad\;\; &= 60 \\
-120x_1 - 40x_2 - 60x_3 \qquad\qquad\qquad + z &= 0,
\end{aligned}
$$

with x_1, x_2, x_3, s_1, s_2, and s_3 all nonnegative.

Set up the initial simplex tableau.

$$
\begin{array}{cccccccc}
x_1 & x_2 & x_3 & s_1 & s_2 & s_3 & z & \\
\left[\begin{array}{ccccccc|c}
1 & 1 & 1 & 1 & 0 & 0 & 0 & 100 \\
10 & 4 & 7 & 0 & 1 & 0 & 0 & 500 \\
1 & 1 & 1 & 0 & 0 & -1 & 0 & 60 \\
\hline
-120 & -40 & -60 & 0 & 0 & 0 & 1 & 0
\end{array}\right]
\end{array}
$$

This tableau gives the solution

$$x_1 = 0, \quad x_2 = 0, \quad x_3 = 0, \quad s_1 = 100, \quad s_2 = 500, \quad s_3 = -60.$$

But this is not a feasible solution, since s_3 is negative. All the variables in any feasible solution must be nonnegative if the solution is to correspond to a corner point of the region of feasible solutions.

When a negative value of a variable appears in the solution, row operations are used to transform the matrix until a solution is found in which all variables are nonnegative. Here the problem is the -1 in a column corresponding to a basic variable. If the number in that row of the right-hand column were 0, we could simply multiply this row by -1 to remove the negative from the column. But we cannot do this with 60 in the right-hand column. Instead, we find the positive entry that is farthest to the left in the third row (the row containing the -1); namely, the 1 in row 3, column 1. We will pivot using this column. (Actually, any column with a positive entry in row 3 will do; we chose the column farthest to the left arbitrarily.*) Use quotients as before to find the pivot, which is the 10 in row 2, column 1. Then use row operations to get the following tableau.

$$
\begin{array}{cccccccc}
 & x_1 & x_2 & x_3 & s_1 & s_2 & s_3 & z \\
-R_2 + 10R_1 \to R_1 & \left[\begin{array}{c}0\end{array}\right. & 6 & 3 & 10 & -1 & 0 & 0 & 500 \\
 & 10 & 4 & 7 & 0 & 1 & 0 & 0 & 500 \\
-R_2 + 10R_3 \to R_3 & 0 & 6 & 3 & 0 & -1 & -10 & 0 & 100 \\
12R_2 + R_4 \to R_4 & 0 & 8 & 24 & 0 & 12 & 0 & 1 & 6000
\end{array}
$$

Notice from the s_3 column that $-10s_3 = 100$, so s_3 is still negative. We therefore apply the procedure again. The 6 in row 3, column 2, is the positive entry farthest to the left in row 3, and by investigating quotients, we see that it is also the pivot. This leads to the following tableau.

---

*We use this rule for simplicity. There are, however, more complicated methods for choosing the pivot element that require, on average, fewer pivots to find the solution.

$$
\begin{array}{c}
\begin{array}{cccccccc}
\; & x_1 & x_2 & x_3 & s_1 & s_2 & s_3 & z \\
\end{array} \\
\begin{array}{l}
-R_3 + R_1 \rightarrow R_1 \\
-2R_3 + 3R_2 \rightarrow R_2 \\
\\
-4R_3 + 3R_4 \rightarrow R_4
\end{array}
\left[
\begin{array}{ccccccc|c}
0 & 0 & 0 & 10 & 0 & 10 & 0 & 400 \\
30 & 0 & 15 & 0 & 5 & 20 & 0 & 1300 \\
0 & 6 & 3 & 0 & -1 & -10 & 0 & 100 \\
0 & 0 & 60 & 0 & 40 & 40 & 3 & 17{,}600
\end{array}
\right]
\end{array}
$$

The value of s_3 is now 0 and the solution is feasible. We now continue with the simplex method until an optimal solution is found. We check for negative indicators, but since there are none, we have merely to create a 1 in each column corresponding to a basic variable or z.

$$
\begin{array}{c}
\begin{array}{cccccccc}
\; & x_1 & x_2 & x_3 & s_1 & s_2 & s_3 & z \\
\end{array} \\
\begin{array}{l}
R_1/10 \rightarrow R_1 \\
R_2/30 \rightarrow R_2 \\
R_3/6 \rightarrow R_3 \\
R_4/3 \rightarrow R_4
\end{array}
\left[
\begin{array}{ccccccc|c}
0 & 0 & 0 & 1 & 0 & 1 & 0 & 40 \\
1 & 0 & \frac{1}{2} & 0 & \frac{1}{6} & \frac{2}{3} & 0 & \frac{130}{3} \\
0 & 1 & \frac{1}{2} & 0 & -\frac{1}{6} & -\frac{5}{3} & 0 & \frac{50}{3} \\
0 & 0 & 20 & 0 & \frac{40}{3} & \frac{40}{3} & 1 & \frac{17{,}600}{3}
\end{array}
\right]
\end{array}
$$

The solution is

$$
x_1 = \frac{130}{3} = 43\frac{1}{3}, \quad x_2 = \frac{50}{3} = 16\frac{2}{3}, \quad x_3 = 0, \quad z = \frac{17{,}600}{3} = 5866.67.
$$

For maximum profit with this new constraint, the farmer should plant $43\frac{1}{3}$ acres of potatoes, $16\frac{2}{3}$ acres of corn, and no cabbage. The profit will be $5866.67, less than the $6000 profit if the farmer were to plant only 50 acres of potatoes. Because of the additional constraint that at least 60 acres must be planted, the profit is reduced. Notice that $s_1 = 40$. This is the slack variable for the constraint that no more than 100 acres are available. It indicates that 40 of the 100 available acres are still unused.

NOTE If we ever reach a point where a surplus variable still has a negative solution, but there are no positive elements left in the row, then the problem has no feasible solution. ■

The procedure we have followed is a simplified version of the **two-phase method**, which is widely used for solving problems with mixed constraints. To see the complete method, including how to handle some complications that may arise, see *Linear Programming: An Introduction with Applications* by Alan Sultan, Academic Press, 1993.

In the previous section we solved standard minimum problems using duals. If a minimizing problem has mixed $\leq$ and $\geq$ constraints, the dual method cannot be used. We solve such problems with the method presented in this section. To see how, consider the simple fact: When a number t gets smaller, then $-t$ gets larger, and vice versa. For instance, if t goes from 6 to 1 to 0 to -8, then $-t$ goes from -6 to -1 to 0 to 8. Thus, if w is the objective function of a minimizing linear programming problem, the feasible solution that produces the minimum value of w also produces the maximum value of $z = -w$, and vice versa. Therefore, to solve a minimization problem with objective function w, we need only solve the maximization problem with the same constraints and objective function $z = -w$.

In summary, the following steps are involved in solving the nonstandard problems in this section.

SOLVING A NONSTANDARD PROBLEM

1. If necessary, convert the problem to a maximization problem.
2. Add slack variables and subtract surplus variables as needed.
3. Write the initial simplex tableau.
4. If any basic variable has a negative value, locate the nonzero number in that variable's column, and note what row it is in.
5. In the row located in Step 4, find the positive entry that is farthest to the left, and note what column it is in.
6. In the column found in Step 5, choose a pivot by investigating quotients.
7. Use row operations to change the other numbers in the pivot column to 0.
8. Continue Steps 4 through 7 until all basic variables are nonnegative. If it ever becomes impossible to continue, then the problem has no feasible solution.
9. Once a feasible solution has been found, continue to use the simplex method until the optimal solution is found.

In the next example, we use this method to solve a minimization problem with mixed constraints.

EXAMPLE 1 **Minimization**

Minimize $\quad w = 3y_1 + 2y_2$

subject to: $\quad y_1 + 3y_2 \leq 6$

$\qquad\qquad 2y_1 + y_2 \geq 3$

with $\qquad y_1 \geq 0, \; y_2 \geq 0.$

▶**Solution** Change this to a maximization problem by letting z equal the *negative* of the objective function: $z = -w$. Then find the *maximum* value of

$$z = -w = -3y_1 - 2y_2.$$

The problem can now be stated as follows.

$$\begin{aligned}
\text{Maximize} \quad & z = -3y_1 - 2y_2 \\
\text{subject to:} \quad & y_1 + 3y_2 \leq 6 \\
& 2y_1 + y_2 \geq 3 \\
\text{with} \quad & y_1 \geq 0, \; y_2 \geq 0.
\end{aligned}$$

To begin, we add slack and surplus variables, and rewrite the objective function.

$$\begin{aligned}
y_1 + 3y_2 + s_1 \qquad\qquad &= 6 \\
2y_1 + y_2 \qquad - s_2 \qquad &= 3 \\
3y_1 + 2y_2 \qquad\qquad + z &= 0
\end{aligned}$$

Set up the initial simplex tableau.

$$
\begin{array}{ccccc}
y_1 & y_2 & s_1 & s_2 & z \\
\end{array}
$$

$$
\left[\begin{array}{ccccc|c}
1 & 3 & 1 & 0 & 0 & 6 \\
2 & 1 & 0 & -1 & 0 & 3 \\
3 & 2 & 0 & 0 & 1 & 0
\end{array}\right]
$$

The solution $y_1 = 0$, $y_2 = 0$, $s_1 = 6$, and $s_2 = -3$, is not feasible. Row operations must be used to get a feasible solution. We start with s_2 which has a -1 in row 2. The positive entry farthest to the left in row 2 is the 2 in column 1. The element in column 1 that gives the smallest quotient is 2, so it becomes the pivot. Pivoting produces the following matrix.

$$
\begin{array}{ccccc}
y_1 & y_2 & s_1 & s_2 & z \\
\end{array}
$$

$$
\begin{array}{c}
-R_2 + 2R_1 \rightarrow R_1 \\
\\
-3R_2 + 2R_3 \rightarrow R_3
\end{array}
\left[\begin{array}{ccccc|c}
0 & 5 & 2 & 1 & 0 & 9 \\
2 & 1 & 0 & -1 & 0 & 3 \\
0 & 1 & 0 & 3 & 2 & -9
\end{array}\right]
$$

Now $s_2 = 0$, so the solution is feasible. Furthermore, there are no negative indicators, so the solution is optimal. Divide row 1 by 2, row 2 by 2, and row 3 by 2 to find the final solution: $y_1 = 3/2$ and $y_2 = 0$. Since $z = -w = -9/2$, the minimum value is $w = 9/2$.

An important application of linear programming is the problem of minimizing the cost of transporting goods. This type of problem is often referred to as a *transportation problem* or *warehouse problem*. Some problems of this type were included in the exercise sets in previous chapters. The next example is based on Exercise 51 from Section 2.2, in which the transportation costs were set equal to $10,640. We will now use the simplex method to minimize the transportation costs.

EXAMPLE 2   **Transportation Problem**

An auto manufacturer sends cars from two plants, I and II, to dealerships A and B located in a midwestern city. Plant I has a total of 28 cars to send, and plant II has 8. Dealer A needs 20 cars, and dealer B needs 16. Transportation costs per car based on the distance of each dealership from each plant are $220 from I to A, $300 from I to B, $400 from II to A, and $180 from II to B. How many cars should be sent from each plant to each of the two dealerships to minimize transportation costs? Use the simplex method to find the solution.

▶**Solution**   To begin, let

$$y_1 = \text{the number of cars shipped from I to A;}$$
$$y_2 = \text{the number of cars shipped from I to B;}$$
$$y_3 = \text{the number of cars shipped from II to A;}$$
and
$$y_4 = \text{the number of cars shipped from II to B.}$$

Plant I has only 28 cars to ship, so

$$y_1 + y_2 \leq 28.$$

Similarly, plant II has only 8 cars to ship, so

$$y_3 + y_4 \leq 8.$$

Since dealership A needs 20 cars and dealership B needs 16 cars,

$$y_1 + y_3 \geq 20 \quad \text{and} \quad y_2 + y_4 \geq 16.$$

The manufacturer wants to minimize transportation costs, so the objective function is

$$w = 220y_1 + 300y_2 + 400y_3 + 180y_4.$$

Now write the problem as a system of linear equations, adding slack or surplus variables as needed, and let $z = -w$.

$$
\begin{aligned}
y_1 + y_2 \qquad\qquad\quad + s_1 \qquad\qquad\qquad\qquad &= 28 \\
y_3 + y_4 \quad + s_2 \qquad\qquad\qquad &= 8 \\
y_1 \qquad + y_3 \qquad\qquad - s_3 \qquad\qquad &= 20 \\
y_2 \qquad + y_4 \qquad\qquad\qquad - s_4 \quad &= 16 \\
220y_1 + 300y_2 + 400y_3 + 180y_4 \qquad\qquad\qquad\quad + z &= 0
\end{aligned}
$$

Set up the initial simplex tableau.

$$
\begin{array}{ccccccccc|c}
y_1 & y_2 & y_3 & y_4 & s_1 & s_2 & s_3 & s_4 & z & \\
1 & 1 & 0 & 0 & 1 & 0 & 0 & 0 & 0 & 28 \\
0 & 0 & 1 & 1 & 0 & 1 & 0 & 0 & 0 & 8 \\
1 & 0 & 1 & 0 & 0 & 0 & -1 & 0 & 0 & 20 \\
0 & 1 & 0 & 1 & 0 & 0 & 0 & 1 & 0 & 16 \\
\hline
220 & 300 & 400 & 180 & 0 & 0 & 0 & 0 & 1 & 0
\end{array}
$$

Because $s_3 = -20$, we choose the positive entry farthest to the left in row 3, which is the 1 in column 1. After forming the necessary quotients, we find that the 1 is also the pivot, leading to the following tableau.

$$
\begin{array}{llcccccccc|c}
& y_1 & y_2 & y_3 & y_4 & s_1 & s_2 & s_3 & s_4 & z & \\
-R_3 + R_1 \to R_1 & 0 & 1 & -1 & 0 & 1 & 0 & 1 & 0 & 0 & 8 \\
& 0 & 0 & 1 & 1 & 0 & 1 & 0 & 0 & 0 & 8 \\
& 1 & 0 & 1 & 0 & 0 & 0 & -1 & 0 & 0 & 20 \\
& 0 & 1 & 0 & 1 & 0 & 0 & 0 & -1 & 0 & 16 \\
\hline
-220R_3 + R_5 \to R_5 & 0 & 300 & 180 & 180 & 0 & 0 & 220 & 0 & 1 & -4400
\end{array}
$$

We still have $s_4 = -16$. Verify that the 1 in row 1, column 2, is the next pivot, leading to the following tableau.

$$
\begin{array}{llcccccccc|c}
& y_1 & y_2 & y_3 & y_4 & s_1 & s_2 & s_3 & s_4 & z & \\
& 0 & 1 & -1 & 0 & 1 & 0 & 1 & 0 & 0 & 8 \\
& 0 & 0 & 1 & 1 & 0 & 1 & 0 & 0 & 0 & 8 \\
& 1 & 0 & 1 & 0 & 0 & 0 & -1 & 0 & 0 & 20 \\
-R_1 + R_4 \to R_4 & 0 & 0 & 1 & 1 & -1 & 0 & -1 & -1 & 0 & 8 \\
\hline
-300R_1 + R_5 \to R_5 & 0 & 0 & 480 & 180 & -300 & 0 & -80 & 0 & 1 & -6800
\end{array}
$$

We still have $s_4 = -8$. Choosing column 3 to pivot, there is a tie between rows 2 and 4. Observe that if we choose row 4, we will remove s_4 from the set of basic variables. This would be a smart next move. But our algorithm says to choose the row nearest the top, so we will do this and see where it leads.

$$
\begin{array}{c}
R_2 + R_1 \rightarrow R_1 \\
\\
-R_2 + R_3 \rightarrow R_3 \\
-R_2 + R_4 \rightarrow R_4 \\
-480R_2 + R_5 \rightarrow R_5
\end{array}
\begin{array}{ccccccccc}
y_1 & y_2 & y_3 & y_4 & s_1 & s_2 & s_3 & s_4 & z \\
\left[\begin{array}{cccccccc|c}
0 & 1 & 0 & 1 & 1 & 1 & 1 & 0 & 0 & 16 \\
0 & 0 & 1 & 1 & 0 & 1 & 0 & 0 & 0 & 8 \\
1 & 0 & 0 & -1 & 0 & -1 & -1 & 0 & 0 & 12 \\
0 & 0 & 0 & 0 & -1 & -1 & -1 & -1 & 0 & 0 \\
0 & 0 & 0 & -300 & -300 & -480 & -80 & 0 & 1 & -10{,}640
\end{array}\right]
\end{array}
$$

Now $s_4 = 0$. There is still a -1 in column 8, but this can be removed by multiplying row 4 by -1. We then have the feasible solution

$$y_1 = 12, \quad y_2 = 16, \quad y_3 = 8, \quad y_4 = 0, \quad s_1 = 0, \quad s_2 = 0, \quad s_3 = 0, \quad s_4 = 0,$$

with $w = 10{,}640$. But there are still negative indicators in the bottom row, so we can keep going. After three more tableaus, we find that

$$y_1 = 20, \quad y_2 = 8, \quad y_3 = 0, \quad y_4 = 8,$$

with $w = 8240$. Therefore, the manufacturer should send 20 cars from plant I to dealership A and 8 cars to dealership B. From plant II, 8 cars should be sent to dealership B and none to dealership A. The transportation cost will then be $8240, a savings of $2400 over the original stated cost of $10,640.

When one or more of the constraints in a linear programming problem is an equation, rather than an inequality, there is no need for a slack or surplus variable. The simplex method requires an additional variable, however, for *each* constraint. To meet this condition, an **artificial variable** is added to each equation. These variables are called artificial variables because they have no meaning in the context of the original problem. The first goal of the simplex method is to eliminate any artificial variables as basic variables, since they must have a value of 0 in the solution.

EXAMPLE 3 **Artificial Variables**
In the transportation problem discussed in Example 2, it would be more realistic for the dealerships to order exactly 20 and 16 cars, respectively. Solve the problem with these two equality constraints.

▶Solution Using the same variables, we can state the problem as follows.

$$\text{Minimize} \quad w = 220y_1 + 300y_2 + 400y_3 + 180y_4$$
$$\text{subject to:} \quad y_1 + y_2 \le 28$$
$$y_3 + y_4 \le 8$$
$$y_1 + y_3 = 20$$
$$y_2 + y_4 = 16$$

with all variables nonnegative.

The corresponding system of equations requires slack variables s_1 and s_2 and two artificial variables that we shall call a_1 and a_2, to remind us that they require special handling. The system

$$
\begin{array}{rcl}
y_1 + y_2 \hspace{3cm} + s_1 \hspace{2.5cm} & = & 28 \\
y_3 + y_4 \hspace{0.5cm} + s_2 \hspace{2cm} & = & 8 \\
y_1 \hspace{1cm} + y_3 \hspace{2.5cm} + a_1 \hspace{0.8cm} & = & 20 \\
y_2 \hspace{1cm} + y_4 \hspace{2.5cm} + a_2 & = & 16 \\
220y_1 + 300y_2 + 400y_3 + 180y_4 \hspace{2.5cm} + z & = & 0
\end{array}
$$

produces a tableau exactly the same as in Example 2, except that the columns labeled s_3 and s_4 in that example are now labeled a_1 and a_2. We proceed as we did in Example 2, except that we must first perform pivot operations to eliminate the artificial variables a_1 and a_2. To accomplish this, we simply find a row in which an artificial variable exists and then pivot on the leftmost positive entry in that row that is not in an artificial variable column. Once an artificial variable becomes nonbasic (so that its value is zero), we drop that column from further consideration. In fact, that column may then be omitted from the tableau. When all of the artificial variables have either been eliminated or have a value of zero, the solution will proceed as in Example 2 and will give the same result. In other problems, equality constraints can result in a higher cost.

CAUTION If the artificial variables cannot be made equal to zero, the problem has no feasible solution. ∎

NOTE Another way to handle this situation is by solving for y_3 and y_4 in terms of y_1 and y_2. Then proceed with the usual method for standard problems. ∎

Applications requiring the simplex method often have constraints that have a zero on the right-hand side. For example, in Exercise 33 of Section 4.2 a person wants to walk at least twice as many hours as she hikes. This results in one of the constraints $x_1 - 2x_2 \le 0$ or $-x_1 + 2x_2 \ge 0$. For the purposes of using the simplex method to solve problems in the standard maximum form, it is always better to write constraints in the first form, since the first constraint can be readily handled by the basic simplex method by adding a slack variable.

Several linear programming models in actual use are presented on the Web site for this textbook. These models illustrate the usefulness of linear programming. In most real applications, the number of variables is so large that these problems could not be solved without using methods (like the simplex method) that can be adapted to computers.

▶ 4.4 Exercises

Rewrite each system of inequalities as a system of linear equations, adding slack variables or subtracting surplus variables as necessary.

1. $2x_1 + 3x_2 \le 8$
$x_1 + 4x_2 \ge 7$

2. $3x_1 + 7x_2 \le 9$
$4x_1 + 5x_2 \ge 11$

3. $2x_1 + x_2 + 2x_3 \le 50$
$x_1 + 3x_2 + x_3 \ge 35$
$x_1 + 2x_2 \hspace{1cm} \ge 15$

4. $2x_1 \hspace{1cm} + x_3 \le 40$
$x_1 + x_2 \hspace{1cm} \ge 18$
$x_1 \hspace{1cm} + x_3 \ge 20$

Convert each problem into a maximization problem.

5. Minimize $w = 3y_1 + 4y_2 + 5y_3$

subject to: $y_1 + 2y_2 + 3y_3 \geq 9$

$y_2 + 2y_3 \geq 8$

$2y_1 + y_2 + 2y_3 \geq 6$

with $y_1 \geq 0, \quad y_2 \geq 0, \quad y_3 \geq 0.$

6. Minimize $w = 8y_1 + 3y_2 + y_3$

subject to: $7y_1 + 6y_2 + 8y_3 \geq 18$

$4y_1 + 5y_2 + 10y_3 \geq 20$

with $y_1 \geq 0, \quad y_2 \geq 0, \quad y_3 \geq 0.$

7. Minimize $w = y_1 + 2y_2 + y_3 + 5y_4$

subject to: $y_1 + y_2 + y_3 + y_4 \geq 50$

$3y_1 + y_2 + 2y_3 + y_4 \geq 100$

with $y_1 \geq 0, \quad y_2 \geq 0, \quad y_3 \geq 0, \quad y_4 \geq 0.$

8. Minimize $w = y_1 + y_2 + 7y_3$

subject to: $5y_1 + 2y_2 + y_3 \geq 125$

$4y_1 + y_2 + 6y_3 \leq 75$

$6y_1 + 8y_2 \geq 84$

with $y_1 \geq 0, \quad y_2 \geq 0, \quad y_3 \geq 0.$

Use the simplex method to solve.

9. Find $x_1 \geq 0$ and $x_2 \geq 0$ such that

$x_1 + 2x_2 \geq 24$

$x_1 + x_2 \leq 40$

and $z = 12x_1 + 10x_2$ is maximized.

10. Find $x_1 \geq 0$ and $x_2 \geq 0$ such that

$2x_1 + x_2 \geq 20$

$2x_1 + 5x_2 \leq 80$

and $z = 6x_1 + 2x_2$ is maximized.

11. Find $x_1 \geq 0, x_2 \geq 0,$ and $x_3 \geq 0$ such that

$x_1 + x_2 + x_3 \leq 150$

$x_1 + x_2 + x_3 \geq 100$

and $z = 2x_1 + 5x_2 + 3x_3$ is maximized.

12. Find $x_1 \geq 0, x_2 \geq 0,$ and $x_3 \geq 0$ such that

$x_1 + x_2 + x_3 \leq 15$

$4x_1 + 4x_2 + 2x_3 \geq 48$

and $z = 2x_1 + x_2 + 3x_3$ is maximized.

13. Find $x_1 \geq 0$ and $x_2 \geq 0$ such that

$x_1 + x_2 \leq 100$

$2x_1 + 3x_2 \leq 75$

$x_1 + 4x_2 \geq 50$

and $z = 5x_1 - 3x_2$ is maximized.

14. Find $x_1 \geq 0$ and $x_2 \geq 0$ such that

$x_1 + 2x_2 \leq 18$

$x_1 + 3x_2 \geq 12$

$2x_1 + 2x_2 \leq 24$

and $z = 5x_1 - 10x_2$ is maximized.

15. Find $y_1 \geq 0, y_2 \geq 0,$ and $y_3 \geq 0$ such that

$5y_1 + 3y_2 + 2y_3 \leq 150$

$5y_1 + 10y_2 + 3y_3 \geq 90$

and $w = 10y_1 + 12y_2 + 10y_3$ is minimized.

16. Minimize $w = 3y_1 + 2y_2 + 3y_3$

subject to: $2y_1 + 3y_2 + 6y_3 \leq 60$

$y_1 + 4y_2 + 5y_3 \geq 40$

with $y_1 \geq 0, \quad y_2 \geq 0, \quad y_3 \geq 0.$

Solve using artificial variables.

17. Maximize $z = 3x_1 + 2x_2$

subject to: $x_1 + x_2 = 50$

$4x_1 + 2x_2 \geq 120$

$5x_1 + 2x_2 \leq 200$

with $x_1 \geq 0, \quad x_2 \geq 0.$

18. Maximize $z = 5x_1 + 7x_2$

subject to: $x_1 + x_2 = 15$

$2x_1 + 4x_2 \geq 30$

$3x_1 + 5x_2 \geq 10$

with $x_1 \geq 0, \quad x_2 \geq 0.$

19. Minimize $w = 32y_1 + 40y_2 + 48y_3$

subject to: $20y_1 + 10y_2 + 5y_3 = 200$

$25y_1 + 40y_2 + 50y_3 \leq 500$

$18y_1 + 24y_2 + 12y_3 \geq 300$

with $y_1 \geq 0, \quad y_2 \geq 0, \quad y_3 \geq 0.$

20. Minimize $w = 15y_1 + 12y_2 + 18y_3$

subject to: $y_1 + 2y_2 + 3y_3 \leq 12$

$3y_1 + y_2 + 3y_3 \geq 18$

$y_1 + y_2 + y_3 = 10$

with $y_1 \geq 0, \quad y_2 \geq 0, \quad y_3 \geq 0.$

21. Explain how, in any linear programming problem, the value of the objective function can be found without using the number in the lower right-hand corner of the final tableau.

22. Explain why, for a maximization problem, you write the negative of the coefficients of the objective function on the bottom row, while, for a minimization problem, you write the coefficients themselves.

▶ Applications

23. *Transportation* Southwestern Oil supplies two distributors in the Northwest from two outlets, S_1 and S_2. Distributor D_1 needs at least 3000 barrels of oil, and distributor D_2 needs at least 5000 barrels. The two outlets can each furnish up to 5000 barrels of oil. The costs per barrel to ship the oil are given in the table.

Outlets	Distributors	
	D_1	D_2
S_1	$30	$20
S_2	$25	$22

There is also a shipping tax per barrel as given in the table below. Southwestern Oil is determined to spend no more than $40,000 on shipping tax.

	D_1	D_2
S_1	$2	$6
S_2	$5	$4

a. How should the oil be supplied to minimize shipping costs?

b. Find and interpret the values of any nonzero slack or surplus variables.

24. *Transportation* Change Exercise 23 so that the two outlets each furnish exactly 5000 barrels of oil, with everything else the same. Use artificial variables to solve the problem, following the steps outlined in Example 3.

25. *Finance* A bank has set aside a maximum of $25 million for commercial and home loans. Every million dollars in commercial loans requires 2 lengthy application forms, while every million dollars in home loans requires 3 lengthy application forms. The bank cannot process more than 72 application forms at this time. The bank's policy is to loan at least four times as much for home loans as for commercial loans. Because of prior commitments, at least $10 million will be used for these two types of loans. The bank earns 10% on commercial loans and 12% on home

loans. What amount of money should be allotted for each type of loan to maximize the interest income?

26. *Blending Seed* Topgrade Turf lawn seed mixture contains three types of seed: bluegrass, rye, and Bermuda. The costs per pound of the three types of seed are 16 cents, 14 cents, and 12 cents, respectively. In each batch there must be at least 25% bluegrass seed, and the amount of Bermuda must be no more than 2/3 the amount of rye. To fill current orders, the company must make at least 6000 lb of the mixture. How much of each kind of seed should be used to minimize cost?

27. *Blending Seed* Change Exercise 26 so that the company must make exactly 6000 lb of the mixture. Use artificial variables to solve the problem.

28. *Investments* Karen Guardino has decided to invest a $100,000 inheritance in government securities that earn 7% per year, municipal bonds that earn 6% per year, and mutual funds that earn an average of 10% per year. She will spend at least $40,000 on government securities, and she wants at least half the inheritance to go to bonds and mutual funds. Government securities have an initial fee of 2%, municipal bonds have an initial fee of 1%, and mutual funds have an initial fee of 3%. Karen has $2400 available to pay initial fees. How much should be invested in each way to maximize the interest yet meet the constraints? What is the maximum interest she can earn?

29. *Transportation* The manufacturer of a popular personal computer has orders from two dealers. Dealer D_1 wants at least 32 computers, and dealer D_2 wants at least 20 computers. The manufacturer can fill the orders from either of two warehouses, W_1 or W_2. There are 25 computers on hand at W_1, and 30 at W_2. The costs (in dollars) to ship one computer to each dealer from each warehouse are given below.

Warehouse	Dealer	
	D_1	D_2
W_1	$14	$12
W_2	$12	$10

a. How should the orders be filled to minimize shipping costs?

b. Find and interpret the values of any nonzero slack or surplus variables.

30. *Blending Chemicals* Natural Brand plant food is made from three chemicals, labeled I, II, and III. In each batch of the plant food, the amounts of chemicals II and III must be in the ratio of 4 to 3. The amount of nitrogen must be at least 30 kg. The percent of nitrogen in the three chemicals is 9%, 4%, and 3%, respectively. If the three chemicals cost $1.09, $0.87, and $0.65 per kilogram, respectively, how much of each should be used to minimize the cost of producing at least 750 kg of the plant food?

31. *Blending Gasoline* A company is developing a new additive for gasoline. The additive is a mixture of three liquid ingredients, I, II, and III. For proper performance, the total amount of additive must be at least 10 oz per gal of gasoline. However, for safety reasons, the amount of additive should not exceed 15 oz per gal of gasoline. At least 1/4 oz of ingredient I must be used for every ounce of ingredient II, and at least 1 oz of ingredient III must be used for every ounce of ingredient I. If the costs of I, II, and III are $0.30, $0.09, and $0.27 per oz, respectively, find the mixture of the three ingredients that produces the minimum cost of the additive. How much of the additive should be used per gal of gasoline?

32. *Blending a Soft Drink* A popular soft drink called Sugarlo, which is advertised as having a sugar content of no more than 10%, is blended from five ingredients, each of which has some sugar content. Water may also be added to dilute the mixture. The sugar content of the ingredients and their costs per gallon are given below.

	Ingredient					
	1	*2*	*3*	*4*	*5*	*Water*
Sugar Content (%)	0.28	0.19	0.43	0.57	0.22	0
Cost ($/gal)	0.48	0.32	0.53	0.28	0.43	0.04

At least 0.01 of the content of Sugarlo must come from ingredients 3 or 4, 0.01 must come from ingredients 2 or 5, and 0.01 from ingredients 1 or 4. How much of each ingredient should be used in preparing 15,000 gal of Sugarlo to minimize the cost?

33. *Calorie Expenditure* Joe Vetere's exercise regimen includes light calisthenics, swimming, and playing the drums. He has at most 10 hours per week to devote to these activities. He wants the total time he does calisthenics and plays the drums to be at least twice as long as he swims. His neighbors, however, will tolerate no more than 4 hours per week on the drums. According to a Web site,* a 190-pound person like Joe will burn an average of 388 calories per hour doing calisthenics, 518 calories per hour swimming, and 345 calories per hour playing the drums. In Section 4.2, Exercise 34, Joe found that he could maximize calories burned in an exercise routine that did not include playing the drums as part of his exercise plan.

a. Joe really likes to play the drums and insists that his exercise plan include at least 1 hour of playing the drums per week. With this added constraint, now how many hours per week should Joe spend on each exercise to maximize the number of calories he burns? What is the maximum number of calories he will burn?

b. Without the added constraint from part a, Joe's maximum calorie expenditure was $4313\frac{1}{3}$ calories. Compare this number with the new optimal solution. What conclusions can you draw when additional constraints are placed on a problem?

Chapter 4 Review

▶ *Chapter Summary*

In this chapter, we introduced the simplex method, which is a procedure for solving any linear programming problem. To apply this method, we first had to write the problem as a standard maximization problem in matrix form. This form tells us an initial basic feasible solution, which the simplex method uses to determine other basic feasible solutions. Each successive iteration of the simplex method gives us a new basic feasible solution, whose objective function value is greater than or equal to the objective function value of the previous basic feasible solution. We then introduced duality, which tells us that every time we solve a linear programming problem, we are

---

*http://www.nutristrategy.com/activitylist4.htm.

actually solving two problems—a maximization problem and a minimization problem. This has far-reaching consequences in the field of operations research and decision sciences, including the fact that standard minimization problems can be solved by the simplex method. Finally, we extended the simplex method to solve problems that are not standard because they have inequalities going in both directions (and perhaps equalities as well).

LINEAR PROGRAMMING: THE SIMPLEX METHOD SUMMARY

Standard Maximum Form
A linear programming problem is in standard maximum form if the following conditions are satisfied.

1. The objective function is to be maximized.

2. All variables are nonnegative.

3. All remaining constraints are stated in the form

$$a_1x_1 + a_2x_2 + \cdots + a_nx_n \leq b \qquad \text{with } b \geq 0.$$

Simplex Method
1. Determine the objective function.

2. Write all the necessary constraints.

3. Convert each constraint into an equation by adding a slack variable in each.

4. Set up the initial simplex tableau.

5. Locate the most negative indicator. If there are two such indicators, choose the one farther to the left.

6. Form the necessary quotients to find the pivot. Disregard any quotients with 0 or a negative number in the denominator. The smallest nonnegative quotient gives the location of the pivot. If all quotients must be disregarded, no maximum solutions exist. If two quotients are both equal and smallest, choose the pivot in the row nearest the top of the matrix.

7. Use row operations to change all other numbers in the pivot column to zero by adding a suitable multiple of the pivot row to a positive multiple of each row.

8. If the indicators are all positive or 0, this is the final tableau. If not, go back to step 5 and repeat the process until a tableau with no negative indicators is obtained.

9. Read the solution from the final tableau.

Standard Minimum Form
A linear programming problem is in standard minimum form if the following conditions are satisfied.

1. The objective function is to be minimized.

2. All variables are nonnegative.

3. All remaining constraints are stated in the form

$$a_1y_1 + a_2y_2 + \cdots + a_ny_n \geq b \qquad \text{with } b \geq 0.$$

Theorem of Duality
The objective function w of a minimization linear programming problem takes on a minimum value if and only if the objective function z of the corresponding dual maximization problem takes on a maximum value. The maximum value of z equals the minimum value of w.

Solving a Standard Minimum Problem with Duals
1. Find the dual standard maximization problem.

2. Solve the maximization problem using the simplex method.

3. The minimum value of the objective function w is the maximum value of the objective function z.

4. The optimum solution is given by the entries in the bottom row of the columns corresponding to the slack variables, so long as the entry in the z column is equal to 1.

Solving a Nonstandard Problem

1. If necessary, convert the problem to a maximization problem.

2. Add slack variables and subtract surplus variables as needed.

3. Write the initial simplex tableau.

4. If any basic variable has a negative value, locate the nonzero number in that variable's column, and note what row it is in.

5. In the row located in step 4, find the positive entry that is farthest to the left, and note what column it is in.

6. In the column found in step 5, choose a pivot by investigating quotients.

7. Use row operations to change the other numbers in the pivot column to 0.

8. Continue steps 4 through 7 until all basic variables are nonnegative. If it ever becomes impossible to continue, then the problem has no feasible solution.

9. Once a feasible solution has been found, continue to use the simplex method until the optimal solution is found.

Artificial Variables

When one or more of the constraints in a linear programming problem is an equation, rather than an inequality, an artificial variable is added to each equation. Proceed with the simplex method and then delete the column associated with an artificial variable once it becomes nonbasic. If in the optimal solution an artificial variable has a positive value, then the original problem does not have a solution.

 **Key Terms**

simplex method	indicators	**4.3** standard minimum	**4.4** surplus variable
4.1 standard maximum	basic variable	form	two-phase method
form	basic feasible solution	dual	artificial variable
slack variable	pivot	transpose	
simplex tableau	**4.2** sensitivity analysis	shadow costs	

Concept Check

Determine whether each of the following statements is true or false, and explain why.

1. The simplex method can be used to solve all linear programming problems.

2. If the feasible region of a linear programming problem is unbounded, then the objective function value is unbounded.

3. A linear programming problem in standard maximization form always has a feasible solution.

4. A linear programming problem in standard minimization form always has a feasible solution.

5. A linear programming problem in standard maximization form always has a finite optimal solution.

6. The tableau below for a linear program in standard maximization form shows that it has no finite maximum value.

$$\begin{array}{ccccc} x_1 & x_2 & s_1 & s_2 & z \\ \left[\begin{array}{ccccc|c} -1 & 1 & 0 & 1 & 0 & 1 \\ -4 & 0 & 1 & -2 & 0 & 3 \\ \hline -1 & 0 & 0 & 2 & 1 & 4 \end{array}\right] \end{array}$$

7. One must always use the minimum quotient when choosing a pivot row.

8. If there is a 0 in the right-hand column, we can disregard it when determining the quotients used to choose the pivot row.

9. One must always pick the most negative number in the indicator row when choosing the pivot column.

10. A basic variable can be assigned a value of zero by the simplex method.

11. A slack variable of a linear programming problem in standard maximization form may become negative during the intermediate stages of the simplex method.

12. The dual of the dual of a linear programming problem is the original problem.

13. The simplex method guarantees that each iteration will yield a feasible solution whose objective function value is bigger than the objective function value of all previous solutions.

▶ *Chapter 4 Review Exercises*

1. When is it necessary to use the simplex method rather than the graphical method?

2. What can you conclude if a surplus variable cannot be made nonnegative?

For each problem, (a) add slack variables or subtract surplus variables, and (b) set up the initial simplex tableau.

3. Maximize $z = 2x_1 + 7x_2$
subject to: $4x_1 + 6x_2 \le 60$
$3x_1 + x_2 \le 18$
$2x_1 + 5x_2 \le 20$
$x_1 + x_2 \le 15$
with $x_1 \ge 0, \ x_2 \ge 0.$

4. Maximize $z = 25x_1 + 30x_2$
subject to: $3x_1 + 5x_2 \le 47$
$x_1 + x_2 \le 25$
$5x_1 + 2x_2 \le 35$
$2x_1 + x_2 \le 30$
with $x_1 \ge 0, \ x_2 \ge 0.$

5. Maximize $z = 5x_1 + 8x_2 + 6x_3$
subject to: $x_1 + x_2 + x_3 \le 90$
$2x_1 + 5x_2 + x_3 \le 120$
$x_1 + 3x_2 \ge 80$
with $x_1 \ge 0, \ x_2 \ge 0, \ x_3 \ge 0.$

6. Maximize $z = 4x_1 + 6x_2 + 8x_3$
subject to: $x_1 + x_2 + 2x_3 \ge 200$
$8x_1 + 6x_3 \le 400$
$3x_1 + 5x_2 + x_3 \le 300$
with $x_1 \ge 0, \ x_2 \ge 0, \ x_3 \ge 0.$

Use the simplex method to solve each maximization linear programming problem with the given initial tableau.

7.

x_1	x_2	x_3	s_1	s_2	z	
4	5	2	1	0	0	18
2	8	6	0	1	0	24
−5	−3	−6	0	0	1	0

8.

x_1	x_2	s_1	s_2	z	
2	7	1	0	0	14
2	3	0	1	0	10
−2	−4	0	0	1	0

9.

x_1	x_2	x_3	s_1	s_2	s_3	z	
1	2	2	1	0	0	0	50
3	1	0	0	1	0	0	20
1	0	2	0	0	−1	0	15
−5	−3	−2	0	0	0	1	0

10.

x_1	x_2	s_1	s_2	s_3	z	
3	6	−1	0	0	0	28
1	1	0	1	0	0	12
2	1	0	0	1	0	16
−1	−2	0	0	0	1	0

Convert each problem into a maximization problem and then solve each problem using both the dual method and the method of Section 4.4.

11. Minimize $\quad w = 10y_1 + 15y_2$

subject to: $\quad y_1 + y_2 \geq 17$

$\quad\quad\quad\quad 5y_1 + 8y_2 \geq 42$

with $\quad\quad y_1 \geq 0, \; y_2 \geq 0.$

12. Minimize $\quad w = 22y_1 + 44y_2 + 33y_3$

subject to: $\quad y_1 + 2y_2 + y_3 \geq 3$

$\quad\quad\quad\quad y_1 \quad\quad + y_3 \geq 3$

$\quad\quad\quad\quad 3y_1 + 2y_2 + 2y_3 \geq 8$

with $\quad\quad y_1 \geq 0, \; y_2 \geq 0, \; y_3 \geq 0.$

13. Minimize $\quad w = 7y_1 + 2y_2 + 3y_3$

subject to: $\quad y_1 + y_2 + 2y_3 \geq 48$

$\quad\quad\quad\quad y_1 + y_2 \quad\quad \geq 12$

$\quad\quad\quad\quad\quad\quad\quad y_3 \geq 10$

$\quad\quad\quad\quad 3y_1 \quad + y_3 \geq 30$

with $\quad\quad y_1 \geq 0, \; y_2 \geq 0, \; y_3 \geq 0.$

The following are the final tableaus of minimization problems. State the solution and the minimum value of the objective function for each problem.

14.

y_1	y_2	y_3	s_1	s_2	z	
0	1	0	5	3	0	7
1	0	0	-2	1	0	15
0	0	1	-6	2	0	23
0	0	0	2	9	1	-53

15.

y_1	y_2	s_1	s_2	s_3	s_4	z	
0	0	3	0	1	1	0	2
1	0	-2	0	2	0	0	8
0	1	7	0	0	0	0	12
0	0	1	1	-4	0	0	1
0	0	5	0	8	0	1	-62

16.

y_1	y_2	y_3	s_1	s_2	z	
0	0	1	-1	2	0	14
1	2	0	0	4	0	11
0	3	0	10	6	1	-120

Use the simplex method to solve each problem. (You may need to use artificial variables.)

17. Maximize $\quad z = 20x_1 + 30x_2$

subject to: $\quad 5x_1 + 10x_2 \leq 120$

$\quad\quad\quad\quad 10x_1 + 15x_2 \geq 200$

with $\quad\quad x_1 \geq 0, \; x_2 \geq 0.$

18. Minimize $\quad w = 4y_1 + 2y_2$

subject to: $\quad y_1 + 3y_2 \geq 6$

$\quad\quad\quad\quad 2y_1 + 8y_2 \leq 21$

with $\quad\quad y_1 \geq 0, \; y_2 \geq 0.$

19. Maximize $\quad z = 10x_1 + 12x_2$

subject to: $\quad 2x_1 + 2x_2 = 17$

$\quad\quad\quad\quad 2x_1 + 5x_2 \geq 22$

$\quad\quad\quad\quad 4x_1 + 3x_2 \leq 28$

with $\quad\quad x_1 \geq 0, \; x_2 \geq 0.$

20. Minimize $\quad w = 24y_1 + 30y_2 + 36y_3$

subject to: $\quad 5y_1 + 10y_2 + 15y_3 \geq 1200$

$\quad\quad\quad\quad y_1 + y_2 + y_3 \leq 50$

with $\quad\quad y_1 \geq 0, \; y_2 \geq 0, \; y_3 \geq 0.$

21. What types of problems can be solved using slack, surplus, and artificial variables?

22. What kind of problems can be solved using the method of duals?

23. In solving a linear programming problem, you are given the following initial tableau.

$$\begin{bmatrix} 4 & 2 & 3 & 1 & 0 & 0 & 9 \\ 5 & 4 & 1 & 0 & 1 & 0 & 10 \\ -6 & -7 & -5 & 0 & 0 & 1 & 0 \end{bmatrix}$$

a. What is the problem being solved?

b. If the 1 in row 1, column 4 were a -1 rather than a 1, how would it change your answer to part a?

c. After several steps of the simplex algorithm, the following tableau results.

$$\left[\begin{array}{cccccc|c} 3 & 0 & 5 & 2 & -1 & 0 & 8 \\ 11 & 10 & 0 & -1 & 3 & 0 & 21 \\ \hline 47 & 0 & 0 & 13 & 11 & 10 & 227 \end{array}\right]$$

What is the solution? (List only the values of the original variables and the objective function. Do not include slack or surplus variables.)

d. What is the dual of the problem you found in part a?

e. What is the solution of the dual you found in part d? (Do not perform any steps of the simplex algorithm; just examine the tableau given in part c.)

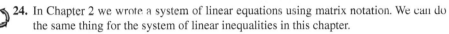

24. In Chapter 2 we wrote a system of linear equations using matrix notation. We can do the same thing for the system of linear inequalities in this chapter.

a. Find matrices A, B, C, and X such that the maximization problem in Example 1 of Section 4.1 can be written as

Maximize CX

subject to: $AX \le B$

with $X \ge 0$.

(*Hint:* Let B and X be column matrices, and C a row matrix.)

b. Show that the dual of the problem in part a can be written as

Minimize YB

subject to: $YA \ge C$

with $Y \ge 0$,

where Y is a row matrix.

c. Show that for any feasible solutions X and Y to the original and dual problems, respectively, $CX \le YB$. (*Hint:* Multiply both sides of $AX \le B$ by Y on the left. Then substitute for YA.)

d. For the solution X to the maximization problem and Y to the dual, it can be shown that

$$CX = YB$$

is always true. Verify this for Example 1 of Section 4.1. What is the significance of the value in CX (or YB)?

▶ Applications

For Exercises 25–28, (**a**) *select appropriate variables;* (**b**) *write the objective functions;* (**c**) *write the constraints as inequalities.*

BUSINESS AND ECONOMICS

25. *Production* The Bronze Forge produces and ships three different hand-crafted bronze plates: a dogwood-engraved cake plate, a wheat-engraved bread plate, and a lace-engraved dinner plate. Each cake plate requires $15 in materials, 5 hours of labor, and $6 to ship. Each bread plate requires $10 in materials, 4 hours of labor, and $5 to ship. Each dinner plate requires $8 in materials, 4 hours of labor, and $5 to deliver. The profit on the cake plate is $15, on the bread plate is $12, and on the dinner plate is $5. The company has available up to 2700 hours of labor per week. Each week, they can spend at most $1500 on materials and $1200 on delivery. How many of each plate should the company produce to maximize their weekly profit? What is their maximum profit?

26. *Investments* An investor is considering three types of investments: a high-risk venture into oil leases with a potential return of 15%, a medium-risk investment in stocks with a 9% return, and a relatively safe bond investment with a 5% return. He has $50,000 to invest. Because of the risk, he will limit his investment in oil leases and stocks to 30% and his investment in oil leases and bonds to 50%. How much should he invest in each to maximize his return, assuming investment returns are as expected?

27. *Profit* The Aged Wood Winery makes two white wines, Fruity and Crystal, from two kinds of grapes and sugar. One gallon of Fruity wine requires 2 bushels of Grape A, 2 bushels of Grape B, 2 lb of sugar, and produces a profit of $12. One gallon of Crystal wine requires 1 bushel of Grape A, 3 bushels of Grape B, 1 lb of sugar, and produces a profit of $15. The winery has available 110 bushels of grape A, 125 bushels of grape B, and 90 lb of sugar. How much of each wine should be made to maximize profit?

28. *Production Costs* Cauchy Canners produces canned whole tomatoes and tomato sauce. This season, the company has available 3,000,000 kg of tomatoes for these two products. To meet the demands of regular customers, it must produce at least 80,000 kg of sauce and 800,000 kg of whole tomatoes. The cost per kilogram is $4 to produce canned whole tomatoes and $3.25 to produce tomato sauce. Labor agreements require that at least 110,000 person-hours be used. Each kilogram can of sauce requires 3 minutes for one worker, and each kilogram can of whole tomatoes requires 6 minutes for one worker. How many kilograms of tomatoes should Cauchy use for each product to minimize cost? (For simplicity, assume production of y_1 kg of canned whole tomatoes and y_2 kg of tomato sauce requires $y_1 + y_2$ kg of tomatoes.)

29. Solve Exercise 25.   30. Solve Exercise 26.

31. Solve Exercise 27.   32. Solve Exercise 28.

33. *Canning* Cauchy Canners produces canned corn, beans, and carrots. Demand for vegetables requires it to produce at least 1000 cases per month. Based on past sales, it should produce at least twice as many cases of corn as of

beans, and at least 340 cases of carrots. It costs $10 to produce a case of corn, $15 to produce a case of beans, and $25 to produce a case of carrots.

a. Using the method of surplus variables, find how many cases of each vegetable should be produced to minimize costs. What is the minimum cost?

b. Using the method of duals, find how many cases of each vegetable should be produced to minimize costs. What is the minimum cost?

34. *Food Cost* A store sells two brands of snacks. A package of Sun Hill costs $3 and contains 10 oz of peanuts, 4 oz of raisins, and 2 oz of rolled oats. A package of Bear Valley costs $2 and contains 2 oz of peanuts, 4 oz of raisins, and 8 oz of rolled oats. Suppose you wish to make a mixture that contains at least 20 oz of peanuts, 24 oz of raisins, and 24 oz of rolled oats.

a. Using the method of surplus variables, find how many packages of each you should buy to minimize the cost. What is the minimum cost?

b. Using the method of duals, find how many packages of each you should buy to minimize the cost. What is the minimum cost?

c. Suppose the minimum amount of peanuts is increased to 28. Use shadow costs to calculate the total cost in this case.

d. Explain why it makes sense that the shadow cost for rolled oats is 0.

LIFE SCIENCES

35. *Calorie Expenditure* Ginger's exercise regimen includes doing tai chi, riding a unicycle, and fencing. She has at most 10 hours per week to devote to these activities. Her fencing partner can work with her at most only 2 hours per week. She wants the total time she does tai chi to be at least twice as long as she unicycles. According to a Web site,* a 130-pound person like Ginger will burn an average of 236 calories per hour doing tai chi, 295 calories per hour riding a unicycle, and 354 calories per hour fencing. How many hours per week should Ginger spend on each activity to maximize the number of calories she burns? What is the maximum number of calories she will burn?

*http://www.nutristrategy.com/activitylist4.htm.

Using Integer Programming in the Stock-Cutting Problem*

In Chapter 3 Section 3 we noted that some problems require solutions in integers because the resources to be allocated are items that can't be split into pieces, like cargo containers or airplanes. These *integer programming* problems are generally harder than the linear programming problems we have been solving by the simplex method, but often linear programming can be combined with other techniques to solve integer problems. Even if the number of variables and constraints is small, some help from software is usually required. We will introduce integer programming with the basic but important *stock-cutting problem.* (To get a feeling for the issues involved, you may want to try the simple stock-cutting problem given in Exercise 1.)

A paper mill produces rolls of paper that are much wider than most customers require, often as wide as 200 in. The mill then cuts these wide rolls into smaller widths to fill orders for paper rolls to be used in printing and packaging and other applications. The stock-cutting problem is the following:

Given a list of roll widths and the number of rolls ordered for each width, decide how to cut the raw rolls that come from the paper-making machine into smaller rolls so as to fill all the orders with a minimum amount of waste.

Another way to state the problem is: What is the minimum number of raw rolls required to fill the orders? This is an integer problem because the customers have ordered whole numbers of rolls, and each roll is cut in a single piece from one of the raw rolls.

As an example, suppose the paper machine produces rolls 100 in. wide. The manufacturer offers rolls in the following six widths: 14 in., 17 in., 31 in., 33 in., 36 in., and 45 in. (We'll call these the standard widths.) The current orders to be filled are as follows:

Width in Inches	14	17	31	33	36	45
Number Ordered	100	123	239	121	444	87

The cutting machine can make four simultaneous cuts, so a raw roll can be cut into as many as five pieces. With luck, all five pieces might be usable for filling orders, but there will usually be unusable waste on the end, and we also might end up with more rolls of some standard width than we need. We'll consider both the end pieces that are too narrow and any unused standard-width rolls as waste, and this is the waste we want to minimize.

The first question is, what are the possible cutting patterns? We're restricted to at most five standard rolls from any given raw roll, and we'll elect to use as much as possible in each raw roll so that the waste remaining at the end will always be less than 14 in. So, for example, 14|36|45| is a possible pattern, but 14|14|14|14|14| is not, because it has too many cuts, and 45|36| is not, because more than 14 in. is left at the end. (Each vertical bar represents a cut; if the piece on the end happens to be a standard width, then we don't need a cut after it, since we've reached the end of the roll.) This is already a tricky problem, and variations of it appear in many industrial applications involving packing objects of different sizes into a fixed space (for example, packing crates into a container for shipment overseas). In the Exercises we'll ask you to write down some more possible patterns, but finding all of them is a job for a computer, and it turns out that there are exactly 33 possible cutting patterns. In Chapter 8 you'll learn some counting techniques that might help you write the program to find all possible patterns.

The next question is, what's the best we can do? We have to use an integral number of 100-in. raw rolls, and we can find the total "roll-inches" ordered by multiplying the width of each standard roll by the number ordered for this width. This computation is a natural one for the matrix notation that you have learned. If W and O are 6×1 column matrices, then the total roll inches used is W^TO:

$$W = \begin{bmatrix} 14 \\ 17 \\ 31 \\ 33 \\ 36 \\ 45 \end{bmatrix} \quad O = \begin{bmatrix} 100 \\ 123 \\ 239 \\ 121 \\ 444 \\ 87 \end{bmatrix} \quad W^TO = 34{,}792$$

Since each raw roll is 100 in., the best we can do is to use 348 rolls with a total width of 34,800. As a percentage of the raw material, the corresponding waste is

$$\frac{8}{34{,}800} \approx 0.02\%,$$

which represents very low waste. Of course, we'll only reach this target if we can lay out the cutting with perfect efficiency.

*This application is based on material from the following online sources:
The Web site of the Optimization Technology Center at Northwestern University at
http://www.ece.nwu.edu/OTC/. There is a link to a thorough explanation of the stock-cutting problem.
Home page of the Special Interest Group on Cutting and Packing at
http://prodlog.wiwi.uni-halle.de/sicup/index.html.
The linear programming FAQ at http://www.faqs.org/faqs/linear-programming-faq/.

As we noted previously, these integer programming problems are difficult, but many mathematical analysis and spreadsheet programs have built-in optimization routines that can handle problems of modest size. We submitted this problem to one such program, giving it the lists of orders and widths and a list of the 33 allowable cutting patterns. Figure 10 shows the seven cutting patterns chosen by the minimizer software, with a graphical representation, and the total number of times each pattern was used.

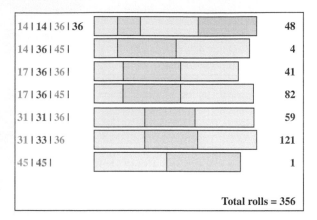

FIGURE 10

With these cutting choices we generate the following numbers of each standard width:

Width	14	17	31	33	36	45
Quantity Produced	100	123	239	121	444	88
Quantity Ordered	100	123	239	121	444	87

We figured that the minimum possible number of raw rolls was 348, so we have used only 8 more than the minimum. In the Exercises you'll figure the percentage of waste with this cutting plan.

Manufacturers of glass and sheet metal encounter a two-dimensional version of this problem: They need to cut the rectangular pieces that have been ordered from a larger rectangular piece of glass or metal, laying out the ordered sizes so as to minimize waste. Besides the extra dimension, this problem is complicated by another constraint: The typical cutting machine can make only "guillotine cuts" that go completely across the sheet being cut, so a cutting algorithm must usually begin with a few long cuts that cut the original rectangle into strips, followed by crossways cuts that begin to create the order sizes. A typical finished cutting layout might look like Figure 11.

The first cuts would be the three vertical cuts labeled 1, 2, and 3, followed by horizontal cuts in each of the four resulting strips, then vertical cuts in these new rectangles, and so on. Areas of waste are marked with **X**. An additional complication in designing the layout is that any given stock rectangle can be oriented in two different directions (unless it's square), so the packing problem has many alternative solutions.

In three dimensions, a comparable problem is to fill a shipping container with smaller boxes (rectangular prisms) with the minimum wasted space. These packing problems are complicated geometric versions of a basic problem called the *knapsack problem*:

Given n objects with weights $w_1, w_2, \ldots, w_n$ and cash values $v_1, v_2, \ldots, v_n$ and a knapsack that can hold a weight of at most W, choose the objects that will pack in the greatest value. In the Exercises you can try a small example, but as soon as n gets large, this problem "explodes," that is, the number of possibilities becomes too large for a trial-and-error solution, even with a computer to do the bookkeeping. The development of good algorithms for cutting and packing problems is an active research specialty in the field of optimization.

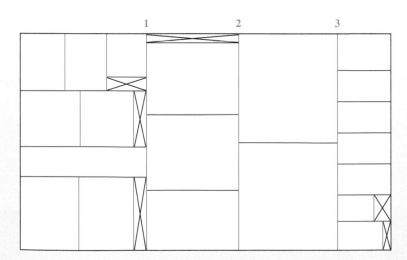

FIGURE 11

EXERCISES

1. Suppose you plan to build a raised flower bed using landscape timbers, which come in 8-ft lengths. You want the bed's outer dimensions to be 6 ft by 4 ft, and you will use three layers of timbers. The timbers are 6 in. by 6 in. in cross section, so if you make the bottom and top layers with 6 ft lengths on the sides and 3 ft lengths on the ends, and the middle layer with 5 ft lengths on the sides and 4 ft lengths on the ends, you could build the bed out of the following lengths.

Plan A	
Length	Number Needed
3 ft	4
4 ft	2
5 ft	2
6 ft	4

a. What is the smallest number of timbers you can buy to build your bed? How will you lay out the cuts? How much wood will you waste?

b. If you overlap the corners in a different way, you can build the bed with this plan:

Plan B	
Length	Number Needed
3 ft	2
4 ft	4
5 ft	4
6 ft	2

Does plan B allow you to build the bed with fewer 8-ft timbers?

c. What is the smallest length for the uncut timbers that would allow you to build the bed with no waste?

2. For the list of standard paper roll widths given earlier, write down four more possible cutting patterns that use at most four cuts and leave less than 14 in. of waste on the end. See if you can find ones that aren't in the list of patterns returned by the optimizer.

3. Four of the 33 possible patterns use up the raw roll with no waste, that is, the widths add up to exactly 100 in. Find these four patterns.

4. For the computer solution of the cutting problem, figure out the percent of the 356 rolls used that is wasted.

5. In our cutting plan, we elected to use up as much as possible of each 100-in. roll with standard widths. Why might it be a better idea to allow leftover rolls that are *wider* than 14 in.?

6. The following table shows the weights of six objects and their values.

Weight	2	2.5	3	3.5	4	4.5
Value	12	11	7	13	10	11

If your knapsack holds a maximum weight of 9, what is the highest value you can pack in?

DIRECTIONS FOR GROUP PROJECT

Suppose you and three of the students from class have met at your house to study and your father questions each of you on what you are learning in college. While this is happening, your mother is busy planning a new raised-bed garden and your sister is attempting to choose which items she will put in a back pack for a field trip. Using the data in Exercises 1 and 6, prepare a presentation for your family on the value of what you're learning in college.

Appendix A

Graphing Equations

GRAPHING EQUATIONS

OBJECTIVES

1 Plot ordered pairs.

2 Determine whether an ordered pair of numbers is a solution to an equation in two variables.

3 Graph linear equations.

4 Graph nonlinear equations.

OBJECTIVE 1 ▶ Plotting ordered pairs. Graphs are widely used today in newspapers, magazines, and all forms of newsletters. A few examples of graphs are shown here.

Percent of Sales Completed Using Cards*

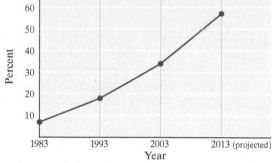

Source: The Nilson Report

*These include credit or debit cards, prepaid cards and EBT (electronic benefits transfer) cards.

Percent of People Who Go to the Movies

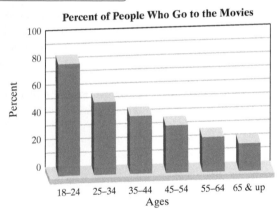

Source: TELENATION/Market Facts, Inc.

To review how to read these graphs, we review their origin—the rectangular coordinate system. One way to locate points on a plane is by using a **rectangular coordinate system,** which is also called a **Cartesian coordinate system** after its inventor, René Descartes (1596–1650).

A rectangular coordinate system consists of two number lines that intersect at right angles at their 0 coordinates. We position these axes on paper such that one number line is horizontal and the other number line is then vertical. The horizontal number line is called the *x***-axis** (or the axis of the **abscissa**), and the vertical number line is called the *y***-axis** (or the axis of the **ordinate**). The point of intersection of these axes is named the **origin.**

Notice in the left figure below that the axes divide the plane into four regions. These regions are called **quadrants.** The top-right region is quadrant I. Quadrants II, III, and IV are numbered counterclockwise from the first quadrant as shown. The *x*-axis and the *y*-axis are not in any quadrant.

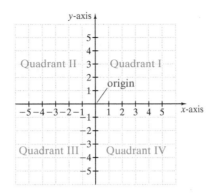

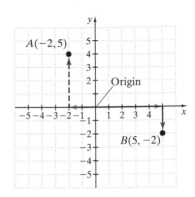

Each point in the plane can be located, or **plotted,** or graphed by describing its position in terms of distances along each axis from the origin. An **ordered pair,** represented by the notation (x, y), records these distances.

For example, the location of point A in the figure on the right on the previous page is described as 2 units to the left of the origin along the x-axis and 5 units upward parallel to the y-axis. Thus, we identify point A with the ordered pair $(-2, 5)$. Notice that the order of these numbers is *critical*. The x-value -2 is called the **x-coordinate** and is associated with the x-axis. The y-value 5 is called the **y-coordinate** and is associated with the y-axis.

Compare the location of point A with the location of point B, which corresponds to the ordered pair $(5, -2)$. Can you see that the order of the coordinates of an ordered pair matters? Also, two ordered pairs are considered equal and correspond to the same point if and only if their x-coordinates are equal and their y-coordinates are equal.

Keep in mind that **each ordered pair corresponds to exactly one point in the real plane and that each point in the plane corresponds to exactly one ordered pair.** Thus, we may refer to the ordered pair (x, y) as the point (x, y).

EXAMPLE 1   Plot each ordered pair on a Cartesian coordinate system and name the quadrant or axis in which the point is located.

a. $(2, -1)$ **b.** $(0, 5)$ **c.** $(-3, 5)$ **d.** $(-2, 0)$ **e.** $\left(-\frac{1}{2}, -4\right)$

f. $(1.5, 1.5)$

Solution   The six points are graphed as shown.

a. $(2, -1)$ lies in quadrant IV.

b. $(0, 5)$ is on the y-axis.

c. $(-3, 5)$ lies in quadrant II.

d. $(-2, 0)$ is on the x-axis.

e. $\left(-\frac{1}{2}, -4\right)$ is in quadrant III.

f. $(1.5, 1.5)$ is in quadrant I.

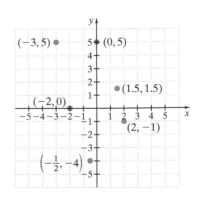

PRACTICE

1   Plot each ordered pair on a Cartesian coordinate system and name the quadrant or axis in which the point is located.

a. $(3, -4)$ **b.** $(0, -2)$ **c.** $(-2, 4)$ **d.** $(4, 0)$ **e.** $\left(-1\frac{1}{2}, -2\right)$
f. $(2.5, 3.5)$

Notice that the y-coordinate of any point on the x-axis is 0. For example, the point with coordinates $(-2, 0)$ lies on the x-axis. Also, the x-coordinate of any point on the y-axis is 0. For example, the point with coordinates $(0, 5)$ lies on the y-axis. These points that lie on the axes do not lie in any quadrants.

Concept Check ☑

Which of the following correctly describes the location of the point $(3, -6)$ in a rectangular coordinate system?

a. 3 units to the left of the y-axis and 6 units above the x-axis

b. 3 units above the x-axis and 6 units to the left of the y-axis

c. 3 units to the right of the y-axis and 6 units below the x-axis

d. 3 units below the x-axis and 6 units to the right of the y-axis

Many types of real-world data occur in pairs. The graph below was shown at the beginning of this section. Notice the paired data $(2013, 57)$ and the corresponding plotted point, both in blue.

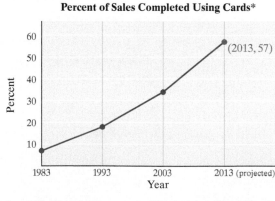

Percent of Sales Completed Using Cards*

Source: The Nilson Report

*These include credit or debit cards, prepaid cards and EBT (electronic benefits transfer) cards.

This paired data point, $(2013, 57)$, means that in the year 2013, it is predicted that 57% of sales will be completed using some type of card (credit, debit, etc.).

OBJECTIVE 2 ▶ Determining whether an ordered pair is a solution. Solutions of equations in two variables consist of two numbers that form a true statement when substituted into the equation. A convenient notation for writing these numbers is as ordered pairs. A solution of an equation containing the variables x and y is written as a pair of numbers in the order (x, y). If the equation contains other variables, we will write ordered pair solutions in alphabetical order.

EXAMPLE 2   Determine whether $(0, -12)$, $(1, 9)$, and $(2, -6)$ are solutions of the equation $3x - y = 12$.

Solution   To check each ordered pair, replace x with the x-coordinate and y with the y-coordinate and see whether a true statement results.

Let $x = 0$ and $y = -12$.

$$3x - y = 12$$
$$3(0) - (-12) \overset{?}{=} 12$$
$$0 + 12 \overset{?}{=} 12$$
$$12 = 12 \quad \text{True}$$

Let $x = 1$ and $y = 9$.

$$3x - y = 12$$
$$3(1) - 9 \overset{?}{=} 12$$
$$3 - 9 \overset{?}{=} 12$$
$$-6 = 12 \quad \text{False}$$

Let $x = 2$ and $y = -6$.

$$3x - y = 12$$
$$3(2) - (-6) \overset{?}{=} 12$$
$$6 + 6 \overset{?}{=} 12$$
$$12 = 12 \quad \text{True}$$

Thus, $(1, 9)$ is not a solution of $3x - y = 12$, but both $(0, -12)$ and $(2, -6)$ are solutions. ☐

PRACTICE

2   Determine whether $(1, 4)$, $(0, 6)$, and $(3, 4)$ are solutions of the equation $4x + y = 8$.

OBJECTIVE 3 ▶ Graphing linear equations. The equation $3x - y = 12$, from Example 2, actually has an infinite number of ordered pair solutions. Since it is impossible to list all solutions, we visualize them by graphing.

A few more ordered pairs that satisfy $3x - y = 12$ are $(4, 0)$, $(3, -3)$, $(5, 3)$, and $(1, -9)$. These ordered pair solutions along with the ordered pair solutions from Example 2 are plotted on the following graph. The graph of $3x - y = 12$ is the single line containing these points. Every ordered pair solution of the equation corresponds to a point on this line, and every point on this line corresponds to an ordered pair solution.

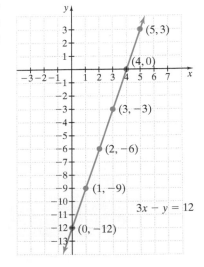

x	y	$3x - y = 12$
5	3	$3 \cdot 5 - 3 = 12$
4	0	$3 \cdot 4 - 0 = 12$
3	-3	$3 \cdot 3 - (-3) = 12$
2	-6	$3 \cdot 2 - (-6) = 12$
1	-9	$3 \cdot 1 - (-9) = 12$
0	-12	$3 \cdot 0 - (-12) = 12$

The equation $3x - y = 12$ is called a linear equation in two variables, and **the graph of every linear equation in two variables is a line.**

Linear Equation in Two Variables

A linear equation in two variables is an equation that can be written in the form

$$Ax + By = C$$

where A and B are not both 0. This form is called **standard form.**

Some examples of equations in standard form:

$$3x - y = 12$$
$$-2.1x + 5.6y = 0$$

▶ **Helpful Hint**

Remember: A linear equation is written in standard form when all of the variable terms are on one side of the equation and the constant is on the other side.

Many real-life applications are modeled by linear equations. Suppose you have a part-time job at a store that sells office products.

Your pay is \$3000 plus 20% or $\frac{1}{5}$ of the price of the products you sell. If we let x represent products sold and y represent monthly salary, the linear equation that models your salary is

$$y = 3000 + \frac{1}{5}x$$

(Although this equation is not written in standard form, it is a linear equation. To see this, subtract $\frac{1}{5}x$ from both sides.)

Some ordered pair solutions of this equation are below.

Products Sold	x	0	1000	2000	3000	4000	10,000
Monthly Salary	y	3000	3200	3400	3600	3800	5000

For example, we say that the ordered pair $(1000, 3200)$ is a solution of the equation $y = 3000 + \frac{1}{5}x$ because when x is replaced with 1000 and y is replaced with 3200, a true statement results.

$$y = 3000 + \frac{1}{5}x$$

$$3200 \stackrel{?}{=} 3000 + \frac{1}{5}(1000) \quad \text{Let } x = 1000 \text{ and } y = 3200.$$

$$3200 \stackrel{?}{=} 3000 + 200$$

$$3200 = 3200 \qquad \qquad \text{True}$$

A portion of the graph of $y = 3000 + \frac{1}{5}x$ is shown in the next example.

Since we assume that the smallest amount of product sold is none, or 0, then x must be greater than or equal to 0. Therefore, only the part of the graph that lies in Quadrant I is shown. Notice that the graph gives a visual picture of the correspondence between products sold and salary.

▶ Helpful Hint

A line contains an infinite number of points and each point corresponds to an ordered pair that is a solution of its corresponding equation.

EXAMPLE 3   Use the graph of $y = 3000 + \frac{1}{5}x$ to answer the following questions.

a. If the salesperson has $8000 of products sold for a particular month, what is the salary for that month?

b. If the salesperson wants to make more than $5000 per month, what must be the total amount of products sold?

Solution

a. Since x is products sold, find 8000 along the x-axis and move vertically up until you reach a point on the line. From this point on the line, move horizontally to the left until you reach the y-axis. Its value on the y-axis is 4600, which means if $8000 worth of products is sold, the salary for the month is $4600.

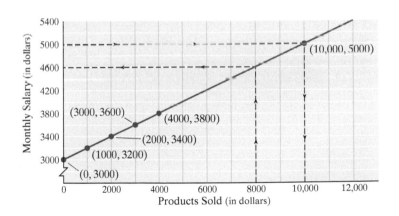

b. Since y is monthly salary, find 5000 along the y-axis and move horizontally to the right until you reach a point on the line. Either read the corresponding x-value from the labeled ordered pair, or move vertically downward until you reach the x-axis. The corresponding x-value is 10,000. This means that $10,000 worth of products sold gives a salary of $5000 for the month. For the salary to be greater than $5000, products sold must be greater that $10,000.   □

PRACTICE
3 Use the graph in Example 3 to answer the following questions.

a. If the salesperson has $6000 of products sold for a particular month, what is the salary for that month?

b. If the salesperson wants to make more than $4800 per month, what must be the total amount of products sold?

Recall from geometry that a line is determined by two points. This means that to graph a linear equation in two variables, just two solutions are needed. We will find a third solution, just to check our work. To find ordered pair solutions of linear equations in two variables, we can choose an x-value and find its corresponding y-value, or we can choose a y-value and find its corresponding x-value. The number 0 is often a convenient value to choose for x and also for y.

EXAMPLE 4 Graph the equation $y = -2x + 3$.

Solution This is a linear equation. (In standard form it is $2x + y = 3$.) Find three ordered pair solutions, and plot the ordered pairs. The line through the plotted points is the graph. Since the equation is solved for y, let's choose three x-values. We'll choose 0, 2, and then -1 for x to find our three ordered pair solutions.

Let $x = 0$	Let $x = 2$	Let $x = -1$
$y = -2x + 3$	$y = -2x + 3$	$y = -2x + 3$
$y = -2 \cdot 0 + 3$	$y = -2 \cdot 2 + 3$	$y = -2(-1) + 3$
$y = 3$ Simplify.	$y = -1$ Simplify.	$y = 5$ Simplify.

The three ordered pairs $(0, 3)$, $(2, -1)$ and $(-1, 5)$ are listed in the table and the graph is shown.

x	y
0	3
2	-1
-1	5

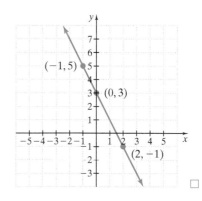

PRACTICE
4 Graph the equation $y = -3x - 2$.

Notice that the graph crosses the y-axis at the point $(0, 3)$. This point is called the **y-intercept.** (You may sometimes see just the number 3 called the y-intercept.) This graph also crosses the x-axis at the point $\left(\dfrac{3}{2}, 0\right)$ This point is called the **x-intercept.**

(You may also see just the number $\dfrac{3}{2}$ called the x-intercept.)

Since every point on the y-axis has an x-value of 0, we can find the y-intercept of a graph by letting $x = 0$ and solving for y. Also, every point on the x-axis has a y-value of 0. To find the x-intercept, we let $y = 0$ and solve for x.

Finding x- and y-Intercepts

To find an x-intercept, let $y = 0$ and solve for x.
To find a y-intercept, let $x = 0$ and solve for y.

EXAMPLE 5   Graph the linear equation $y = \dfrac{1}{3}x$.

Solution   To graph, we find ordered pair solutions, plot the ordered pairs, and draw a line through the plotted points. We will choose x-values and substitute in the equation. To avoid fractions, we choose x-values that are multiples of 3. To find the y-intercept, we let $x = 0$.

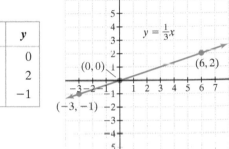

x	y
0	0
6	2
-3	-1

$$y = \frac{1}{3}x$$

If $x = 0$, then $y = \dfrac{1}{3}(0)$, or 0.

If $x = 6$, then $y = \dfrac{1}{3}(6)$, or 2.

If $x = -3$, then $y - \dfrac{1}{3}(-3)$, or -1.

> **Helpful Hint**
>
> Notice that by using multiples of 3 for x, we avoid fractions.

> **Helpful Hint**
>
> Since the equation $y = \dfrac{1}{3}x$ is solved for y, we choose x-values for finding points. This way, we simply need to evaluate an expression to find the x-value, as shown.

This graph crosses the x-axis at $(0, 0)$ and the y-axis at $(0, 0)$. This means that the x-intercept is $(0, 0)$ and that the y-intercept is $(0, 0)$.   □

PRACTICE
5   Graph the linear equation $y = -\dfrac{1}{2}x$.

OBJECTIVE 4 ▶ Graphing nonlinear equations. Not all equations in two variables are linear equations, and not all graphs of equations in two variables are lines.

EXAMPLE 6   Graph $y = x^2$.

Solution   This equation is not linear because the x^2 term does not allow us to write it in the form $Ax + By = C$. Its graph is not a line. We begin by finding ordered pair solutions. Because this graph is solved for y, we choose x-values and find corresponding y-values.

If $x = -3$, then $y = (-3)^2$, or 9.

If $x = -2$, then $y = (-2)^2$, or 4.

If $x = -1$, then $y = (-1)^2$, or 1.

If $x = 0$, then $y = 0^2$, or 0.

If $x = 1$, then $y = 1^2$, or 1.

If $x = 2$, then $y = 2^2$, or 4.

If $x = 3$, then $y = 3^2$, or 9.

x	y
-3	9
-2	4
-1	1
0	0
1	1
2	4
3	9

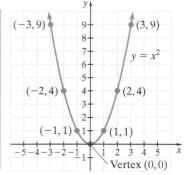

Study the table a moment and look for patterns. Notice that the ordered pair solution $(0, 0)$ contains the smallest y-value because any other x-value squared will give a positive result. This means that the point $(0, 0)$ will be the lowest point on the graph. Also notice that all other y-values correspond to two different x-values. For example, $3^2 = 9$ and also $(-3)^2 = 9$. This means that the graph will be a mirror image of itself across the y-axis. Connect the plotted points with a smooth curve to sketch the graph.

This curve is given a special name, a parabola. We will study more about parabolas in later chapters. ☐

PRACTICE

6   Graph $y = 2x^2$.

EXAMPLE 7   Graph the equation $y = |x|$.

Solution   This is not a linear equation since it cannot be written in the form $Ax + By = C$. Its graph is not a line. Because we do not know the shape of this graph, we find many ordered pair solutions. We will choose x-values and substitute to find corresponding y-values.

If $x = -3$, then $y = |-3|$, or 3.

If $x = -2$, then $y = |-2|$, or 2.

If $x = -1$, then $y = |-1|$, or 1.

If $x = 0$, then $y = |0|$, or 0.

If $x = 1$, then $y = |1|$, or 1.

If $x = 2$, then $y = |2|$, or 2.

If $x = 3$, then $y = |3|$, or 3.

x	y
-3	3
-2	2
-1	1
0	0
1	1
2	2
3	3

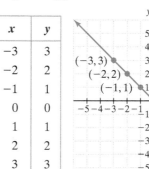

Again, study the table of values for a moment and notice any patterns.

From the plotted ordered pairs, we see that the graph of this absolute value equation is V-shaped. ☐

PRACTICE

7   Graph $y = -|x|$.

Graphing Calculator Explorations

In this section, we begin a study of graphing calculators and graphing software packages for computers. These graphers use the same point plotting technique that we introduced in this section. The advantage of this graphing technology is, of course, that graphing calculators and computers can find and plot ordered pair solutions much faster than we can. Note, however, that the features described in these boxes may not be available on all graphing calculators.

The rectangular screen where a portion of the rectangular coordinate system is displayed is called a **window.** We call it a **standard window** for graphing when both the x- and y-axes display coordinates between -10 and 10. This information is often displayed in the window menu on a graphing calculator as

$\text{Xmin} = -10$

$\text{Xmax} = 10$

$\text{Xscl} = 1$ The scale on the x-axis is one unit per tick mark.

$\text{Ymin} = -10$

$\text{Ymax} = 10$

$\text{Yscl} = 1$ The scale on the y-axis is one unit per tick mark.

To use a graphing calculator to graph the equation $y = -5x + 4$, press the $\boxed{\text{Y} =}$ key and enter the keystrokes

(Check your owner's manual to make sure the "negative" key is pressed here and not the "subtraction" key.)

The top row should now read $Y_1 = -5x + 4$. Next press the $\boxed{\text{GRAPH}}$ key, and the display should look like this:

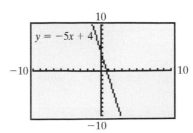

Use a standard window and graph the following equations. (Unless otherwise stated, we will use a standard window when graphing.)

1. $y = -3.2x + 7.9$

2. $y = -x + 5.85$

3. $y = \frac{1}{4}x - \frac{2}{3}$

4. $y = \frac{2}{3}x - \frac{1}{5}$

5. $y = |x - 3| + 2$

6. $y = |x + 1| - 1$

7. $y = x^2 + 3$

8. $y = (x + 3)^2$

VOCABULARY & READINESS CHECK

Determine the coordinates of each point on the graph.

1. Point A
2. Point B
3. Point C
4. Point D
5. Point E
6. Point F
7. Point G
8. Point H

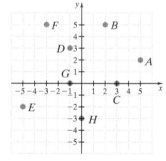

Without graphing, visualize the location of each point. Then give its location by quadrant or x- or y-axis.

9. $(2, 3)$
10. $(0, 5)$
11. $(-2, 7)$
12. $(-3, 0)$
13. $(-1, -4)$
14. $(4, -2)$
15. $(0, -100)$
16. $(10, 30)$
17. $(-10, -30)$
18. $(0, 0)$
19. $(-87, 0)$
20. $(-42, 17)$

APPENDIX A
EXERCISE SET

MyMathLab   PRACTICE WATCH DOWNLOAD READ REVIEW

Plot each point and name the quadrant or axis in which the point lies. See Example 1.

1. $(3, 2)$
2. $(2, -1)$
3. $(-5, 3)$
4. $(-3, -1)$
5. $\left(5\frac{1}{2}, -4\right)$
6. $\left(-2, 6\frac{1}{3}\right)$
7. $(0, 3.5)$
8. $(-5.2, 0)$
9. $(-2, -4)$
10. $(-4.2, 0)$

Given that x is a positive number and that y is a positive number, determine the quadrant or axis in which each point lies. See Example 1.

11. $(x, -y)$
12. $(-x, y)$
13. $(x, 0)$
14. $(0, -y)$
15. $(-x, -y)$
16. $(0, 0)$

Determine whether each ordered pair is a solution of the given equation. See Example 2.

17. $y = 3x - 5; (0, 5), (-1, -8)$

18. $y = -2x + 7; (1, 5), (-2, 3)$

19. $-6x + 5y = -6; (1, 0), \left(2, \frac{6}{5}\right)$

20. $5x - 3y = 9; (0, 3), \left(\frac{12}{5}, -1\right)$

21. $y = 2x^2; (1, 2), (3, 18)$

22. $y = 2|x|; (-1, 2), (0, 2)$

23. $y = x^3; (2, 8), (3, 9)$

24. $y = x^4; (-1, 1), (2, 16)$

25. $y = \sqrt{x} + 2; (1, 3), (4, 4)$

26. $y = \sqrt[3]{x} - 4; (1, -3), (8, 6)$

MIXED PRACTICE

Determine whether each equation is linear or not. Then graph the equation by finding and plotting ordered-pair solutions. See Examples 3 through 7.

27. $x + y = 3$

28. $y - x = 8$

29. $y = 4x$

30. $y = 6x$

31. $y = 4x - 2$

32. $y = 6x - 5$

33. $y = |x| + 3$

34. $y = |x| + 2$

35. $2x - y = 5$

36. $4x - y = 7$

37. $y = 2x^2$

38. $y = 3x^2$

39. $y = x^2 - 3$

40. $y = x^2 + 3$

41. $y = -2x$

42. $y = -3x$

43. $y = -2x + 3$

44. $y = -3x + 2$

45. $y = |x + 2|$

46. $y = |x - 1|$

47. $y = x^3$
  (*Hint:* Let $x = -3, -2, -1, 0, 1, 2$.)

48. $y = x^3 - 2$
  (*Hint:* Let $x = -3, -2, -1, 0, 1, 2$.)

49. $y = -|x|$

50. $y = -x^2$

51. $y = \frac{1}{3}x - 1$

52. $y = \frac{1}{2}x - 3$

53. $y = -\frac{3}{2}x + 1$

54. $y = -\frac{2}{3}x + 1$

REVIEW AND PREVIEW

Solve the following equations. See Section 2.1.

55. $3(x - 2) + 5x = 6x - 16$

56. $5 + 7(x + 1) = 12 + 10x$

57. $3x + \frac{2}{5} = \frac{1}{10}$

58. $\frac{1}{6} + 2x = \frac{2}{3}$

Solve the following inequalities. See Section 2.4.

59. $3x \le -15$

60. $-3x > 18$

61. $2x - 5 > 4x + 3$

62. $9x + 8 \le 6x - 4$

CONCEPT EXTENSIONS

Solve. See the Concept Check in this section.

63. Which correctly describes the location of the point $(-1, 5.3)$ in a rectangular coordinate system?

  a. 1 unit to the right of the y-axis and 5.3 units above the x-axis

  b. 1 unit to the left of the y-axis and 5.3 units above the x-axis

  c. 1 unit to the left of the y-axis and 5.3 units below the x-axis

  d. 1 unit to the right of the y-axis and 5.3 units below the x-axis

64. Which correctly describes the location of the point $\left(0, -\frac{3}{4}\right)$ in a rectangular coordinate system?

  a. on the x-axis and $\frac{3}{4}$ unit to the left of the y-axis

  b. on the x-axis and $\frac{3}{4}$ unit to the right of the y-axis

  c. on the y-axis and $\frac{3}{4}$ unit above the x-axis

  d. on the y-axis and $\frac{3}{4}$ unit below the x-axis

For Exercises 65 through 68, match each description with the graph that best illustrates it.

65. Moe worked 40 hours per week until the fall semester started. He quit and didn't work again until he worked 60 hours a week during the holiday season starting mid-December.

66. Kawana worked 40 hours a week for her father during the summer. She slowly cut back her hours to not working at all during the fall semester. During the holiday season in December, she started working again and increased her hours to 60 hours per week.

67. Wendy worked from July through February, never quitting. She worked between 10 and 30 hours per week.

68. Bartholomew worked from July through February. The rest of the time, he worked between 10 and 40 hours per week. During the holiday season between mid-November and the beginning of January, he worked 40 hours per week.

a.

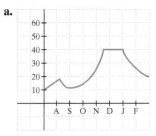

b.

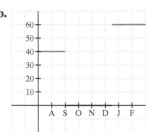

c.

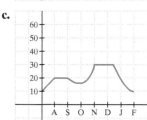

d.

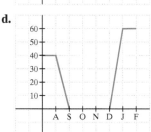

69. What was the first year that the price for a first-class stamp rose above $0.25?

70. What was the first year that the price for a first-class stamp rose above $0.30?

71. Why do you think that this graph is shaped the way it is?

72. The U.S. Postal Service issued first-class stamps as far back as 1885. The cost for a first-class stamp then was $0.02. By how much had it increased by 2007?

73. Graph $y = x^2 - 4x + 7$. Let $x = 0, 1, 2, 3, 4$ to generate ordered pair solutions.

74. Graph $y = x^2 + 2x + 3$. Let $x = -3, -2, -1, 0, 1$ to generate ordered pair solutions.

△75. The perimeter y of a rectangle whose width is a constant 3 inches and whose length is x inches is given by the equation

$$y = 2x + 6$$

a. Draw a graph of this equation.

b. Read from the graph the perimeter y of a rectangle whose length x is 4 inches.

x inches

3 inches

76. The distance y traveled in a train moving at a constant speed of 50 miles per hour is given by the equation

$$y = 50x$$

where x is the time in hours traveled.

a. Draw a graph of this equation.

b. Read from the graph the distance y traveled after 6 hours.

The graph below shows first-class postal rates and the years it increased. Use this graph for Exercises 69 through 72.

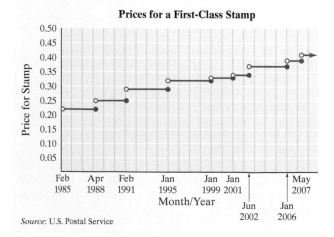

Prices for a First-Class Stamp

Source: U.S. Postal Service

*For income tax purposes, Jason Verges, owner of Copy Services, uses a method called **straight-line depreciation** to show the loss in value of a copy machine he recently purchased. Jason assumes that he can use the machine for 7 years. The following graph shows the value of the machine over the years. Use this graph to answer Exercises 77 through 82.*

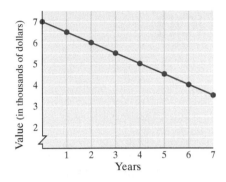

77. What was the purchase price of the copy machine?

78. What is the depreciated value of the machine in 7 years?

79. What loss in value occurred during the first year?

80. What loss in value occurred during the second year?

81. Why do you think that this method of depreciating is called straight line depreciation?

82. Why is the line tilted downward?

83. On the same set of axes, graph $y = 2x$, $y = 2x - 5$, and $y = 2x + 5$. What patterns do you see in these graphs?

84. On the same set of axes, graph $y = 2x$, $y = x$, and $y = -2x$. Describe the differences and similarities in these graphs.

85. Explain why we generally use three points to graph a line, when only two points are needed.

Write each statement as an equation in two variables. Then graph each equation.

86. The y-value is 5 more than three times the x-value.

87. The y-value is -3 decreased by twice the x-value.

88. The y-value is 2 more than the square of the x-value.

89. The y-value is 5 decreased by the square of the x-value.

Use a graphing calculator to verify the graphs of the following exercises.

90. Exercise 39

91. Exercise 40

92. Exercise 47

93. Exercise 48

Appendix B

Sequences, Series, and Summation Notation

If someone asked you to list all natural numbers that are perfect squares, you might begin by writing

$$1, 4, 9, 16, 25, 36$$

But you would soon realize that it is impossible to actually list all the perfect squares, since there are an infinite number of them. However, you could represent this collection of numbers in several different ways. One common method is to write

$$1, 4, 9, \ldots, n^2, \ldots \quad n \in N$$

where N is the set of natural numbers. A list of numbers such as this is generally called a *sequence*.

Sequences

Consider the function f given by

$$f(n) = 2n + 1 \tag{1}$$

where the domain of f is the set of natural numbers N. Note that

$$f(1) = 3, \quad f(2) = 5, \quad f(3) = 7, \quad \ldots$$

The function f is an example of a sequence. In general, a **sequence** is a function with domain a set of successive integers. Instead of the standard function notation used in equation (1), sequences are usually defined in terms of a special notation.

The range value $f(n)$ is usually symbolized more compactly with a symbol such as a_n. Thus, in place of equation (1), we write

$$a_n = 2n + 1$$

and the domain is understood to be the set of natural numbers unless something is said to the contrary or the context indicates otherwise. The elements in the range are called **terms of the sequence**; a_1 is the first term, a_2 is the second term, and a_n is the **nth term**, or **general term**.

$$a_1 = 2(1) + 1 = 3 \qquad \text{First term}$$
$$a_2 = 2(2) + 1 = 5 \qquad \text{Second term}$$
$$a_3 = 2(3) + 1 = 7 \qquad \text{Third term}$$
$$\vdots$$
$$a_n = 2n + 1 \qquad \text{General term}$$

The ordered list of elements

$$3, 5, 7, \ldots, 2n + 1, \ldots$$

obtained by writing the terms of the sequence in their natural order with respect to the domain values is often informally referred to as a sequence. A sequence also may be represented in the abbreviated form $\{a_n\}$, where a symbol for the nth term is written within braces. For example, we could refer to the sequence $3, 5, 7, \ldots, 2n + 1, \ldots$ as the sequence $\{2n + 1\}$.

If the domain of a sequence is a finite set of successive integers, then the sequence is called a **finite sequence**. If the domain is an infinite set of successive integers, then the sequence is called an **infinite sequence**. The sequence $\{2n + 1\}$ discussed above is an infinite sequence.

EXAMPLE 1   **Writing the Terms of a Sequence** Write the first four terms of each sequence:

(A) $a_n = 3n - 2$ (B) $\left\{ \dfrac{(-1)^n}{n} \right\}$

SOLUTION   (A) $1, 4, 7, 10$ (B) $-1, \dfrac{1}{2}, \dfrac{-1}{3}, \dfrac{1}{4}$

Matched Problem 1   Write the first four terms of each sequence:

(A) $a_n = -n + 3$ (B) $\left\{ \dfrac{(-1)^n}{2^n} \right\}$

Now that we have seen how to use the general term to find the first few terms in a sequence, we consider the reverse problem. That is, can a sequence be defined just by listing the first three or four terms of the sequence? And can we then use these initial terms to find a formula for the nth term? In general, without other information, the answer to the first question is no. Many different sequences may start off with the same terms. Simply listing the first three terms (or any other finite number of terms) does not specify a particular sequence.

What about the second question? That is, given a few terms, can we find the general formula for at least one sequence whose first few terms agree with the given terms? The answer to this question is a qualified yes. If we can observe a simple pattern in the given terms, we usually can construct a general term that will produce that pattern. The next example illustrates this approach.

EXAMPLE 2 **Finding the General Term of a Sequence** Find the general term of a sequence whose first four terms are

(A) $3, 4, 5, 6, \ldots$ (B) $5, -25, 125, -625, \ldots$

SOLUTION   (A) Since these terms are consecutive integers, one solution is $a_n = n, n \geq 3$. If we want the domain of the sequence to be all natural numbers, another solution is $b_n = n + 2$.

(B) Each of these terms can be written as the product of a power of 5 and a power of -1:

$$5 = (-1)^0 5^1 = a_1$$
$$-25 = (-1)^1 5^2 = a_2$$
$$125 = (-1)^2 5^3 = a_3$$
$$-625 = (-1)^3 5^4 = a_4$$

If we choose the domain to be all natural numbers, a solution is

$$a_n = (-1)^{n-1} 5^n$$

Matched Problem 2   Find the general term of a sequence whose first four terms are

(A) $3, 6, 9, 12, \ldots$ (B) $1, -2, 4, -8, \ldots$

In general, there is usually more than one way of representing the nth term of a given sequence (see the solution of Example 2A). However, unless something is stated to the contrary, we assume that the domain of the sequence is the set of natural numbers N.

Series and Summation Notation

If $a_1, a_2, a_3, \ldots, a_n, \ldots$ is a sequence, the expression

$$a_1 + a_2 + a_3 + \cdots + a_n + \cdots$$

is called a **series**. If the sequence is finite, the corresponding series is a **finite series**. If the sequence is infinite, the corresponding series is an **infinite series**. We consider only finite series in this section. For example,

$$1, 3, 5, 7, 9 \qquad \textit{Finite sequence}$$
$$1 + 3 + 5 + 7 + 9 \qquad \textit{Finite series}$$

Notice that we can easily evaluate this series by adding the five terms:

$$1 + 3 + 5 + 7 + 9 = 25$$

Series are often represented in a compact form called **summation notation**. Consider the following examples:

$$\sum_{k=3}^{6} k^2 = 3^2 + 4^2 + 5^2 + 6^2$$
$$= 9 + 16 + 25 + 36 = 86$$

$$\sum_{k=0}^{2} (4k + 1) = (4 \cdot 0 + 1) + (4 \cdot 1 + 1) + (4 \cdot 2 + 1)$$
$$= 1 + 5 + 9 = 15$$

In each case, the terms of the series on the right are obtained from the expression on the left by successively replacing the **summing index** k with integers, starting with the number indicated below the **summation sign** Σ and ending with the number that appears above Σ. The summing index may be represented by letters other than k and may start at any integer and end at any integer greater than or equal to the starting integer. If we are given the finite sequence

$$\frac{1}{2}, \frac{1}{4}, \frac{1}{8}, \ldots, \frac{1}{2^n}$$

the corresponding series is

$$\frac{1}{2} + \frac{1}{4} + \frac{1}{8} + \cdots + \frac{1}{2^n} = \sum_{j=1}^{n} \frac{1}{2^j}$$

where we have used j for the summing index.

EXAMPLE 3   **Summation Notation** Write

$$\sum_{k=1}^{5} \frac{k}{k^2 + 1}$$

without summation notation. Do not evaluate the sum.

SOLUTION $\displaystyle \sum_{k=1}^{5} \frac{k}{k^2 + 1} = \frac{1}{1^2 + 1} + \frac{2}{2^2 + 1} + \frac{3}{3^2 + 1} + \frac{4}{4^2 + 1} + \frac{5}{5^2 + 1}$

$$= \frac{1}{2} + \frac{2}{5} + \frac{3}{10} + \frac{4}{17} + \frac{5}{26}$$

Matched Problem 3   Write

$$\sum_{k=1}^{5} \frac{k + 1}{k}$$

without summation notation. Do not evaluate the sum.

If the terms of a series are alternately positive and negative, we call the series an **alternating series**. The next example deals with the representation of such a series.

EXAMPLE 4   **Summation Notation** Write the alternating series

$$\frac{1}{2} - \frac{1}{4} + \frac{1}{6} - \frac{1}{8} + \frac{1}{10} - \frac{1}{12}$$

using summation notation with

(A) The summing index k starting at 1

(B) The summing index j starting at 0

SOLUTION   (A) $(-1)^{k+1}$ provides the alternation of sign, and $1/(2k)$ provides the other part of each term. So, we can write

$$\frac{1}{2} - \frac{1}{4} + \frac{1}{6} - \frac{1}{8} + \frac{1}{10} - \frac{1}{12} = \sum_{k=1}^{6} \frac{(-1)^{k+1}}{2k}$$

(B) $(-1)^{j}$ provides the alternation of sign, and $1/[2(j+1)]$ provides the other part of each term. So, we can write

$$\frac{1}{2} - \frac{1}{4} + \frac{1}{6} - \frac{1}{8} + \frac{1}{10} - \frac{1}{12} = \sum_{j=0}^{5} \frac{(-1)^{j}}{2(j+1)}$$

Matched Problem 4   Write the alternating series

$$1 - \frac{1}{3} + \frac{1}{9} - \frac{1}{27} + \frac{1}{81}$$

using summation notation with

(A) The summing index k starting at 1

(B) The summing index j starting at 0

    Summation notation provides a compact notation for the sum of any list of numbers, even if the numbers are not generated by a formula. For example, suppose that the results of an examination taken by a class of 10 students are given in the following list:

$$87, 77, 95, 83, 86, 73, 95, 68, 75, 86$$

If we let $a_1, a_2, a_3, \ldots, a_{10}$ represent these 10 scores, then the average test score is given by

$$\frac{1}{10} \sum_{k=1}^{10} a_k = \frac{1}{10}(87 + 77 + 95 + 83 + 86 + 73 + 95 + 68 + 75 + 86)$$

$$= \frac{1}{10}(825) = 82.5$$

More generally, in statistics, the **arithmetic mean** $\bar{a}$ of a list of n numbers $a_1, a_2, \ldots, a_n$ is defined as

$$\bar{a} = \frac{1}{n} \sum_{k=1}^{n} a_k$$

EXAMPLE 5   **Arithmetic Mean**   Find the arithmetic mean of $3, 5, 4, 7, 4, 2, 3$, and 6.

SOLUTION $\bar{a} = \dfrac{1}{8}\displaystyle\sum_{k=1}^{8} a_k = \dfrac{1}{8}(3 + 5 + 4 + 7 + 4 + 2 + 3 + 6) = \dfrac{1}{8}(34) = 4.25$

Matched Problem 5   Find the arithmetic mean of $9, 3, 8, 4, 3$, and 6.

Appendix B Exercises

A

Write the first four terms for each sequence in Problems 1–6.

1. $a_n = 2n + 3$

2. $a_n = 4n - 3$

3. $a_n = \dfrac{n + 2}{n + 1}$

4. $a_n = \dfrac{2n + 1}{2n}$

5. $a_n = (-3)^{n+1}$

6. $a_n = \left(-\dfrac{1}{4}\right)^{n-1}$

7. Write the 10th term of the sequence in Problem 1.

8. Write the 15th term of the sequence in Problem 2.

9. Write the 99th term of the sequence in Problem 3.

10. Write the 200th term of the sequence in Problem 4.

In Problems 11–16, write each series in expanded form without summation notation, and evaluate.

11. $\displaystyle\sum_{k=1}^{6} k$

12. $\displaystyle\sum_{k=1}^{5} k^2$

13. $\displaystyle\sum_{k=4}^{7}(2k - 3)$

14. $\displaystyle\sum_{k=0}^{4}(-2)^k$

15. $\displaystyle\sum_{k=0}^{3}\dfrac{1}{10^k}$

16. $\displaystyle\sum_{k=1}^{4}\dfrac{1}{2^k}$

Find the arithmetic mean of each list of numbers in Problems 17–20.

17. $5, 4, 2, 1$, and 6

18. $7, 9, 9, 2$, and 4

19. $96, 65, 82, 74, 91, 88, 87, 91, 77$, and 74

20. $100, 62, 95, 91, 82, 87, 70, 75, 87$, and 82

B

Write the first five terms of each sequence in Problems 21–26.

21. $a_n = \dfrac{(-1)^{n+1}}{2^n}$

22. $a_n = (-1)^n(n - 1)^2$

23. $a_n = n[1 + (-1)^n]$

24. $a_n = \dfrac{1 - (-1)^n}{n}$

25. $a_n = \left(-\dfrac{3}{2}\right)^{n-1}$

26. $a_n = \left(-\dfrac{1}{2}\right)^{n+1}$

In Problems 27–42, find the general term of a sequence whose first four terms agree with the given terms.

27. $-2, -1, 0, 1, \ldots$

28. $4, 5, 6, 7, \ldots$

29. $4, 8, 12, 16, \ldots$

30. $-3, -6, -9, -12, \ldots$

31. $\frac{1}{2}, \frac{3}{4}, \frac{5}{6}, \frac{7}{8}, \ldots$

32. $\frac{1}{2}, \frac{2}{3}, \frac{3}{4}, \frac{4}{5}, \ldots$

33. $1, -2, 3, -4, \ldots$

34. $-2, 4, -8, 16, \ldots$

35. $1, -3, 5, -7, \ldots$

36. $3, -6, 9, -12, \ldots$

37. $1, \frac{2}{5}, \frac{4}{25}, \frac{8}{125}, \ldots$

38. $\frac{4}{3}, \frac{16}{9}, \frac{64}{27}, \frac{256}{81}, \ldots$

39. $x, x^2, x^3, x^4, \ldots$

40. $1, 2x, 3x^2, 4x^3, \ldots$

41. $x, -x^3, x^5, -x^7, \ldots$

42. $x, \dfrac{x^2}{2}, \dfrac{x^3}{3}, \dfrac{x^4}{4}, \ldots$

Write each series in Problems 43–50 in expanded form without summation notation. Do not evaluate.

43. $\displaystyle\sum_{k=1}^{5}(-1)^{k+1}(2k - 1)^2$

44. $\displaystyle\sum_{k=1}^{4}\dfrac{(-2)^{k+1}}{2k + 1}$

45. $\displaystyle\sum_{k=2}^{5}\dfrac{2^k}{2k + 3}$

46. $\displaystyle\sum_{k=3}^{7}\dfrac{(-1)^k}{k^2 - k}$

47. $\displaystyle\sum_{k=1}^{5} x^{k-1}$

48. $\displaystyle\sum_{k=1}^{3}\dfrac{1}{k}x^{k+1}$

49. $\displaystyle\sum_{k=0}^{4}\dfrac{(-1)^k x^{2k+1}}{2k + 1}$

50. $\displaystyle\sum_{k=0}^{4}\dfrac{(-1)^k x^{2k}}{2k + 2}$

Write each series in Problems 51–54 using summation notation with

(A) The summing index k starting at $k = 1$

(B) The summing index j starting at $j = 0$

51. $2 + 3 + 4 + 5 + 6$

52. $1^2 + 2^2 + 3^2 + 4^2$

53. $1 - \frac{1}{2} + \frac{1}{3} - \frac{1}{4}$

54. $1 - \frac{1}{3} + \frac{1}{5} - \frac{1}{7} + \frac{1}{9}$

Write each series in Problems 55–58 using summation notation with the summing index k starting at $k = 1$.

55. $2 + \dfrac{3}{2} + \dfrac{4}{3} + \cdots + \dfrac{n+1}{n}$

56. $1 + \dfrac{1}{2^2} + \dfrac{1}{3^2} + \cdots + \dfrac{1}{n^2}$

57. $\dfrac{1}{2} - \dfrac{1}{4} + \dfrac{1}{8} - \cdots + \dfrac{(-1)^{n+1}}{2^n}$

58. $1 - 4 + 9 - \cdots + (-1)^{n+1}n^2$

C

In Problems 59–62, discuss the validity of each statement. If the statement is true, explain why. If not, give a counterexample.

59. For each positive integer n, the sum of the series
$1 + \dfrac{1}{2} + \dfrac{1}{3} + \cdots + \dfrac{1}{n}$ is less than 4.

60. For each positive integer n, the sum of the series
$\dfrac{1}{2} + \dfrac{1}{4} + \dfrac{1}{8} + \cdots + \dfrac{1}{2^n}$ is less than 1.

61. For each positive integer n, the sum of the series
$\dfrac{1}{2} - \dfrac{1}{4} + \dfrac{1}{8} - \cdots + \dfrac{(-1)^{n+1}}{2^n}$ is greater than or equal to $\dfrac{1}{4}$.

62. For each positive integer n, the sum of the series
$1 - \dfrac{1}{2} + \dfrac{1}{3} - \dfrac{1}{4} + \cdots + \dfrac{(-1)^{n+1}}{n}$ is greater than or equal to $\dfrac{1}{2}$.

*Some sequences are defined by a **recursion formula**—that is, a formula that defines each term of the sequence in terms of one or more of the preceding terms. For example, if $\{a_n\}$ is defined by*

$$a_1 = 1 \quad and \quad a_n = 2a_{n-1} + 1 \quad for\ n \geq 2$$

then

$$a_2 = 2a_1 + 1 = 2 \cdot 1 + 1 = 3$$
$$a_3 = 2a_2 + 1 = 2 \cdot 3 + 1 = 7$$
$$a_4 = 2a_3 + 1 = 2 \cdot 7 + 1 = 15$$

and so on. In Problems 63–66, write the first five terms of each sequence.

63. $a_1 = 2$ and $a_n = 3a_{n-1} + 2$ for $n \geq 2$

64. $a_1 = 3$ and $a_n = 2a_{n-1} - 2$ for $n \geq 2$

65. $a_1 = 1$ and $a_n = 2a_{n-1}$ for $n \geq 2$

66. $a_1 = 1$ and $a_n = -\tfrac{1}{3}a_{n-1}$ for $n \geq 2$

If A is a positive real number, the terms of the sequence defined by

$$a_1 = \frac{A}{2} \quad and \quad a_n = \frac{1}{2}\left(a_{n-1} + \frac{A}{a_{n-1}}\right) \quad for\ n \geq 2$$

can be used to approximate $\sqrt{A}$ to any decimal place accuracy desired. In Problems 67 and 68, compute the first four terms of this sequence for the indicated value of A, and compare the fourth term with the value of $\sqrt{A}$ obtained from a calculator.

67. $A = 2$ **68.** $A = 6$

69. The sequence defined recursively by $a_1 = 1$, $a_2 = 1$, $a_n = a_{n-1} + a_{n-2}$ for $n \geq 3$ is called the *Fibonacci sequence*. Find the first ten terms of the Fibonacci sequence.

70. The sequence defined by $b_n = \dfrac{\sqrt{5}}{5}\left(\dfrac{1 + \sqrt{5}}{2}\right)^n$ is related to

the Fibonacci sequence. Find the first ten terms (to three decimal places) of the sequence $\{b_n\}$ and describe the relationship.

Answers to Matched Problems

1. (A) $2, 1, 0, -1$ (B) $\tfrac{-1}{2}, \tfrac{1}{4}, \tfrac{-1}{8}, \tfrac{1}{16}$

2. (A) $a_n = 3n$ (B) $a_n = (-2)^{n-1}$

3. $2 + \tfrac{3}{2} + \tfrac{4}{3} + \tfrac{5}{4} + \tfrac{6}{5}$

4. (A) $\displaystyle\sum_{k=1}^{5} \frac{(-1)^{k-1}}{3^{k-1}}$ (B) $\displaystyle\sum_{j=0}^{4} \frac{(-1)^j}{3^j}$

5. 5.5

Appendix C
Solving Systems of Equations Using Determinants

OBJECTIVES

1 Define and Evaluate a 2×2 Determinant.

2 Use Cramer's Rule to Solve a System of Two Linear Equations in Two Variables.

3 Define and Evaluate a 3×3 Determinant.

4 Use Cramer's Rule to Solve a System of Three Linear Equations in Three Variables.

We have solved systems of two linear equations in two variables in four different ways: graphically, by substitution, by elimination, and by matrices. Now we analyze another method called **Cramer's rule.**

OBJECTIVE 1 ▶ Evaluating 2×2 determinants. Recall that a matrix is a rectangular array of numbers. If a matrix has the same number of rows and columns, it is called a **square matrix.** Examples of square matrices are

$$\begin{bmatrix} 1 & 6 \\ 5 & 2 \end{bmatrix} \qquad \begin{bmatrix} 2 & 4 & 1 \\ 0 & 5 & 2 \\ 3 & 6 & 9 \end{bmatrix}$$

A **determinant** is a real number associated with a square matrix. The determinant of a square matrix is denoted by placing vertical bars about the array of numbers. Thus,

The determinant of the square matrix $\begin{bmatrix} 1 & 6 \\ 5 & 2 \end{bmatrix}$ is $\begin{vmatrix} 1 & 6 \\ 5 & 2 \end{vmatrix}$.

The determinant of the square matrix $\begin{bmatrix} 2 & 4 & 1 \\ 0 & 5 & 2 \\ 3 & 6 & 9 \end{bmatrix}$ is $\begin{vmatrix} 2 & 4 & 1 \\ 0 & 5 & 2 \\ 3 & 6 & 9 \end{vmatrix}$.

We define the determinant of a 2×2 matrix first. (Recall that 2×2 is read "two by two." It means that the matrix has 2 rows and 2 columns.)

Determinant of a 2×2 Matrix

$$\begin{vmatrix} a & b \\ c & d \end{vmatrix} = ad - bc$$

EXAMPLE 1 Evaluate each determinant

a. $\begin{vmatrix} -1 & 2 \\ 3 & -4 \end{vmatrix}$

b. $\begin{vmatrix} 2 & 0 \\ 7 & -5 \end{vmatrix}$

Solution First we identify the values of $a, b, c,$ and d. Then we perform the evaluation.

243

a. Here $a = -1, b = 2, c = 3,$ and $d = -4.$

$$\begin{vmatrix} -1 & 2 \\ 3 & -4 \end{vmatrix} = ad - bc = (-1)(-4) - (2)(3) = -2$$

b. In this example, $a = 2, b = 0, c = 7,$ and $d = -5.$

$$\begin{vmatrix} 2 & 0 \\ 7 & -5 \end{vmatrix} = ad - bc = 2(-5) - (0)(7) = -10 \qquad \square$$

OBJECTIVE 2 ▶ Using Cramer's rule to solve a system of two linear equations. To develop Cramer's rule, we solve the system $\begin{cases} ax + by = h \\ cx + dy = k \end{cases}$ using elimination. First, we eliminate y by multiplying both sides of the first equation by d and both sides of the second equation by $-b$ so that the coefficients of y are opposites. The result is that

$$\begin{cases} d(ax + by) = d \cdot h \\ -b(cx + dy) = -b \cdot k \end{cases} \quad \text{simplifies to} \quad \begin{cases} adx + bdy = hd \\ -bcx - bdy - -kb \end{cases}$$

We now add the two equations and solve for x.

$$\begin{aligned} adx + bdy &= hd \\ \underline{-bcx - bdy} &= \underline{-kb} \\ adx - bcx \quad &= hd - kb \quad \text{Add the equations.} \\ (ad - bc)x \quad &= hd - kb \\ x \quad &= \frac{hd - kb}{ad - bc} \quad \text{Solve for } x. \end{aligned}$$

When we replace x with $\dfrac{hd - kb}{ad - bc}$ in the equation $ax + by = h$ and solve for y, we find that $y = \dfrac{ak - ch}{ad - bc}$.

Notice that the numerator of the value of x is the determinant of

$$\begin{vmatrix} h & b \\ k & d \end{vmatrix} = hd - kb$$

Also, the numerator of the value of y is the determinant of

$$\begin{vmatrix} a & h \\ c & k \end{vmatrix} = ak - hc$$

Finally, the denominators of the values of x and y are the same and are the determinant of

$$\begin{vmatrix} a & b \\ c & d \end{vmatrix} = ad - bc$$

This means that the values of x and y can be written in determinant notation:

$$x = \frac{\begin{vmatrix} h & b \\ k & d \end{vmatrix}}{\begin{vmatrix} a & b \\ c & d \end{vmatrix}} \quad \text{and} \quad y = \frac{\begin{vmatrix} a & h \\ c & k \end{vmatrix}}{\begin{vmatrix} a & b \\ c & d \end{vmatrix}}$$

For convenience, we label the determinants D, D_x, and D_y.

x-coefficients ⟶

y-coefficients ⟶

$$\begin{vmatrix} a & b \\ c & d \end{vmatrix} = D \qquad \begin{vmatrix} h & b \\ k & d \end{vmatrix} = D_x \qquad \begin{vmatrix} a & h \\ c & k \end{vmatrix} = D_y$$

x-column replaced   y-column replaced
by constants   by constants

These determinant formulas for the coordinates of the solution of a system are known as **Cramer's rule.**

Cramer's Rule for Two Linear Equations in Two Variables

The solution of the system $\begin{cases} ax + by = h \\ cx + dy = k \end{cases}$ is given by

$$x = \frac{\begin{vmatrix} h & b \\ k & d \end{vmatrix}}{\begin{vmatrix} a & b \\ c & d \end{vmatrix}} = \frac{D_x}{D} \qquad y = \frac{\begin{vmatrix} a & h \\ c & k \end{vmatrix}}{\begin{vmatrix} a & b \\ c & d \end{vmatrix}} = \frac{D_y}{D}$$

as long as $D = ad - bc$ is not 0.

When $D = 0$, the system is either inconsistent or the equations are dependent. When this happens, we need to use another method to see which is the case.

EXAMPLE 2   Use Cramer's rule to solve the system

$$\begin{cases} 3x + 4y = -7 \\ x - 2y = -9 \end{cases}$$

Solution   First we find D, D_x, and D_y.

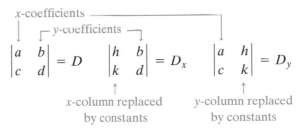

$$\begin{cases} 3x + 4y = -7 \\ x - 2y = -9 \end{cases}$$

$$D = \begin{vmatrix} a & b \\ c & d \end{vmatrix} = \begin{vmatrix} 3 & 4 \\ 1 & -2 \end{vmatrix} = 3(-2) - 4(1) = -10$$

$$D_x = \begin{vmatrix} h & b \\ k & d \end{vmatrix} = \begin{vmatrix} -7 & 4 \\ -9 & -2 \end{vmatrix} = (-7)(-2) - 4(-9) = 50$$

$$D_y = \begin{vmatrix} a & h \\ c & d \end{vmatrix} = \begin{vmatrix} 3 & -7 \\ 1 & -9 \end{vmatrix} = 3(-9) - (-7)(1) = -20$$

Then $x = \dfrac{D_x}{D} = \dfrac{50}{-10} = -5$ and $y = \dfrac{D_y}{D} = \dfrac{-20}{-10} = 2$.

The ordered pair solution is $(-5, 2)$.

As always, check the solution in both original equations. ☐

EXAMPLE 3   Use Cramer's rule to solve the system

$$\begin{cases} 5x + y = 5 \\ -7x - 2y = -7 \end{cases}$$

Solution   First we find D, D_x, and D_y.

$$D = \begin{vmatrix} 5 & 1 \\ -7 & -2 \end{vmatrix} = 5(-2) - (-7)(1) = -3$$

$$D_x = \begin{vmatrix} 5 & 1 \\ -7 & -2 \end{vmatrix} = 5(-2) - (-7)(1) = -3$$

$$D_y = \begin{vmatrix} 5 & 5 \\ -7 & -7 \end{vmatrix} = 5(-7) - 5(-7) = 0$$

Then

$$x = \frac{D_x}{D} = \frac{-3}{-3} = 1 \qquad y = \frac{D_y}{D} = \frac{0}{-3} = 0$$

The ordered pair solution is $(1, 0)$ ☐

OBJECTIVE 3 ▶ Evaluating 3 × 3 determinants. A 3×3 determinant can be used to solve a system of three equations in three variables. The determinant of a 3×3 matrix, however, is considerably more complex than a 2×2 one.

Determinant of a 3 × 3 Matrix

$$\begin{vmatrix} a_1 & b_1 & c_1 \\ a_2 & b_2 & c_2 \\ a_3 & b_3 & c_3 \end{vmatrix} = a_1 \cdot \begin{vmatrix} b_2 & c_2 \\ b_3 & c_3 \end{vmatrix} - a_2 \cdot \begin{vmatrix} b_1 & c_1 \\ b_3 & c_3 \end{vmatrix} + a_3 \cdot \begin{vmatrix} b_1 & c_1 \\ b_2 & c_2 \end{vmatrix}$$

Notice that the determinant of a 3 × 3 matrix is related to the determinants of three 2 × 2 matrices. Each determinant of these 2 × 2 matrices is called a **minor,** and every element of a 3 × 3 matrix has a minor associated with it. For example, the minor of c_2 is the determinant of the 2 × 2 matrix found by deleting the row and column containing c_2.

$$\begin{array}{ccc} a_1 & b_1 & c_1 \\ a_2 & b_2 & c_2 \\ a_3 & b_3 & c_3 \end{array} \qquad \text{The minor of } c_2 \text{ is} \qquad \begin{vmatrix} a_1 & b_1 \\ a_3 & b_3 \end{vmatrix}$$

Also, the minor of element a_1 is the determinant of the 2 × 2 matrix that has no row or column containing a_1.

$$\begin{array}{ccc} a_1 & b_1 & c_1 \\ a_2 & b_2 & c_2 \\ a_3 & b_3 & c_3 \end{array} \qquad \text{The minor of } a_1 \text{ is} \qquad \begin{vmatrix} b_2 & c_2 \\ b_3 & c_3 \end{vmatrix}$$

So the determinant of a 3 × 3 matrix can be written as

$$a_1 \cdot (\text{minor of } a_1) - a_2 \cdot (\text{minor of } a_2) + a_3 \cdot (\text{minor of } a_3)$$

Finding the determinant by using minors of elements in the first column is called **expanding** by the minors of the first column. *The value of a determinant can be found by expanding by the minors of any row or column.* The following **array of signs** is helpful in determining whether to add or subtract the product of an element and its minor.

$$\begin{array}{ccc} + & - & + \\ - & + & - \\ + & - & + \end{array}$$

If an element is in a position marked +, we add. If marked −, we subtract. □

Concept Check ☑

Suppose you are interested in finding the determinant of a 4 × 4 matrix. Study the pattern shown in the array of signs for a 3 × 3 matrix. Use the pattern to expand the array of signs for use with a 4 × 4 matrix.

EXAMPLE 4 Evaluate by expanding by the minors of the given row or column.

$$\begin{vmatrix} 0 & 5 & 1 \\ 1 & 3 & -1 \\ -2 & 2 & 4 \end{vmatrix}$$

a. First column

b. Second row

Solution

a. The elements of the first column are $0, 1$, and -2. The first column of the array of signs is $+, -, +$.

$$\begin{vmatrix} 0 & 5 & 1 \\ 1 & 3 & -1 \\ -2 & 2 & 4 \end{vmatrix} = 0 \cdot \begin{vmatrix} 3 & -1 \\ 2 & 4 \end{vmatrix} - 1 \cdot \begin{vmatrix} 5 & 1 \\ 2 & 4 \end{vmatrix} + (-2) \cdot \begin{vmatrix} 5 & 1 \\ 3 & -1 \end{vmatrix}$$

$$= 0(12 - (-2)) - 1(20 - 2) + (-2)(-5 - 3)$$

$$= 0 - 18 + 16 = -2$$

b. The elements of the second row are $1, 3$, and -1. This time, the signs begin with $-$ and again alternate.

$$\begin{vmatrix} 0 & 5 & 1 \\ 1 & 3 & -1 \\ -2 & 2 & 4 \end{vmatrix} = -1 \cdot \begin{vmatrix} 5 & 1 \\ 2 & 4 \end{vmatrix} + 3 \cdot \begin{vmatrix} 0 & 1 \\ -2 & 4 \end{vmatrix} - (-1) \cdot \begin{vmatrix} 0 & 5 \\ -2 & 2 \end{vmatrix}$$

$$= -1(20 - 2) + 3(0 - (-2)) - (-1)(0 - (-10))$$

$$= -18 + 6 + 10 = -2$$

Notice that the determinant of the 3×3 matrix is the same regardless of the row or column you select to expand by. □

Concept Check ☑

Why would expanding by minors of the second row be a good choice for the determinant

$$\begin{vmatrix} 3 & 4 & -2 \\ 5 & 0 & 0 \\ 6 & -3 & 7 \end{vmatrix} ?$$

OBJECTIVE 4 ▶ Using Cramer's rule to solve a system of three linear equations. A system of three equations in three variables may be solved with Cramer's rule also. Using the elimination process to solve a system with unknown constants as coefficients leads to the following.

Cramer's Rule for Three Equations in Three Variables

The solution of the system $\begin{cases} a_1x + b_1y + c_1z = k_1 \\ a_2x + b_2y + c_2z = k_2 \\ a_3x + b_3y + c_3z = k_3 \end{cases}$ is given by

$$x = \frac{D_x}{D} \qquad y = \frac{D_y}{D} \qquad \text{and} \qquad z = \frac{D_z}{D}$$

where

$$D = \begin{vmatrix} a_1 & b_1 & c_1 \\ a_2 & b_2 & c_2 \\ a_3 & b_3 & c_3 \end{vmatrix} \qquad D_x = \begin{vmatrix} k_1 & b_1 & c_1 \\ k_2 & b_2 & c_2 \\ k_3 & b_3 & c_3 \end{vmatrix}$$

$$D_y = \begin{vmatrix} a_1 & k_1 & c_1 \\ a_2 & k_2 & c_2 \\ a_3 & k_3 & c_3 \end{vmatrix} \qquad D_z = \begin{vmatrix} a_1 & b_1 & k_1 \\ a_2 & b_2 & k_2 \\ a_3 & b_3 & k_3 \end{vmatrix}$$

as long as D is not 0.

Answer to Concept Check:

Two elements of the second row are 0, which makes calculations easier.

EXAMPLE 5   Use Cramer's rule to solve the system

$$\begin{cases} x - 2y + z = 4 \\ 3x + y - 2z = 3 \\ 5x + 5y + 3z = -8 \end{cases}$$

Solution   First we find D, D_x, D_y, and D_z. Beginning with D, we expand by the minors of the first column.

$$D = \begin{vmatrix} 1 & -2 & 1 \\ 3 & 1 & -2 \\ 5 & 5 & 3 \end{vmatrix} = 1 \cdot \begin{vmatrix} 1 & -2 \\ 5 & 3 \end{vmatrix} - 3 \cdot \begin{vmatrix} -2 & 1 \\ 5 & 3 \end{vmatrix} + 5 \cdot \begin{vmatrix} -2 & 1 \\ 1 & -2 \end{vmatrix}$$

$$= 1(3 - (-10)) - 3(-6 - 5) + 5(4 - 1)$$

$$= 13 + 33 + 15 = 61$$

$$D_x = \begin{vmatrix} 4 & -2 & 1 \\ 3 & 1 & -2 \\ -8 & 5 & 3 \end{vmatrix} = 4 \cdot \begin{vmatrix} 1 & -2 \\ 5 & 3 \end{vmatrix} - 3 \cdot \begin{vmatrix} -2 & 1 \\ 5 & 3 \end{vmatrix} + (-8) \cdot \begin{vmatrix} -2 & 1 \\ 1 & -2 \end{vmatrix}$$

$$= 4(3 - (-10)) - 3(-6 - 5) + (-8)(4 - 1)$$

$$= 52 + 33 - 24 = 61$$

$$D_y = \begin{vmatrix} 1 & 4 & 1 \\ 3 & 3 & -2 \\ 5 & -8 & 3 \end{vmatrix} = 1 \cdot \begin{vmatrix} 3 & -2 \\ -8 & 3 \end{vmatrix} - 3 \cdot \begin{vmatrix} 4 & 1 \\ -8 & 3 \end{vmatrix} + 5 \cdot \begin{vmatrix} 4 & 1 \\ 3 & -2 \end{vmatrix}$$

$$= 1(9 - 16) - 3(12 - (-8)) + 5(-8 - 3)$$

$$= -7 - 60 - 55 = -122$$

$$D_z = \begin{vmatrix} 1 & -2 & 4 \\ 3 & 1 & 3 \\ 5 & 5 & -8 \end{vmatrix} = 1 \cdot \begin{vmatrix} 1 & 3 \\ 5 & -8 \end{vmatrix} - 3 \cdot \begin{vmatrix} -2 & 4 \\ 5 & -8 \end{vmatrix} + 5 \cdot \begin{vmatrix} -2 & 4 \\ 1 & 3 \end{vmatrix}$$

$$= 1(-8 - 15) - 3(16 - 20) + 5(-6 - 4)$$

$$= -23 + 12 - 50 = -61$$

From these determinants, we calculate the solution:

$$x = \frac{D_x}{D} = \frac{61}{61} = 1 \quad y = \frac{D_y}{D} = \frac{-122}{61} = -2 \quad z = \frac{D_z}{D} = \frac{-61}{61} = -1$$

The ordered triple solution is $(1, -2, -1)$. Check this solution by verifying that it satisfies each equation of the system. □

VOCABULARY & READINESS CHECK

Evaluate each determinant mentally.

1. $\begin{vmatrix} 7 & 2 \\ 0 & 8 \end{vmatrix}$

2. $\begin{vmatrix} 6 & 0 \\ 1 & 2 \end{vmatrix}$

3. $\begin{vmatrix} -4 & 2 \\ 0 & 8 \end{vmatrix}$

4. $\begin{vmatrix} 5 & 0 \\ 3 & -5 \end{vmatrix}$

5. $\begin{vmatrix} -2 & 0 \\ 3 & -10 \end{vmatrix}$

6. $\begin{vmatrix} -1 & 4 \\ 0 & -18 \end{vmatrix}$

APPENDIX C | EXERCISE SET

Evaluate each determinant. See Example 1.

1. $\begin{vmatrix} 3 & 5 \\ -1 & 7 \end{vmatrix}$

2. $\begin{vmatrix} -5 & 1 \\ 1 & -4 \end{vmatrix}$

3. $\begin{vmatrix} 9 & -2 \\ 4 & -3 \end{vmatrix}$

4. $\begin{vmatrix} 4 & -1 \\ 9 & 8 \end{vmatrix}$

5. $\begin{vmatrix} -2 & 9 \\ 4 & -18 \end{vmatrix}$

6. $\begin{vmatrix} -40 & 8 \\ 70 & -14 \end{vmatrix}$

7. $\begin{vmatrix} \frac{3}{4} & \frac{5}{2} \\ -\frac{1}{6} & \frac{7}{3} \end{vmatrix}$

8. $\begin{vmatrix} \frac{5}{7} & \frac{1}{3} \\ \frac{6}{7} & \frac{2}{3} \end{vmatrix}$

Use Cramer's rule, if possible, to solve each system of linear equations. See Examples 2 and 3.

9. $\begin{cases} 2y - 4 = 0 \\ x + 2y = 5 \end{cases}$

10. $\begin{cases} 4x - y = 5 \\ 3x - 3 = 0 \end{cases}$

11. $\begin{cases} 3x + y = 1 \\ 2y = 2 - 6x \end{cases}$

12. $\begin{cases} y = 2x - 5 \\ 8x - 4y = 20 \end{cases}$

13. $\begin{cases} 5x - 2y = 27 \\ -3x + 5y = 18 \end{cases}$

14. $\begin{cases} 4x - y = 9 \\ 2x + 3y = -27 \end{cases}$

15. $\begin{cases} 2x - 5y = 4 \\ x + 2y = -7 \end{cases}$

16. $\begin{cases} 3x - y = 2 \\ -5x + 2y = 0 \end{cases}$

17. $\begin{cases} \frac{2}{3}x - \frac{3}{4}y = -1 \\ -\frac{1}{6}x + \frac{3}{4}y = \frac{5}{2} \end{cases}$

18. $\begin{cases} \frac{1}{2}x - \frac{1}{3}y = -3 \\ \frac{1}{8}x + \frac{1}{6}y = 0 \end{cases}$

Evaluate. See Example 4.

19. $\begin{vmatrix} 2 & 1 & 0 \\ 0 & 5 & -3 \\ 4 & 0 & 2 \end{vmatrix}$

20. $\begin{vmatrix} -6 & 4 & 2 \\ 1 & 0 & 5 \\ 0 & 3 & 1 \end{vmatrix}$

21. $\begin{vmatrix} 4 & -6 & 0 \\ -2 & 3 & 0 \\ 4 & -6 & 1 \end{vmatrix}$

22. $\begin{vmatrix} 5 & 2 & 1 \\ 3 & -6 & 0 \\ -2 & 8 & 0 \end{vmatrix}$

23. $\begin{vmatrix} 1 & 0 & 4 \\ 1 & -1 & 2 \\ 3 & 2 & 1 \end{vmatrix}$

24. $\begin{vmatrix} 0 & 1 & 2 \\ 3 & -1 & 2 \\ 3 & 2 & -2 \end{vmatrix}$

25. $\begin{vmatrix} 3 & 6 & -3 \\ -1 & -2 & 3 \\ 4 & -1 & 6 \end{vmatrix}$

26. $\begin{vmatrix} 2 & -2 & 1 \\ 4 & 1 & 3 \\ 3 & 1 & 2 \end{vmatrix}$

Use Cramer's rule, if possible, to solve each system of linear equations. See Example 5.

27. $\begin{cases} 3x + z = -1 \\ -x - 3y + z = 7 \\ 3y + z = 5 \end{cases}$

28. $\begin{cases} 4y - 3z = -2 \\ 8x - 4y = 4 \\ -8x + 4y + z = -2 \end{cases}$

29. $\begin{cases} x + y + z = 8 \\ 2x - y - z = 10 \\ x - 2y + 3z = 22 \end{cases}$

30. $\begin{cases} 5x + y + 3z = 1 \\ x - y - 3z = -7 \\ -x + y = 1 \end{cases}$

31. $\begin{cases} 2x + 2y + z = 1 \\ -x + y + 2z = 3 \\ x + 2y + 4z = 0 \end{cases}$

32. $\begin{cases} 2x - 3y + z = 5 \\ x + y + z = 0 \\ 4x + 2y + 4z = 4 \end{cases}$

33. $\begin{cases} x - 2y + z = -5 \\ 3y + 2z = 4 \\ 3x - y = -2 \end{cases}$

34. $\begin{cases} 4x + 5y = 10 \\ 3y + 2z = -6 \\ x + y + z = 3 \end{cases}$

CONCEPT EXTENSIONS

Find the value of x that will make each a true statement.

35. $\begin{vmatrix} 1 & x \\ 2 & 7 \end{vmatrix} = -3$

36. $\begin{vmatrix} 6 & 1 \\ -2 & x \end{vmatrix} = 26$

37. If all the elements in a single row of a determinant are zero, what is the value of the determinant? Explain your answer.

38. If all the elements in a single column of a determinant are 0, what is the value of the determinant? Explain your answer.

Appendix D
Answers to Selected Exercises

Exercises 1.1 (page 15)

1. 3/5 **3.** Not defined **5.** 1 **7.** 5/9 **9.** Not defined **11.** 0 **13.** 2 **15.** $y = -2x + 5$ **17.** $y = -7$
19. $y = -(1/3)x + 10/3$ **21.** $y = 6x - 7/2$ **23.** $x = -8$ **25.** $y = -(1/2)x - 3$ **27.** $x = -6$ **29.** $y = -(3/2)x$
31. $y = x - 7$ **33.** $y = 5x + 4$ **35.** No **39.** a **41.** -4

45.
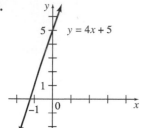

47.
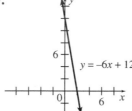

49.
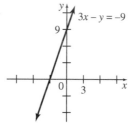

51.
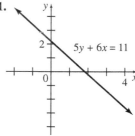

53.
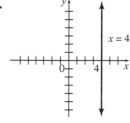

55.
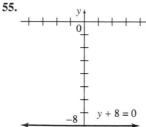

57.
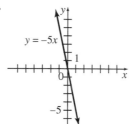

59.
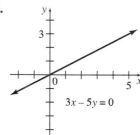

61. a.
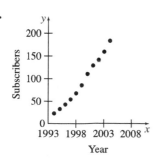

The number of subscribers is increasing and the data appear to be nearly linear.
b. $y = 17.26x - 7.75$ **c.** For 2005, the number of subscribers is 199.4, which is less than the actual number of subscribers.

63. a. $y = 4.23x + 100$ **b.** 176.14, which is more than the actual CPI. **c.** It is increasing at a rate of 4.23 per year.

65. a. $u = 0.85(220 - x) = 187 - 0.85x, l = 0.7(220 - x) = 154 - 0.7x$ **b.** 140 to 170 beats per minute. **c.** 126 to 153 beats per minute. **d.** The women are 16 and 52. Their pulse is 143 beats per minute. **67.** Approximately 86 yr

69. a. $y = 0.115x + 22.2$ **b.** $y = 0.13x + 19.95$ **c.** Women   **d.** 2028   **e.** 28.8 yr   **71. a.** $y = 0.145x + 1.59$ **b.** About 5.94 million   **73. a.** There appears to be a linear relationship.   **b.** $y = 76.9x$ **c.** About 780 megaparsecs (about 1.5×10^{22} mi)   **d.** About 12.4 billion yr

75.   a.

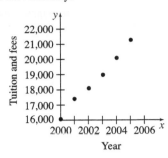

Yes, the data are approximately linear.
b. $y = 1032.6x + 16{,}072$; the slope 1032.6 indicates that tuition and fees have increased approximately \$1033 per year.   **c.** The year 2025 is too far in the future to rely on this equation to predict costs; too many other factors may influence these costs by then.

Exercises 1.2 (page 28)

1. -3 **3.** 22   **5.** 0   **7.** -4 **9.** $7 - 5t$ **11.** True   **13.** True   **19.** If $R(x)$ is the cost of renting a snowboard for x hours, then $R(x) = 2.25x + 10$.   **21.** If $C(x)$ is the cost of parking a car for x half-hours, then $C(x) = 0.75x + 2$.
23. $C(x) = 30x + 100$ **25.** $C(x) = 75x + 550$ **27. a.** \$16   **b.** \$11   **c.** \$6   **d.** 640 watches   **e.** 480 watches
f. 320 watches   **g.**

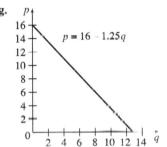

h. 0 watches   **i.** About 1333 watches   **j.** About 2667 watches

k.

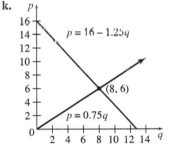

l. 800 watches, \$6

29. a.

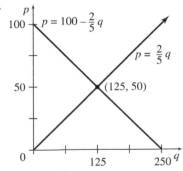

b. 125 tubs, \$50

31. a. $C(x) = 3.50x + 90$ **b.** 17 shirts **c.** 108 shirts **33. a.** $C(x) = 0.097x + 1.32$ **b.** \$1.32 **c.** \$98.32 **d.** \$98.417
e. 9.7¢ **f.** 9.7¢, the cost of producing one additional cup of coffee would be 9.7¢. **35. a.** \$5,100,000 **b.** (1, 100,000) and
(6, 5,100,000); $S(x) = 1,000,000x - 900,000$ **c.** 2991; sales would have to grow much faster than linearly to reach \$1 billion by 2003.
d. $S(x) = 123,000,000x - 1,234,000,000$ **e.** 602,000,000; this is less than the actual sales. **f.** 2009 **37. a.** 3 units **b.** \$3211
c. 13 units **39.** Break-even quantity is about 41 units; produce; $P(x) = 145x - 6000$ **41.** Break-even quantity is -50 units;
impossible to make a profit when $C(x) > R(x)$ for all positive x; $P(x) = -100x - 5000$ (always a loss). **43. a.** 98.6°F
b. 97.7°F and 99.5°F

Exercises 1.3 (page 41)

3. a. **b.** 0.993 **c.** $Y = 0.55x - 0.5$ **d.** 5.55

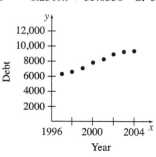
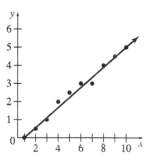

7. a. $Y = -0.2519x + 33.6330$ **b.** 5924 **c.** $r = -0.977$; the line fits the data points very well.

9. a. **b.** $Y = 482.25x - 40,537.5$. The least squares line seems to be a good fit. **c.** $r = 0.987$. This confirms that the least squares line is a good fit. **d.** 2009

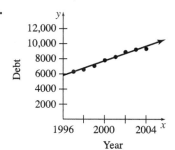

11. a. **b.** 0.959, yes **c.** $Y = 3.98x + 22.7$

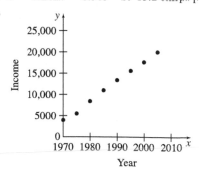
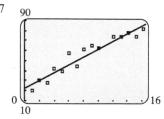

13. a. $Y = 0.212x - 0.315$ **b.** 15.2 chirps per second. **c.** 86.4°F **d.** 0.835
15. a. **b.** $r = 0.999$; yes **c.** $Y = 0.467x + 3.74$ **d.** \$27,090
17. a. $Y = 14.9x + 2820$ **b.** 5060, compared to actual 5000; 6990, compared to actual 7000; 9080, compared to actual 9000 **c.** 6500 BTU air conditioner

19. a. $Y = -0.1358x + 113.94$ **b.** $Y = -0.3913x + 148.98$ **c.** $x \approx 137$; the women will catch up to the men in the year 2037.
d. $r_{men} = -0.9823$; $r_{women} = -0.9487$; both sets of data points closely fit a line with negative slope.
e.

Men's

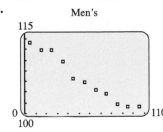

Women's

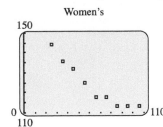

21. a. $Y = 1.121x + 34.27$ **b.** 0.8963 **c.** $3:02$

Concept Check (page 49)

1. False   **2.** False   **3.** True   **4.** False   **5.** True   **6.** False   **7.** True   **8.** False   **9.** False   **10.** False   **11.** False   **12.** True

Chapter 1 Review Exercises (page 50)

3. 1   **5.** $-2/11$ **7.** $-4/3$ **9.** 0   **11.** 5   **13.** $y = (2/3)x - 13/3$ **15.** $y = -x - 3$ **17.** $x = -1$
19. $y = 2x - 10$ **21.** $y = -10$ **23.** $x = -3$

25.

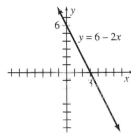

$y = 6 - 2x$

27.

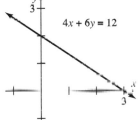

$4x + 6y = 12$

29.

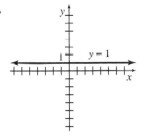

$y = 1$

31.

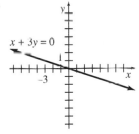

$x + 3y = 0$

33. a. $7/6$; $9/2$ **b.** 2; 2 **c.** $5/2$; $1/2$ **d.**

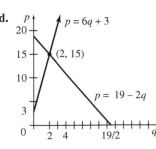

$p = 6q + 3$

$(2, 15)$

$p = 19 - 2q$

e. $15   **f.** 2

35. $D(q) = -0.5q + 72.50$ **37.** $C(x) = 30x + 60$ **39.** $C(x) = 30x + 85$ **41. a.** 5 cartons   **b.** $2000
43. $y = 35.25x + 66.75$ **45.** $I(x) = 180.4x + 27{,}384$

47. a. $r = 0.881$, yes   **b.**

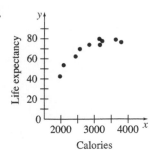

Somewhat, but there is also a nonlinear trend.   **c.** $Y = 0.0173x + 19.3$
d. $Y = 78.1$ yr   **49.** $Y = -0.797x + 201.3$

51. a. $r = 0.749$; yes, but the fit is not very good.   **b.**

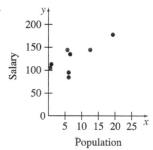

c. $Y = 3.81x + 98.24$ **d.** \$3810

CHAPTER 2 **Systems of Linear Equations and Matrices**

Exercises 2.1 (page 65)

1. $(3, 2)$ **3.** $(1, 3)$ **5.** $(-2, 0)$ **7.** $(0, 2)$ **9.** $(3, -2)$ **11.** $(2, -2)$ **13.** No solution   **15.** $((2y - 4)/3, y)$ **17.** No
19. $(4, 1)$ **21.** $(7, -2)$ **23.** $(1, 2, -1)$ **25.** $(2, 0, 3)$ **27.** $(3, 0, 1)$ **31.** $((-2z - 7)/5, (11z + 21)/5, z)$
33. $((-4z + 28)/5, (z - 7)/5, z)$ **37.** 260 skirts and 270 blouses   **39.** This situation is not possible.   **41.** 24 fives, 8 tens,
and 38 twenties   **43.** Either 10 buffets, 5 chairs, and no tables, or 11 buffets, 1 chair, and 1 table   **45.** $z + 80$ long-sleeve blouses,
$260 - 2z$ short-sleeve blouses, and z sleeveless blouses with $0 \le z \le 130$.   **47. a.** March 23, March 19   **b.** 1991   **49.** 36 field
goals, 28 foul shots   **51.** One possible system is $\begin{cases} x + y = 3 \\ 3x + 2y = 8 \end{cases}$ with solution $(2, 1)$.

Exercises 2.2 (page 80)

1. $\begin{bmatrix} 3 & 1 & | & 6 \\ 2 & 5 & | & 15 \end{bmatrix}$ **3.** $\begin{bmatrix} 2 & 1 & 1 & | & 3 \\ 3 & -4 & 2 & | & -7 \\ 1 & 1 & 1 & | & 2 \end{bmatrix}$ **5.** $x = 2, y = 3$ **7.** $x = 4, y = -5, z = 1$ **9.** Row operations

11. $\begin{bmatrix} 3 & 7 & 4 & | & 10 \\ 0 & 1 & -5 & | & -8 \\ 0 & 4 & 5 & | & 11 \end{bmatrix}$ **13.** $\begin{bmatrix} 1 & 0 & 0 & | & -3 \\ 0 & 3 & 2 & | & 5 \\ 0 & 5 & 3 & | & 7 \end{bmatrix}$ **15.** $\begin{bmatrix} 1 & 0 & 0 & | & 6 \\ 0 & 5 & 0 & | & 9 \\ 0 & 0 & 4 & | & 8 \end{bmatrix}$ **17.** $(2, 3)$ **19.** $(1, 6)$ **21.** No solution

23. $((3y + 1)/6, y)$ **25.** $(4, 1, 0)$ **27.** No solution   **29.** $(-1, 23, 16)$ **31.** $((-9z + 5)/23, (10z - 3)/23, z)$
33. $((-2z + 62)/35, (3z + 5)/7, z)$ **35.** $((9 - 3y - z)/2, y, z)$ **37.** $(0, 2, -2, 1)$; the answers are given in the order x, y, z, w.
39. $(-w - 3, -4w - 19, -3w - 2, w)$ **41.** $(28.9436, 36.6326, 9.6390, 37.1036)$ **43.** row 1: 3/8, 1/6, 11/24; row 2: 5/12, 1/3,
1/4; row 3: 5/24, 1/2, 7/24   **45.** 22 units from Toronto, 56 units from Montreal, and 22 units from Ottawa   **47. a.** 15 deluxe, 10
super-deluxe, 20 ultra   **b.** None   **c.** 9   **49.** 120 vans, 60 small trucks, and 20 large trucks   **51.** Send 12 cars from I to A, 8 cars from
II to A, 16 cars from I to B, and no cars from II to B.   **53.** 18,000 packages of Italian style, 15,000 packages of French style, and
54,000 packages of Oriental style   **55.** Four possibilities: no cases of A and D, 12 cases of B, 8 cases of C; or 1 case of A, 8 cases of

B, 9 cases of C, 1 case of D; or 2 cases of A, 4 cases of B, 10 cases of C, 2 cases of D; or 3 cases of A, no cases of B, 11 cases of C, 3 cases of D **57.** 2340 of the first species, 10,128 of the second species, and 224 of the third species (all are rounded) **59. a.** No **b.** Yes; 150 acres for honeydews, 50 acres for onions, and 20 acres for lettuce **61. a.** $a = -0.1225, b = 2.035, c = 207.9$ **b.** 189.90 **c.** $a = 0.0002202, b = -0.1291, c = 2.079, d = 207.9$ **63. a.** $x_2 + x_3 = 700, x_3 + x_4 = 600$ **b.** $(1000 - x_4, 100 + x_4, 600 - x_4, x_4)$ **c.** $0 \le x_4 \le 600$ **d.** $400 \le x_1 \le 1000, 100 \le x_2 \le 700, 0 \le x_3 \le 600.$ **65. a.** 24 balls, 57 dolls, and 19 cars **b.** None **c.** 48 **d.** 5 balls, 95 dolls, and 0 cars **e.** 52 balls, 1 doll, and 47 cars **67.** 225 singles, 24 doubles, 5 triples, and 8 home runs

Exercises 2.3 (page 91)

1. False; not all corresponding elements are equal. **3.** True **5.** True **7.** 2×2; square; $\begin{bmatrix} 4 & -8 \\ -2 & -3 \end{bmatrix}$

9. 3×4; $\begin{bmatrix} 6 & -8 & 0 & 0 \\ -4 & -1 & -9 & -2 \\ -3 & 5 & -7 & -1 \end{bmatrix}$ **11.** 2×1; column; $\begin{bmatrix} 7 \\ -5 \end{bmatrix}$ **13.** The $n \times m$ zero matrix **15.** $x = 4, y = -8, z = 1$

17. $s - 10, t = 0, r = 7$ **19.** $a = 20, b = 5, c = 0, d = 4, f = 1$ **21.** $\begin{bmatrix} 10 & 4 & -5 & -6 \\ 4 & 5 & 3 & 11 \end{bmatrix}$ **23.** Not possible

25. $\begin{bmatrix} 1 & 5 & 6 & -9 \\ 5 & 7 & 2 & 1 \\ -7 & 2 & 2 & -7 \end{bmatrix}$ **27.** $\begin{bmatrix} 3 & 4 \\ 4 & 8 \end{bmatrix}$ **29.** $\begin{bmatrix} 10 & 2 \\ 10 & 9 \end{bmatrix}$ **31.** $\begin{bmatrix} -12x + 8y & -x + y \\ x & 8x - y \end{bmatrix}$ **33.** $\begin{bmatrix} -x & -y \\ -z & -w \end{bmatrix}$

39. a. Chicago: $\begin{bmatrix} 4.05 & 7.01 \\ 3.27 & 3.51 \end{bmatrix}$, Seattle. $\begin{bmatrix} 4.40 & 6.90 \\ 3.54 & 3.76 \end{bmatrix}$ **b.** $\begin{bmatrix} 4.42 & 7.43 \\ 3.38 & 3.62 \end{bmatrix}$ **41. a.** $\begin{bmatrix} 2 & 1 & 2 & 1 \\ 3 & 2 & 2 & 1 \\ 4 & 3 & 2 & 1 \end{bmatrix}$ **b.** $\begin{bmatrix} 5 & 0 & 7 \\ 0 & 10 & 1 \\ 0 & 15 & 2 \\ 10 & 12 & 8 \end{bmatrix}$ **c.** $\begin{bmatrix} 8 \\ 4 \\ 5 \end{bmatrix}$

43. a. 8 **b.** 3 **c.** $\begin{bmatrix} 85 & 15 \\ 27 & 73 \end{bmatrix}$ **d.** Yes **45. a.** $\begin{bmatrix} 60.0 & 68.3 \\ 63.8 & 72.5 \\ 64.5 & 73.6 \\ 68.2 & 74.9 \end{bmatrix}$ **b.** $\begin{bmatrix} 68.0 & 75.6 \\ 70.7 & 78.1 \\ 72.7 & 79.4 \\ 74.8 & 80.0 \end{bmatrix}$ **c.** $\begin{bmatrix} -8.0 & -7.3 \\ -6.9 & -5.6 \\ -8.2 & -5.8 \\ -6.6 & -5.1 \end{bmatrix}$

47. a. $\begin{bmatrix} 51.4 & 7.9 \\ 59.9 & 11.1 \\ 66.2 & 11.3 \\ 73.8 & 13.3 \\ 78.9 & 16.6 \\ 80.6 & 17.6 \end{bmatrix}$ **b.** $\begin{bmatrix} 44.5 & 7.6 \\ 47.9 & 8.5 \\ 50.8 & 9.2 \\ 53.4 & 9.3 \\ 57.0 & 10.6 \\ 58.4 & 12.1 \end{bmatrix}$ **c.** $\begin{bmatrix} 6.9 & 0.3 \\ 12.0 & 2.6 \\ 15.4 & 2.1 \\ 20.4 & 4.0 \\ 21.9 & 6.0 \\ 22.2 & 5.5 \end{bmatrix}$

Exercises 2.4 (page 103)

1. $\begin{bmatrix} -4 & 8 \\ 0 & 6 \end{bmatrix}$ **3.** $\begin{bmatrix} 12 & -24 \\ 0 & -18 \end{bmatrix}$ **5.** $\begin{bmatrix} -22 & -6 \\ 20 & -12 \end{bmatrix}$ **7.** $2 \times 2; 2 \times 2$ **9.** 3×4; BA does not exist. **11.** AB does not exist; 3×2

13. Columns: rows **15.** $\begin{bmatrix} 8 \\ -1 \end{bmatrix}$ **17.** $\begin{bmatrix} 14 \\ -23 \end{bmatrix}$ **19.** $\begin{bmatrix} -7 & 2 & 8 \\ 27 & -12 & 12 \end{bmatrix}$ **21.** $\begin{bmatrix} -2 & 10 \\ 0 & 8 \end{bmatrix}$ **23.** $\begin{bmatrix} 13 & 5 \\ 25 & 15 \end{bmatrix}$

25. $\begin{bmatrix} 13 \\ 29 \end{bmatrix}$ **27.** $\begin{bmatrix} 7 \\ -33 \\ 4 \end{bmatrix}$ **29.** $\begin{bmatrix} 22 & -8 \\ 11 & -4 \end{bmatrix}$ **31. a.** $\begin{bmatrix} 16 & 22 \\ 7 & 19 \end{bmatrix}$ **b.** $\begin{bmatrix} 5 & -5 \\ 0 & 30 \end{bmatrix}$ **c.** No **d.** No

39. a. $\begin{bmatrix} 6 & 106 & 158 & 222 & 28 \\ 120 & 139 & 64 & 75 & 115 \\ -146 & -2 & 184 & 144 & -129 \\ 106 & 94 & 24 & 116 & 110 \end{bmatrix}$ **b.** Does not exist **c.** No

41. a. $\begin{bmatrix} -1 & 5 & 9 & 13 & -1 \\ 7 & 17 & 2 & -10 & 6 \\ 18 & 9 & -12 & 12 & 22 \\ 9 & 4 & 18 & 10 & -3 \\ 1 & 6 & 10 & 28 & 5 \end{bmatrix}$ **b.** $\begin{bmatrix} -2 & -9 & 90 & 77 \\ -42 & -63 & 127 & 62 \\ 413 & 76 & 180 & -56 \\ -29 & -44 & 198 & 85 \\ 137 & 20 & 162 & 103 \end{bmatrix}$ **c.** $\begin{bmatrix} -56 & -1 & 1 & 45 \\ -156 & -119 & 76 & 122 \\ 315 & 86 & 118 & -91 \\ -17 & -17 & 116 & 51 \\ 118 & 19 & 125 & 77 \end{bmatrix}$

d. $\begin{bmatrix} 54 & -8 & 89 & 32 \\ 114 & 56 & 51 & -60 \\ 98 & -10 & 62 & 35 \\ -12 & -27 & 82 & 34 \\ 19 & 1 & 37 & 26 \end{bmatrix}$ **e.** $\begin{bmatrix} -2 & -9 & 90 & 77 \\ -42 & -63 & 127 & 62 \\ 413 & 76 & 180 & -56 \\ -29 & -44 & 198 & 85 \\ 137 & 20 & 162 & 103 \end{bmatrix}$ **f.** Yes

43. a. $\begin{array}{c} \\ \text{Dept. 1} \\ \text{Dept. 2} \\ \text{Dept. 3} \\ \text{Dept. 4} \end{array} \begin{array}{c} A \quad B \\ \begin{bmatrix} 57 & 70 \\ 41 & 54 \\ 27 & 40 \\ 39 & 40 \end{bmatrix} \end{array}$ **b.** Supplier A: \$164; Supplier B: \$204; Supplier A **45. a.** $\begin{bmatrix} 4.24 & 6.95 \\ 3.42 & 3.64 \end{bmatrix}$ **b.** $\begin{bmatrix} 4.41 & 7.17 \\ 3.46 & 3.69 \end{bmatrix}$

47. a. $\begin{bmatrix} 80 & 40 & 120 \\ 60 & 30 & 150 \end{bmatrix}$ **b.** $\begin{bmatrix} 1/2 & 1/5 \\ 1/4 & 1/5 \\ 1/4 & 3/5 \end{bmatrix}$ **c.** $PF = \begin{bmatrix} 80 & 96 \\ 75 & 108 \end{bmatrix}$ The rows give the average price per pair of footwear sold by each store, and the columns give the state.

49. a. $\begin{bmatrix} 20 & 52 & 27 \\ 25 & 62 & 35 \\ 30 & 72 & 43 \end{bmatrix}$; the rows give the amounts of fat, carbohydrates, and protein, respectively, in each of the daily meals.

b. $\begin{bmatrix} 75 \\ 45 \\ 70 \\ 168 \end{bmatrix}$; the rows give the number of calories in one exchange of each of the food groups. **c.** The rows give the number of calories in each meal.

51. $\begin{bmatrix} 66.7 & 74.4 \\ 69.6 & 77.2 \\ 71.3 & 78.4 \\ 73.7 & 79.2 \end{bmatrix}$ **53. a.** $\begin{bmatrix} 0.036 & 0.014 \\ 0.019 & 0.008 \\ 0.021 & 0.006 \\ 0.014 & 0.008 \\ 0.011 & 0.011 \end{bmatrix}$; $\begin{bmatrix} 283 & 1628 & 218 & 199 & 425 \\ 361 & 2038 & 286 & 227 & 460 \\ 473 & 2494 & 362 & 252 & 484 \\ 627 & 2978 & 443 & 278 & 499 \\ 839 & 3518 & 539 & 320 & 513 \end{bmatrix}$ **b.** $\begin{array}{c} \\ 1960 \\ 1970 \\ 1980 \\ 1990 \\ 2002 \end{array} \begin{array}{c} \textit{Births} \quad \textit{Deaths} \\ \begin{bmatrix} 53.159 & 24.561 \\ 65.962 & 29.950 \\ 80.868 & 36.086 \\ 97.838 & 42.973 \\ 118.488 & 51.327 \end{bmatrix} \end{array}$

Exercises 2.5 (page 116)

1. Yes **3.** No **5.** No **7.** Yes **9.** No; the row of all zeros makes it impossible to get all the 1's in the diagonal of the identity matrix, no matter what matrix is used as an inverse.

11. $\begin{bmatrix} 0 & 1/2 \\ -1 & 1/2 \end{bmatrix}$ **13.** $\begin{bmatrix} 2 & 1 \\ 5 & 3 \end{bmatrix}$ **15.** No inverse **17.** $\begin{bmatrix} 1 & 0 & 0 \\ 0 & -1 & 0 \\ -1 & 0 & 1 \end{bmatrix}$ **19.** $\begin{bmatrix} 15 & 4 & -5 \\ -12 & -3 & 4 \\ -4 & -1 & 1 \end{bmatrix}$ **21.** No inverse

23. $\begin{bmatrix} -11/2 & -1/2 & 5/2 \\ 1/2 & 1/2 & -1/2 \\ -5/2 & 1/2 & 1/2 \end{bmatrix}$ **25.** $\begin{bmatrix} 1/2 & 1/2 & -1/4 & 1/2 \\ -1 & 4 & -1/2 & -2 \\ -1/2 & 5/2 & -1/4 & -3/2 \\ 1/2 & -1/2 & 1/4 & 1/2 \end{bmatrix}$ **27.** $(5, 1)$ **29.** $(2, 1)$ **31.** $(15, 21)$

33. No inverse, $(-8y - 12, y)$ **35.** $(-8, 6, 1)$ **37.** $(-36, 8, -8)$ **39.** No inverse, no solution for system

41. $(-7, -34, -19, 7)$

51. Entries are rounded to four places. $\begin{bmatrix} -0.0447 & -0.0230 & 0.0292 & 0.0895 & -0.0402 \\ 0.0921 & 0.0150 & 0.0321 & 0.0209 & -0.0276 \\ -0.0678 & 0.0315 & -0.0404 & 0.0326 & 0.0373 \\ 0.0171 & -0.0248 & 0.0069 & -0.0003 & 0.0246 \\ -0.0208 & 0.0740 & 0.0096 & -0.1018 & 0.0646 \end{bmatrix}$

53. Entries are rounded to four places $\begin{bmatrix} 0.0394 & 0.0880 & 0.0033 & 0.0530 & -0.1499 \\ -0.1492 & 0.0289 & 0.0187 & 0.1033 & 0.1668 \\ -0.1330 & -0.0543 & 0.0356 & 0.1768 & 0.1055 \\ 0.1407 & 0.0175 & -0.0453 & -0.1344 & 0.0655 \\ 0.0102 & -0.0653 & 0.0993 & 0.0085 & -0.0388 \end{bmatrix}$ **55.** Yes

57. $\begin{bmatrix} 1.51482 \\ 0.053479 \\ -0.637242 \\ 0.162629 \end{bmatrix}$ **59. a.** $\begin{bmatrix} 72 \\ 48 \\ 60 \end{bmatrix}$ **b.** $\begin{bmatrix} 2 & 4 & 2 \\ 2 & 1 & 2 \\ 2 & 1 & 3 \end{bmatrix}\begin{bmatrix} x_1 \\ x_2 \\ x_3 \end{bmatrix} = \begin{bmatrix} 72 \\ 48 \\ 60 \end{bmatrix}$ **c.** 8 type I, 8 type II, and 12 type III

61. a. $10,000 at 6%, $10,000 at 6.5%, and $5000 at 8% **b.** $14,000 at 6%, $9000 at 6.5%, and $7000 at 8% **c.** $24,000 at 6%, $4000 at 6.5%, and $12,000 at 8% **63. a.** 50 Super Vim, 75 Multitab, and 100 Mighty Mix **b.** 75 Super Vim, 50 Multitab, and 60 Mighty Mix **c.** 80 Super Vim, 100 Multitab, and 50 Mighty Mix **65. a.** $262, -161, -12, 186, -103, -22, 264, -168, -9,$ $208, -134, -5, 224, -152, 5, 92, -50, -3$ **b.** $\begin{bmatrix} 1.75 & 2.5 & 3 \\ -0.25 & -0.5 & 0 \\ -0.25 & -0.5 & -1 \end{bmatrix}$ **c.** happy birthday

Exercises 2.6 (page 125)

1. $\begin{bmatrix} 60 \\ 50 \end{bmatrix}$ **3.** $\begin{bmatrix} 6.43 \\ 26.12 \end{bmatrix}$ **5.** $\begin{bmatrix} 10 \\ 18 \\ 10 \end{bmatrix}$ **7.** $33:47:23$ **9.** $\begin{bmatrix} 7697 \\ 4205 \\ 6345 \\ 4106 \end{bmatrix}$ (rounded)

11. About 1440 metric tons of wheat and 1938 metric tons of oil. **13.** About 1511 units of agriculture, 1712 units of manufacturing, and 1414 units of transportation. **15.** About 3077 units of agriculture, about 2564 units of manufacturing, and about 3179 units of transportation **17. a.** 7/4 bushels of yams and $15/8 \approx 2$ pigs **b.** 167.5 bushels of yams and $153.75 \approx 154$ pigs **19.** About 848 units of agriculture, about 516 units of manufacturing, and about 2970 units of households **21.** About 195 million lb of agriculture, about 26 million lb of manufacturing, and about 13.6 million lb of energy **23.** In millions of dollars, the amounts are about 532 for natural resources, about 481 for manufacturing, about 805 for trade and services, and about 1185 for personal consumption.

25. a. $\begin{bmatrix} 1.67 & 0.56 & 0.56 \\ 0.19 & 1.17 & 0.06 \\ 3.15 & 3.27 & 4.38 \end{bmatrix}$ **b.** These multipliers imply that if the demand for one community's output increases by $1, then the output in the other community will increase by the amount in the row and column of that matrix. For example, if the demand for Hermitage's output increases by $1, then output from Sharon will increase by $0.56, Farrell by $0.06, and Hermitage by $4.38.

27. 3 units of coal to every 4 units of steel **29.** 6 units of mining to every 8 units of manufacturing and 5 units of communication

Concept Check (page 130)

1. False **2.** False **3.** True **4.** True **5.** False **6.** True **7.** False **8.** False **9.** True **10.** False **11.** False **12.** False
13. True **14.** True **15.** False **16.** True

Chapter 2 Review Exercises (page 131)

3. $(1, -4)$ **5.** $(-1, 2, 3)$ **7.** $(-9, 3)$ **9.** $(7, -9, -1)$ **11.** $(6 - 7z/3, 1 + z/3, z)$ **13.** $3 \times 2; a = 2, x = -1, y = 4,$
$p = 5, z = 7$ **15.** 3×3 (square); $a = -12, b = 1, k = 9/2, c = 3/4, d = 3, l = -3/4, m = -1, p = 3, q = 9$

17. $\begin{bmatrix} 0 & -16 \\ -10 & -18 \end{bmatrix}$ **19.** Not possible **21.** $\begin{bmatrix} 2 & 50 \\ 1 & -15 \\ -3 & 45 \end{bmatrix}$ **23.** $\begin{bmatrix} 6 & 18 & -24 \\ 1 & 3 & -4 \\ 0 & 0 & 0 \end{bmatrix}$ **25.** $\begin{bmatrix} 15 \\ 16 \\ 1 \end{bmatrix}$ **27.** $\begin{bmatrix} -7/19 & 4/19 \\ 3/19 & 1/19 \end{bmatrix}$

29. No inverse **31.** $\begin{bmatrix} -1/4 & 1/6 \\ 0 & 1/3 \end{bmatrix}$ **33.** No inverse **35.** $\begin{bmatrix} 1/4 & 1/2 & 1/2 \\ 1/4 & -1/2 & 1/2 \\ 1/8 & -1/4 & -1/4 \end{bmatrix}$ **37.** No inverse

39. Matrix A has no inverse. Solution: $(-2y + 5, y)$ **41.** $X = \begin{bmatrix} 6 \\ 15 \\ 16 \end{bmatrix}$ **43.** $(34, \quad 9)$ **45.** $(1, 2, 3)$ **47.** $\begin{bmatrix} 725.7 \\ 305.9 \\ 166.7 \end{bmatrix}$

49. 8000 standard, 6000 extra large **51.** 150,000 gal were produced at Tulsa, 225,000 gal at New Orleans, and 180,000 gal at
Ardmore **53. a.** $\begin{bmatrix} 3170 \\ 2360 \\ 1800 \end{bmatrix}$ **b.** $\begin{bmatrix} x \\ y \\ z \end{bmatrix}$ **c.** $\begin{bmatrix} 10 & 5 & 8 \\ 12 & 0 & 4 \\ 0 & 10 & 5 \end{bmatrix} \begin{bmatrix} x \\ y \\ z \end{bmatrix} = \begin{bmatrix} 3170 \\ 2360 \\ 1800 \end{bmatrix}$ **d.** $\begin{bmatrix} 150 \\ 110 \\ 140 \end{bmatrix}$

55. a. $\begin{bmatrix} 1.300 & 0.045 & 0.567 & 0.012 & 0.068 & 0.020 \\ 0.204 & 1.030 & 0.183 & 0.004 & 0.022 & 0.006 \\ 0.155 & 0.038 & 1.120 & 0.020 & 0.114 & 0.034 \\ 0.018 & 0.021 & 0.028 & 1.080 & 0.016 & 0.033 \\ 0.537 & 0.525 & 0.483 & 0.279 & 1.730 & 0.419 \\ 0.537 & 0.346 & 0.497 & 0.536 & 0.087 & 1.940 \end{bmatrix}$; every \$1 of increased demand for livestock will result in an increase of

production demand of \$0.204 in crops **b.** In millions of dollars, produce \$3855 in livestock, \$1476 in crops, \$2726 in food products, \$1338 in mining and manufacturing, \$8439 in households, and \$10,256 in other business sectors.
57. a. $b + c$ **b.** A is tumorous, B is bone, and C is healthy **c.** For patient X, A and C are healthy; B is tumorous. For patient Y, A and B are tumorous; C is bone. For patient Z, A could be healthy or tumorous; B and C are healthy. **59.** About 20 head and face injuries, 12 concussions, 3 neck injuries, and 55 other injuries. **61.** $W_1 \approx 110$ lb and $W_2 \approx 134$ lb **63. a.** $x = 1$ and $y = 1/2$
b. $x = 1, y = 1,$ and $z = -1$ **65.** 60 singles, 27 doubles, 3 triples, and 45 home runs

CHAPTER 3 | Linear Programming: The Graphical Method

Exercises 3.1 (page 145)

1.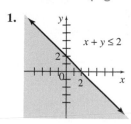

3.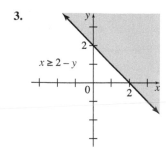

5.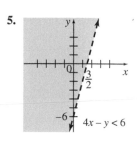

7.

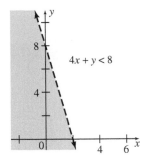

$4x + y < 8$

9.

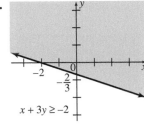

$x + 3y \geq -2$

11.

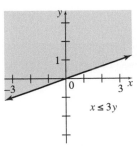

$x \leq 3y$

13.

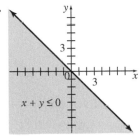

$x + y \leq 0$

15.

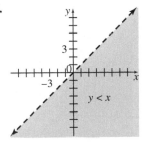

$y < x$

17.

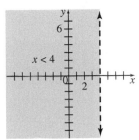

$x < 4$

19.

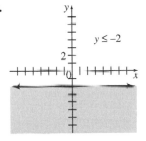

$y \leq -2$

21.

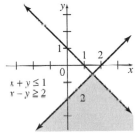

$x + y \leq 1$
$x - y \geq 2$

23.

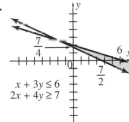

$x + 3y \leq 6$
$2x + 4y \geq 7$

25.

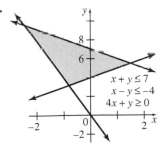

$x + y \leq 7$
$x - y \leq -4$
$4x + y \geq 0$

27.

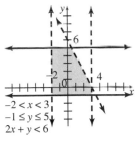

$-2 < x < 3$
$-1 \leq y \leq 5$
$2x + y < 6$

29.

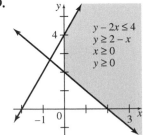

$y - 2x \leq 4$
$y \geq 2 - x$
$x \geq 0$
$y \geq 0$

31.

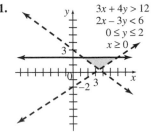

$3x + 4y > 12$
$2x - 3y < 6$
$0 \leq y \leq 2$
$x \geq 0$

33.

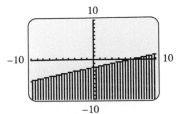

35.

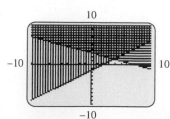

37. B: ≤, ≤, ≤; **C:** ≥, ≥, ≤; **D:** ≤, ≥, ≤; **E:** ≤, ≤, ≥; **F:** ≤, ≥, ≥; **G:** ≥, ≥, ≥

39. a.

	Shawls	Afghans		Total
Number Made	x	y		
Spinning Time	1	2	≤	8
Dyeing Time	1	1	≤	6
Weaving Time	1	4	≤	14

b.

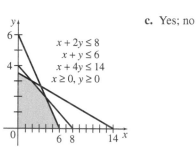

$x + 2y \le 8$
$x + y \le 6$
$x + 4y \le 14$
$x \ge 0, y \ge 0$

c. Yes; no

41. a. $x \ge 4y$; $0.06x + 0.08y \ge 1.6$; $x + y \le 30$; $x \ge 0$; $y \ge 0$ **b.**

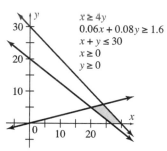

$x \ge 4y$
$0.06x + 0.08y \ge 1.6$
$x + y \le 30$
$x \ge 0$
$y \ge 0$

43. a. $x \le (1/2)y$; $x + y \le 800$; $x \ge 0$; $y \ge 0$ **b.**

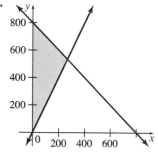

45. a. $x + y \ge 7$; $2x + y \ge 10$; $x + y \le 9$; $x \ge 0$; $y \ge 0$ **b.**

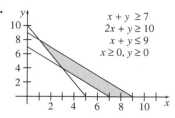

$x + y \ge 7$
$2x + y \ge 10$
$x + y \le 9$
$x \ge 0, y \ge 0$

Exercises 3.2 (page 152)

1. a. Maximum of 29 at $(7, 4)$; minimum of 10 at $(0, 5)$ **b.** Maximum of 35 at $(3, 8)$; minimum of 8 at $(4, 1)$
3. a. Maximum of 9 at $(0, 12)$; minimum of 0 at $(0, 0)$ **b.** Maximum of 12 at $(8, 0)$; minimum of 0 at $(0, 0)$

5. a. No maximum; minimum of 16 at $(0, 8)$ **b.** No maximum; minimum of 18 at $(3, 4)$ **c.** No maximum; minimum of 21 at $(13/2, 2)$ **d.** No maximum; minimum of 12 at $(12, 0)$ **7.** Minimum of 24 when $x = 6$ and $y = 0$ **9.** Maximum of 46 when $x = 6$ and $y = 8$ **11.** Maximum of 1500 when $x = 150$ and $y = 0$, as well as when $x = 50$ and $y = 100$ and all points on the line between **13.** No solution **15. a.** Maximum of 204 when $x = 18$ and $y = 2$ **b.** Maximum of 588/5 when $x = 12/5$ and $y = 39/5$ **c.** Maximum of 102 when $x = 0$ and $y = 17/2$ **17.** b

Exercises 3.3 (page 160)

1. Let x be the number of product A produced and y be the number of product B. Then $3x + 5y \le 60$. **3.** Let x be the number of calcium carbonate supplements and y be the number of calcium citrate supplements. Then $600x + 250y \ge 1500$. **5.** Let x be the number of pounds of $8 coffee and y be the number of $10 coffee. Then $x + y \ge 40$. **7.** 45 to plant I and 32 to plant II, for a minimum cost of $2630 **9. a.** 6 units of policy A and 16 units of policy B, for a minimum premium cost of $940 **b.** 30 units of policy A and 0 units of policy B, for a minimum premium cost of $750 **11. a.** 500 type I and 1000 type II **b.** Maximum revenue is $275. **c.** If the price of the type I bolt exceeds 20¢, then it is more profitable to produce 1050 type I bolts and 450 type II bolts. **13. a.** 120 kg of the half-and-half mix and 120 kg of the other mix, for a maximum revenue of $1980 **b.** 0 kg of the half-and-half mix and 200 kg of the other mix, for a maximum revenue of $2200 **15. a.** 40 gal from dairy I and 60 gal from dairy II, for a maximum butterfat of 3.4% **b.** 10 gal from dairy I and 20 gal from dairy 2. No. **17.** $10 million in bonds and $20 million in mutual funds, or $5 million in bonds and $22.5 million in mutual funds (or any solution on the line in between those two points), for a maximum annual interest of $2 million **19.** a **21. a.** Three of pill 1 and two of pill 2, for a minimum cost of $1.05 per day **b.** 12 surplus units of vitamin A. No. **23.** 4 ounces of fruit and 2 ounces of nuts, for a minimum of 140 calories **25.** 0 plants and 18 animals, for a minimum of 270 hours

Concept Check (page 164)

1. False **2.** True **3.** False **4.** False **5.** False **6.** False **7.** True **8.** False **9.** False **10.** True **11.** True **12.** True **13.** True

Chapter 3 Review Exercises (page 165)

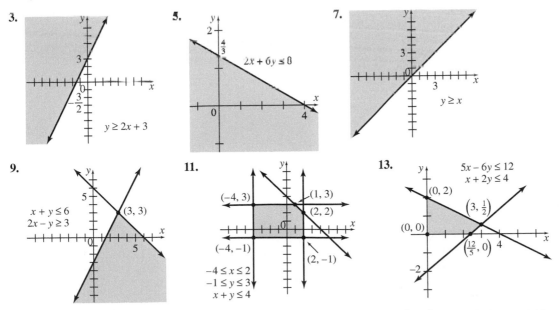

15. Maximum of 22 at $(3, 4)$; minimum of 0 at $(0, 0)$ **17.** Maximum of 24 at $(0, 6)$ **19.** Minimum of 40 at any point on the segment connecting $(0, 20)$ and $(10/3, 40/3)$

23. a.

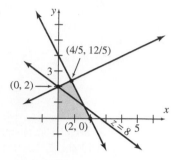

b.

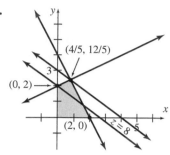

25. Let x = number of batches of cakes and y = number of batches of cookies. Then $x \geq 0$, $y \geq 0$, $2x + (3/2)y \leq 15$, and $3x + (2/3)y \leq 13$.

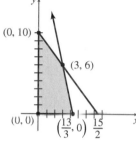

27. a. 3 batches of cakes and 6 batches of cookies, for a maximum profit of $210   **b.** If the profit per batch of cookies increases by more than $2.50 (to $22.50), then it will be more profitable to make 10 batches of cookies and no batches of cake.   **29.** 7 packages of gardening mixture and 2 packages of potting mixture, for a maximum income of $31   **31.** Produce no runs of type I and 7 runs of type II, for a minimum cost of $42,000.   **33.** 0 acres for millet and 2 acres for wheat, for a maximum harvest of 1600 lb

---

CHAPTER 4 | Linear Programming: The Simplex Method

Exercises 4.1 (page 175)

1. $x_1 + 2x_2 + s_1 = 6$ **3.** $2.3x_1 + 5.7x_2 + 1.8x_3 + s_1 = 17$ **5. a.** 3   **b.** s_1, s_2, s_3 **c.** $2x_1 + 3x_2 + s_1 = 15$; $4x_1 + 5x_2 + s_2 = 35$; $x_1 + 6x_2 + s_3 = 20$ **7. a.** 2   **b.** s_1, s_2 **c.** $7x_1 + 6x_2 + 8x_3 + s_1 = 118$; $4x_1 + 5x_2 + 10x_3 + s_2 = 220$
9. $x_1 = 0, x_2 = 4, x_3 = 0, s_1 = 0, s_2 = 8, z = 28$ **11.** $x_1 = 0, x_2 = 0, x_3 = 8, s_1 = 0, s_2 = 6, s_3 = 7, z = 12$ **13.** $x_1 = 0, x_2 = 20,$
$x_3 = 0, s_1 = 16, s_2 = 0, z = 60$ **15.** $x_1 = 0, x_2 = 0, x_3 = 12, s_1 = 0, s_2 = 9, s_3 = 8, z = 36$
17. $x_1 = 0, x_2 = 250, x_3 = 0, s_1 = 0, s_2 = 50, s_3 = 200, z = 1000$

19.
$$\begin{array}{ccccc|c} x_1 & x_2 & s_1 & s_2 & z & \\ 4 & 2 & 1 & 0 & 0 & 5 \\ 1 & 2 & 0 & 1 & 0 & 4 \\ \hline -7 & -1 & 0 & 0 & 1 & 0 \end{array}$$

21.
$$\begin{array}{cccccc|c} x_1 & x_2 & s_1 & s_2 & s_3 & z & \\ 1 & 1 & 1 & 0 & 0 & 0 & 10 \\ 5 & 2 & 0 & 1 & 0 & 0 & 20 \\ 1 & 2 & 0 & 0 & 1 & 0 & 36 \\ \hline -1 & -3 & 0 & 0 & 0 & 1 & 0 \end{array}$$

23.
$$\begin{array}{ccccc|c} x_1 & x_2 & s_1 & s_2 & z & \\ 3 & 1 & 1 & 0 & 0 & 12 \\ 1 & 1 & 0 & 1 & 0 & 15 \\ \hline -2 & -1 & 0 & 0 & 1 & 0 \end{array}$$

25. If x_1 is the number of simple figures, x_2 is the number of figures with additions, and x_3 is the number of computer-drawn sketches, find $x_1 \geq 0, x_2 \geq 0, x_3 \geq 0, s_1 \geq 0, s_2 \geq 0, s_3 \geq 0, s_4 \geq 0$ so that $20x_1 + 35x_2 + 60x_3 + s_1 = 2200$, $x_1 + x_2 + x_3 + s_2 = 400$, $-x_1 - x_2 + x_3 + s_3 = 0$, $-x_1 + 2x_2 + s_4 = 0$, and $z = 95x_1 + 200x_2 + 325x_3$ is maximized.

$$\begin{array}{cccccccc|c} x_1 & x_2 & x_3 & s_1 & s_2 & s_3 & s_4 & z & \\ 20 & 35 & 60 & 1 & 0 & 0 & 0 & 0 & 2200 \\ 1 & 1 & 1 & 0 & 1 & 0 & 0 & 0 & 400 \\ -1 & -1 & 1 & 0 & 0 & 1 & 0 & 0 & 0 \\ -1 & 2 & 0 & 0 & 0 & 0 & 1 & 0 & 0 \\ \hline -95 & -200 & -325 & 0 & 0 & 0 & 0 & 1 & 0 \end{array}$$

27. If x_1 is the number of redwood tables made, x_2 is the number of stained Douglas fir tables made, and x_3 is the number of stained white spruce tables made, find $x_1 \geq 0, x_2 \geq 0, x_3 \geq 0, s_1 \geq 0, s_2 \geq 0$, $s_3 \geq 0$ so that $8x_1 + 7x_2 + 8x_3 + s_1 = 720, 2x_2 + 2x_3 + s_2 = 480$, $159x_1 + 138.85x_2 + 129.35x_3 + s_3 = 15,000$, and $z = x_1 + x_2 + x_3$ is maximized.

x_1	x_2	x_3	s_1	s_2	s_3	z	
8	7	8	1	0	0	0	720
0	2	2	0	1	0	0	480
159	138.85	129.35	0	0	1	0	15,000
−1	−1	−1	0	0	0	1	0

29. If x_1 is the number of newspaper ads run, x_2 is the number of Internet banner ads run, and x_3 is the number of TV ads run, find $x_1 \geq 0, x_2 \geq 0, x_3 \geq 0, s_1 \geq 0, s_2 \geq 0, s_3 \geq 0, s_4 \geq 0$ so that $400x_1 + 20x_2 + 2000x_3 + s_1 = 8000, x_1 + s_2 = 30$, $x_2 + s_3 = 60, x_3 + s_4 = 10$, and $z = 4000x_1 + 3000x_2 + 10,000x_3$ is maximized.

x_1	x_2	x_3	s_1	s_2	s_3	s_4	z	
400	20	2000	1	0	0	0	0	8000
1	0	0	0	1	0	0	0	30
0	1	0	0	0	1	0	0	60
0	0	1	0	0	0	1	0	10
−4000	−3000	−10,000	0	0	0	0	1	0

Exercises 4.2 (page 185)

1. Maximum is 30 when $x_1 = 10, x_2 = 0, x_3 = 0, s_1 = 6$, and $s_2 = 0$.   **3.** Maximum is 8 when $x_1 = 4, x_2 = 0, s_1 = 8, s_2 = 2$, and $s_3 = 0$.   **5.** Maximum is 264 when $x_1 = 16, x_2 = 4, x_3 = 0, s_1 = 0, s_2 = 16$, and $s_3 = 0$.   **7.** Maximum is 25 when $x_1 = 0$, $x_2 = 5, s_1 = 20$, and $s_2 = 0$.   **9.** Maximum is 120 when $x_1 = 0, x_2 = 10, s_1 = 0, s_2 = 40$, and $s_3 = 4$.   **11.** Maximum is 944 when $x_1 = 118, x_2 = 0, x_3 = 0, s_1 = 0$, and $s_2 = 102$.   **13.** Maximum is 3300 when $x_1 = 240, x_2 = 60, x_3 = 0, x_4 = 0, s_1 = 0$, and $s_2 = 0$.   **15.** No maximum   **17.** Maximum is 70,818.18 when $x_1 = 181.82, x_2 = 0, x_3 = 454.55, x_4 = 0, x_5 = 1363.64$, $s_1 = 0, s_2 = 0, s_3 = 0$, and $s_4 = 0$.   **21.** 6 churches and 2 labor unions, for a maximum of $1000 per month   **23. a.** Assemble 1000 Royal Flush poker sets, 3000 Deluxe Diamond poker sets, and 0 Full House poker sets, for a maximum profit of $104,000. **b.** $s_4 = 1000$; there are 1000 unused dealer buttons.   **25. a.** No racing or touring bicycles and 2700 mountain bicycles   **b.** Maximum profit is $59,400   **c.** No; there are 1500 units of aluminum left; $s_2 = 1500$.   **27. a.** 17 newspaper ads, 60 Internet banner ads, and no TV ads, for a maximum exposure of 248,000   **29. a.** 3   **b.** 4   **c.** 3   **31.** $200, $66.67, $300, $100   **33.** Rachel should run 3 hours, bike 4 hours, and walk 8 hours, for a maximum calorie expenditure of 6313 calories.   **35. a.** 163.6 kg of food P, none of Q, 1090.9 kg of R, 145.5 kg of S   **b.** Maximum is 87,454.5.   **c.** Yes; none   **37.** 12 minutes to the senator, 9 minutes to the congresswoman, and 6 minutes to the governor, for a maximum of 1,050,000 viewers

Exercises 4.3 (page 199)

1. $\begin{bmatrix} 1 & 3 & 1 \\ 2 & 2 & 10 \\ 3 & 1 & 0 \end{bmatrix}$ **3.** $\begin{bmatrix} 4 & 7 & 5 \\ 5 & 14 & 0 \\ -3 & 20 & -2 \\ 15 & -8 & 23 \end{bmatrix}$

5. Minimize $w = 5y_1 + 4y_2 + 15y_3$ subject to $y_1 + y_2 + 2y_3 \geq 4, y_1 + y_2 + y_3 \geq 3, y_1 + 3y_3 \geq 2$, with $y_1 \geq 0, y_2 \geq 0$, and $y_3 \geq 0$.   **7.** Maximize $z = 150x_1 + 275x_2$ subject to $x_1 + 2x_2 \leq 3, x_1 + 2x_2 \leq 6, x_1 + 3x_2 \leq 4, x_1 + 4x_2 \leq 1$, with $x_1 \geq 0$ and $x_2 \geq 0$.   **9.** Minimum is 14 when $y_1 = 0$ and $y_2 = 7$.   **11.** Minimum is 40 when $y_1 = 10$ and $y_2 = 0$.   **13.** Minimum is 100 when $y_1 = 0, y_2 = 100$, and $y_3 = 0$.   **15.** a   **17. a.** 1800 small test tubes and 900 large test tubes, for a minimum cost of $459 **b.** The shadow cost is 17 cents; total cost is $510.   **19. a.** Maximize $z = x_1 + 1.5x_2$ subject to $x_1 + 2x_2 \leq 200, 4x_1 + 3x_2 \leq 600$, $0 \leq x_2 \leq 90$, with $x_1 \geq 0$.   **b.** Make 120 bears and 40 monkeys, for a maximum profit of $180.   **c.** Minimize $w = 200y_1 + 600y_2 + 90y_3$ subject to $y_1 + 4y_2 \geq 1, 2y_1 + 3y_2 + y_3 \geq 1.5$, with $y_1 \geq 0, y_2 \geq 0$, and $y_3 \geq 0$.   **d.** $y_1 = 0.6$, $y_2 = 0.1, y_3 = 0, w = 180$ **e.** $186   **f.** $179   **21. a.** 0 g of soybean meal, 8 g of meat byproducts, and 3.6 g of grain, or 0 g of soybean meal, 0 g of meat byproducts, and 10.8 g of grain   **b.** $1.08   **c.** Same as part a   **23.** Make 16 large bowls, no small bowls, and 6 pots, for a minimum time of 104 hours.   **25.** 3 of pill #1 and 2 of pill #2, for a minimum cost of 70¢

Exercises 4.4 (page 209)

1. $2x_1 + 3x_2 + s_1 = 8$; $x_1 + 4x_2 - s_2 = 7$ **3.** $2x_1 + x_2 + 2x_3 + s_1 = 50$; $x_1 + 3x_2 + x_3 - s_2 = 35$; $x_1 + 2x_2 - s_3 = 15$
5. Change the objective function to maximize $z = -3y_1 - 4y_2 - 5y_3$. The constraints are not changed. **7.** Change the objective
function to maximize $z = -y_1 - 2y_2 - y_3 - 5y_4$. The constraints are not changed. **9.** Maximum is 480 when $x_1 = 40$
and $x_2 = 0$. **11.** Maximum is 750 when $x_1 = 0$, $x_2 = 150$, and $x_3 = 0$. **13.** Maximum is 135 when $x_1 = 30$ and $x_2 = 5$.
15. Minimum is 108 when $y_1 = 0$, $y_2 = 9$, and $y_3 = 0$. **17.** Maximum is 400/3 when $x_1 = 100/3$ and $x_2 = 50/3$.
19. Minimum is 512 when $y_1 = 6$, $y_2 = 8$, and $y_3 = 0$. **23. a.** Ship 200 barrels of oil from supplier S_1 to distributor D_1; ship
2800 barrels of oil from supplier S_2 to distributor D_1; ship 2800 barrels of oil from supplier S_1 to distributor D_2; ship 2200 barrels of
oil from supplier S_2 to distributor D_2. Minimum cost is \$180,400. **b.** $s_3 = 2000$; S_1 could furnish 2000 more barrels of oil. **25.**
Make \$3,000,000 in commercial loans and \$22,000,000 in home loans, for a maximum return of \$2,940,000. **27.** Use 1500 lb of
bluegrass, 2700 lb of rye, and 1800 lb of Bermuda, for a mininum cost of \$834. **29. a.** Ship 2 computers from W_1 to D_1, 20 computers from W_1 to D_2, 30 computers from W_2 to D_1, and 0 computers from W_2 to D_2, for a minimum cost of \$628. **b.** $s_3 = 3$; warehouse W_1 has 3 more computers that it could ship. **31.** 5/3 oz of I, 20/3 oz of II, 5/3 oz of III, for a minimum cost of \$1.55 per
gal; 10 oz of the additive should be used per gal of gasoline. **33. a.** Joe should do $5\frac{2}{3}$ hours of calisthenics, $3\frac{1}{3}$ hours of swimming,
and 1 hour of playing the drums, for a maximum calorie expenditure of $4270\frac{1}{3}$ calories.

Concept Check (page 214)

1. True **2.** False **3.** True **4.** False **5.** False **6.** True **7.** True **8.** False **9.** False **10.** True **11.** False **12.** True
13. False

Chapter 4 Review Exercises (page 215)

1. When the problem has more than two variables **3. a.** $4x_1 + 6x_2 + s_1 = 60$; $3x_1 + x_2 + s_2 = 18$; $2x_1 + 5x_2 + s_3 = 20$;
$x_1 + x_2 + s_4 = 15$ **b.**

x_1	x_2	s_1	s_2	s_3	s_4	z	
4	6	1	0	0	0	0	60
3	1	0	1	0	0	0	18
2	5	0	0	1	0	0	20
1	1	0	0	0	1	0	15
-2	-7	0	0	0	0	1	0

5. a. $x_1 + x_2 + x_3 + s_1 = 90$; $2x_1 + 5x_2 + x_3 + s_2 = 120$; $x_1 + 3x_2 - s_3 = 80$ **b.**

x_1	x_2	x_3	s_1	s_2	s_3	z	
1	1	1	1	0	0	0	90
2	5	1	0	1	0	0	120
1	3	0	0	0	-1	0	80
-5	-8	-6	0	0	0	1	0

7. Maximum is 33 when $x_1 = 3$, $x_2 = 0$, $x_3 = 3$, $s_1 = 0$, and $s_2 = 0$. **9.** Maximum is 76.67 when $x_1 = 6.67$, $x_2 = 0$, $x_3 = 21.67$,
$s_1 = 0$, $s_2 = 0$, and $s_3 = 35$. **11. Dual Method** Solve the dual problem: Maximize $17x_1 + 42x_2$ subject to $x_1 + 5x_2 \leq 10$,
$x_1 + 8x_2 \leq 15$. **Method of Section 4.4** Change the objective function to maximize $z = -10y_1 - 15y_2$. The constraints are not
changed. Minimum is 170 when $y_1 = 17$ and $y_2 = 0$. **13. Dual Method** Solve the dual problem: Maximize
$48x_1 + 12x_2 + 10x_3 + 30x_4$ subject to $x_1 + x_2 + 3x_4 \leq 7$, $x_1 + x_2 \leq 2$, $2x_1 + x_3 + x_4 \leq 3$. **Method of Section 4.4** Change the
objective function to maximize $z = -7y_1 - 2y_2 - 3y_3$. The constraints are not changed. Minimum is 98 when $y_1 = 4$, $y_2 = 8$, and
$y_3 = 18$. **15.** Minimum of 62 when $y_1 = 8$, $y_2 = 12$, $s_1 = 0$, $s_2 = 1$, $s_3 = 0$, and $s_4 = 2$ **17.** Maximum of 480 when $x_1 = 24$
and $x_2 = 0$ **19.** Maximum of 102 when $x_1 = 0$ and $x_2 = 8.5$ **21.** Problems with constraints involving "$\leq$" can be solved using
slack variables, while those involving "$\geq$" or "$=$" can be solved using surplus and artificial variables, respectively. **23. a.** Maximize $z = 6x_1 + 7x_2 + 5x_3$, subject to $4x_1 + 2x_2 + 3x_3 \leq 9$, $5x_1 + 4x_2 + x_3 \leq 10$, with $x_1 \geq 0$, $x_2 \geq 0$, $x_3 \geq 0$. **b.** The first
constraint would be $4x_1 + 2x_2 + 3x_3 \geq 9$. **c.** $x_1 = 0$, $x_2 = 2.1$, $x_3 = 1.6$, and $z = 22.7$ **d.** Minimize $w = 9y_1 + 10y_2$, subject
to $4y_1 + 5y_2 \geq 6$, $2y_1 + 4y_2 \geq 7$, $3y_1 + y_2 \geq 5$, with $y_1 \geq 0$, $y_2 \geq 0$. **e.** $y_1 = 1.3$, $y_2 = 1.1$, and $w = 22.7$ **25. a.** Let $x_1 = $
number of cake plates, $x_2 = $ number of bread plates, and $x_3 = $ number of dinner plates. **b.** $z = 15x_1 + 12x_2 + 5x_3$

c. $15x_1 + 10x_2 + 8x_3 \leq 1500$; $5x_1 + 4x_2 + 4x_3 \leq 2700$; $6x_1 + 5x_2 + 5x_3 \leq 1200$ **27. a.** Let $x_1 =$ number of gallons of Fruity wine and $x_2 =$ number of gallons of Crystal wine to be made.   **b.** $z = 12x_1 + 15x_2$ **c.** $2x_1 + x_2 \leq 110$; $2x_1 + 3x_2 \leq 125$; $2x_1 + x_2 \leq 90$ **29.** Produce no cake plates, 150 bread plates, and no dinner plates, for a maximum profit of $1800.   **31.** 36.25 gal of Fruity and 17.5 gal of Crystal, for a maximum profit of $697.50   **33. a and b** Produce 660 cases of corn, 0 cases of beans, and 340 cases of carrots, for a minimum cost of $15,100.   **35.** Ginger should do $5\frac{1}{3}$ hours of tai chi, $2\frac{2}{3}$ hours of riding a unicycle, and 2 hours of fencing, for a maximum calorie expenditure of $2753\frac{1}{3}$ calories.

Appendix A
Practice Exercises

1.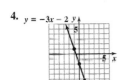

a. Quadrant IV   **b.** y-axis   **c.** Quadrant II   **d.** x-axis   **e.** Quadrant III   **f.** Quadrant I
2. yes, no, yes   **3. a.** $4200   **b.** more than $9000

4. $y = -3x - 2$ 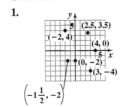   **5.**   **6.** $y = 2x^2$ **7.**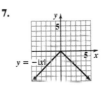

Graphing Calculator Explorations

1. 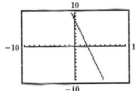   **3.** 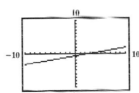   **5.**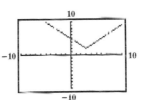

7.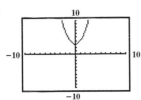

Vocabulary and Readiness Check
1. $(5, 2)$ **3.** $(3, 0)$ **5.** $(-5, -2)$ **7.** $(-1, 0)$ **9.** QI   **11.** QII   **13.** QIII   **15.** y-axis   **17.** QIII   **19.** x-axis

Exercise Set
1. Quadrant I   **3.** Quadrant II   **5.** Quadrant IV   **7.** y-axis   **9.** Quadrant III

11. Quadrant IV   **13.** x-axis   **15.** Quadrant III   **17.** no; yes   **19.** yes; yes   **21.** yes; yes   **23.** yes; no   **25.** yes; yes

27. linear

29. linear

31. linear

33. not linear

35. linear

37. not linear

39. not linear

41. linear

43. linear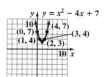

45. not linear

47. not linear

49. not linear

51. linear

53. linear

55. -5 **57.** $-\dfrac{1}{10}$ **59.** $(-\infty, -5]$

61. $(-\infty, -4)$ **63.** b   **65.** b   **67.** c   **69.** 1991   **71.** answers may vary   **73.**

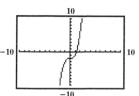

75. a.   **b.** 14 in.   **77.** $7000   **79.** $500   **81.** Depreciation is the same from year to year.

83. 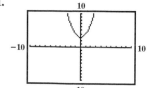   ; answers may vary   **85.** answers may vary   **87.** $y = -3 - 2x$;

89. $y = 5 - x^2$;   **91.**   **93.**

Appendix B

1. $5, 7, 9, 11$ **3.** $\frac{3}{2}, \frac{4}{3}, \frac{5}{4}, \frac{6}{5}$ **5.** $9, -27, 81, -243$ **7.** 23 **9.** $\frac{101}{100}$ **11.** $1 + 2 + 3 + 4 + 5 + 6 = 21$ **13.** $5 + 7 + 9 + 11 = 32$
15. $1 + \frac{1}{10} + \frac{1}{100} + \frac{1}{1,000} = \frac{1,111}{1,000}$ **17.** 3.6 **19.** 82.5 **21.** $\frac{1}{2}, -\frac{1}{4}, \frac{1}{8}, -\frac{1}{16}, \frac{1}{32}$ **23.** $0, 4, 0, 8, 0$ **25.** $1, -\frac{3}{2}, \frac{9}{4}, -\frac{27}{8}, \frac{81}{16}$ **27.** $a_n = n - 3$
29. $a_n = 4n$ **31.** $a_n = (2n - 1)/2n$ **33.** $a_n = (-1)^{n+1}n$ **35.** $a_n = (-1)^{n+1}(2n - 1)$ **37.** $a_n = \left(\frac{2}{5}\right)^{n-1}$ **39.** $a_n = x^n$
41. $a_n = (-1)^{n+1}x^{2n-1}$ **43.** $1 - 9 + 25 - 49 + 81$ **45.** $\frac{4}{7} + \frac{8}{9} + \frac{16}{11} + \frac{32}{13}$ **47.** $1 + x + x^2 + x^3 + x^4$

49. $x - \dfrac{x^3}{3} + \dfrac{x^5}{5} - \dfrac{x^7}{7} + \dfrac{x^9}{9}$

51. (A) $\displaystyle\sum_{k=1}^{5}(k+1)$ (B) $\displaystyle\sum_{j=0}^{4}(j+2)$ **53.** (A) $\displaystyle\sum_{k=1}^{4}\dfrac{(-1)^{k+1}}{k}$ (B) $\displaystyle\sum_{j=0}^{3}\dfrac{(-1)^j}{j+1}$ **55.** $\displaystyle\sum_{k=1}^{n}\dfrac{k+1}{k}$

57. $\displaystyle\sum_{k=1}^{n}\dfrac{(-1)^{k+1}}{2^k}$

59. False   **61.** True   **63.** $2, 8, 26, 80, 242$ **65.** $1, 2, 4, 8, 16$ **67.** $1, \frac{3}{2}, \frac{17}{12}, \frac{577}{408}; a_4 = \frac{577}{408} \approx 1.414\,216, \sqrt{2} \approx 1.414\,214$

69. $1, 1, 2, 3, 5, 8, 13, 21, 34, 55$

Appendix C

Vocabulary and Readiness Check
1. 56   **3.** -32 **5.** 20

Exercise Set Appendix C

1. 26   **3.** -19 **5.** 0   **7.** $\dfrac{13}{6}$ **9.** $(1, 2)$ **11.** $\{(x, y)\,|\,3x + y = 1\}$ **13.** $(9, 9)$ **15.** $(-3, -2)$ **17.** $(3, 4)$ **19.** 8

21. 0   **23.** 15   **25.** 54   **27.** $(-2, 0, 5)$ **29.** $(6, -2, 4)$ **31.** $(-2, 3, -1)$ **33.** $(0, 2, -1)$ **35.** 5   **37.** 0; answers may vary